# Seeking the Promised Land

Mormons have long had an outsized presence in American culture and politics, but they remain largely unknown to most Americans. Recent years have seen the political prominence of Mormons taken to a new level, thanks to developments including the presidential candidacy of Republican Mitt Romney, the high-profile involvement of Mormons in the campaign for California's Proposition 8 (anti–gay marriage), and the ascendancy of Democrat Harry Reid to the position of Senate Majority Leader. This book provides the most thorough examination ever written of Mormons' place in the American political landscape – what Mormons are like politically and how non-Mormons respond to Mormon candidates. However, this is a book about more than Mormons. As a religious subculture in a pluralistic society, Mormons are a case study of how a religious group balances distinctiveness and assimilation – a question faced by all faiths.

David E. Campbell is Professor of Political Science at the University of Notre Dame and the founding director of the Rooney Center for the Study of American Democracy. He is the coauthor (with Robert Putnam) of *American Grace: How Religion Divides and Unites Us*, which received both the 2011 Woodrow Wilson Award from the American Political Science Association and the Wilbur Award from the Religious Communicators Council for the best nonfiction book of 2010. He is also the author of *Why We Vote: How Schools and Communities Shape Our Civic Life*.

John C. Green is director of the Ray C. Bliss Institute of Applied Politics and Distinguished Professor of Political Science at the University of Akron. He also serves as a senior research advisor at the Pew Forum on Religion & Public Life. He is the author of *The Faith Factor: How Religion Influences American Elections* and the coauthor of *The Diminishing Divide: Religion's Changing Role in American Politics*, *The Bully Pulpit: The Politics of Protestant Clergy*, and *Religion and the Culture Wars*.

J. Quin Monson is Associate Professor of Political Science, former director of the Center for the Study of Elections and Democracy, and a Mollie and Karl Butler Young Scholar in Western Studies at the Charles Redd Center for Western Studies at Brigham Young University. Monson's research has appeared in journals such as *Public Opinion Quarterly*, *Political Research Quarterly*, *Political Analysis*, *Political Behavior*, and the *Journal for the Scientific Study of Religion*. He is the coeditor of several monographs on congressional and presidential elections and contributes regularly to a blog called *Utah Data Points*.

# Cambridge Studies in Social Theory, Religion and Politics

*Editors*

DAVID C. LEEGE, University of Notre Dame
KENNETH D. WALD, University of Florida, Gainesville
RICHARD L. WOOD, University of New Mexico

The most enduring and illuminating bodies of late-nineteenth-century social theory – by Marx, Weber, Durkheim, and others – emphasized the integration of religion, polity, and economy through time and place. Once a staple of classic social theory, however, religion gradually lost the interest of many social scientists during the twentieth century. The recent emergence of phenomena such as Solidarity in Poland; the dissolution of the Soviet empire; various South American, Southern African, and South Asian liberation movements; the Christian Right in the United States; and Al Qaeda have reawakened scholarly interest in religiously based political conflict. At the same time, fundamental questions are once again being asked about the role of religion in stable political regimes, public policies, and constitutional orders. The series Cambridge Studies in Social Theory, Religion and Politics produces volumes that study religion and politics by drawing upon classic social theory and more recent social scientific research traditions. Books in the series offer theoretically grounded, comparative, empirical studies that raise "big" questions about a timely subject that has long engaged the best minds in social science.

*Titles in the Series*

# Seeking the Promised Land

## Mormons and American Politics

**DAVID E. CAMPBELL**
*University of Notre Dame*

**JOHN C. GREEN**
*University of Akron*

**J. QUIN MONSON**
*Brigham Young University*

CAMBRIDGE
UNIVERSITY PRESS

# CAMBRIDGE
## UNIVERSITY PRESS

32 Avenue of the Americas, New York NY 10013-2473, USA

Cambridge University Press is part of the University of Cambridge.

It furthers the University's mission by disseminating knowledge in the pursuit of education, learning and research at the highest international levels of excellence.

www.cambridge.org
Information on this title: www.cambridge.org/9781107027978

© David E. Campbell, John C. Green, and J. Quin Monson 2014

First published 2014

*A catalogue record for this publication is available from the British Library*

*Library of Congress Cataloguing in Publication data*
Campbell, David E.
Seeking the Promised Land: Mormons and American Politics / David E. Campbell, University of Notre Dame; John C. Green, University of Akron; J. Quin Monson, Brigham Young University.
    pages   cm. – (Cambridge studies in social theory, religion and politics)
ISBN 978-1-107-02797-8 – ISBN 978-1-107-66267-4 (paperback)
1. Mormons – Political activity – United States.   2. Church of Jesus Christ of Latter-day Saints – Political activity.   3. Church of Jesus Christ of Latter-day Saints – Doctrines.
4. Mormon Church – Political activity.   5. Christianity and politics – Church of Jesus Christ of Latter-day Saints.   6. Christianity and politics – United States.   I. Green, John Clifford, 1953–   II. Monson, J. Quin.   III. Title.
BX8643.P6C36   2014
320.973088'2893–dc23        2013048105

ISBN 978-1-107-02797-8 Hardback
ISBN 978-1-107-66267-4 Paperback

*For Kirsten, Katie, and Soren;*
*Kate, Anna, Alex, Sadie, and Josephine;*
*Lynn, Brendan, Darcy, Russell, and Caroline*

# Contents

# Preface

This is a book about Mormons and American politics, a religious community and a subject that frequently elicit strong reactions. Some readers will have a negative perception of Mormons, others will have a positive view, and some will be Mormons themselves. Still others will not have a prior opinion one way or the other and are reading this book out of curiosity (or perhaps because it was assigned in a class). Since our readers will come to this subject with different backgrounds, let us explain ours.

We recognize that it is unusual to highlight authors' personal, especially religious, backgrounds in a work of empirical social science. But owing to the fervent opinions Mormonism can engender, many readers will undoubtedly wonder about our connections to the faith. Readers who would rather not know our religious perspectives should stop reading this and skip to Chapter 1. Perhaps, upon finishing the book, they can try to guess our religions and then come back to find out whether they are right.

Our team consists of two Mormons and a non-Mormon. J. Quin Monson is LDS and teaches at Brigham Young University, the LDS Church's flagship university. He grew up in the Mormon heartland of Utah. Mormonism is to his hometown, Provo, what chocolate is to Hershey, Pennsylvania. Furthermore, his extended family has deep roots within Mormonism (although he is not related to LDS Church President Thomas B. Monson). David E. Campbell is also LDS and teaches at the University of Notre Dame. He hails from Medicine Hat, Alberta, Canada – a community where Mormons are a relatively small share of the population. His extended family members are a mixture of Mormons and non-Mormons.

In other words, Monson was born, raised, and still lives in the midst of Mormonism's "Zion." Campbell, on the other hand, was raised and now lives in what Utah Mormons call the "mission field" (an environment where Mormons are a minority). The genesis of this book dates from when Campbell and Monson were both undergraduates at BYU, majoring in political science and on their way to graduate school. It was in the food court of BYU's student center that they hatched a plan to one day write a book on Mormons and politics. Even then they recognized that because of their varying life experiences, they bring different perspectives to their understanding of Mormon culture.

John C. Green provides still another perspective. He is a United Methodist who teaches at the University of Akron, a public university in Ohio. He has long been interested in American religious pluralism, including the fact that it is more often honored in preaching than observance. It is worth noting that the terms "Mormon" and "Methodist" were originally coined by critics, but then proudly adopted by the targets of the criticism.

While our biographies are likely relevant to some readers, we nonetheless hope that attention to our religious backgrounds does not overshadow our professional expertise. As a parallel, we point to the bounty of excellent scholarship on African Americans and politics – some of which is written by black scholars and some of which is not. To those who may worry that Mormon scholars cannot write objectively about Mormons, we paraphrase John F. Kennedy, who famously said that he was not the "Catholic candidate for president but the Democratic Party's candidate, who happens also to be a Catholic" (1960). Likewise, Monson and Campbell are not Mormon political scientists but political scientists who happen also to be Mormons. To those who are concerned that a non-Mormon cannot understand the intricacies of Mormonism, we note that even though Green is a not a member of the faith, he nonetheless has a deep familiarity with it. He has done many years of "field work" among Mormons, beginning with a childhood spent in Colorado around many Latter-day Saints. As a team, we rely on insider knowledge to detect nuances within Mormon culture while also drawing on an outsider perspective when translating "Mormonisms" to those unfamiliar with that culture.

In writing this book, we have had to decide how much of Mormonism to explain and how to explain it. This is not a book on all things Mormon, but rather an analysis of Mormons' place in American politics. Accordingly, we have made our choices by keeping our focus on those aspects of the LDS faith and culture that are *politically* pertinent. Unlike much that is written about Mormonism, our objective is not to be devotional or polemical. We cover some potentially uncomfortable aspects of Mormonism – particularly polygamy and the restrictive racial policies of its past – because they have political relevance. But neither do we dwell on them at the expense of ignoring politically salient aspects of Mormonism that perhaps do not garner as much attention from other sources. At all times, we have stuck to the facts.

In sum, we hope to provide a theoretically grounded, empirically informed examination of Mormons' place in American politics – with perspectives from both inside and outside the faith.

# Acknowledgments

Many of the ideas in this book have been percolating for years, having taken shape in our conversations with each other, as well as with mentors, colleagues, and students. But refining our ideas, collecting the data, and producing the actual manuscript happened rather quickly, thanks to supportive institutions and the assistance of good friends. Financial support for the data collection was jointly supplied by the Francis and Kathleen Rooney Center for the Study of American Democracy at the University of Notre Dame, the Ray C. Bliss Institute of Applied Politics at the University of Akron, and the Center for the Study of Elections and Democracy at Brigham Young University. The political science departments at Notre Dame and BYU also granted leave to David C. Campbell and J. Quin Monson that allowed them to focus on writing.

The series editor, Ken Wald, has been helpful and encouraging throughout the process, offering crucial advice and substantive input every step of the way. We gathered as an author team at Brigham Young University in November 2012 for a small conference with a group of friends and colleagues to review early chapter drafts, for data analysis, and to set a course for the remaining work. We are grateful to Brian Cannon and the Charles Redd Center for Western Studies at Brigham Young University for funding this conference. We likewise owe a debt of gratitude to Clyde Wilcox, Frances Lee, Chris Karpowitz, Paul Edwards, and Kelly Patterson for their conference participation and careful review at that early stage. They were encouraging while also steering us toward additional analysis and writing that have made the book thorough enough to interest specialists in religion and politics but also informative and accessible to a general audience. We are also grateful to two anonymous reviewers for their suggestions.

The original data collection for the book was all done through YouGov. Samantha Luks and Ashley Grosse were especially helpful with their expertise in conducting the Peculiar People Survey and the Mormon Perceptions Study. Available data about Mormons has exploded in recent years, largely because of the Pew Forum on Religion & Public Life. We have especially benefited from the "Mormons in America" data and report and the large-scale Religious Landscape survey. At a time when government funding for political science research is drying up, Pew demonstrates the value in public-spirited data collection. The work of David Magleby and Kelly Patterson with the Utah Colleges Exit Poll has provided a tremendous data resource and also sparked an intellectual curiosity for questions about Mormons and politics among their former students (including both Campbell and Monson).

We were aided in our work by a number of student research assistants who faithfully toiled with us on the project. We thank them for their long hours and careful work on what could at times be tedious tasks. They include Zach Smith, Kali Smith, Brian Reed, Madison Daines, and Jordan Stauss at Brigham Young University. In particular, Zach provided tremendous assistance on a variety of data analysis tasks and Brian contributed heavily to the ecological inference analysis of Utah Mormons. Other research assistance was provided by the staff and students at the University of Akron, including Angie Wynar, Michael Kohler, Britney Raies, Ian Schwarber, and Marilyn Johnson, who contributed heavily to the case studies of Mormon presidential candidates, trends in Mormon officer holders, and mentions of Mormon candidates in the *New York Times*. We are especially grateful to Jonathan Schwartz for the brilliant idea to use the Pew Religious Landscape survey questions about former religious affiliation to compare current and former Mormons. Janet Lykes Bolois deserves praise for her copyediting expertise.

Feedback on early drafts of our work was also provided by the participants in a seminar at the University of Florida and the weekly research workshop of Notre Dame's Rooney Center. As the manuscript progressed, we also received helpful input on sections of the book from Geoff Layman, Christina Wolbrecht, Robert Millet, Kirsten Campbell, and Lynn Green. Finally, a project like this always requires patience and support from those closest to us, particularly our spouses and children. Our families provide just the right balance of support and distraction to make doing a project like this possible and even pleasant.

PART I

MORMONS AS AN ETHNO-RELIGIOUS GROUP

I

# Meet the Mormons

In 1996, *Time* magazine named Stephen R. Covey one of the twenty-five most influential Americans. His best-known book, *The Seven Habits of Highly Effective People* (1990), has long been a staple of bookstores and best-seller lists, having sold more than 25 million copies. Covey built a self-help empire teaching executives how to employ his habits to make an effective business. When he passed away in 2012, his *New York Times* obituary noted that "more than two-thirds of Fortune 500 companies" had sought his advice (D. Martin 2012). Covey also consulted with political leaders, winning praise from Democrats like President Bill Clinton and Republicans like Newt Gingrich. His advice even extended beyond the boardroom to the family room with a follow-up book on creating highly effective families (Covey 1997). With his bipartisan appeal, folksy wisdom, and sunny disposition, Covey was part Norman Vincent Peale, part Dale Carnegie.

Covey was also a Mormon, a member of the Church of Jesus Christ of Latter-day Saints.[1] Far from merely a peripheral aspect of his life and work, Covey's Mormonism served as the foundation for his famous seven habits. Fellow Mormon and Harvard Business School professor Clayton Christensen told the *Economist* that "the seven habits are essentially a secular distillation of Mormon teaching" (*Economist* 2012). Indeed, prior to writing *The Seven Habits*, Covey published a book for a Mormon audience, *The Spiritual Roots of Human Relations* (1970), which employed many of the same concepts.

Covey is only one example among many of how Mormons seemingly stand at the center of American culture – they are the "quintessential Americans," as columnist George Will put it back in 1979 (cited in R. L. Moore 1986, 43). In

[1] The full name is the Church of Jesus Christ of Latter-day Saints. For the sake of brevity and variety, we often refer to it here as either the Church (when the context makes our meaning clear) or the LDS Church. Members of the Church are referred to as Mormons, Latter-day Saints, LDS Church members, or, occasionally, Church members. As we use them, these terms are fully interchangeable synonyms.

1959, the Mormon Tabernacle Choir won a Grammy for its recording of "The Battle Hymn of the Republic." In the 1970s, Donny and Marie Osmond were America's sweethearts, with hits on the pop charts and a top-rated television variety show. In 2002, Mormons received very positive press coverage during the Winter Olympics hosted by Salt Lake City, a city founded by Mormons and today the worldwide headquarters for the LDS Church.

Those Olympics were run by Mitt Romney. He was given the job of running the Olympics in the wake of a bribery scandal and financial difficulties that were threatening to tarnish the Games. As head of Bain Capital, Romney had specialized in the art of the turnaround. And turn around the Olympics he did, as they made a profit and were generally thought to be a success (Gold 2012). His business background no doubt made him an attractive choice to take the reins of a troubled Olympics. But given that the games were held in Utah, his religious background certainly mattered too. Like Covey, Romney is a Mormon, with deep family roots in the LDS Church.

Five years later, Mitt Romney was running for president. Given the importance of religion to many American voters, one might think that belonging to the "quintessentially American" church would be a political asset – and especially in the Republican primaries, where conservative values are a boon. Instead, Romney was confronted with suspicion regarding his religion, from both the left and the right. Editorialists argued that voters were "thoroughly justified" in opposing a Mormon presidential candidate on the grounds of his religion (Weisberg 2006; Linker 2006). Romney's leading opponent in the primaries, former Southern Baptist pastor Mike Huckabee, subtly raised suspicions about his religion (Chafets 2007). Out on the hustings, anti-Mormon sentiment was anything but subtle. For example, many South Carolina voters were sent an unsigned eight-page anti-Mormon diatribe in 2007 (Spencer 2007).

In this context, a Gallup poll found that 28 percent of Americans openly said they would not vote for a Mormon presidential candidate, a number essentially unchanged since 1967 – when Mitt Romney's father, Michigan governor George Romney, also ran for president. Interestingly, this was roughly the same percentage of Americans who said that they would not vote for a Catholic candidate in 1960, when John F. Kennedy was running for president (Jones 2007).

Given the controversy over his religion, it should not be surprising that in both 2008 and 2012, Romney generally steered clear of discussing it. In today's religion-soaked presidential campaigns – especially among Republicans – his religious reticence stood out. This is not to say, however, that he ignored the "Mormon question." In 2007, during his first run for the presidency, Romney sought to address concerns about his Mormonism in a speech delivered in College Station, Texas, evoking memories of a comparable speech delivered by Kennedy during the 1960 presidential campaign, also in Texas. In that speech, Romney walked a fine line. On the one hand, he spoke of his core belief in Jesus, leading to a remarkable statement for someone running for the secular office of the presidency: "I believe that Jesus Christ is the Son of God and the Savior of mankind." On the other hand, he declined to discuss the "distinctive doctrines" of his church and instead invoked his belief in a common set of "moral values" found in nearly all religious traditions (Romney 2007).

In his 2012 campaign, Romney delivered no comparable speech about his faith, and mostly tried to keep the focus on his business background. To the extent that his religion was mentioned, it was generally either journalists reporting on the millions of dollars he has donated to the LDS Church (Montgomery, Yang, and Rucker 2012) or friends of Romney describing his time as a lay leader in his church ministering to members of his congregation (S. Holland 2012). Through his highlighting of these aspects of Mormonism, Americans unfamiliar with the faith were introduced to the tight bonds Mormons form with one another, and the often-extraordinary investment of time and money they make in their church.

This book is about the seeming paradox of Mormonism in American life, as revealed by the contrast between Stephen Covey and Mitt Romney. If Mormons are the quintessential Americans, Covey and Romney could be considered the quintessential Mormons – or, at least, they are exemplars of how Mormons are often presented and perceived. Both are toothsome family men who achieved considerable professional and financial success. Yet whatever similarities they share, the contrast in their public reception is telling. Covey wrote a book that has sold 25 million copies by distilling his Mormon beliefs into secular language, with no antagonism toward the peculiar features of his faith. Romney ran for president and, despite stressing his faith's commonalities with other American religions, faced antagonism over Mormonism's distinctiveness. Who better represents the place of Mormons in today's America: Covey or Romney? Are the Latter-day Saints a "quintessentially American" faith or a "peculiar people" set apart?

The paradox is that Mormons are both. Just as light has the properties of both a particle and a wave, so are Mormons best understood as being simultaneously in the mainstream and on the fringes of American society. Mormons have a strong sense of internal solidarity, powering a degree of voluntarism unmatched by any other religious group in America. They are an optimistic and patriotic people known for their upright living, family values, good health, and generous ways. However, the same faith that fosters these all-American virtues also includes unique beliefs and practices that create external tensions with other Americans. Many simply consider Mormons to be different and praiseworthy or odd but innocuous, while others see Mormons as clannish, exotic, or even heretical – a "peculiar people" in one way or another.

WHY THIS BOOK?

Why a whole book about Mormons and politics? One reason is the lack of attention Mormons have received from social scientists. In the contemporary United States, there are as many Mormons as Jews – roughly 2 percent of the population – and contrary to the stable Jewish population, Mormonism is often described as being among the fastest-growing religions in America.[2] Yet there has been far less research on Mormonism than on Judaism, let alone work that has focused specifically on Mormons and politics.[3]

Size and growth rates alone would admittedly be weak rationales for a book about the politics of any group. There are as many owners of hamsters and guinea pigs in the United States as there are Mormons, and the number of Zumba dancers is growing much more rapidly than the membership rolls of the LDS Church.[4] But neither owners of small rodents nor dance exercise fads occupy the kind of cultural or political niche that Mormons do.

Mormonism's place in American culture is perhaps best illustrated by the hit Broadway play *The Book of Mormon: The Musical*, written by Trey Parker and Matt Stone of *South Park* fame. Imagine musical theater that spoofs, say, Presbyterianism. Somehow it would lack the same comedic punch. Nor is this the first time that Mormons have been featured in popular culture, as they have appeared in fiction – usually as villains – since the nineteenth century (Givens 1997).

Whatever their portrayal in fiction, in reality Mormons have long walked the halls of power. Many Mormons hold high political office, such as Senate Majority Leader Harry Reid (Democrat) and the long-serving senior senator from Utah, Orrin Hatch (Republican). In Congress, Mormons have consistently been represented in numbers slightly greater than their share of the population. From the 106th (1999–2000) to the 113th (2013–14) Congresses, the proportion of Mormon members has hovered around 3 percent. A number of Mormons have also run for the presidency, a legacy that includes the quixotic campaign of Mormonism's founder, Joseph Smith, in 1844. The twentieth century saw the presidential campaigns of George Romney (1968), Mo Udall

---

[2] While there is no question that the LDS Church is growing, the precise rate of growth is a matter of controversy. According to membership statistics provided by the LDS Church, the Church grew by 30 percent between 1990 and 2008. Using the American Religious Identification Survey, sociologists Rick Phillips and Ryan T. Cragun put the LDS growth rate during that same period at 16 percent. Using other membership statistics reported by the LDS Church, the *Salt Lake Tribune* reports that the LDS growth rate from 2000 to 2010 was 18 percent. The discrepancies result from different methods of counting membership. While the LDS Church reports anyone baptized into the Church as a member, a survey like the ARIS counts only those people who self-identify as Mormon. See *Mormons in the United States 1990–2008* for more details (Phillips and Cragun 2011); also see Stack (2012b).

[3] There are, however, a few notable exceptions. They include *Latter-Day Political Views* (Fox 2006); *Mormons in American Politics: From Persecution to Power* (Perry and Cronin 2012); and *LDS in the USA: Mormonism and the Making of American Culture* (Trepanier and Newswander 2012). We acknowledge these authors for being in the vanguard of studying Mormonism's impact on American politics, and are grateful for their insights.

[4] According to Gallup, 2 percent of Americans own a hamster or guinea pig (http://www.gallup.com/poll/25969/americans-their-pets.aspx). For details on the explosive growth of Zumba, see Rusli (2012).

(1976), and Orrin Hatch (2000), while the twenty-first century brought both Jon Huntsman, Jr. (2012) and Mitt Romney (2008, 2012). Romney has come closest to winning the presidency, having received the 2012 Republican nomination but ultimately losing in a tight race to Barack Obama.

Even if Trey Parker and Matt Stone had not written their self-described "atheist's love note to Mormonism" (Jardin 2011) and Mitt Romney had never run for president, a detailed treatment of Mormons' place in contemporary American politics would be long overdue. Because Mormon voters are politically distinctive, they warrant an in-depth examination. In being distinctive, they can also inform a theoretical understanding of how religion and politics intersect. The politics of the Mormon rank and file are often shaped by their religion, sometimes in surprising ways. Although Mormons are overwhelmingly Republicans, Harry Reid reminds us of Mormons' partisan diversity. And notwithstanding that most Mormons are Republicans and self-described conservatives, on some issues their religious beliefs cause them to depart from the canon of conservative thought.

Mormons also challenge the prevailing trend within American religion whereby boundaries between religious communities have blurred and distinctions eroded (Putnam and Campbell 2010). Mormonism draws bright lines around its adherents with a set of distinctive beliefs and practices. Latter-day Saints are an example of what scholars call an "ethno-religious" political group, in which religion and ethnicity forge a strong sense of identity. Irish Catholics, Dutch Calvinists, and German Jews are good examples of ethno-religious groups in the past (Green 2007). Mormons represent a contemporary case of a group whose identity is shaped by their religion in ways that closely resemble an ethnic group, even if the group is not defined as ethnic per se.

Many scholars have argued that ethno-religious tensions have largely been supplanted by a new type of political grouping, in which religious traditionalists and progressives face off in dueling alliances that cut across religious communities. The divisions between conservative and liberal Catholics – and the alliances of these groups with their ideological counterparts among Protestants – are good examples. This development is known by many names: "religious restructuring" (Wuthnow 1990), "culture war politics" (J. D. Hunter 1991), "the new religion gap" (Green 2007), and the "coalition of the religious" (Putnam and Campbell 2010).

Mormons challenge this new paradigm in two respects. First, they hold to highly traditional values and yet fit uneasily with other religious traditionalists, especially evangelical Protestants. Second, Mormons offer a unique window into the persistence of ethno-religious groups in a pluralistic society. Mormons are not an archeological discovery, an ancient people isolated on the margins of modern society. Founded in the United States in the nineteenth century, the Latter-day Saints have become a global religion, well adapted to the modern world and yet offering a clear alternative to it. Mormons are a paradigmatic case of a vital religious group that has only slowly found acceptance in the American social and political mainstream. In this sense, the experience of Mormons may be helpful in understanding the future of other ethno-religious groups in the American religious mosaic, such as Muslims, Hindus, and Buddhists.

### WHO ARE THE MORMONS?

A group cannot be studied until it is defined. For our purposes, "Mormon" or its synonym, "Latter-day Saint," refers to members of the Church of Jesus Christ of Latter-day Saints. In this approach, Mormonism is defined much like Catholicism, with both traditions demarcated by membership in one worldwide church. Like Catholicism, Mormonism has also produced a few schismatic groups that identify with the broader tradition, but such groups are dwarfed in size, if not public attention, by a single dominant institution (in the case of Mormons, the Salt Lake City–based LDS Church). And as with Catholicism, history is important to the definition of Mormonism.

As every Mormon child can tell you, Joseph Smith had what Mormons call his "First Vision" in 1820, at the age of fourteen. In this initial theophany, Mormons believe Smith came face-to-face with God and Jesus Christ. This inaugural revelatory experience was followed by a series of other visions and divine visitations. In the ensuing years, an angel revealed to Smith the location of plates, made of gold, containing the record of an ancient Hebraic civilization in the Americas whose progenitors traveled from the Holy Land to the New World in Old Testament times. Smith translated the plates with divine assistance and published the translation as the *Book of Mormon* (Mormon being the name of a prominent figure within the book). As God's prophet, Smith formed a church in 1830, initially called the Church of Christ.[5]

The young church grew, and its members came together and formed tight-knit communities. They were often pejoratively called "Mormonites" or "Mormons." The latter nickname was accepted by the faith's early adherents, and it has stuck ever since. Mormonism's early days brought a grim pattern – a gathering in a particular place, rising tension with the surrounding communities, and then an exodus to gather anew someplace else. In 1837, most Mormons moved from Ohio to Missouri, and then, facing an extermination order issued by Missouri's governor, moved again across the Mississippi River to Illinois in 1838. Smith named the new gathering place Nauvoo, where he

---

[5] We can only provide a précis of Mormon history here. For more thorough treatments, see:

> *The Mormon People: The Making of An American Faith*, by Matthew Bowman (2012a, Random House)
>
> *The Mormon Experience: A History of the Latter-day Saints*, by Leonard J. Arrington and Davis Bitton (1992, University of Illinois Press)
>
> *Mormonism: The Story of a New Religious Tradition*, by Jan Shipps (1985, University of Illinois Press)

simultaneously served as mayor, general of the city's military force, and prophet of the Church.

The Mormons prospered in their "kingdom on the Mississippi" (Flanders 1975), but by 1844 tensions had risen again. Rumors of polygamy among the upper strata of LDS leaders were circulating, having been put into print by a newspaper published by some of the Church's former officials. In his capacity as mayor of Nauvoo, Smith had the newspaper's press destroyed, which led to his imprisonment in the county seat of Carthage, Illinois. Joseph was joined in jail by his brother Hyrum and two other prominent Church leaders. On June 27, 1844, a mob stormed the jail with guns blazing. Joseph and Hyrum Smith were shot and killed. Smith's murder – known to Mormons as the Martyrdom – was a critical juncture for the young Church. In the immediate aftermath of his death, it was not clear if anyone would succeed the charismatic young prophet, and if Mormonism would fade as just another failed utopian experiment of the Second Great Awakening.

Far from fading away, Mormonism carried on under the leadership of Brigham Young. Most – but not all – Mormons accepted Young as Smith's successor. "Brother Brigham" became the Mormons' Moses (Arrington 1986). Their troubles did not end with Smith's murder, and Young made the decision to lead his people on a mass exodus to what they hoped would be their promised land. The Mormons left Nauvoo and immigrated to present-day Utah, which was then part of Mexico. They soon established settlements throughout the Mountain West.[6] For years, a steady stream of Mormon converts, many from Europe, made the arduous trek to "the place which God ... prepared, far away in the West."[7]

Upon settling in their western enclave, in 1852 LDS leaders openly acknowledged the practice of polygamy, or "plural marriage," as the Mormons themselves called it. Polygamy was highly controversial and led to decades of conflict between the Mormons and the federal government, including a military expedition, pursuit of Church leaders by federal authorities, a series of federal laws designed to thwart polygamy by targeting the LDS Church and its assets, and, finally, an 1879 Supreme Court decision that polygamy was not a form of free exercise of religion protected by the U.S. Constitution. Polygamy long delayed Utah from becoming a state.

---

[6] Some Mormons did not recognize Young as their new leader and instead followed others who claimed to be Smith's successor. The largest of these groups eventually formed the Reorganized Church of Jesus Christ of Latter Day Saints (RLDS), initially led by Joseph Smith's son, Joseph Smith III. Among the RLDS was Emma Smith, Joseph Smith's first – that is, pre-polygamy – wife and Mormonism's "founding mother." Today, the RLDS Church has been renamed the Community of Christ. Headquartered in Missouri, with a membership of approximately 120,000, the Community of Christ bears diminishing resemblance to today's LDS Church. When we speak of Mormons, we do not mean members of the Community of Christ, or any other offshoot from the dissension following Smith's death.

[7] Lyrics from the Mormon hymn, "Come, Come Ye Saints."

A watershed in Mormon history came in 1890, when the fourth president of the LDS Church, Wilford Woodruff, announced that the Church would no longer sanction plural marriages. The "Manifesto," as it came to be called, did not bring polygamy to a screeching halt, but it did apply the brakes. In the immediate wake of the Manifesto, there was ambiguity regarding its full implications. For example, questions remained about the status of preexisting polygamous marriages and whether such marriages could be performed outside the territory of the United States. Notwithstanding these unresolved questions, the polygamy ban was enough for Utah to be granted statehood in 1896, and by the beginning of the twentieth century the polygamy era drew to a close. Any uncertainty about the status of polygamy was resolved in 1905, when two of the Church's twelve apostles were forced to resign from their ecclesiastical positions after defying the church president's edict and continuing to officiate at polygamous weddings (Flake 2004).

Just as the death of Joseph Smith caused one critical juncture, the end of polygamy brought another. Some "fundamentalist" sects never accepted the prohibition on polygamy and continue the practice today (Van Wagoner 1989). These fundamentalists are not members of the LDS Church, which treats polygamy as an offense that warrants excommunication. Indeed, as we detail further in Chapter 3, among members of the LDS Church, polygamy meets with greater moral disapproval than premarital sex – which is saying something, given Mormons' moral conservatism. While the number of polygamists is tiny, they elicit equal parts public fascination and revulsion such that they attract a lot of attention. In recent years, this has included the reality TV show "Sister Wives" and the dramatic series "Big Love." Recent years have also seen the high-profile prosecution of Warren Jeffs, leader of the Fundamentalist Church of Jesus Christ of Latter-Day Saints, as his marriage to teenage wives led to a conviction for the sexual assault of minors (*Associated Press* 2011). These fundamentalist polygamists are not included in our definition of Mormons, because the Church does not accept them as members and they, in turn, do not recognize the authority of the leadership of the Church of Jesus Christ of Latter-day Saints.

## WHAT DO MORMONS BELIEVE?

An examination of LDS beliefs brings the Mormon paradox to light – the juxtaposition of being both the "quintessential American church" and a "peculiar people." To anyone accustomed to Protestantism or Catholicism, attending an LDS sacrament meeting (worship service) would reveal a blend of both the familiar and unfamiliar. The meeting would include many common Christian themes. Mormons believe the Bible to be holy scripture and draw lessons from both the Old and New Testaments. Mormons freely speak of Christ as their Savior, celebrating the nativity at Christmas and the resurrection at Easter. They take communion and sing many hymns found in the songbooks of other churches. But such a visitor would hear much that is unfamiliar – a sampling might include quotations from the *Book of Mormon* and other uniquely Mormon scripture, references to modern prophets and apostles, or a sermon on the importance of temple rites that are restricted only to devout members of the LDS Church.

This combination of beliefs shared with other Christians and doctrines found exclusively among Latter-day Saints has led to a long-standing dispute over whether Mormons should be considered Christians. Among Mormons themselves, there is no debate. According to a recent survey, 97 percent say they are Christians. In contrast, one-third of the general population says they are not (Pew Forum on Religion & Public Life 2012a, 20). While we say more about this debate in Chapter 7, for now we note how it exemplifies the Mormon paradox. No one can dispute that Mormons believe in Christ and describe themselves as Christians. However, neither can anyone dispute that Latter-day Saints have distinctive beliefs and practices, including their theology regarding Christ.

The debate over whether Mormons are Christians thus boils down to whether their distinctiveness from other Christian denominations outweighs the commonalities shared with them, particularly Protestantism. Mormons' ambivalent place among Christian denominations is illustrated by Mormons' own ambivalence about the cross. While Mormons use pictures and statues of Christ, their modern iconography does not include the cross – the defining symbol of Christianity.[8] Mormons explain that this practice reflects an emphasis on the life and resurrection of Christ over his death (Hinckley 2005). To members of some denominations, the cross's absence merely underscores that Mormons are not wholly Christian.

Given that many readers will be unacquainted with the beliefs and practices of the LDS faith, we provide a crash course in Mormonism 101. A full-length exposition of LDS beliefs would require another book,[9] but we offer a précis focused specifically on those distinctive aspects of the LDS faith that have political relevance. For the purposes of our brief introduction to Mormonism, we organize the wide array of LDS beliefs into three essential themes: history, authority, and family.

---

[8] The story of Mormons' aversion to the cross illustrates a primary theme of this book: that the LDS Church selectively chooses ways to emphasize Mormonism's distinctiveness, and that those markers of distinctiveness change over time. While today Mormons avoid the cross as a symbol, with the theological justification that they prefer to emphasize the life rather than death of Jesus, this attitude is a twentieth-century innovation. Prior to that, Mormons regularly used the cross as one among many LDS symbols (Stack 2009).

[9] Book-length synopses of Mormon theology include:

*The God Who Weeps: How Mormonism Makes Sense of Life*, by Terryl L. Givens and Fiona Givens (2012, Ensign Peak)
*Mormonism: A Very Short Introduction*, by Richard L. Bushman (2008, Oxford University Press)
*What Do Mormons Believe?* by Rex E. Lee (1992, Deseret Book)

## History

Scholars of Mormonism often quip that instead of theology, Mormons have history.[10] While this statement is obviously an exaggeration, it speaks to a truth about the LDS faith. To understand Mormonism, one must learn Mormon history, as the foundation of the LDS religion rests on a series of historical events that involve God and other divine emissaries communicating with Joseph Smith (and other early Church leaders). Mormons have no formal catechism but they nonetheless speak of "having a testimony," meaning that they can say they know that the fundamentals of the faith are true. When Latter-day Saints "bear their testimony" – declare their core convictions, usually in a worship meeting – they often speak of knowing through personal inspiration that key events from both ancient scripture and nineteenth-century Mormon history really happened.

Among these catechism-like fundamentals is the conviction that Joseph Smith literally spoke with a corporeal God and Jesus Christ. This aspect of Mormon history has such significance that the First Vision (always capitalized) is often portrayed in song and art. Many Mormons make a pilgrimage of sorts to visit the vision's location in upstate New York – known as the "sacred grove" – which today is a historic site operated by the LDS Church. Equally fundamental is a personal spiritual witness that Joseph Smith translated the golden plates into the *Book of Mormon*, and that it contains a genuine record of flesh-and-blood people who traveled from the biblical Holy Land to the Americas. To underscore that the *Book of Mormon* is to be understood as history, not metaphor, the Church annually stages a summer outdoor pageant in that same area of upstate New York with a cast of hundreds dramatizing the events and people described in the *Book of Mormon*.

Similarly, Mormons understand the Old and New Testaments to be a historical record: Moses actually parted the Red Sea and Jesus was physically resurrected from the dead. It is not accurate to describe Mormons as biblical literalists, at least not in the sense that they believe the Bible to be inerrant, because they also believe that parts of the Biblical text have become corrupted during a lengthy period of apostasy stretching from the dawn of the Common Era to Joseph Smith. Mormons are better described as scriptural empiricists rather than literalists – scripture describes real people and real events, even if some biblical language has been removed or altered.

## Authority

Joseph Smith, Mormons believe, was a prophet chosen by God to restore Christ's church as it existed in the days of the New Testament. He was given God's priesthood, which in turn meant that he – and those whom he ordained to

---

[10]  While this witticism is often repeated among the Mormon cognoscenti, we have been unable to determine the original source for it (but not for a lack of trying).

the same priesthood – had the authority to act in God's name. Smith was not just a prophet in the sense of crying repentance to his people. He was also the leader of his people, complete with an administrative role. Hence, Joseph Smith held the dual roles of "prophet" and "president" of the Church. As prophet, he was authorized to receive revelation from God on behalf of the entire Church. As president, he had ultimate responsibility for the operation of the Church.

Today, Joseph Smith's successor is colloquially, and affectionately, referred to by Mormons as "the prophet," although his official title is actually president of the Church. Latter-day Saints believe that as prophet, he receives revelation from God, and thus that there is an "open canon" – not only is the *Book of Mormon* scripture coequal with the Bible, but so can revelations received by the prophet be canonized as scripture. As president, he sits at the apex of a centrally organized and financed organization with a clear hierarchy and lines of authority. The Church president is the only person with the authority to receive divine direction for the entire Church, although in practice he governs in consultation with both of his two counselors – a troika known as the First Presidency – and the Quorum (council) of the Twelve Apostles. While the Mormon buck stops at the desk of the Church president, the organizational structure is a corporate-style arrangement, with specific areas of responsibility delegated to church-wide, regional, and local leaders.

The collective nature of modern LDS Church governance is important for understanding the exercise of prophetic authority. Even though contemporary Mormons speak (and even sing) of "following the prophet," in modern practice all public announcements, policy changes, and official interpretations of LDS doctrine are issued in the collective voice of the top echelon of LDS leaders, who are all considered "prophets, seers, and revelators." Such announcements from the "Brethren," as they are often called by Church members, come only after consultation, deliberation, and complete consensus – not unlike the cabinet of a Westminster-style Parliament or the magisterium of the Catholic Church. As a result, change can take a long time. But when change comes it is implemented rapidly from the top down, as the lines of authority are clearly defined and the Church leadership speaks with one voice. Mormons do not have a formal doctrine that the prophet or the "Brethren" are infallible, but they do believe, as one past Church president put it, "The Lord will never permit me or any other man who stands as President of this Church to lead you astray."[11] In Chapter 6, we show experimental evidence that Mormons follow their church authorities on political as well as spiritual matters.

To Mormons, "authority" is not limited to the top echelon of Church leaders. The importance of authority extends into every local LDS ward (congregation).

[11] This quotation is found in a book of LDS scripture known as the *Doctrine and Covenants*. Specifically, it comes from "Excerpts from Three Addresses by President Wilford Woodruff Regarding the Manifesto," which immediately follow the text of Official Declaration 1 (also known as The Manifesto, the statement officially repealing polygamy).

Each ward is overseen by a bishop, a lay minister who has the same sorts of responsibilities as a pastor, priest, or rabbi. Just as the Church president receives divine inspiration for the whole Church, a bishop has the authority to receive God's guidance for his ward. Bishops are not elected, nor do they have formal training as clergy. They are "called" to their position by those leaders in the next level up in the hierarchy (a "stake," roughly comparable to a diocese).[12] This call typically comes without any specific preparation and often without warning. Upon receiving the call – that is, being asked to serve – bishops continue working in their lay occupation, as Mormons have no professional, full-time clergy at the local level. The typical bishop performs his considerable pastoral duties on top of whatever else he does to make a living, whether he is a dentist, schoolteacher, accountant, or so forth.

The concept of authority extends beyond leadership to the rites of the Church, as they can only be performed by those who have been ordained to the LDS priesthood. In one sense, this authority is shared widely, as it includes virtually every active male member of the LDS Church. Fathers usually perform baby blessings, baptisms, and blessings of the sick; teenage boys typically prepare and distribute "the sacrament" (the LDS version of communion).

But while the ranks of the priesthood encompass nearly every active male Mormon, they do not include any women. Thus women are unable to perform rites such as blessings and baptisms. Nor do they serve as bishops or occupy many other ecclesiastical roles. Instead, women serve in the leadership of various sub-organizations within the Church, including the "Relief Society" (women's auxiliary) and programs for children and teenage girls.

### Family

Although history and authority are fundamental to the LDS belief system, the family is its linchpin. Many religions have a high regard for families and speak of family values, but in none does the family have the same theological significance as Mormonism. One cannot understand the contemporary LDS worldview without reference to the faith's unique doctrinal emphasis on family relationships. To understand the theological importance of family, in turn, requires some explanation of LDS temples. The temple is at the heart of modern Mormonism; the family is at the heart of the temple.

Latter-day Saints believe that family relationships can endure beyond the grave, not just as a vague sympathy-card notion, but as part of a holistic set of beliefs about the nature of God and salvation. The Mormon heaven consists of familial relationships that extend into eternity. However, only those who have been bound together – in LDS parlance, "sealed" – will enjoy these familial

---

[12] The term "stake" derives from Isaiah and, apropos of our discussion of the sacred tabernacle, refers to the stakes that hold a tent (Isaiah 54:2) or tabernacle (Isaiah 33:20) in place. Note that all biblical references in this book are to the King James Version.

bonds in the afterlife. To be sealed is an ordinance (or rite, what other faiths would call a sacrament). Sealings take place in LDS temples, which are different than local churches. LDS churches are fairly nondescript, multipurpose buildings open to all and used for everything from Sunday worship to Boy Scout troop meetings to basketball tournaments. Temples, which are generally larger in size, far fewer in number, and often designed as architectural landmarks, are used only for a small set of religious rites, including but not limited to sealings.[13]

Access to LDS temples is restricted to practicing Mormons who have received a recommend to enter the temples by their local leaders. To receive a temple recommend – a small piece of paper about the size of a driver's license – Church members are interviewed by first a bishop and then a "stake president" (regional leader).[14] In each interview they answer a standardized series of questions about their adherence to the faith, both in belief and behavior. After questions about basic theological beliefs, they are asked whether they affirm the basic historical claims related to the Church's founding and if they support the Church's current leaders. Other questions include whether they are honest, pay a full tithe to the Church, follow the Mormon health code, and are sexually chaste (if unmarried) or, if married, completely faithful to their spouse. Temple recommends must be renewed biennially, requiring a fresh set of interviews each time.

This process requires "active" (practicing) Mormons to regularly affirm the fundamentals of their faith, in order to be deemed "worthy" (the LDS term) to have access to the Church's temples. Note that these interviews reflect the LDS emphasis on both history and authority – the former because Latter-day Saints avow both the reality and significance of the events surrounding the birth of the Church, and the latter because Church members can only be granted access to the temples, and thus the pinnacle of LDS worship, with the assent of their local and regional leaders. Obtaining a temple recommend also reinforces the seriousness with which devout Mormons take the temple experience. LDS sermons often mention the sacrifices that many Mormons have made to worship at a temple, especially Church members who live far from the nearest one. The importance of family fuels this desire to reach a temple.

Sociologically, the emphasis on affirming the fundamentals of the faith in order to gain access to the most sacred of spaces creates a symbolic border around believing Mormons. It reinforces the Mormon sense of otherness from both secular society and other religions, while also differentiating between Mormons who are at the core of the faith versus those on the periphery. Adding to the sense of being "set apart" is the confidential nature of the temple ceremonies. Not only is access to the temple limited, but the Church emphasizes to members that they are

---

[13] A sealing often constitutes a couple's wedding or, if they are already married, can be performed as a sort of second wedding, even many years after their initial wedding ceremony. Any children subsequently born to a couple who have been sealed are also considered sealed to the parents. If a married couple already has children, they are sealed to the couple as part of the rite.

[14] Those renewing a recommend can meet with one of the bishop's two counselors (assistants).

not to discuss the details of the temple rituals publicly. In the words of the LDS Church's website, "Temple covenants and ordinances, including the words used, are too sacred to be discussed in detail outside the temple. By avoiding discussion of these sacred things outside the temple, we protect them from mocking, ridicule, or disrespect. Do not be casual when talking about your experiences in the temple."[15]

Theologically, the importance of temple worship extends beyond the binding together of nuclear families – husband, wife, and children. Mormons believe that all human beings are children of the same God and thus constitute one extended family. As a reflection of this belief, Latter-day Saints regularly refer to one another as "brother" and "sister." While this practice occurs in other religions as well, for Mormons these labels are freighted with theological significance. Mormons believe that God wants all of His children to be linked together through a multigenerational chain of interconnected sealings that form a vast family tree. Those believers who have forged such familial bonds will enjoy the highest plane of existence in the next life. It is this belief that leads to the oft-repeated claim that Mormons believe that they can become gods. As an LDS Church president memorably summarized this aspect of Mormon theology: "As man is, God once was. As God is, man may become."[16]

However, as Jana Riess, a careful observer of Mormonism, notes, while LDS doctrine does include the possibility of deification, in practice "many Mormons no longer think about the topic at all; it has become an insignificant aspect of contemporary theological expression" (2011). Instead, they more often speak of spending eternity in the presence of God and their loved ones. In the words of Terryl and Fiona Givens, to Mormons, "heaven consists of those relationships that matter most to us now" (2012).

In the past, sealings were not restricted to one husband, one wife, and their children, as they included polygamous marriages (Van Wagoner 1989).[17] Eventually, however, the current practice of sealings among one man, one woman, and their children became the norm. But since most people are parents as well as children, these sealings are a link across generations. Parents are to be sealed to their children, but also to their own parents. Children who are sealed to their own parents often become sealed to a spouse; that couple will then have children who are sealed to them. Sealings are also done retroactively for ancestors who are no longer living, thus creating a vast chain of familial bonds that expands exponentially through each branch of a family tree. Such sealings for the deceased are performed vicariously; the people participating in the ceremony stand in for deceased family members.

---

[15] Quoted from http://www.lds.org/church/temples/frequently-asked-questions (accessed October 7, 2013).

[16] This couplet was penned by Lorenzo Snow.

[17] Technically, these marriages were polygynous, not polygamous, because they consisted of multiple women married to a single man.

Sealings, are not the only rites performed in the temple, however. Latter-day Saints believe participation in other temple ceremonies to be essential to returning to God. These include an initiation rite and the "endowment," a relatively lengthy ceremony that, like many elements of a Catholic Mass, is virtually identical regardless of the temple, country, or even language in which it is conducted. As with sealings, temple-goers experience these ceremonies once for themselves, but in subsequent visits to the temple they undertake the rites on behalf of specific people who are no longer living, often (and ideally) their own ancestors.

These rites-for-the-deceased also include baptism, which in the LDS tradition is done by full immersion. One's own baptism happens outside the temple at a minimum age of eight years old, but baptisms for the deceased take place within temples. Mormons do not hold that the souls of the deceased automatically become members of the LDS Church – and do not count them in their membership statistics – but believe instead that in the afterlife the departed can choose whether or not to accept baptism, and other rites, done on their behalf. Because LDS temple rites serve to bond family members across generations, Latter-day Saints place great emphasis on genealogical research in order to identify their ancestors, so that temple rites can be performed for them.[18]

The centrality of the temple within LDS theology represents a perfect illustration of the tension within Mormonism between being distinctive and seeking mainstream acceptance. Within the LDS Church, repeated emphasis is placed on worshipping in the temple often – which is separate from regular Sunday worship services and, as noted, requires a Church member to meet specific requirements of both belief and behavior. Mormon children often sing a song with the lyrics, "I love to see the temple; I'm going there some day." LDS lessons and sermons also regularly reinforce that Mormons should plan on getting married (sealed) in a temple and, thus, to a fellow devout Church member. Mormons take great pride in their temples, particularly the prominent "landmark" temples, such as those in Salt Lake City, Washington, DC, and Los Angeles, which include visitors' centers staffed by LDS missionaries. Many Mormons have a picture of one or more temples in their homes. A Mormon's first time participating in the temple rites is a significant rite of passage, not unlike a Jewish bar or bat mitzvah or a Catholic confirmation (although, unlike these other ceremonies, it typically takes place in one's late teens or early twenties). In short, aspiring to participate in the rites of the temple permeates the culture of Mormonism.

However, the confidential nature of temple worship raises suspicion among some non-Mormons. Except for public tours conducted before they are formally

---

[18] Recent years have seen controversy over this practice, as some Mormons had been entering the names of Holocaust victims to whom they were not related into the vast database used for the proxy ceremonies. The LDS Church has affirmed that Church members should only input the genealogical records of their own ancestors (Stack 2012a).

dedicated, temples are closed to non-Mormons (and Church members who do not meet the requirements for admission). Those tours are of the interior of the building, but do not include details of the ceremonies themselves.

Because LDS temples are both celebrated and criticized, the very language used to describe aspects of LDS temple worship is fraught. What Mormons celebrate as *inspirational*, critics of the Church see as *sinister*. Mormons describe the temple ceremonies as *sacred*; critics say they are *secret*. And perhaps most fraught of all is the temple "garment," or underclothing that devout Mormons receive as part of the temple's initiation rite, and which they are required to wear for the rest of their lives. To critics of the Church, garments are an object of ridicule. To those without much of an opinion about Mormonism, they might seem strange. To Latter-day Saints, garments are a "reminder of the sacred covenants they have made with the Lord and also as a protection against temptation and evil" (Asay 1997).[19] In this way, they are similar to symbolic underclothing worn by the devout of other faiths, including the Catholics' scapular, the orthodox Jews' *tallit katan*, and the Sikhs' *kacchera*. And however garments are perceived by non-Mormons, they serve as a highly tangible boundary marker for Mormons themselves. In the words of historian Matthew Bowman, "they remind both Mormons and everybody else that these people are of a different faith" (2012b).

While garments may be the most tangible example of how LDS temple worship forges a strong sense of religious identity, the totality of the temple experience contributes both to Mormons' high levels of religious commitment and strong bonds with fellow Church members. Historian John Turner describes the temple as creating an "extended, ecclesial family" (2012, 141) as Mormons began their arduous emigration from Illinois to Utah, forging a sense of peoplehood and fortifying them against hardship. The specific challenges faced by Mormons differ today, but their temples still serve to bind them together and steel them against a world that they often see as antithetical to their values.

The familial bonds forged in temples extend beyond Mormons now living, as according to LDS theology, every person who has ever lived must have these religious ordinances performed on their behalf. This theological imperative not only motivates the Mormon emphasis on genealogical research, it means that temple-going Mormons believe that they are playing a role in weaving all of humanity into a vast network of interlocking, eternal relationships.

This brief introduction to Mormonism only scratches the surface. We could say more about the Mormon health code, the faith's emphasis on sexual chastity, the importance Mormons place on self-sufficiency, the LDS system of caring for the poor and needy, Mormons' belief in the payment of a literal tithe (10 percent of one's income) to the Church, and the Church's extensive missionary force of young men and women. Indeed, many of these aspects of Mormonism will arise in the pages to follow.

---

[19]  In this talk, Elder Carlos E. Asay was quoting a letter written by the LDS Church's First Presidency in 1988 to local leaders of the Church.

But this brief discussion highlights beliefs and practices that are – or can become – politically relevant. For example, in later chapters we see that a large majority of Mormons believe that the U.S. Constitution is divinely inspired, a historical claim that resonates with their understanding that God prepared the United States as the nation where Christ's true Church could be restored. Similarly, Mormon teachings about the authority of their Church leaders help explain why so many Latter-day Saints responded with alacrity when the LDS hierarchy mobilized them to support California's Proposition 8 (an initiative to write a ban on gay marriage into the state constitution). The family's theological primacy perhaps helps illuminate why the issue of gay marriage – framed as a threat to the traditional family – has such potency among Latter-day Saints. The strong bonds formed among Mormons, facilitated by the nature of temple worship, foster an unrivaled level of religious vitality, but can also close Mormons off from extensive interaction with non-Mormons, making them ripe for suspicion. Wariness of Mormons can be exacerbated by some of their seemingly "exotic" beliefs and practices, causing potential harm to the electoral prospects of LDS politicians.

WHAT ARE MORMONS LIKE?

In round numbers, there are roughly 15 million members of the LDS Church worldwide, approximately 6 million of whom live in the United States.[20] In keeping with the theme of being quintessentially American in some ways but highly distinctive in others, Mormons are both similar to and different from the rest of the American population. Compared to other Americans, Mormons are predominantly white and married, moderately better educated, and more likely to be in the middle class.

As shown in Table 1.1, 85 percent of Mormons describe their race as white, compared to 70 percent of non-Mormons. Reflecting the emphasis on families within Mormonism, nearly 71 percent of adult Mormons are married, compared to 54 percent of the rest of the population. They also have more children than the general population. Of married respondents, Mormons have an average of 3.5 children, compared to a national average of 2.2. Fewer Mormons report having less than a high school diploma than non-Mormons (9 percent versus 14 percent), while more Mormons report having some post-secondary schooling (but less than a four-year degree) than the rest of the population – 36 percent compared to 27 percent. Mormons are about as likely to have a four-year or postgraduate degree as are non-Mormons.

Mormons are also more likely than the general population to report a household income between $50,000 and $75,000 (22 percent versus 17 percent); this means Mormons are more likely than others to be in the middle of the income

[20] http://www.mormonnewsroom.org/facts-and-stats (accessed October 7, 2013).

TABLE 1.1. *A Demographic Profile of Mormons*

|                                         | Mormons | Non-Mormons |
|-----------------------------------------|---------|-------------|
| **Race (%)**                            |         |             |
| White                                   | 85      | 70          |
| Black                                   | 3       | 11          |
| Hispanic                                | 7       | 12          |
| **Marital Status (%)**                  |         |             |
| Married                                 | 71      | 54          |
| Living with someone                     | 3       | 6           |
| Divorced                                | 8       | 10          |
| Never been married                      | 12      | 19          |
| **Children**                            |         |             |
| Number of children                      | 3.5     | 2.2         |
| **Education (%)**                       |         |             |
| Less than high school                   | 9       | 14          |
| High school                             | 27      | 32          |
| Some college, technical school, etc.    | 36      | 27          |
| College degree (4 year)                 | 18      | 16          |
| Postgraduate degree                     | 10      | 11          |
| **Income (%)**                          |         |             |
| Fewer than $50,000                      | 47      | 53          |
| $50,000–$74,999                         | 22      | 17          |
| $75,000–$150,000                        | 25      | 22          |
| More than $150,000                      | 7       | 8           |

*Source*: Pew U.S. Religious Landscape Survey, 2007; General Social Survey, 2000–10 (for number of children, which includes married respondents only)

distribution, as the median household income in the United States is roughly $50,000. Mormons are less likely to report an income below $50,000, but about as likely to report an income between $75,000 and $150,000, or more than $150,000.[21] Prominent Latter-day Saints like Mitt Romney may suggest a stereotype of Mormons as wealthy, but the data suggest that the modal Mormon is better described as middle class – another example of their quintessential "American-ness."

As shown in Figure 1.1, American Mormons are largely concentrated in Utah, with a critical mass in Idaho, Nevada, Wyoming, and Arizona – a historical

[21] These numbers are derived from the Pew U.S. Religious Landscape Survey, a very large, nationally representative survey of the American population. With a total of 35,556 respondents, the data include 581 Mormons, a far larger sample than in most other national surveys. The statistics reported here are very similar to those found in the American Religious Identification Survey (Phillips and Cragun 2011), an even larger national survey that has not yet been released for secondary analysis. See Data Appendix for more details on the Pew U.S. Religious Landscape survey and other survey data used throughout the book.

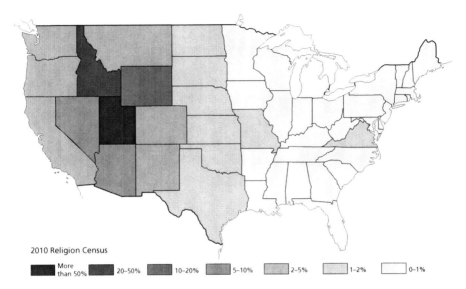

FIGURE 1.1. Percentage of Mormons

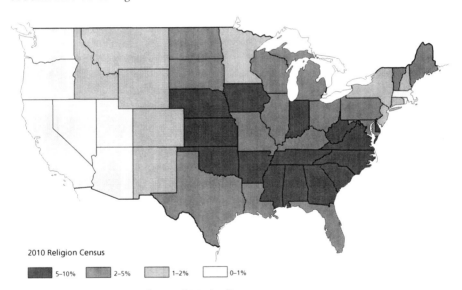

FIGURE 1.2. Percentage of United Methodists

vestige of the Mormon migration to the Mountain West in the nineteenth century. For comparison, Figures 1.2 and 1.3 display the geographic dispersion of United Methodists and Southern Baptists. Methodists share some historical parallels with Mormonism, as both were "frontier faiths" in the nineteenth century, while Southern Baptists, like Mormons, have historical roots in one region of the country. Yet neither Methodists nor Southern Baptists – indeed, no other religious

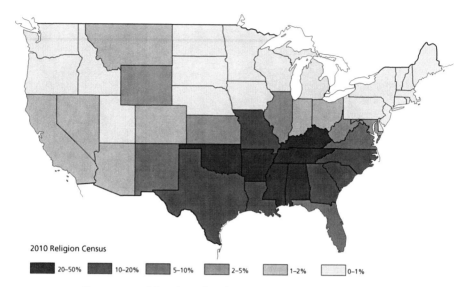

FIGURE 1.3. Percentage of Southern Baptists
*Source:* Association of Statisticians of American Religious Bodies

group – are as concentrated in one area of the country, as "Mormons are the most geographically isolated and uniquely distributed religious group in the U.S." (Phillips and Cragun 2011, 2). Nonetheless, the days of Mormons' seclusion are long gone, as they have diffused throughout the country.

PLAN OF THE BOOK

In centering on the paradox of Mormons as "quintessential Americans" and a "peculiar people," this book examines how both features affect the politics of Mormons and the political reaction to Mormons by other Americans. Part I (Chapters 1–3) delineates the boundaries that define Mormons as an ethno-religious group. Part II (Chapters 4–6) examines the implications of those boundaries for the political behavior of Mormons. Part III (Chapters 7–9) then examines how these boundaries create public perceptions of Mormonism and how those perceptions affect the political behavior of non-Mormons.

Part I: Mormons as an Ethno-Religious Group

This chapter has provided a brief introduction to Mormonism as a religion and Mormons as a people. Chapter 2 then develops a theoretical framework for understanding Mormons as an ethno-religious group with a distinctive subculture. Chapter 3 uses a wealth of data, including a new survey of Mormons we have conducted, to go deep into the religious and social distinctiveness of Latter-day Saints – what they believe, how they behave, and their sense of belonging. In addition to showing the distinctiveness of Mormons' religious belief and behavior when compared to adherents of other traditions, this chapter also shows that not all Mormons are alike. They differ in their level of religious activity, attitudes toward authority, their own self-identity as Mormons, and their immersion in Mormon-centered social networks.

## Part II: Political Behavior of Mormons

Chapters 4 and 5 describe the political ramifications of Mormons' distinctiveness. Mormons, we shall see, are politically peculiar – sometimes in unexpected ways. They are predominantly Republican, but have not always been so. They are overwhelmingly conservative, but with a twist on key issues. When LDS teachings are out of step with conservative orthodoxy, Mormons generally follow their church over their party. Chapter 6 examines Mormon political mobilization in more detail, by analyzing how Mormons react when they receive political cues from their religious leaders. Drawing on the literature regarding political persuasion and mobilization, we discuss how Mormonism creates the conditions for effective persuasion, and rapid, intense – but infrequent – political mobilization. We also put the political influence of LDS leaders to the test by examining whether they can move Mormons' opinion against their natural political predisposition, to the left instead of the right. (They can.)

## Part III: The Consequences of Distinctiveness

Part III begins with Chapter 7, which examines public opinion toward Mormons both in the past and present. Mormons' distinctiveness is a mixed blessing, as it leads to both positive and negative stereotypes circulating in the cultural ether. On balance, negative information is more common, which means that most Americans "store" more negative than positive impressions of Mormons in their mental filing systems. We find that Mormons face this negativity, at least in part, because of the limited social connections between Mormons and non-Mormons, combined with most Americans' relative lack of accurate information about the LDS religion. This sets the stage for Chapter 8, where we examine the political consequences of Americans' attitudes toward Mormons with case studies of LDS presidential candidates. Different candidates have dealt with their Mormonism in different ways – and with different results. Key to these differences is the degree to which a candidate's religion is politicized.

Chapter 9 then examines how attitudes toward Mormons affected Mitt Romney in 2008 and 2012, when the supply of information about Mormonism increased – particularly in 2008, when Romney's religion was novel. Initially, the only voters untroubled by Romney's Mormonism were those who had the preexisting condition of personal knowledge of or about Mormons. By Election Day 2012, however, for most voters partisanship trumped any concerns about religion. Romney's religion mattered a lot to a few voters, but mattered little to most. This chapter also asks whether Romney's candidacy has affected attitudes toward Mormons. In spite of the LDS Church's efforts to present itself as politically neutral, we will show that attitudes toward Mormons have become sharply polarized along partisan lines. Whether this polarization will persist remains an open question.

Chapter 10 concludes by considering how Mormonism presents a challenge to religious pluralism in America. While the last fifty years have seen most other religious boundaries blur, Mormons have remained distinctive – even if their distinguishing characteristics have undergone change. While other groups are religiously distinctive too, arguably none can match the Latter-day Saints' combination of distinctiveness, size, and growth.

From the beginning of Mormonism, Latter-day Saints have had an uneasy relationship with the rest of American society. Upon describing his first revelations, Joseph Smith describes being met with ridicule. As the "Mormon movement" grew, ridicule became violence, until eventually Mormons consciously reenacted the journey of the ancient Israelites as they trekked to what they hoped would be their promised land. In the years since, Mormons have employed four broad strategies to address their paradoxical place in American society – separation, assimilation, engagement, and alignment – each with its own benefits and costs, and each with a different conception of the promised land. Mormons are thus a test of America's promise of religious pluralism. Can a group be both distinctive and accepted?

# 2

# The Sacred Tabernacle

## Mormons as an Ethno-Religious Group

Most people do not take kindly to being described as "peculiar," finding the term pejorative and perhaps even insulting. Not Mormons. In a national survey of Latter-day Saints we conducted, 79 percent agreed that they can be described as a "peculiar people," echoing the frequent use of this phrase within LDS circles.[1] If the willing adoption of peculiar as a label seems, well, peculiar, we should note that the phrase is biblical, used in both the Old and New Testaments to describe God's people. The apostle Peter speaks of converts to Christianity as "a chosen generation, a royal priesthood, a holy nation, a peculiar people" (1 Peter 2:9), echoing the language in Deuteronomy describing the Israelites as "a holy people . . . a peculiar people" (Deuteronomy 14:2). In this context, peculiar does not mean strange so much as "chosen." Mormons often use the term with a hint of wry humor, while also relishing the differentness that comes with being a practicing member of their faith.

Mormons' self-perception of their peculiarity is empirically accurate. As we will detail in the pages to follow, Mormons are highly distinctive in many ways – religiously, culturally, and politically. In this chapter, we argue that Mormons are an example of an "ethno-religious" group – one of many in American history and society – characterized by a distinctive subculture. The Mormon subculture is peculiar: it has the high level of group solidarity typically associated with ethnicity, nationality, or race, but this ethnic-like character is the product of religion. We call this subculture the "sacred tabernacle." However, high solidarity with insiders comes at the price of high tension with outsiders. This trade-off is the theme of this chapter and, indeed, this whole book.

---

[1] See the details of the Peculiar People Survey in Data Appendix; this survey will be discussed further in Chapter 3.

AN ETHNIC GROUP?

We are hardly the first to note Mormons' peculiarity. Owing to their distinctiveness, some scholars have described Mormons as an ethnic group. To our knowledge, however, none has gone as far as a report from a U.S. Army officer in 1861:

Whether owing to the practice of a purely sensual and material religion, to the premature development of the passions, or to isolation, there is, nevertheless, an expression of countenance and a style of feature, which may be styled the Mormon expression and style; an expression compounded of sensuality, cunning, suspicion, and a smirking self-conceit. The yellow, sunken, cadaverous visage; the greenish-colored eyes; the thick, protuberant lips; the low forehead; the light, yellowish hair; and the lank, angular person, constitute an appearance so characteristic of the new race. (Givens 1997, 136)

These words were written at a time when Mormons were the scourge of America and the federal government had sent the Army to quell their supposed rebellion in the far-off and isolated Utah territory. Once the transcontinental railroad ended Utah's isolation, the LDS Church ended polygamy, and Utah's statehood ended Mormons' political segregation, tensions simmered down. Even though the precise contours of Mormons' distinctiveness changed – polygamy was out, but strict adherence to an abstemious health code was in – there could be no doubt that the Latter-day Saints were indeed a peculiar people (Alexander 1996; Fluhman 2012).

Even if Mormons do not have unique physical characteristics (i.e. a "new race"), are they sociologically distinctive enough to be considered an ethnic group? The question is more than idle speculation, as answering it helps us understand Mormons' niche in American society. As we consider whether Mormons can be classified as an ethnic group, our key criterion should be whether the label helps or hinders our understanding of Mormonism.

If ethnicity simply refers to a sense of collective belonging (Varshney 2007), Mormons definitely qualify. The contemporary Latter-day Saints certainly are characterized by a high level of internal solidarity. As shown in Figure 2.1, Mormons rate their fellow Mormons more positively than do members of any other group – a higher rating than Hispanics give Hispanics, African Americans give African Americans, and Jews give Jews.

In addition, Mormons have a strong sense of group identity. In a national survey of Mormons, we found that 90 percent agreed that "when I talk about Mormons, I usually say 'we' rather than 'they.'" And Mormons are 20 percentage points more likely than the rest of the American population to say that they prefer to buy goods and services from "someone who shares your religious beliefs," a common stereotype of ethnic "clannishness."[2] Furthermore, Mormons are perceived as different by fellow Americans, often in a negative light (see Chapter 7).

---

[2] More precisely, according to the 2006 Faith Matters survey, 46 percent of Mormons say that they prefer to "buy from someone who shares your religious beliefs if you have a chance," sometimes, most of the time, or always. Among the rest of the population, 27 percent say that they prefer to do

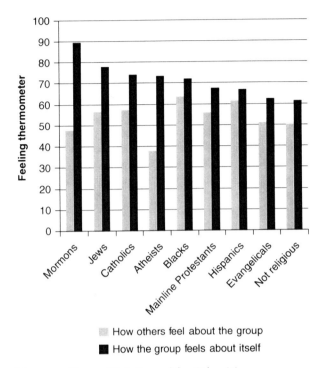

FIGURE 2.1. Mormons Have a High Regard for Other Mormons
Perceptions Are a "feeling thermometer," ranging from 0 to 100
*Source:* Faith Matters Survey, 2011

However, membership in Mormonism is not defined by genealogical descent, which Kanchan Chandra (2006) argues is the essential characteristic of ethnicity. While many Mormons are born into the faith, large numbers are converts. In the same spirit as Chandra, Donald Horowitz (1985) writes of a continuum between birth and choice; the former makes a stronger claim on ethnicity than the latter. As a proselytizing religion, Mormons would seem to be on the choice end of the spectrum, thus weakening any claim to ethnic status. In contrast, racial groups, such as African Americans, are closer to the birth end of spectrum. Race is also a powerful source of internal solidarity and external tension that is regularly likened to ethnicity.[3]

For Mormons, however, the birth-choice distinction is not so clear-cut because their theology places great emphasis on familial relationships (see Chapter 1).

business with someone who has the same religious beliefs. Evangelicals are similar, as 47 percent say that they prefer to do business with their coreligionists.

[3] Even racial identity, however, can be a matter of choice. See Barack Obama's *Dreams from My Father* for a case study (2004).

While, like members of many other faiths, Mormons speak of being symbolically "reborn" when baptized, they also refer more literally to being members of the "House of Israel." One of the faith's rites even involves declaring an individual Mormon to be descended from one of the biblical tribes of Israel (either literally or by adoption; the declaration typically does not specify).[4] This Judaic reference is one way that Mormons forge a sense of community, extending back to the biblical prophet Abraham – likewise, Mormons often refer to their Church as "Israel." Mormons are also known for their prodigious genealogical work, motivated by the belief that family relationships can extend beyond the grave. Many Latter-day Saints today also trace their genealogy to the Mormon pioneers who often suffered great hardship emigrating to the Mountain West. Even those Mormons who do not have a direct family tie to the pioneers are encouraged to claim this sacralized journey as part of their heritage. Thus, while many Mormons are "made," not "born," a convert to Mormonism joins a community replete with references to the sort of familial bonds common to ethnic groups that are unambiguously hereditary.

Language is another marker of ethnicity. Even though modern Latter-day Saints do not have their own tongue per se, they did once, in fact, have an indigenous language. Known as the Deseret alphabet, it was invented in the 1800s to help Mormon immigrants who spoke a smorgasbord of languages to communicate with one another (Arrington and Bitton 1992). The Deseret alphabet did not endure, but its legacy of a group bound together by a distinctive argot has. And anyone who has spent time with a group of Mormons can attest that they have their own vocabulary that often requires translation for outsiders. Just for starters, congregations are "wards," while dioceses are "stakes." With their distinctive vocabulary, Mormons resemble second-generation members of ethnic groups whose English is peppered with terms and expressions from their ancestral tongue.

Ethnicity is often linked to nationality, especially in the United States (M. Gordon 1966). This connection is due to the presence of a steady stream of immigrants, first from northern and western Europe, later from southern and eastern Europe, and now from Latin America, Asia, and Africa. In this sense, ethnicity is fostered when a people are nurtured for generations in a particular place, be it Ireland, Poland, or Swaziland. Since Mormons come from all these places, they do not have a single nationality. However, *Mormonism* does have a nation of origin – the United States. Mormonism was founded in the dynamic context of the new American nation. Joseph Smith's initial religious visions occurred in the "burned-over district" in western New York, a place consumed by the intensity of the Second Great Awakening and the location of numerous religious and social innovations (Cross 1981). Smith and his followers shared many of the values of the era, including individual freedom, personal holiness,

---

[4] Known as a "patriarchal blessing," this rite not only includes a declaration of lineage from a tribe of Israel but also personalized instruction and encouragement.

economic self-sufficiency, and the providential origins of the United States. Hostile reaction to Smith's peculiar theology and the eventual migration of Mormons to Utah nurtured a sense of nationhood in the generations that followed (see Chapter 1). This perspective was at once strongly American and uniquely Mormon in character.

Because of their distinctiveness, some scholars have described Mormons in explicitly ethnic terms. For example, the *Harvard Encyclopedia of American Ethnic Groups* includes an entry for Mormons (May 1980). Likewise, sociologist Thomas O'Dea came to live in Utah in the 1950s and wrote what is generally considered to be the first sociological study of Mormons by someone outside the faith. In describing the Mormon experience in America, O'Dea wrote that "The Mormon group came closer to evolving an ethnic identity on this continent than did any other comparable group. Moreover, it was a genuine, locally and independently conceived, ethnicity, born and nurtured on this side of the water and not imported from abroad" (1957, 116). Decades later, Laurence Moore wrote that "A sense of difference has persisted so strongly among Mormons that they have probably gained an ethnic as well a religious identity, thus becoming like the Jewish people they have always emulated" (1986, 44).

Although both O'Dea and Moore invoke ethnicity, note the hints of equivocation from both. O'Dea writes that Mormons came *closer* to ethnicity than anyone else, not that they necessarily achieved it. Likewise, Moore describes Mormons as *probably* having gained an ethnic identity. While a case can be made for classifying Mormons as an ethnic group, the taxonomy seems fraught, as it rests precariously on both a contested definition of ethnicity and a particular interpretation of LDS theology. Our answer to the question of whether Mormons are accurately labeled as an ethnic group is that, on balance, the label obscures more than it reveals. We concur with Armand Mauss, who argues that "although Mormons might have once become a separate ethnic group in America, they never actually did" (Mauss 1994, 46). He asks, "If Mormons of all sizes, shapes, colors, cultures, and geographic origins can comprise an ethnic group then who, one wonders, cannot?" (64).

Nonetheless, we take seriously those scholars who argue for the ethnic character of Mormonism. Definitional quibbles aside, their main point stands: Mormonism is something more than just another religious denomination. Even those who avoid the label of "ethnic" nonetheless settle on labels that go beyond a denominational label. In lieu of ethnicity, others have described Mormons as a "tribe" (Kotkin 1993) and a "people" (Bloom 1992; Bowman 2012a). In this regard, Mormons resemble the ethnic communities among American Jews (D. D. Moore 1981), Catholics (Greeley 1976), and Muslims (Pew Forum on Religion & Public Life 2011; Ewing 2008).

In short, what makes a Methodist a Methodist differs from what makes a Mormon a Mormon. For our purposes, what matters is that Mormons' distinctiveness, at least in some contexts, produces high levels of internal solidarity and strong external tension that *resemble* an ethnic group. What Terryl Givens writes about Mormons in the nineteenth century applies today as well: "The debate as to what term most accurately categorizes Mormonism is not the point here. Clearly, the group transcended merely denominational status fairly early in the nineteenth century, and was *represented* as something akin to an ethnic community" (1997, 17, emphasis in original).

## MORMONISM AS A SUBCULTURE

In an era of theological "mushiness" (Douthat 2012), where few Americans have much religious literacy (Prothero 2007), and even practical distinctions between faiths are generally either unknown or ignored, what explains Mormons' peculiarity? Why have they not morphed into being just another denomination among many? The puzzle is even more daunting upon consideration of what *does not* explain Mormons' peculiarity, as perceived by themselves or others. Consider theories that religious "sects" are a product of isolation, whether geographic, social, or economic (J. D. Hunter 1983; Crawford 1980; Wood and Hughes 1984). Although Mormons once fit this description, contra such explanations, modern Mormons are far from isolated. Geographically, Latter-day Saints have diffused across the United States and, increasingly, the globe. Socially, Mormons no longer live in a "sheltered enclave," segregating themselves from broader American society like the Old Order Amish or some ultraorthodox Jews. Economically, Mormons are hardly deprived (see Chapter 1). Far from being shunted into a far-off corner of society, Mormons are fully integrated into the heart of American institutions such as business (J. Willard Marriott of the eponymous hotel chain), literature (Stephenie Meyer, *Twilight* author), sports (Steve Young, San Francisco 49ers), entertainment (the Osmonds, David Archuleta of *American Idol*), and, of course, politics (Mitt Romney, Harry Reid, and Glenn Beck come to mind). Isolation may well have explained Mormon peculiarity in the nineteenth century, but not in the twenty-first.

Mormons are not segregated from American culture but instead engaged with it. This engagement lies at the heart of a compelling explanation for Mormons' distinctiveness: the theory of subcultural identity. Employed by sociologist Christian Smith and his colleagues (1998) to explain American evangelicalism, it illuminates the Mormon case as well. The term "subcultural identity" refers to a group, religious or otherwise, that combines points of contact with, as well as points of distinction from, the broader culture. The subculture is thus a part of the larger culture, overlapping with it in some respects, but in tension with it in others. That tension feeds the subculture's vitality. The recognition of such tension in religious subcultures is not unique to Mormons, a point well illustrated by Rodney Clapp's (1996) call for the "church" to be a "peculiar people" and the common use of the term to describe other American religious groups (Noll and Harlow 2007). Thus, the fact that

Mormons are peculiar does not make them unique; their uniqueness lies in what makes them peculiar.

Subcultural identity theory shares some similarities with the theory that "strict churches are strong" (Finke and Stark 2005; Iannaccone 1994). Rooted in the assumptions of market economics, the strict church theory holds that in order to thrive, religions must have what economists call high barriers to entry – such as prohibitions on sexual activity, a strict health code, or a dress code. Religions that ask for a lot provide the deepest meaning in their members' lives. They also screen out free riders, making it easier to overcome the usual dilemma of collective action, since the group members all have a deep commitment to the same cause. Mormonism is the archetypal case of successful strictness. Appropriately, one of the leading proponents of the strictness theory of religious vitality, Rodney Stark (1984; 1996), has also projected sustained, long-term growth for Mormonism.

However, while strictness might be necessary for religious vitality – and there is even debate about that (Marwell 1996; Norris and Inglehart 2011; Voas, Olson, and Crockett 2002) – it is clearly not sufficient. Plenty of religions with high barriers to entry have foundered. Subcultural identity theory adds another ingredient to explain the endurance and growth of a high-demand faith. To thrive, a religion must reinforce its distinctiveness through engagement with the broader culture in which it is embedded. Here are Smith et al.'s words applying subcultural identity theory to evangelicalism. We have added the word "Mormonism" alongside their original references to "evangelicalism" below to demonstrate that the theory applies to the LDS case as well.

American evangelicalism [Mormonism], we contend, is strong not because it is shielded against, but because it is – or at least perceives itself to be – embattled with forces that seem to oppose or threaten it. Indeed, evangelicalism [Mormonism], we suggest, *thrives* on distinction, engagement, tension, conflict, and threat. Without these, evangelicalism [Mormonism] would lose its identity and purpose and grow languid and aimless. (Smith et al. 1998, 89)

The tension integral to forging a subcultural identity arises from social boundaries that the subgroup draws between itself and other groups. Smith et al. refer to these boundaries as symbolic, but some can be tangible as well. For contemporary evangelicals, the principal boundary is between them and "the world." As Smith et al. describe it, "the world" is a nebulous concept, but essentially refers to what devout evangelicals seek to avoid – a sinful society rife with temptation.

Mormons also speak of standing firm against such temptations, "being *in* but not *of* the world." For Mormons this language is more than rhetorical, as they have many points of departure from the mores of American society. Mormons have made abstention from alcohol, tobacco, coffee, and tea a hallmark of their religious orthodoxy; accordingly, a 2013 study by Gallup finds that Mormons are the religious group least likely to smoke (Newport and Himelfarb 2013). And while in the nineteenth century the Mormon practice of polygamy led to the

caricature of Mormon men as licentious, today Mormons are accurately characterized as upholding traditional views on sexuality. According to the 2012
Pew Mormons in America survey,[5] 79 percent of Mormons say that sex between
unmarried adults is morally wrong compared to only 35 percent of the general
population. Mormons also diverge from the growing acceptance of homosexuality. Sixty-five percent of Mormons say that homosexuality should be discouraged by society, compared to 33 percent of the general public (Pew Forum
on Religion & Public Life 2012a).

Mormons also *see* themselves as being in tension with American society.
Two-thirds of Mormons say that their values are threatened in America today –
about the same percentage as evangelicals, and higher than any other religious
group.[6] Similarly, in a different survey Mormons were most likely to say
that their values are threatened by "Hollywood and the entertainment industry," the primary conveyor of popular culture. Sixty-eight percent of Mormons
agree that they feel threatened by Hollywood, compared to 53 percent of
evangelicals and 38 percent of the general population.[7]

Mormons are not the only religious subculture, whether we are speaking of
the present or the past. Perhaps the largest and best known is the Catholic
subculture, particularly in the late nineteenth and early twentieth centuries
(O'Brien 1968). In the face of an often hostile Protestantism, Catholics developed their subculture and institutions to support it, including schools, colleges,
hospitals, charities, and even professional associations – paralleling and yet
engaging with American society (Greeley 1967). Traditionally, Catholics worried about "the world, the flesh, and the devil" as the main sources of temptation. Although the boundaries of the Catholic subculture have diminished since
the middle of the twentieth century, it is still a touchstone of Catholic identity
(P. Steinfels 2003; D'Antonio, Dillon, and Gautier 2013). Today, evangelical
Christians have also created a subculture of their own, complete with organizations, institutions, and entertainment that are self-consciously Christian (Smith
et al. 1998). Like Catholics of yesteryear and evangelicals today, Mormons have
also developed a set of subcultural institutions that run parallel to those of the
broader culture. There are LDS bookstores, novels, movies, pop music, match-
making websites, universities and other educational institutions, and so on.[8]

---

[5] See Data Appendix for details of the Pew Mormons in American Survey.
[6] These results are from the Faith Matters survey, conducted by Robert Putnam and David
    Campbell. See their book *American Grace: How Religion Divides and Unites Us* (2010) for
    more details about the survey.
[7] See Data Appendix for details of the Pew U.S. Religious Landscape Survey.
[8] There are a few LDS private elementary and secondary schools and a small LDS home-schooling
    population. Most LDS youth attend public schools but supplement their secular education with a
    daily religious class. Known as "seminary," it is either held before the school day in areas with a
    small concentration of LDS Church members, or during the school day (release time) in areas
    where Mormons have a critical mass. Release-time seminary classes are held in LDS-owned

Although Mormons have drawn clear boundaries with the world, by which they mean a society that has embraced values antithetical to their own, it is not their only line of demarcation. In Chapter 1, we described history, authority, and family as the defining features of the LDS belief system, which intertwine to form a sharp boundary between Mormonism and all other religions, especially the forms of Christianity that predominate in America.

From its founding, Mormonism has made the audacious claim that Joseph Smith received his prophetic call after literally speaking with God. The restoration channeled through Joseph Smith was necessary, Mormons believe, because of what they call the great apostasy, a historical period that stretches from shortly after the establishment of early Christianity to Joseph Smith's revelations. During this time, the truth was corrupted and the line of God's authority had been broken. Joseph Smith wrote of hearing from God's own mouth that he was not to join an existing church, "for they were all wrong" and "all their creeds were an abomination in his sight."[9] This historical claim to authority is regularly reinforced within Mormon culture. Twice a year, believing Mormons worldwide raise their right hands in unison to signify that they "sustain" or believe the Church's president and other top leaders to be "prophets, seers, and revelators," having received the same mantle as Joseph Smith.

Attend any LDS meeting and you are likely to hear Church members repeat the common Mormon expression that "they know the Church is true," which means, of course, that all other churches are not. According to the Pew U. S. Religious Landscape Survey, Mormons are far and away the religious group most likely to say that "my religion is the one, true faith leading to eternal life" (see Chapter 3). At the risk of understatement, this core Mormon belief makes for a substantial boundary with people of other religions.[10]

---

buildings that are typically built very close to public high schools. At the postsecondary level, there are a number of LDS universities, including one that is independent of the LDS Church but nonetheless defines itself as having a "Latter-day Saint environment" (Southern Virginia University). For Mormon students not enrolled in LDS schools, the Church offers a college-level version of seminary classes (known in LDS parlance as "Institutes of Religion," they are much like Jewish Hillel Houses or Catholic Newman Centers).

[9] *Joseph Smith History*, verse 19. This canonized history is found in the LDS book of scripture known as *The Pearl of Great Price*.

[10] As one reviewer has noted, the LDS belief that theirs is the "only true and living church" (an oft-repeated phrase among Mormons) does not preclude that other religions have some truth – just not all of it. LDS apostle Elder Dallin H. Oaks has spoken of the way Mormons declare that their Church is true. "Sometimes we do this in a way that gives great offense to people who belong to other churches or who subscribe to other philosophies. But God has not taught us anything that should cause us to feel superior to other people. Certainly all churches and philosophies have elements of truth in them, some more than others" (Oaks 2010) Interestingly, the comments left below this article on the lds.org website illustrate how rank and file Mormons speak of their Church as true, typically without the nuance suggested by Oaks. One commenter writes, "Only this church can help all to understand how to gain true salvation and eternal life. This is amazing to know and something I wish people could accept, but as this article says, it is not 'politically correct' and is therefore shunned in society."

These concepts of history, authority, and family are not merely vestiges of religious doctrines once believed and now ignored. They are the core tenets of modern Mormonism, regularly taught and widely espoused by Latter-day Saints. As we describe in Chapter 3, there are many uniquely Mormon beliefs that are nearly universally held within the faith. Among these are that the *Book of Mormon* is scripture, that the LDS Church is led by a prophet, and that LDS temple ceremonies bind families together to endure beyond the grave.

With its doctrinal emphasis on exclusivity, Mormonism has drawn a clear boundary with other faiths. Over the arc of the LDS Church's history, its distinctive theology and practices – ranging from polygamy in the past to temple rites in the present – have generally accentuated the sharpness of that boundary. Because of this distinctiveness, Jan Shipps (1985), an eminent scholar of Mormon history, calls Mormonism a "new world religion."

Such exclusive faith claims are not unique to Mormons, of course. Historically, Catholics maintained they represented the true "apostolic church," while Jews regarded themselves as God's "chosen people." These claims once fostered tensions with Protestants, although they have largely abated today. Perhaps the best-known example of religious exclusiveness is the fundamentalist movement of the early twentieth century, a progenitor of contemporary evangelical Protestantism. In a fashion similar to Mormons, fundamentalists sought to restore the New Testament faith, and drew sharp religious boundaries with other Protestants, Catholics, Jews – and Mormons. The aggressiveness and intensity of religious exclusiveness may have declined in response to increased pluralism in the United States, but it is still a feature of some religious subcultures (Putnam and Campbell 2010).

Mormons have clearly flourished by sharply drawing two boundaries – one with secular society ("the world") and the other with other religions. Or, phrased differently, Mormons are fighting a "two-front war." We use the term "war" with our tongues planted firmly in our cheeks, but as a metaphor it is apropos. Mormons themselves often use martial metaphors, speaking of putting on the "armor of God" and likening Mormon youth to a group of young ("stripling") soldiers described in the *Book of Mormon*. The meaning is purely allegorical, but the imagery is telling nonetheless.[11] In adopting such militaristic rhetoric, Mormons reinforce their self-identity as a besieged minority, and mimic comparable language found in other religious subcultures, for example, the *Knights* of Columbus or the Salvation *Army*.

An important element of subcultural identity theory is that boundaries defining distinctiveness need not remain static. As befitting subcultures that engage with a dynamic wider culture in which they are embedded, their specific elements

---

[11]  For example, see the talk (sermon) by Elder Boyd K. Packer, a senior LDS apostle and next in line to become Church president: "How to Survive in Enemy Territory." In this address, Elder Packer speaks of how "the adversary [i.e. Satan] has infiltrated the world around you. He is in homes, entertainment, the media, language – everything around you" (Packer 2012).

of distinction change in response to broader trends in society. Smith et al. (1998, 102) write of how religious traditions "creatively renegotiate and strategically adapt their beliefs and practices to perform more robustly in a modern context." In keeping with this dynamic aspect of the theory, Mormons have not always drawn the same boundaries they do today. Renegotiation and adaptation has characterized Mormonism throughout its history.

In its earliest days, Mormonism was defined by a physical gathering to Zion, first in Ohio, then Missouri, then Illinois, then the Mountain West. New converts would leave their homes to immigrate to these new frontiers – for many a promised land, where they could find refuge from persecution. Upon settling in the West, the boundaries that set Mormons apart were not merely symbolic, but instead the very tangible Rocky Mountains. Having found sanctuary, Mormons continued to gather but now were known, and reviled, for the practice of plural marriage. Not all Mormons practiced polygamy, but it was nonetheless the defining feature of the faith. However, eventually it ended.[12]

Likewise, Mormons ceased to gather, as converts to the faith were encouraged to stay in place and build Zion in their own communities. Kathleen Flake has argued that with the end of polygamy – the primary boundary between Mormons and the rest of America – Mormons turned to an emphasis on the faith's founding as a new theological boundary marker. Specifically, Mormons began to stress the First Vision of the teenage Joseph Smith, his initial revelatory experience in which he came face-to-face with God. "New emphasis on the First Vision successfully reframed the Latter-day Saints' necessary sense of otherness to fit safely within the politics of American religion" (2004, 120). The boundary had been transformed to emphasize the New Testament theme of restoration – and thus apostasy – rather than the Old Testament practice of polygamy. The opening decades of the twentieth century were also when LDS leaders made abstinence from alcohol, tobacco, coffee, and tea obligatory rather than optional, creating another mark of distinctiveness (Alexander 1996).

Similarly, Armand Mauss has described how Mormonism has undergone periods of accommodation and retrenchment. In the former, boundaries are blurred. In the latter – including the current era – they are sharpened. "It is as though Mormons spent the first half of the twentieth century striving to become more like Episcopalians, only to reverse course with the approach of the twenty-first century and begin emulating the Southern Baptists instead" (Mauss 1994, 8).

When Mormons today speak of themselves as a peculiar people, they are nearly always referring to the "first front" of the two-front war – the distinctions between Mormons and what they see as an increasingly libertine society. Latter-day Saints invoke the military symbolism mentioned earlier as motivation to resist the temptations of the world. Historically, however, the second front – distinctions between Mormons and other faiths – was the focus within the faith.

---

[12] As discussed in Chapter 1, today polygamy is perpetuated only by schismatic groups of self-described fundamentalists excommunicated from the LDS Church.

Mormon missionaries, literature, and sermons made much of apostasy and restoration, often with pointed criticism of other faiths. Non-Mormons were referred to as "gentiles," a term that some Mormons still use today to describe those outside their faith (however, this is typically done drolly).

Today, the second front is handled with greater ambivalence. While Mormons continue to teach of past apostasy, in current practice actual criticism of other faiths is rare. The LDS Church has also made a conscious effort to identify itself as a Christian faith. In 1995, the official logo for the Church's name was redesigned so that the words "Jesus Christ" are larger than the rest (Stack 2012f); in 1982, the subtitle "another testament of Jesus Christ" was added to the *Book of Mormon*. Over the past generation, Jesus has increasingly been referred to in sermons by LDS leaders and featured in Church publications (Shepherd and Shepherd 1984; Prothero 2003). During this same period, major addresses at church-wide general conferences and Church publications have placed greater emphasis on the grace of Christ, thus underscoring that, like Protestants and Catholics, Mormons believe that salvation comes through Jesus (Millet 2007).

In addition, recent years have seen efforts by LDS leaders to foster good relations with other faiths, particularly leaders and scholars within the evangelical Protestant and Catholic traditions, who are in agreement on issues such as same-sex marriage. As we shall see, these efforts at détente along the second front have not fully assuaged Protestants' – particularly evangelicals' – concerns about Mormon theology. While Mormons' primary attention is on the first front, skirmishes along the second front continue.

Here, too, there are parallels with other faiths. For example, Catholics have experimented with separatism (Kane 1994), struggled with assimilation (Greeley 1977), negotiated accommodations (Seidler 1986), and searched for allies in the public square (M. O. Steinfels 2004a; M. O. Steinfels 2004b). Catholics are an especially useful point of comparison because of their strong communal character in a highly individualist society (D'Antonio 2001).[13]

THE SACRED TABERNACLE

Subcultural identity theory explains the vigor of Mormonism in terms of the way it fosters a strong sense of internal solidarity. To this point, we have stressed the similarities between evangelicalism and Mormonism, in order to justify applying to Mormons a theory developed to explain why evangelicals are "embattled and thriving." We have also drawn some attention to the similarities between Catholicism and Mormonism. Admittedly, when viewed from a distance, the two religious traditions share some common traits with Mormons – more,

---

[13] A rich literature has documented the impact of the Catholic subculture on politics (Leege and Welch 1989) as well as the impact of religious diversity on Catholic politics (M. R. Welch and Leege 1991).

perhaps, than most members of these faiths recognize. In the words of Matthew Bowman (2012a, xvii), while Mormons have "a decidedly Protestant devotion to scripture and suspicion of trained clergy," they couple it with "a sacramentalism and priesthood reminiscent of Catholicism." Like evangelicals, Mormons place great emphasis on scripture. But unlike evangelicals, Mormon scripture does not end with the Bible, and even includes continuing revelation from God and thus an open canon. Also like evangelicals, Mormons stress local congregational leadership, but like the Catholic Church, the LDS Church has a hierarchical structure. However, unlike Catholics, religious authority is far more centralized among the Latter-day Saints (D'Antonio 1994).

In still other ways, Mormons are also like Jews. Not only are there are about as many Mormons as Jews in America; Mormons have adopted some of the language of Judaism, and many of Mormonism's rituals have a Judaic flavor. And while the analogy is not perfect, the geographic presence of Mormons in their "promised land" of Utah has parallels to Jews' relationship to Israel. Indeed, during the migration led by Brigham Young, Mormons explicitly thought of themselves as reenacting the exodus of the biblical children of Israel, even referring to themselves as the Camp of Israel. It is not a coincidence that Utah has a Jordan River, and that Salt Lake City – like ancient Jerusalem – has a temple at its center.

Mormonism could also be said to have characteristics reminiscent of other religious traditions. As detailed in Chapter 3, they have a level of religious fervor comparable to black Protestants. Like Jehovah's Witnesses, they emphasize proselytizing. Like Seventh-Day Adventists, they have a strict health code. However, analogies to other religions only extend so far. There are clear differences between Mormonism and other faiths. To convert to Mormonism means more than joining a church; it means becoming part of a people. In Kathleen Flake's (2004, 56) memorable phrase, if America is the nation with the soul of a church, Mormonism is the church with the soul of a nation.

The peculiar Mormon subculture can be usefully described with the metaphor of a "sacred tabernacle." This metaphor has roots in Peter Berger's (1990) well-known concept of the "sacred canopy," a society with widely shared religious beliefs, and thus a common sense of ultimate meaning. For Berger, belief systems are maintained in the absence of a competing worldview. This metaphor thus well describes religions that dominate a culture, such as Catholicism in European history. Subcultural identity theory, in contrast, argues that religions can thrive when facing an oppositional worldview. To explain how, Smith et al. (1998, 106) use the apt metaphor of the "sacred umbrella."

Canopies are expansive, immobile, and held up by props beyond the reach of those covered. Umbrellas, on the other hand, are small, handheld, and portable – like the faith-sustaining religious worlds that modern people construct for themselves. . . . In the pluralistic, modern world, people don't need macro-encompassing sacred cosmoses to maintain their religious beliefs. They only need "sacred umbrellas," small, portable, accessible, relational worlds – religious reference groups – "under" which their beliefs can make complete sense.

An umbrella brings to a mind a very individualized style of religion, which accurately describes contemporary evangelicalism. Mormonism, however, is not so individualized. As we have noted, a collective sense of peoplehood permeates Mormonism. In the past, that solidarity was manifest by building cities and creating a communal economic system. Today, Mormons' peoplehood arises from tight-knit communities dispersed throughout the globe that subtly weave together numerous strands of culture. Theologically, the Mormon concept of salvation does not center on individuals going to heaven, but on family bonds that endure through eternity. Culturally, Mormons have a strong sense of group identity. Operationally, while Mormons no longer gather in a single geographic place, their faith puts into action the adage to "think global, act local," as Mormon communalism centers on active participation in their wards. Sociologically, Mormons build social bonds with one another, with high rates of homophily (friendships with fellow Mormons) and endogamy (marriage between Mormons).

With so many communal aspects to their faith, Mormons are not individuals sheltering under their own personal umbrellas. Yet neither do modern Mormons live under a canopy in sheltered communities. Latter-day Saints are found all over the United States – the world, really – in places where their views and lifestyle are decidedly in the minority, but where they have formed a thriving community nonetheless. The Mormon case calls for a metaphor that lies in between the expansive reach of a canopy and the individualism of an umbrella.

The image of a *sacred tabernacle* captures the way Mormons create tight-knit communities wherever they are found. In the Old Testament, the tabernacle was the tentlike structure that served as a temple for the children of Israel as they wandered in the wilderness. Like a canopy, the tabernacle was relatively large and had a communal purpose. Individual Israelites did not have their own tabernacles; there was only one. But, more like an umbrella, it was portable, and erected wherever the children of Israel made camp. Similarly, the Mormon style of communalism can be moved nearly anywhere, and especially into hostile landscapes. While the centralized authority and standardized structure of the LDS Church ensures that every Mormon ward has a common organization, the shared ethnic-like subculture provides each ward's religious vitality. While moveable, once erected, the sacred tabernacle fully encompasses Mormons. In this regard, Mormonism cuts across the conventional sociological categories: from within the sacred tabernacle, Mormonism looks like a "church," but from outside of the sacred tabernacle, it looks like a "sect."

The sacred tabernacle allows us to identify Mormons as an "ethno-religious group," a subculture where ethnicity and religion are mutually reinforcing. But for Mormons, it is *religion* that defines the subculture. It is precisely because Mormons are not an ethnic group in a strict sense that we can make the case for their overt religious distinctiveness. Ethnicity and religion are not mutually reinforcing (as with, say, Irish Catholics), but rather, it is religion that generates ethnic-like qualities. Nor is "Mormon" a passive, hereditary ethnic identity like, say, being Irish. Rather, it is the embrace of Mormon beliefs and behaviors that creates a Mormon identity. Unlike most other Americans, Mormons appear to substitute their religious identity for an ethnic identity. It is as though their religion supplants identification with an ethnic group, and in so doing the religion produces the ethnic-like characteristics of the sacred tabernacle (Putnam and Campbell 2010).

## THE POLITICAL RELEVANCE OF PECULIARITY

Describing the sacred tabernacle still leaves open the question of its political relevance. Does being a subculture – a peculiar people – matter politically? History and contemporary social science suggest it does.

Political historians have made a convincing case that in the nineteenth century American politics was characterized by ethno-religious (or "ethno-cultural") groups. Party affiliation was closely linked to identities that fused ethnicity and religion – Irish Catholics, Scotch-Irish Presbyterians, German Jews, and so on. Such religiously inflected political divisions persisted into the twentieth century, most palpably with tensions between Catholics and Protestants. Opposition to Al Smith, the first Catholic to win a major party's presidential nomination, and John F. Kennedy, the first and thus far only Catholic to become president, went far beyond the usual partisan parameters. As Catholics running in a majority-Protestant nation, they endured suspicion regarding their religion, which at times became quite ugly (Casey 2008; Prendergrast 1999). They ran poorly among Protestants but won big among their fellow Catholics. In Kennedy's case, he did especially well among fellow Irish-Catholics, a fusion of an ethnic and religious identity (Converse 1966; Wilson 2007).

The campaigns of Smith and Kennedy inflamed Catholic–Protestant tensions, but they only poured fuel on a fire that was already smoldering. For the first seventy years or so of the twentieth century many voters' partisan allegiances were determined by their religious affiliation – what has been dubbed the "old religion gap" (Green 2007). Put another way, the subcultural identity of the United States' many ethno-religious groups was the chief vehicle by which religion mattered politically (Leege, Lieske, and Wald 1991). While the old religion gap refers specifically to politics, it also reflects the religious landscape of the past. Writing in the mid-twentieth century, Will Herberg (1960) described a tripartite ethno-religious division in America – Protestant, Catholic, and Jew. These three religious traditions stood alongside one another in American society, an informal analog to the pillar system of the Netherlands.

However, the social tumult of the 1960s shook the pillars until they fell, leading to what Robert Wuthnow (1990) describes as a "restructuring of American religion." New alliances were made across the old borders that separated religious traditions. The defining axis was now religious traditionalism, or "orthodoxy" – and this "new religion gap" mostly replaced the old. Theologically conservative Protestants and Catholics, and to a lesser extent

Orthodox Jews, found common cause, both religiously and politically. James Davison Hunter (1991) provocatively declared this state of affairs to be a culture war, with traditionalist believers of many religious traditions squaring off against modernists, often within the same religious family. Writing twenty years ago, Wuthnow and Hunter were describing the erosion of some religious boundaries and the emergence of others. A few years later, David Leege, Kenneth Wald, and colleagues (2002) demonstrated the political significance of these shifting boundaries, as the "politics of cultural differences" created new fault lines in American elections. More recently, Robert Putnam and David Campbell (2010) have described a blurring of religious boundaries altogether, owing to a highly fluid environment in which Americans move freely from one religion to another. While ethno-religious politics did not disappear, it became far less important among white Americans (Wald, Silverman, and Fridy 2005).

Mormons stand out as an exception to these trends. In describing how American religion has been restructured, Wuthnow emphasizes the importance of symbolic boundaries drawn between religious groups. For most of the American religious landscape, these boundaries have been redrawn and, increasingly, erased. As we have suggested, for Mormons the boundaries have remained sharply defined. They are as peculiar as ever.

Mormons challenge the paradigm that American religion has been restructured into traditionalist and progressive camps, displacing the old religious divisions that characterized a period of ethno-religious politics in the past. They do so from a position that, at first glance, appears to place them in the heart of the traditionalist coalition. But, as we shall show in later chapters, Mormons are distinctive among traditionalists and, on some issues, even transcend the traditionalists' camp. Rumors of the death of ethno-religious politics have been greatly exaggerated.

To say that Mormons are a glowing ember from the old ethno-religious political divisions, however, requires an examination of the literature from whence the concept sprang. The ethno-religious school of political history emerged as a response to the widespread belief among historians and political scientists that voting patterns and partisan allegiances of the nineteenth century could be explained solely on materialist or economic grounds. Scholars of the ethno-religious school argued that voting in the nineteenth and early twentieth centuries was often along religious, not economic, lines (R. J. Jensen 1971; Kleppner 1979; Kleppner 1987; Swierenga 1971). This literature has produced a wealth of empirical research, both qualitative and quantitative, that convincingly makes the case that ethnically tinged religious affiliations shaped the political landscape of nineteenth-century America. The raison d'être of the ethno-religious school has been to counter the materialist focus that has long prevailed in empirical election analysis. To find that religion matters, the reasoning goes, means that economic considerations are not the sole explanation for election outcomes. Instead, "negative reference group antagonisms, conflicts of custom and lifestyle, and differences in religious values and worldviews" are at the root of political conflict (McCormick 1974, 352).[14]

The ethno-religious literature has carefully documented how religious tensions characterized American politics in an age of sharply defined religious differences. It teaches us that religious divisions can have political meaning, and that such religiously inspired political conflict has long characterized the American political system. Ethno-religious divisions of the past are an instructive template for the present.

Self-evidently, describing the politics of today in ethno-religious terms presupposes the existence of a group or groups that can be defined as ethno-religious, and not simply ethnic. While the term "ethno-religious" may imply that religion is subsumed by ethnicity, historian Richard Jensen argues that political conflict in the nineteenth century was driven more by the religious than the ethnic side of the equation. In his assessment, "theology, rather than language, customs, or heritage, was the foundation of cultural and political subgroups in America" (1971, 82). To claim that Mormons are a vestige of the old ethno-religious cleavages in American politics, then, requires salient *religious* differences between Mormons and others. It is not enough for Mormons to be a peculiar people – their peculiarity must be rooted in their religion.

As we have seen, both theaters in Mormons' two-front war result from the religious characteristics of Latter-day Saints. Mormonism defines itself in opposition to secular society, both in lifestyle and worldview. The LDS lifestyle embraces a traditional family structure, conservative sexual attitudes, modest dress, an avoidance of profanity and R-rated entertainment, and complete abstention from alcohol and tobacco. The Mormon worldview includes an emphasis on God-given authority, and a clear sense of right and wrong. In terms of lifestyle, Mormons would appear to be in sync with other cultural conservatives, particularly those who also have traditionalist views on gender and sexuality, and thus are fighting in the same cultural foxholes as Mormons. In particular, evangelicals and Mormons would seem to be natural allies. And in some political skirmishes, they have been. Yet Mormon–evangelical cooperation is constrained by the Mormons' worldview, specifically the belief that theirs is the only true church. Conversely, cooperation is also hindered by evangelicals' rejection of Mormonism as a cultish and false religion.

These disagreements have not been limited to genteel debates over matters of abstract doctrinal matters. Contention between Mormons and their antagonists can be heated, and has historically even led to violence on both sides (Mason

---

[14] There is one important contrast between the tensions experienced by Mormons today and ethno-religious cleavages of the past. Historically, ethno-religious political conflict fueled partisan differences. Members of pietistic ("low church") religions voted Republican, while members of the ritualistic ("high church") religions voted Democratic. The case of contemporary Latter-day Saints is qualitatively different, as much of the friction between Mormons and non-Mormons exists within the ranks of the Republican Party.

2011; Walker, Turley, and Leonard 2011). Today, physical violence is a thing of the past, but participants in evangelical–Mormon disputes still throw sharp rhetorical elbows. There is a cottage industry of anti-Mormon literature, films, and websites ridiculing Mormon beliefs, accusing Mormons of not being Christians, and labeling Mormonism a heretical cult. In response, Mormon apologists often employ incendiary rhetoric as defenders of their faith (Stack 2012c). One need only read the comments posted online whenever a news story about Mormons is published to see that Mormonism can elicit strong reactions from both its supporters and detractors. We suspect that the tension between Mormons and evangelicals is further exacerbated by competition for converts, as both groups actively proselytize.

Reactions to Mitt Romney illustrate the ethno-religious character of objections to his faith. He faced criticism, and even ridicule, from a secular perspective for the distinctive beliefs and practices of Mormonism. This is not unlike what believers of many stripes face, particularly devout evangelical Protestants. Yet Romney also faced criticism from within the traditionalist coalition, specifically from evangelicals – including the description of his faith as a cult (Oppel and Eckholm 2011). However, we stress that as illuminating as the Romney case might be, the themes we discuss go beyond any single candidate. Our objective is a general understanding of Mormons' role in American politics, and society more broadly.

## CONCLUSION

In tandem, the two theoretical perspectives we have introduced illuminate the political significance of Mormons' peculiarity. First, subcultural identity theory explains the sociological causes and consequences of Mormons' sense of peoplehood, and why and how the sacred tabernacle enables Mormons to thrive even in the face of a culture that they perceive as a threat to their beliefs. Second, the ethno-religious school of political history shows us how a distinctive ethno-religious group can trigger a political reaction from others. For Mormons, that reaction falls along two lines, both secular ("the world") and religious ("gentiles"). Together, these theories establish a framework for understanding contemporary Mormonism and its place in American politics. Mormons operate within a sacred tabernacle, characterized both by high internal solidarity and high external tensions. In Chapter 3, we will take a close look at the tabernacle, both inside and out.

# 3

## A Peculiar People?

### Mormon Religious Distinctiveness

In many ways, Dee Dee Squires is a typical Mormon. She is a native of Charleston, South Carolina and converted to Mormonism shortly after graduating from college in 1975. Her husband, whom she married in 1983, is also a convert, and they have three sons (G. Hill 2005). Dee Dee's self-created profile on Mormon.org, an official church web site designed for outreach by ordinary Mormons, provides a window into her background and shows that she is a typical Mormon in ways that go beyond marriage and family.[1] First, she is very involved in her local Mormon ward (congregation) as well as her community, having had many "callings" (volunteer jobs that fill pastoral roles). These callings can range from teaching children's classes to coordinating humanitarian service for congregation members to leading the ward's program for teenage boys or girls. In describing herself, she writes:

I have especially enjoyed being a Visiting Teacher, assigned to visit other female members on a monthly basis and to befriend them truly as "sisters." I have also enjoyed organizing service projects in the community for our congregation (Ward), such as working with "Habitat for Humanity" to build a home for a disadvantaged family, or working with a large local, historic cemetery to mow the grass and straighten headstones. It is such a wonderful feeling working side-by-side with our fellow members, wearing a yellow "Mormon Helping Hands" T-shirt, serving in a project together to benefit someone or some group that needed assistance. I love the way the Church is so well organized and members are ready to serve together when called upon. (Squires 2012)

The commitment that Mormons demonstrate, especially within their ward, distinguishes them from their neighbors and helps define the contours of the

---

[1] In 2010 the Church of Jesus Christ of Latter-day Saints launched a newly overhauled edition of its signature web site for a non-Mormon audience at Mormon.org. Within months, Mormons had created thousands of profiles. In launching the new site, the church explicitly stated that one of its goals is to ease interaction between Mormons and non-Mormons such that "many myths and misconceptions vanish" (Holman 2010).

secular boundary of the "sacred tabernacle" described in Chapter 2, or what we have called the first front of the two-front war.

Dee Dee's profile also reveals the unique beliefs of Mormons. She writes:

As it says in Amos 3:7 of the Old Testament: "Surely the Lord God will do nothing, but he revealeth his secret unto his servants the prophets." Yes, we have a living prophet on the earth today to guide us during THESE times. Each age – each year – gives us different challenges that need the fine-tuned help of those who have the mantle of prophecy from our Heavenly Father. Of course, each one of us is also entitled to the whispering of the spirit to guide each of us in our daily lives as we study the scriptures and pray for guidance for ourselves and our families. (Squires 2012)

As we will see, Dee Dee's statement of belief in a living prophet is a defining characteristic of Mormons, and one of a number of uniquely Mormon beliefs and practices that mark the religious boundary of the sacred tabernacle, and the second front in the two-front war.

The dual boundaries encourage a high degree of conformity within the sacred tabernacle, but there is also room for diversity. Notice above that Dee Dee expresses her belief that Mormons are able to receive individual-level guidance from "the spirit" (the Holy Ghost or Holy Spirit), a belief in personal revelation unmediated by religious leaders. Kara Kimball, a recent college graduate who studied family life and human development, provides another example of this aspect within Mormon theology:

My favorite aspect about this church is that . . .[it] encourages individuals to find truth on their own. Individual/personal revelation is what sets this church apart from others. We believe agency is an essential component and an important part of God's plan. Individuals have the right to make choices for themselves. . .All people are encouraged by our prophet to study the teachings of this church and then pray to God to find out if they are true. (Kimball 2014)

Terryl Givens sums it up this way: "Mormonism is, after all, a religion in which the authority of the one living prophet at the head of the church is every bit as literal and all-encompassing as that of Moses over the children of Israel. But it is also a religion in which . . . all members are vouchsafed the right to personal, literal, dialogic revelation with God" (2007, xiv).

In this chapter, we expand on the framework from Chapter 2 of Mormons as an ethno-religious group by describing their distinctive beliefs and practices. This description reveals the dual boundaries of the sacred tabernacle and shows the degree to which Mormons are a "peculiar people." The secular boundary of the sacred tabernacle can be seen in the differences between Mormons and American society in general. The religious boundary can be seen in the ways Mormons differ from adherents of other religions. This chapter also looks at diversity within the sacred tabernacle, developing four measures of what might be called "Mormon-ness": level of *activity*, adherence to *authority*, strength of *identity*, and degree of *insularity*.

INSIDE THE SACRED TABERNACLE: A DISTINCTIVE FAITH

The secular boundary of the sacred tabernacle is the first front of the two-front war explained in Chapter 2, pitting Mormons against secular American society. We can delineate this first boundary by comparing Mormons to other religious traditions and the American public in general, using survey questions asked in common across religious traditions. The religious boundary of the sacred tabernacle, or the second front, pits Mormons against other religions, especially Protestants and Catholics. We can delineate this religious boundary of the sacred tabernacle by demonstrating theological distinctiveness through data from survey questions about uniquely Mormon beliefs.

At this point, it is worth discussing what we can and cannot learn about Mormon distinctiveness from surveys. Making valid comparisons of religious beliefs and behaviors across religious traditions is very difficult. Although some beliefs and practices are common enough to ask members of different religious traditions about, such questions may be interpreted differently across traditions. And it makes little sense to ask members of other religious traditions about the beliefs and behaviors that are truly distinctive to one religious tradition (e.g. asking Presbyterians whether they keep *kosher*).

Still, it is helpful to situate Mormons in the American religious landscape by comparing Mormons to other Christians on standard measures of religious belief and behaviors that are common enough to allow a cautious comparison. As we will see, Mormons score high on nearly all such measures. This pattern arises in part because Mormons do hold some basic beliefs and behaviors in common with members of other faiths, and in part because Mormons can map their peculiar beliefs onto standard questions (although for some questions this mapping is easier than for others). But such differences only hint at the unique character of the Latter-day Saints as an ethno-religious group. To capture Mormon distinctiveness more fully, we will turn to special measures of Mormon theology and practice in the Peculiar People Survey, which included only self-identified Mormons.

But even special surveys of Mormons have limitations. To be interviewed as a Mormon in a national survey, respondents must self-identify as affiliated with the LDS Church. In other words, one has to actively choose the designation of Mormon. A person whose name appears on the official membership rolls of the Church of Jesus Christ of Latter-day Saints but has become disaffected with the Church may or may not still self-identify as a Mormon. A high-profile example of the disjuncture between Church records and self-identification surfaced in the 2012 political season, when reporters discovered that Florida U.S. Senator Marco Rubio had joined the LDS Church as a preteen. Senator Rubio now identifies as a Catholic, but absent an official request for removal, it is likely that his name remains on the LDS Church's records (Burr 2012a; Coppins 2012).

Our need to rely on self-identified Mormons undoubtedly produces high estimates of practices such as church attendance that would certainly differ from a survey based on a full sample from official LDS Church records.[2] This said, our sample of self-identified Mormons in the Peculiar People Survey produces estimates that are very consistent with other surveys of self-identified Mormons.[3] Fortunately, the Pew U.S. Religious Landscape Survey also asks about former religious affiliation on a massive national sample, large enough that we can examine differences between current and former Mormons.[4] This enables us to see whether Mormon distinctiveness is found among those who once self-identified as Mormons, but no longer do. Roughly 30 percent of people raised in the LDS Church no longer identify as Mormon.

### The Secular Boundary: Distinctiveness on Common Religious Beliefs and Practices

Mormons' high level of religiosity represents a sharp boundary with secular society. Table 3.1 summarizes a series of standard questions from the Pew U.S. Religious Landscape Survey that are common enough to be asked of members of a wide variety of religions in America. To facilitate comparison, we created a simple additive index, scoring a point for each instance that a survey respondent crosses the particular belief threshold listed in the table, such as being "absolutely certain" that God exists (found in the last row of the table).

Mormons have the highest percentage of adherents who agree with six of the ten religious belief items listed (see Table 3.1). For example, while most religious Americans believe in life after death, Mormons appear to believe in an afterlife almost universally (98 percent). Similarly high proportions of Mormons are "absolutely certain" in their belief in God (91 percent) and express an affirmative belief in heaven (95 percent). Three-quarters or more of Americans hold these beliefs, including large majorities of the other major Christian traditions. (Further examples of beliefs common to Mormons and other Christians can be found in Table 3.3.)

Belief in hell drops off considerably among Mormons, to 59 percent, far behind evangelical Protestants and black Protestants (both at 82 percent), but is at about the same level as among Catholics. This difference may reflect

---

[2] Even if we had access to Church membership records to draw a sample, we would likely still see a lower response rate from those who are not currently active in the faith, in part due to the fact that many "inactive" Mormons would choose not to participate in a survey about religion or would not be reachable because the contact information on file would be outdated. For an example of such a survey see Cornwall et al. (1986).

[3] See Data Appendix for the details of the Peculiar People Survey.

[4] We define "former Mormons" as those who were previously affiliated, using the question, "Thinking about when you were a child, in what religion were you raised, if any?" but who no longer self-identify as Mormons. A variety of other definitions could be used that incorporate religious belief and behavior, but this one afforded the most straightforward definition and also provides a reasonably large enough sample size of former Mormons (N = 166) to allow for comparisons. See Data Appendix for details of the Pew U.S. Religious Landscape Survey.

TABLE 3.1. *Religious Beliefs in Terms Common to Other Traditions*

| Question | Response option | Mormon | Former Mormon | Evangelical Protestant | Mainline Protestant | Catholic | Black Protestant | General public |
|---|---|---|---|---|---|---|---|---|
| Believe in God | % Yes, absolutely certain | 91% | 64% | 91% | 75% | 74% | 92% | 77% |
| Believe in life after death | % Yes | 98% | 78% | 86% | 78% | 77% | 79% | 74% |
| Believe in heaven | % Yes | 95% | 72% | 86% | 77% | 82% | 91% | 74% |
| Believe in hell | % Yes | 59% | 53% | 82% | 56% | 60% | 82% | 59% |
| Miracles still occur | % Completely Agree | 80% | 40% | 61% | 42% | 47% | 58% | 47% |
| Angels and demons are active in the world | % Completely Agree | 59% | 32% | 61% | 31% | 35% | 59% | 40% |
| My religion is the one, true faith leading to eternal life | % Closer to own view | 57% | 5% | 36% | 12% | 16% | 34% | 24% |
| There is only one true way to interpret the teachings of my religion | % Closer to own view | 54% | 13% | 41% | 14% | 19% | 39% | 27% |
| My church should preserve its traditional beliefs and practices | % Closer to own view | 68% | 23% | 59% | 34% | 36% | 48% | 44% |

(continued)

TABLE 3.1 (continued)

| Question | Response option | Mormon | Former Mormon | Evangelical Protestant | Mainline Protestant | Catholic | Black Protestant | General public |
|---|---|---|---|---|---|---|---|---|
| Clear and absolute standards for right and wrong | % Completely Agree | 46% | 34% | 51% | 33% | 38% | 41% | 39% |
| Average on 10-point index | | 7.1 | 4.2 | 6.6 | 4.5 | 4.9 | 6.2 | 5.4 |

*Source:* Pew U.S. Religious Landscape Survey, 2007

*Notes:* Question wording from Pew Landscape Survey

- "Do you believe in God or a universal spirit?" and "How certain are you about this belief? Are you absolutely certain, fairly certain, not too certain, or not at all certain?"

- "Do you believe in life after death?"

- "Do you think there is a heaven, where people who have led good lives are eternally rewarded?"

- "Do you think there is a hell, where people who have led bad lives and die without being sorry are eternally punished?"

- "Miracles still occur today as in ancient times. Do you completely agree, mostly agree, mostly disagree, or completely disagree?"

- "Angels and demons are active in the world. Do you completely agree, mostly agree, mostly disagree, or completely disagree?"

- "Now, as I read a pair of statements, tell me whether the FIRST statement or the SECOND statement comes closer to your own views even if neither is exactly right. First/next: My religion is the one, true faith leading to eternal life, OR Many religions can lead to eternal life."

- "Thinking about your religion, which of the following statements comes CLOSEST to your view? My church or denomination should preserve its traditional beliefs and practices, or adjust traditional beliefs and practices in light of new circumstances, or adopt modern beliefs and practices."

- "There are clear and absolute standards for what is right and wrong. Do you completely agree, mostly agree, mostly disagree, or completely disagree?"

Mormon distinctiveness. While "hell" is a term familiar to Mormons, it would not be the one most commonly used to describe an afterlife of condemnation. Rather, Mormons might more commonly refer to differing "degrees of glory" or even to "outer darkness." Thus, even on a point of commonality, the language of Mormon theology provides further evidence of distinctiveness (see the religious boundary section later in this chapter). There may be a similar language difference for Catholics due to their concept of purgatory.

It is worth noting, however, that Mormons resemble evangelical and black Protestants on one belief about the supernatural: that angels and demons are active in the world. In contrast, a relatively low proportion of Catholics and mainline Protestants subscribe to a belief in the supernatural. Mormons score the highest of all the religious groups when it comes to belief in another supernatural occurrence, the present-day reality of miracles.

Mormons also score highest on measures of religious particularism – far higher than any other religious tradition. More than two-thirds of Mormons agree that their church should "maintain its traditions," almost three-fifths agree with the statement that "my religion is the one, true faith leading to eternal life" (57 percent), and a clear majority agrees that there is "only one true way to interpret the teachings of my religion" (54 percent).[5]

The bottom line is that when Mormons are compared with other religious traditions on belief questions in which the traditions share enough in common to make comparisons possible, Mormons show an unusual level of cohesiveness and conformity. This conclusion is illustrated by a summary of the ten beliefs measure at the bottom of Table 3.1, where Mormons score an average of 7.1, followed closely by evangelical Protestants (6.6) and black Protestants (6.2), but trailed by mainline Protestants (4.5), Roman Catholics (4.9), and the American public as a whole (5.4).

The Pew U.S. Religious Landscape Survey data in Table 3.1 also allows us to compare current Mormons with former Mormons across the same array of general religious beliefs. Former Mormons do not maintain any of the distinctiveness of current Mormons – if anything, they become distinctive for the *absence* of religious belief, having the lowest level of agreement on several individual items. They also have the lowest score on the ten-item summary index. Leaving

---

[5] Given that a belief in the LDS Church as "the one true church" is a bedrock Mormon doctrine, some readers may wonder why "only" 57 percent of Mormons describe their religion this way. First, by way of comparison, we note that the two groups with the next highest percentages are evangelicals and black Protestants, but at 36 and 34 percent respectively, they are well below Mormons. Second, the other option for this question is "many religions can lead to eternal life," which could also be considered true according to LDS theology, since Mormons believe that many religions contain fundamental truths. According to LDS beliefs, people who were not Latter-day Saints while living can learn and accept the complete gospel in a state of existence after they die, and have baptism (and other rites) performed on their behalf. See Chapter 1 for more explanation. Thus, even though 57 percent may not seem high, it is high relative to other religions and in light of the ambiguity with which LDS respondents can interpret this question.

the sacred tabernacle erases the boundary between these former Mormons and secular society. Or, perhaps, former Mormons did not form the boundary in the first place, and opted to leave Mormonism as a result.

Further evidence of the secular boundary of the sacred tabernacle is buttressed by a similar examination of religious practices – what people do rather than what they believe. Table 3.2 lists a series of ten religious behaviors common enough among Americans to be asked in a national survey. Mormons are the most likely to do nine of the ten activities on the list. This pattern includes being an official member of the Church (92 percent), praying daily (82 percent), attending church weekly (76 percent), reading scripture weekly or more (76 percent), attending social activities at church at least monthly (68 percent), participating in prayer or study group once a week (64 percent), volunteering through church at least monthly (59 percent), looking to religion for moral guidance (58 percent), and meditating once a week (56 percent).

Mormons score third, behind evangelical Protestants and black Protestants, when asked how frequently they "share your beliefs with non-believers or people from other religious backgrounds." Forty-seven percent of Mormons report doing so at least monthly, compared to 55 percent of black Protestants and 52 percent of evangelicals.[6] The summary measure of religious behavior shows Mormons with the highest average, at 7.2 out of 10. Once again, evangelical Protestants (6.0) and black Protestants (6.2) are close on the heels of Mormons, followed at a distance by mainline Protestants (4.1), Catholics (3.7), and the public as a whole (4.8). In other words, Mormons have both individualistic and communitarian aspects to their lived religion, exhibiting more private devotion than evangelical Protestants (whose faith is highly personalized) and communal activities than Catholics (whose faith has a strong dose of communitarianism).

Table 3.2 also includes data for former Mormons. Whereas 76 percent of Mormons attend church, only 23 percent of former Mormons do (presumably in another denomination). Even on activities not tied to a particular church or congregation, like daily prayer, only 47 percent of former Mormons report doing so, compared to 82 percent of Mormons. Once again, former Mormons

---

[6] This pattern may be surprising given the emphasis Mormons place on missionary work and the relatively high proportions of young Mormons who serve voluntary church missions. This question about sharing beliefs is another example of how the wording of a question may reveal Mormon distinctiveness. We speculate that for many Mormons to "share your beliefs" may be interpreted through the lens of their former full-time missionary service or interaction with current full-time missionaries. That is, Mormons may have a high bar for counting something as "sharing your beliefs," akin to the formal proselytizing associated with the Church's full-time missionaries rather than casual conversations about their beliefs with friends and neighbors. Or perhaps the relatively high degree of insularity among Mormons (see below) limits their exposure to people who are not Mormon and thus do not already believe as they do. Even in light of such linguistic idiosyncrasies, the broad pattern is clear: Mormons report extensive and uniform religious practice that is distinctive among Americans.

TABLE 3.2. *Religious Behaviors in Terms Common to Other Traditions*

| Question | Response option | Mormon | Former Mormon | Evangelical Protestant | Mainline Protestant | Catholic | Black Protestant | General public |
|---|---|---|---|---|---|---|---|---|
| Attend church | % Once a week or more | **76%** | 23% | 58% | 35% | 41% | 59% | 39% |
| Read the Scriptures | % Weekly or more | **76%** | 28% | 60% | 27% | 21% | 60% | 35% |
| Pray | % Daily | **82%** | 47% | 78% | 54% | 58% | 80% | 58% |
| Volunteer through the Church | % Once a month or more | **59%** | 22% | 31% | 23% | 19% | 37% | 26% |
| Attend social activities at church | % Once a month or more | **68%** | 31% | 50% | 37% | 25% | 55% | 39% |
| Official members of your church | % Yes | **92%** | 40% | 74% | 64% | 67% | 83% | 61% |
| Participate in prayer or scripture study groups or religious education programs | % Once a week | **64%** | 12% | 41% | 16% | 13% | 44% | 23% |
| Meditate | % Once a week | **56%** | 33% | 46% | 35% | 36% | 55% | 39% |
| Share your beliefs | % Once a month or more | **47%** | 17% | 52% | 26% | 23% | **55%** | 36% |

*(continued)*

TABLE 3.2 (*continued*)

| Question | Response option | Mormon | Former Mormon | Evangelical Protestant | Mainline Protestant | Catholic | Black Protestant | General public |
|---|---|---|---|---|---|---|---|---|
| Look for guidance most | % Religion | 58% | 15% | 52% | 24% | 22% | 43% | 29% |
| Average on 10-point index | | 7.2 | 4.4 | 6.0 | 4.1 | 3.8 | 6.2 | 4.8 |

*Source:* Pew U.S. Religious Landscape Survey, 2007

*Notes:* Question wording from Pew Landscape Survey

- "Aside from weddings and funerals, how often do you attend religious services... more than once a week, once a week, once or twice a month, a few times a year, seldom, or never?"
- "Please tell me how often you do each of the following. First, how often do you [read scripture outside of religious services]: would you say at least once a week, once or twice a month, several times a year, seldom, or never?"
- "People practice their religion in different ways. Outside of attending religious services, do you pray several times a day, once a day, a few times a week, once a week, a few times a month, seldom, or never?"
- "And still thinking about the church or house of worship where you attend religious services most often, please tell me how often, if ever, you do each of the following. First, how often do you [do community volunteer work through your place of worship]: would you say at least once a week, once or twice a month, several times a year, seldom or never?"
- "And still thinking about the church or house of worship where you attend religious services most often, please tell me how often, if ever, you do each of the following. First, how often do you [participate in social activities, such as meals, club meetings, or other gatherings there]: would you say at least once a week, once or twice a month, several times a year, seldom or never?"
- "Are you or your family official members of a local church or house of worship?"
- "Please tell me how often you do each of the following. First, how often do you [participate in prayer groups, scripture study groups or religious education programs]: would you say at least once a week, once or twice a month, several times a year, seldom, or never?"
- "Please tell me how often you do each of the following. First, how often do you [meditate]: would you say at least once a week, once or twice a month, several times a year, seldom, or never?"
- "Please tell me how often you do each of the following. First, how often do you [share your faith with non-believers or people from other religious backgrounds]: would you say at least once a week, once or twice a month, several times a year, seldom, or never?"
- "When it comes to questions of right and wrong, which of the following do you look to most for guidance? Would you say religious teachings and beliefs, philosophy and reason, practical experience and common sense, or scientific information (randomized)?"

have far less religious commitment than current Mormons, and less even than the general population.

This high level of religiosity shown by Mormons also carries over into their volunteer work within the church. Our data on Mormons are consistent with the work of other scholars, particularly research on Mormons' high rate of voluntarism within their Church. A study led by University of Pennsylvania scholar Ram Cnaan surveyed Mormons at their church services and found that the vast majority of church-attending Mormons (94 percent) held a calling in their local congregation (Cnaan, Evans, and Curtis 2012). Similarly, in the Peculiar People Survey we found that 68 percent of all Mormons, and 90 percent of those who attend church every week, hold a calling. The survey also asked, "In an average week, how many hours do you spend on your calling or callings?" Among all Mormons, 27 percent report spending five or more hours a week in church service, although the number of hours varies greatly by the nature of the calling. We also asked respondents to list their calling(s) with an open-ended question and then coded the list into five groups based on the level of responsibility within the church. For those who are among the lay leadership of their ward (11 percent of the total sample), 71 percent spend five or more hours and 27 percent spend more than 11 hours a week.[7] As we will explain further in Chapter 6, this high rate of voluntarism extends outside the sacred tabernacle too, as Mormons often participate in community volunteering. All of this voluntarism provides Mormons with skills, experience, and social networks that can be directed, with great effect, toward a political cause (Verba, Schlozman, and Brady 1995).

One mark of Mormons' religious distinctiveness, therefore, is simply their high level of religiosity both in terms of beliefs and behavior. Such measures clearly demarcate the boundary between Mormons and secular society, the first front in the two-front war.

## Religious Boundary: Distinctive Mormon Beliefs and Practices

Latter-day Saints' religious distinctiveness extends beyond beliefs and practices held in common with other traditions to a set of doctrines and practices unique to Mormonism. These uniquely Mormon doctrines form the boundaries of the second front of the two-front war, whereby Mormons clearly separate

---

[7] We coded the callings into five groups. "Leaders" (11 percent) are defined as those who head an organization within a congregation and/or have counselors, assistants, or a committee under them. In Mormon terms, these individuals would attend a monthly leadership meeting at the congregation level called the "Ward Council." "Other Leadership" (21 percent) is generally defined as counselors, assistants, or committee members. The one exception is counselors to the ward bishop who, because of their extensive leadership responsibilities and central participation in directing the ward, are coded as "Leaders." "Teachers" (11 percent) are those called to positions that involve teaching as the main responsibility. "Other" (25 percent) is a catchall category for callings with less responsibility to direct other church members. Finally, a fifth group (32 percent) includes those without callings or who did not report a calling.

themselves from other religions. They hold to beliefs that are distinctive enough to give real meaning to Mormons' self-description as a peculiar people.

One of the most distinctive of Mormons' beliefs lies in their view of scripture. In the Pew U.S. Religious Landscape Survey, belief in the literalism of the Bible, or other scripture where relevant,[8] was assessed using two questions that allow respondents to be categorized into three main groups. First, respondents were asked whether their faith's holy book is the "word of God" or is "a book written by men and is not the word of God." If they answered that it is the word of God, they were then asked whether it should be "taken literally, word for word" or if "not everything is to be taken literally." In response to the first question, 90 percent of Mormons believe the Bible to be the word of God. However, in response to the follow-up question, only 35 percent express a belief that the Bible is the word of God *and* should be taken literally. In comparison, 59 percent of evangelical Protestants and 62 percent of black Protestants are literalists.

Mormons have difficulty mapping their beliefs onto the standard options offered in the typical Bible survey question, especially the phrase "word for word." One of the Church's "Articles of Faith," a list of beliefs authored by Church founder Joseph Smith and taught to Mormon children as a kind of catechism, states, "We believe the Bible to be the word of God as far as it is translated correctly."[9] For Mormons, Biblical literalism takes a distinctive turn when they try to match "word for word" in the question wording with the phrase "as far as it is translated correctly" in the Articles of Faith.

The Article of Faith mentioning the Bible finishes with a prominent point of Mormon theological distinctiveness: "We also believe the *Book of Mormon* to be the word of God." Here there is no qualification about whether it is translated correctly. Examples of Mormons' religious distinctiveness abound, but belief in the divine provenance of the *Book of Mormon* is a central belief unique to Latter-day Saints. According to the Pew Mormons in America Survey, 91 percent of Mormons believe that the *Book of Mormon* was "written by ancient prophets and translated by Joseph Smith."[10] Similarly, in our Peculiar People Survey, 96 percent of Mormons say that they believe the *Book of Mormon* to be a record of real events and people.

Table 3.3 lists some LDS beliefs that are distinctive and emphasized within the faith. For example, belief in the *Book of Mormon* is the essence of what it means to be a Mormon. Other essential and distinctive Mormon beliefs include a rejection of the doctrine of the Trinity, a belief that Joseph Smith was a modern prophet, the continuing prophetic leadership of the LDS Church, and the eternal significance of the rites performed in LDS temples.

---

[8]  For Jews the question referenced the Torah, for Muslims the Qur'an.

[9]  The thirteen "Articles of Faith" summarize basic Mormon beliefs. As a group, they are a relatively short summary of beliefs printed on cards given away by Mormon missionaries.

[10] See Data Appendix for details of the Pew Mormons in America Survey.

TABLE 3.3.  *Illustrative Examples of What Is Distinctive, Emphasized, and Currently Practiced in Mormon Theology*

---

Not Distinctive and Emphasized
• Belief in God
• Belief in the Resurrection of Jesus Christ
• Belief in the Old and New Testament

Distinctive and Emphasized
• Belief in the Book of Mormon
• God the Father and Jesus Christ are distinct and corporeal beings (i.e. no Trinity)
• Joseph Smith was a prophet
• The current president of the Church is a living prophet
• Temple rites

Distinctive But Not Emphasized
• The Garden of Eden was located in Missouri
• Have a supply of food for emergencies or disasters

Once Distinctive But Now Abandoned
• Polygamy (officially stopped in 1890)
• Men of African descent were not ordained to priesthood (all men eligible for priesthood beginning in 1978)

---

On all these theological points, Mormons overwhelmingly subscribe to the doctrines of their church. Nearly all Mormons endorse the LDS view of a God separate from his son Jesus, both of whom have corporeal form. In the Pew Mormons in America Survey, 94 percent of Mormons said that they believe that "God the Father and Jesus Christ are separate, physical beings." Ninety-four percent also believe that the president of the LDS Church is "a prophet of God." Ninety-five percent of self-identified Mormons believe that "families can be bound together eternally in temple ceremonies."

These beliefs are all highly distinctive and arguably unique to Latter-day Saints. Indeed, some of them are considered heretical to many Protestants and Catholics and thus define the boundary between Mormons and members of other religions. These distinctions provide the theological rationale for critics of Mormonism to define it as a non-Christian religion, notwithstanding the beliefs that Mormons share with other faiths (see Chapter 7 for more discussion).

These beliefs do not exhaust the many ways that Mormons are distinctive, even if not always unique. Mormons also abide by the "Word of Wisdom," a health code that includes abstention from tobacco, coffee, and alcohol. Certainly, these strictures separate Mormons from secular society. Following the Word of Wisdom is even included in the questions that faithful Mormons are asked to obtain a recommend to enter a temple (see Chapter 2). Obviously, Mormons are not alone in having such a health code. Seventh-Day Adventists have similar dietary restrictions, and a number of faiths prohibit alcohol consumption. Jews have *kosher*, Muslims *halal*, and many Catholics abstain from meat during Lent. Yet even if not unique, Mormons' adherence to their health code is a palpable social marker, reinforced every time a Church member declines a glass of wine at dinner or walks past a Starbucks. Nor are dietary restrictions the only such markers. Similarly, Mormons' emphasis on sexual chastity and modesty in dress also mark them as distinctive in contemporary society.

It is also important to note that some theological beliefs within Mormonism allow for personal interpretation, a point that will become more important as we try to measure the religious diversity among Latter-day Saints. For example, virtually all Mormons would agree that "keeping the Sabbath Day holy" includes attendance at church meetings, but defining appropriate activities beyond that opens the door to a variety of views. Mormons also have a clear restriction on viewing pornography, but a gray area exists about whether or not to avoid all R-rated movies. Even the health code contains ambiguity, as Mormons disagree on whether the restrictions on coffee and tea should extend to caffeinated soda (officially, they do not).[11]

Like most religions, Mormonism encompasses a wide range of doctrines, but – also like most other faiths – not all of the teachings "on the books" receive equal attention. Table 3.3 also includes LDS beliefs and practices that are distinctive, but are not emphasized in the contemporary Church. The song "I Believe," sung in the Broadway musical *The Book of Mormon* provides several examples of distinctive Mormon beliefs that sound even more exotic when summarized with one line of a catchy tune, for example, "I believe that the Garden of Eden was in Jackson County, Missouri." While this view is certainly something that can be attributed to Mormon founder Joseph Smith, it is hardly ever mentioned in a typical LDS sermon or Sunday School lesson.

Likewise, Mormons are encouraged to be prepared for disasters or personal emergencies by storing food.[12] While this practice can be portrayed in the press as a survivalist fixation, food storage is actually a part of larger emphasis on self-reliance. Currently the Church encourages members to maintain a three-month supply of food, as well as a "seventy-two-hour kit" of essentials in case of a disaster (just as the Department of Homeland Security encourages all Americans to do).[13] We chose to classify food storage as "less emphasized"

---

[11]  For example, in response to a segment on Mormons aired by NBC's "Rock Center" in August 2012, the Church posted a statement online that said, in part, "Finally, another small correction: Despite what was reported, the Church revelation spelling out health practices … does not mention the use of caffeine. The Church's health guidelines prohibit alcoholic drinks, smoking or chewing of tobacco, and 'hot drinks' – taught by Church leaders to refer specifically to tea and coffee" (Church of Jesus Christ of Latter-day Saints 2012b). This statement was updated from a previous version that read, "the church does not prohibit the use of caffeine" and that the "hot drinks" reference "does not go beyond [tea and coffee]" (Stack 2012d), illustrating that expressing a definitive view on caffeine is difficult, even for Church public affairs employees.

[12]  See https://www.lds.org/topics/food-storage (accessed October 7, 2013).

[13]  See http://www.ready.gov/build-a-kit (accessed October 7, 2013).

because it is something not uniformly practiced by Mormons (and not required to be a member in good standing). The Pew Mormons in America Survey reveals that while 82 percent of Mormons engage in some kind of food storage, only 70 percent of those who store food, or 57 percent of all Mormons, have the requisite three-month supply or more – a majority, but not overwhelmingly so.

Table 3.3 also lists some Mormon beliefs that were once distinctive but have since been abandoned. The first is polygamy. The second is the practice of not ordaining men of African descent to the Priesthood (also a one-liner in "I Believe" from Broadway's *The Book of Mormon*). Because these topics are telling examples of how Mormonism was historically so distinct (and because one cannot have a book about Mormons and politics and ignore polygamy and race), a brief digression on these topics is in order. Discussing them in detail provides two case studies of a distinctive aspect of Mormon theology. Mormons believe in continuing revelation, allowing for abrupt changes in doctrine and practice. Perhaps ironically, while the changes regarding polygamy and race lessened Mormons' distinctiveness from other Americans, they nonetheless reinforce the continuity of a still quite peculiar belief in a living prophet.

### Polygamy

Polygamy (or, as nineteenth-century Mormons called it, "plural marriage") was introduced by Joseph Smith to a select group of Mormons in the 1840s before the exodus west, publicly acknowledged by the Church in 1852, and then officially discontinued in 1890 (Daynes 2001). More than a century after it was discontinued, it remains an issue with which Mormons are often associated (see Chapter 7). Much ink has been spilled on the origins, justification, and consequences of polygamy, but for our purposes the following facts are relevant.

First, even though not all Mormons were involved in polygamous marriages, many were, especially among the leadership cadre. More importantly, it was not simply a marital arrangement but had a theological rationale as well, and so was an integral part of the faith (Daynes 2001; Van Wagoner 1989; S. B. Gordon 2002). Second, the practice of polygamy as sanctioned by the LDS Church ended long ago. In 1890, Church president Wilford Woodruff issued a Manifesto declaring an end to plural marriage. The Manifesto came after decades of escalating tension with the federal government, including federal legislation disincorporating the LDS Church and a landmark U.S. Supreme Court case that placed polygamy outside the constitutional protections afforded religious free exercise. In the wake of the Manifesto, polygamy did not end immediately, but by the beginning of the twentieth century the polygamy era was over. Anyone practicing polygamy was, and continues to be, excommunicated from the LDS Church. The small fundamentalist sects that still engage in the practice are wholly estranged from the Church of Jesus Christ of Latter-day Saints. Third, while the practice of polygamy among Mormons has long been abandoned, the theological justification for it still exists, as part of canonized Mormon scripture.[14]

Given these three facts, how do Mormons feel about polygamy today? To answer this question, the Pew Mormons in America Survey included a question about whether polygamy is "morally acceptable, morally wrong, or not a moral issue." Eighty-six percent said that it is morally wrong, with another 11 percent saying that it is not a moral issue, leaving only 2 percent who say that it is morally acceptable. By way of comparison, more Mormons believe polygamy to be morally wrong than say the same about sex between unmarried adults (79 percent), having an abortion (74 percent), or drinking alcohol (54 percent). Clearly, regardless of any theological traces that remain, Mormons today see polygamy as immoral.


## Race

Alongside polygamy, perhaps the next most visible and controversial issue in Mormon history is the LDS Church's past policy regarding race. Prior to 1978, black men could be baptized in the Church but were denied the LDS priesthood, thus preventing them from holding any leadership positions or participating in LDS temple marriages and other temple rites. Today, even many Latter-day Saints are not aware of the sweeping implications of the previous racial restrictions within the Church, as they affected black women as well as men. For example, black women were also prohibited from temple worship and black teenage boys could not have a leadership role within LDS-sponsored Boy Scout troops, a very important element of Mormon culture.

Admittedly, these restrictions had little practical effect within the Church, since there were, understandably, very few black Mormons (and the LDS Church generally avoided active proselytizing among blacks). Nonetheless, the restrictions drew a lot of vocal criticism from outside the Church and heartache within it. Numerous universities, for example, refused to allow their sports teams to compete against Church-sponsored Brigham Young University. Many Latter-day Saints – including some Church authorities – pushed quietly for a change in the policy behind the scenes (Mauss 2003; Bush, Jr. 1973; Prince and Wright 2005).

Change came in June of 1978, when LDS Church President Spencer W. Kimball and the other top church leaders announced that they had received a revelation from God ending the racial restriction on the priesthood, similar to President Wilford Woodruff's divinely sanctioned Manifesto that ended

---

[14] See the *Doctrine and Covenants*, section 132. While the church has officially repudiated polygamy, in Mormon theology a marriage in an LDS temple is referred to as a "sealing" for "time and all eternity." Current church policy allows a man with a deceased wife to be sealed again to another woman, but a woman with a deceased husband cannot be sealed to another husband. She can only enter into a civil marriage, which according to LDS theology will dissolve upon death.

polygamy.[15] The origins of the ban have been pinpointed by the Church to an 1852 policy made by second Church President Brigham Young, who departed from the more progressive stance taken by Joseph Smith. After a long silence on the question, the Church has now suggested that the ban was also part of the racist American culture of its time. No detailed explanation for why it was lifted has been provided either, except to say that worldwide Church growth "seemed increasingly incompatible with the priesthood and temple restrictions" and that it was changed under divine direction.[16] To critics of the Church, the change in policy was merely a convenient way around an increasingly untenable restriction in the wake of the Civil Rights movement. To faithful Mormons, it is an example of how God guides His prophet. Just as with polygamy, believing Latter-day Saints do not deny that there was outside pressure on the Church to change, but believe that change could only come when God revealed that it was His will to do so.

Once the priesthood ban was lifted, "all worthy males" were entitled to the priesthood, regardless of race or color. While the LDS Church does not report membership statistics by race, it is clear that today there are many black men who have been ordained to the priesthood, including one of the Church's full-time general authorities.

We characterize LDS teachings on race as distinctive but not because a policy of racial exclusion within the religion was unique. Many denominations once had similar restrictions, although few maintained them as long as the LDS Church. Rather, Mormons' distinctiveness on race lies in the theological rationale that developed to justify the ban. While the precise origins of the ban are obscure, once in place it was then justified with the same reasoning used by other religions for their forms of religious apartheid. Like members of many other faiths, many Mormons believed that black skin was the mark of Cain, the first murderer, and thus God's way of signifying a person's inferiority or spiritual unworthiness. In the Mormon context, skin color had particular spiritual significance, since the *Book of Mormon* contains references to dark skin as a curse from God for a people's collective unrighteousness.[17]

---

[15] For the official canonized language of the Manifesto see "Official Declaration 1" in the LDS Church's *Doctrine and Covenants* (see: https://www.lds.org/scriptures/dc-testament/od/1). The announcement ending racial restrictions on the priesthood is "Official Declaration 2" (see: https://www.lds.org/scriptures/dc-testament/od/2) (both accessed on October 7, 2013).

[16] A brief article by the LDS Church was released in December 2013 and provides more detail about the origins and end to the priesthood ban. See "Race and the Priesthood" at http://www.lds.org/topics/race-and-the-priesthood?lang=eng (accessed January 31, 2014). See Mauss (2003) for a more detailed discussion.

[17] For example, one *Book of Mormon* verse states, "And he had caused the cursing to come upon them, yea, even a sore cursing, because of their iniquity. For behold, they had hardened their hearts against him, and they had become like unto a flint; wherefore, as they were white, and exceedingly fair and delightsome, that they might not be enticing unto my people the Lord God did cause a skin of blackness to come upon them" (*Book of Mormon*, 2nd Nephi 5:21). The Mormon folk doctrines about race more commonly tie back to stories about Cain than to the *Book of Mormon*, perhaps because the *Book of Mormon* also contains verses like this one, just a few pages later: "God inviteth them all to come unto him and partake of his goodness; and he denieth none that come unto him,

Over time, a folk doctrine arose to offer a further – and distinctively LDS – justification for the racial restriction (Crapo 1987). The folk doctrine built on the fundamental tenet of LDS theology that every person existed in a spiritual form prior to mortality (that part is official doctrine). The folk (that is, unofficial) part of the doctrine held that blacks were unable to hold the priesthood because they were tepid or neutral in the "war in heaven" – a confrontation between the followers of God and Lucifer prior to the Earth's creation. Essentially, black skin was a sign not only of a genealogical link to Cain, but an earthly punishment for ambivalence toward God in a spiritual realm. While the link to Cain was a connection made in other traditions to justify racially discriminatory policies, the folk doctrine was unique to Latter-day Saints, as it was rooted in the distinctive Mormon doctrine of a premortal existence (Bush, Jr. 1973).

Variations of this folk doctrine circulated widely among the LDS rank- and-file rank-and-file members throughout the twentieth century, and were taught by some Church leaders, including Joseph Fielding Smith, who later served as Church president. Current Church leaders and official statements have repudiated the folk doctrine as a rationale for the ban, although no statement from the Church has gone so far as to describe the ban itself as a mistake.[18] This example

black and white, bond and free, male and female; and he remembereth the heathen; and all are alike unto God, both Jew and Gentile" (*Book of Mormon*, 2nd Nephi 26:33).

[18]   In December 2013 the Church released an article that briefly reviews the history of the ban concluding, "Over time, Church leaders and members advanced many theories to explain the priesthood and temple restrictions. None of these explanations is accepted today as the official doctrine of the Church." See "Race and the Priesthood" at http://www.lds.org/topics/race-and-the-priesthood?lang=eng (accessed, January 31, 2014). Prior to this, the official explanations were limited to individual church leaders. For example, Elder Jeffrey R. Holland, a member of the Church's Quorum of the Twelve Apostles and thus part of the top leadership, distanced the Church from past statements on race in an interview for the PBS documentary "The Mormons."

Elder Jeffrey R. Holland: One clear-cut position is that the folklore must never be perpetuated.... I have to concede to my earlier colleagues.... They, I'm sure, in their own way, were doing the best they knew to give shape to [the policy], to give context for it, to give even history to it. All I can say is however well intended the explanations were, I think almost all of them were inadequate and/or wrong.... It probably would have been advantageous to say nothing, to say we just don't know, and, [as] with many religious matters, whatever was being done was done on the basis of faith at that time. But some explanations were given and had been given for a lot of years.... At the very least, there should be no effort to perpetuate those efforts to explain why that doctrine existed. I think, to the extent that I know anything about it, as one of the newer and younger ones to come along ... we simply do not know why that practice, that policy, that doctrine was in place (Public Broadcasting Service (PBS) 2006).

Another Apostle, Dallin H. Oaks, provided similar language about the incorrectness of past explanations for the ban on the tenth anniversary of the policy being changed: "We can put reasons to commandments. When we do, we're on our own. Some people put reasons to ... [the ban] and they turned out to be spectacularly wrong" (*Associated Press* 1988). In 2013, the LDS Church announced a new edition of the LDS scriptures that includes the following statement as a preface to "Official Declaration 2" that ended the racial ban: "During Joseph Smith's lifetime, a few black male members of the Church were ordained to the priesthood. Early in its history, Church leaders stopped conferring the priesthood on black males of African descent. Church records offer no clear insights into the origins of this practice." The entire preface and declaration are at https://www.lds.org/scriptures/dc-testament/od/2?lang=eng (accessed October 7, 2013).

reveals the cohesiveness of the sacred tabernacle: once a belief gets "under the tent," so to speak, it can spread quickly among Mormons, despite having no official sanction. It can then take considerable effort by Church authorities to change the belief. This is another parallel between polygamy and the policy on race – both have officially ended but vestiges of past justification still linger.[19]

For this reason, we were curious to know whether the particular folk doctrine that blacks "sat on the sidelines" in the war in heaven still holds sway among rank-and-file Mormons, so we asked about it on the Peculiar People Survey.[20] Using LDS terminology, our question read as follows: "In the past, some Mormons have said that blacks had to wait to hold the priesthood because they were less valiant in the war in heaven, or the premortal existence." We first asked whether respondents had ever heard this teaching and, if yes, whether they agreed with it.[21] Only 45 percent of Mormons said that they have ever heard the teaching on race (see Figure 3.1). Of those who are aware of the racial folk doctrine, 22 percent say that they agree (but only 5 percent say that they strongly agree). When we combine awareness and agreement, this means that 90 percent of Mormons have either never heard of this particular teaching or, if they have, do not agree with it.[22]

Young Mormons are slightly less likely to be aware of the racial folk doctrine than their elders and more likely to disagree with it if they have. Among Mormons born since the priesthood ban ended in 1978 (below 35 years of

---

[19] We do not have reliable data on Mormons' attitudes regarding the racial folk doctrine from an earlier era, but anecdotal evidence suggests that the belief was once prevalent. In his book *All Abraham's Children: Changing Mormon Conceptions of Race and Lineage*, sociologist Armand Mauss notes that BYU professor Eugene England used to administer surveys to his students on the subject and as late as the 1990s still found that a majority of his students believed the old folklore associated with the racial restrictions on the priesthood. The folk doctrine on race may never have achieved more universal acceptance because, while it was widely known, the doctrine was not canonized in scripture or taught frequently, likely allowing some Mormons to individually dissent from the norm (2003, 249).

[20] Fortunately, we conducted our survey before the *Washington Post* brought attention to the issue by publishing an interview with a professor of religion at Brigham Young University in which he repeated the folklore and then attempted to explain why blacks could not hold the LDS priesthood until 1978 with racist analogies (J. Horowitz 2012). The Church took the unusual step of repudiating the statements, saying that they "absolutely do not represent the teachings and doctrines" of the church. We can thus be sure that this latest imbroglio did not affect our respondents' attitudes.

[21] We were taught a lesson in the uneven awareness of the racial folk doctrine while designing the Peculiar People Survey. Originally, we drafted a question on this subject that stated the doctrine and asked respondents to indicate whether they agree or disagree with it. However, when we pilot-tested the questionnaire with a group of LDS students at Brigham Young University, we were struck that many had never heard of it.

[22] Awareness of the folk doctrine is related to involvement in Mormon culture and practices. Sixty percent of Mormons who have been church members all their lives and have done full-time missionary service have heard of the doctrine. However, greater awareness of the folk doctrine does not increase agreement with it. We suspect that awareness reflects exposure to both speculation on the topic inside, and criticism from outside, the LDS Church.

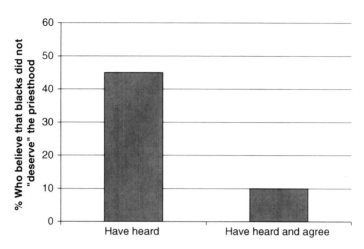

FIGURE 3.1. Few Mormons Today Have Heard, Let Alone Agree, That Blacks Did Not "Deserve" the Priesthood

*The folk doctrine was described as "In the past, some Mormons have said that blacks had to wait to hold the priesthood because they were less valiant in the war in heaven, or the premortal existence."*

Source: Peculiar People Survey, 2012

age), just 40 percent have heard of it but only 5 percent are both aware and agree (merely 1 percent strongly agree). As with polygamy, Mormons' attitudes regarding race suggest that even if the LDS Church has not officially labeled the priesthood ban as a mistake, Mormons themselves have discarded it. Looking forward, it is likely that this folk doctrine will literally die off as older generations pass on.

Given that polygamy and a racially restrictive priesthood are in the past, it might seem odd to include them in a chapter on Mormons' distinctiveness. Admittedly, devoid of historical context, contemporary disapproval of polygamy and disavowal of the folk doctrine on race may seem unremarkable, but in light of LDS history both are telling. These were not minor issues within the faith, but instead put the LDS Church in the glare of the public spotlight over its practices, policies, and doctrines. The turnabouts on both polygamy and race thus inform us about an important distinctive element of LDS theology and culture: things change. More specifically, Latter-day Saints' doctrine that their leaders carry a prophetic mantle and that there is an "open canon" leads to a belief system with the capacity for adjustment. Thus, as seeming counter-examples of Mormons' peculiarity, attitudes on polygamy and race actually underscore an important aspect of LDS distinctiveness. When LDS leaders speak, Mormons listen. Or perhaps it is more accurate to say that when LDS leaders stop speaking about an issue, Mormons stop believing it, although historical inertia might keep some old beliefs around for a while.

## MEASURING "MORMON-NESS"

Thus far in this chapter, we have emphasized the uniformity within the sacred tabernacle. This, however, is only half of the story. A close look within Mormonism reveals that uniformity along some dimensions is balanced with diversity among others. By drawing on the wide range of LDS beliefs and practices included in the Peculiar People Survey, we have created four indices that each reflects a different dimension of "Mormon-ness."[23]

• Activity: degree of religious practice
• Authority: degree of obedience to the institutional church
• Insularity: degree of social separation from the wider society
• Identity: degree of self-conscious affinity with the group

The specific items in each of the indices are found in the appendix to this chapter, Tables 3A.1 through 3A.4. We introduce these measures here because they will be employed in subsequent chapters to explore Mormons' political attitudes and behavior.

The Activity Index (Table 3A.1) includes five items that capture a mix of religious behaviors that combine participation in public meetings (church attendance), support for a religious organization (financial contributions from tithing), and private devotion (individual prayer and scripture reading), along with a question that asks respondents their level of activity within the Church. The Activity Index comes the closest to a traditional religiosity measure commonly used in a variety of political science scholarship about religion and politics (e.g. Kellstedt et al. 1996; Green 2007). It also resembles measures used by sociologists to study the LDS population (Cornwall et al. 1986; Cornwall 1989).[24]

---

[23] For each index, the component questions are rescaled between zero and one so that each item contributes equally to each index. Thus, each of the indices also ranges between zero and five.

[24] We have excluded a few items that could arguably be included. Generally, we opted for a mix of generalizability, parsimony, and reliability:

  • Generalizability, in the sense that items in the Activity Index that could be compared to other religious traditions (except for the self-assessed religious activity question).
  • Parsimony, in the form of a shorter list of comparable length across indices.
  • Reliability, defined as the highest possible Cronbach's Alpha score we could obtain while holding the line on parsimony and generalizability.

For example, we excluded whether or not a person had a current Mormon "temple recommend." To enter a Mormon temple (of which there are 140 in the entire world), Mormons are required to have a kind of "pass" that requires biennial interviews with two levels of ecclesiastical leadership about their adherence to doctrinal and behavioral norms. Even if they do not live close to a temple, Mormons are strongly encouraged to have a recommend as a sign of being in good standing with the Church. However, the questions to obtain a temple recommend span more than one of our indices. Likewise, frequency of temple attendance was excluded because it is far easier to attend a temple in some geographic areas than others. Finally, a subset of the Church's membership will not have had the opportunity to attend the temple yet, either because they are too young or have not been members long enough (one has to have been a member for at least a year). We have also

The Authority Index includes items that reflect Mormons' adherence to authority (Table 3A.2). As explained in Chapter 1, the concept of authority lies at the theological heart of Mormonism, but not all Latter-day Saints interpret the role of authority the same way. One such area of varying interpretation is the potential tension between reliance on church authority versus personal revelation to guide one's life (as exemplified in the profiles of Dee Dee and Kara at the beginning of the chapter). Another is the individual's willingness to call into question church teachings that some find difficult to accept. The items in the Authority Index in some ways resemble "belief orthodoxy" survey items used in the study of other faiths.[25] In this case we have crafted questions specific to Mormons, in order to gauge compliance with religious authority (Green 2007, 49).[26] To use language often employed to describe differences within other religious traditions, these questions place Mormons on a spectrum of traditionalism (Kellstedt and Smidt 1996).

The Insularity Index is modeled after items drawn from Putnam and Campbell (2010, 522–34) about the religious affiliation of one's family and friends (Table 3A.3). The index measures the religious diversity within social networks – the degree to which people insulate themselves from interaction with people of other faiths. Putnam and Campbell find that Mormons exhibit a homogeneity in their religious networks that is only exceeded by Latino Catholics and is about the same as black Protestants (525).[27]

Much scholarship in religion is concerned with "belonging," or identifying with a particular religious denomination or tradition (e.g. Kellstedt et al. 1996; Steensland et al. 2000). Often this research is concerned with the nominal classification of people into one religious tradition versus another. Since our work begins, by definition, with people who self-identify as Mormons, we instead measure "belonging" as their depth of connection to Mormonism as an identity using the Identity Index items listed in Table 3A.4.[28]

---

excluded whether or not a person has a Church calling as well as the amount of time spent on one's calling, since for Church members that is not entirely in their control. Callings are not self-appointed. It is worth noting that all of these items (and others) strongly correlate as expected with items in our Activity Index.

[25] The variables were coded so that those who follow church authority or do not question particular teachings score higher.

[26] This index captures the distinction made by Richard Poll between "Iron Rod" and "Liahona" Mormons (2001). Both are terms from the *Book of Mormon*. The former refers to a "straight and narrow" path to God, symbolizing strict obedience to top-down authority. The latter refers to a divine compass activated by an individual's faith, suggesting a bottom-up form of personal inspiration.

[27] Note that, as we have constructed it, the Insularity Index includes whether the respondent is a convert to the LDS Church. We have included this measure because converts are, almost by definition, more likely to be less insular than lifetime Mormons and, empirically, it loads on this factor in principal components analysis. Our results are substantively unchanged if convert status is removed from this index.

[28] Inspiration for these items comes from their adaptation for use in measuring group identity with political parties by Steve Greene (1999). We thank David Lassen for sharing his adaption of the items for use with Mormons as part of a campaign finance pilot study (2009). Greene and Lassen, in turn, have based their items on research by Fred Mael and Lois Tetrick (1992).

Each of our four indices has a different distribution, as shown in Figure 3.2. The Activity Index is quite skewed, showing that most Mormons do most of the things in the index on a regular basis. The Authority and Identity Indices are also somewhat skewed toward the high end, but not nearly to the same extent as the Activity Index. In other words, there are comparatively more self-identified Mormons who rely on individual inspiration or who express some doubts about fundamental points of Mormon theology than those who are religiously "inactive." This pattern is not surprising. Relying more on

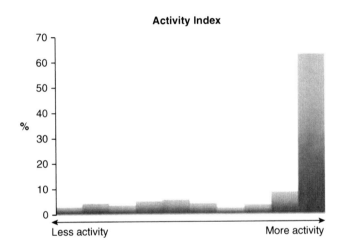

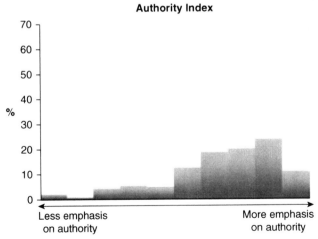

FIGURE 3.2. Dimensions of "Mormon-ness"
*Source:* Peculiar People Survey, 2012

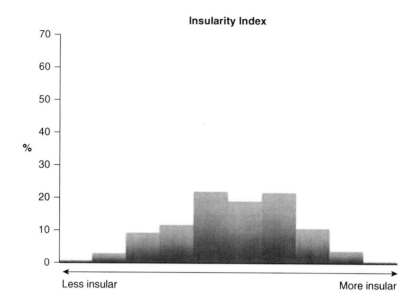

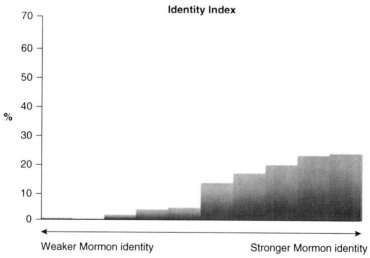

FIGURE 3.2. (cont.)

individual inspiration than top-down authority is well within the boundaries of accepted Mormon theology (Givens 2007). Entertaining doubts about theology is also not forbidden within the church, although the public expression of such doubts may lead to friction and, depending on the severity and circumstances, even excommunication.

The Insularity Index is the most evenly distributed of all, suggesting that Mormons vary in the degree to which they have built bridges to people of other faiths. Below we will see that Mormons' insularity is strongly affected by whether they live in a heavily LDS area.

The similar but varying distributions of the indices suggest that they are related but distinct. The bivariate correlation between them ranges from a low of 0.29 (Identity and Insularity) to a high of 0.57 (Activity and Authority). (A zero correlation means no overlap, while 1.0 means complete overlap.)[29] A better test of their relationship to each other is to estimate a simple set of statistical (regression) models where each of the indices is predicted by the other three indices. The point of the exercise is to see if these indices independently correlate with each other, while controlling for the effects of the other indices, or not. Given the significant correlations between the indices, it is likely that at times they would predict each other. The Activity Index is a significant predictor of the other three, and vice versa, underscoring that Mormonism has expectations for religious practice that are both clear and high. Conversely, the Insularity Index does not predict anything except Activity, suggesting that the social networks represented in the Insularity Index are largely measuring something distinctive. (See Table 3A.5, in the appendix to this chapter, for details.)

The details aside, these statistical models most clearly demonstrate that the four indices are each tapping into "Mormon-ness" from different angles.

UTAH MORMONS

Within Mormon culture, "Utah Mormons" are commonly thought to be different from Mormons who live elsewhere. In a very loose sense, Utah to Mormons is like Israel to Jews, the physical and spiritual center of the faith. The perceived differences extend into the realm of common stereotypes. Perhaps because they are in "Zion" (Mormon lingo for the heartland of the Church), Utah Mormons are perceived by Mormons in the "mission field" (areas where Mormons are a minority) as displaying a "holier-than-thou" attitude about how the Church *should* operate. Many observers of LDS culture would assume that Mormons in Utah differ from those who live outside of Utah in many ways but, perhaps surprisingly, they differ in only a few.

---

[29] Here are the correlations between the four indices:

|            | Activity | Authority | Identity | Insularity |
|------------|----------|-----------|----------|------------|
| Activity   | 1.00     |           |          |            |
| Authority  | 0.57     | 1.00      |          |            |
| Identity   | 0.55     | 0.49      | 1.00     |            |
| Insularity | 0.47     | 0.32      | 0.29     | 1.00       |

The greatest differences appear in terms of social networks – connections and interactions with fellow Mormons. Utah Mormons are more likely to have Mormon family members, spouses, neighbors, and friends. A third of Utah Mormons say that "all" of their family is LDS, compared to 14 percent of non-Utah Mormons. Likewise, when compared to non-Utah Mormons, Church members in Utah are also more likely to have both a spouse who is a member of the Church, as well as one who is currently active in the faith. Finally, and not surprisingly, there are sharp differences for the questions about neighbors and close friends. For neighbors, 90 percent of non-Utah Mormons say "some" or "none" of their friends are Mormon, compared to 68 percent of Utah Mormons who report that "most" of their friends are Mormon. Out of their five closest friends, the average Mormon in Utah has four close friends who are also LDS, while non-Utah Mormons have fewer than three.

On questions measuring religious activity, Utah Mormons are slightly more active and more likely to hold a church calling.[30] However, that is where the differences end. Utah Mormons do not differ substantively in frequency of prayer, temple attendance, or scripture reading, nor in volunteer time, amount of tithing contributed, belief in the reality of the *Book of Mormon*, or the importance of their religion in their lives.[31] When it comes to questions about the role of authority in the Church, Utah Mormons *do not* differ from their non-Utah counterparts.[32] Similarly, the two groups have the same strength of Mormon identity.[33]

While much is made of differences between Utah Mormons and non-Utah Mormons, the "Utah effect" is largely in the social networks Mormons form. Latter-day Saints are more insular when surrounded by fellow LDS members. Otherwise, Utah Mormons and non-Utah Mormons have much more in common with each other than not. These similarities illustrate what we mean by the "portability" of the sacred tabernacle – the self-reinforcing subculture Mormons form wherever they reach a critical mass, whether it be in Provo, Portland, or Pawtucket.

## CONVERTS

As Mormonism is a religion that prioritizes proselytizing, we should not be surprised that a sizeable proportion of Mormons are converts to the faith. According to the Peculiar People Survey, roughly a third of all self-identified

---

[30] There is little difference on callings that required a larger number of hours; the difference came from those who had no callings (non-Utah Mormons) compared to those who had low-hour callings (Utah Mormons).

[31] There are questions where the two groups differed statistically, but the substantive differences are quite small (holding a temple recommend, giving to charity, serving an LDS mission, giving of tithes, and volunteering).

[32] They do not differ on any of the measurements in the Authority Index.

[33] The only exception was the question on whether Mormons are a peculiar people, where the majority of Utah Mormons agreed with the statement while their non-Utah counterparts disagreed overall. On all of the measurements for the Identity Index, there are no differences whatsoever.

Mormons are converts.[34] Just as Mormons frequently draw distinctions between Church members inside and outside of Utah, so too do they distinguish between converts and those who were born in the Church. However, contrary to the assumption that there is no zeal like that of a convert, converts to Mormonism score lower than lifetime Mormons on each measure of "Mormon-ness." They are less religiously active, have a weaker Mormon identity, put less emphasis on authority than personal revelation, and are less likely to have friends, family, and neighbors who are LDS.[35]

The fact that converts are, on average, less engaged with Mormonism provides another example of the sacred tabernacle at work. Mormon converts have spent less time immersed in the LDS subculture than lifetime members, and thus do not exhibit the same degree of religious devotion – reminding us of the importance of community within the LDS faith.

SELF-AWARENESS

As we saw in the previous chapter, Mormons are aware of their distinctiveness, as they willingly embrace the label of a peculiar people. And the more embedded they are in Mormon culture, the more likely they are to describe themselves as peculiar. Figure 3.3 examines agreement by our four indices – Activity, Authority, Insularity, and Identity – by splitting each index into five equal-sized "bins" (quintiles). We display the percentage agreeing with the "peculiar people" label in the bottom and top quintile. In each case, the self-awareness of peculiarity increases dramatically between the bottom and the top. In the Activity Index, only 39 percent of those in the lowest quintile agree, compared to 91 percent of those in the highest quintile. The differences lessen only a little in the other three indices, going from 57 percent to 83 percent on the Authority Index, 61 percent to 78 percent on the Insularity Index, and from 60 percent to 90 percent on the Identity Index. Strikingly, for these three indices over half of Mormons in the lowest category still think of themselves as peculiar.

While Mormons largely embrace the label of peculiar, many are also aware of its downside. While peculiarity fosters religious vitality and identity, it can also bring marginalization and even discrimination. In the Pew Mormons

---

[34] The survey used the LDS Church's own definition of a convert, namely someone baptized at the age of nine or older. "Lifetime" Mormons would have been baptized at eight years old, the minimum age. Obviously, this blunt method of classifying converts does not differentiate between people who joined the LDS Church as children (and thus have essentially grown up Mormon) and those who converted as adults. As a comparison, the Pew Mormons in America Survey asked respondents whether they were "raised Mormon" and classified any current Mormon who said no as a convert. Using this method, 26 percent of Mormons are coded as converts. We leave it to future research to make more fine-grained distinctions among converts to Mormonism.

[35] Since being a convert is part of the full Insularity Index, we compare converts versus lifetime members on the other components of the index. Also, note that these results hold up when controlling for whether or not someone is a Utah Mormon.

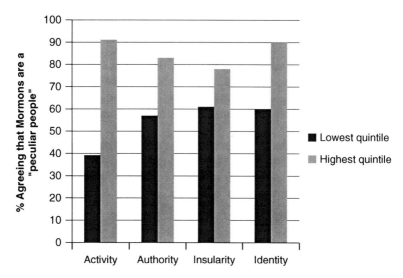

FIGURE 3.3. Agreement with "Peculiar People" Label by Mormon-ness Indices
*Source:* Peculiar People Survey, 2012

in America Survey, a majority of Mormons indicated that discrimination and misperception were among the most important problems facing American Mormons today. Likewise, one-quarter of Latter-day Saints said that there was "a lot of discrimination" against Mormons (2012a). Peculiarity has its pros and cons.

CONCLUSION

Mormons are clearly distinctive in both religious belief and behavior, creating dual social boundaries for the sacred tabernacle and the "two-front war." First, they share a common set of beliefs and high levels of religious activity with members of other religious traditions, especially evangelicals, which set them apart from the rest of American secular society. A second boundary arises between Mormons and other religions – particularly and perhaps ironically, evangelicals – due to uniquely Mormon theology about, among other things, the nature of God, the existence of modern revelation, scripture beyond the Bible, and belief in a living prophet. These distinctive aspects of LDS theology lead some people to wonder whether Mormons should even be considered Christians (see Chapter 7 for more discussion of this controversy). And while specific beliefs and practices within Mormonism can and do change, thus lessening Mormons' distinctiveness in one way, the belief that change comes through divine revelation to God's prophet nonetheless reinforces Mormons' distinctiveness in another way.

Yet Mormons are not all alike and diversity can be found within the sacred tabernacle. There are four dimensions of Mormon-ness, and Latter-day Saints vary on each one. They differ slightly in their degree of Activity, more so on attitudes toward Authority and their strength of Identity, and most of all in their degree of Insularity.

Having described the many ways that Mormons are a peculiar people, in the next two sections of the book we examine the political consequences of that peculiarity, beginning with partisanship and voting behavior.

CHAPTER 3 APPENDIX

TABLE 3A.1. *Activity Index Items and Responses*

Active – "How would you describe your activity in the LDS Church?"
- Not at all active (10%)
- Not too active (9%)
- Somewhat active (17%)
- Very active (64%)

Tithe – "Do you currently pay tithing, that is, donate 10% or more of your income to the LDS Church?"
- Yes (75%)
- No (25%)

Attend – "How often do you attend church?"
- Once a week (72%)
- Once or twice a month (7%)
- A few times a year (5%)
- Seldom (11%)
- Never (5%)

Read – "How often, if ever, do you do the following things: read the scriptures?"
- Daily (39%)
- A few times a week (29%)
- A few times a month (13%)
- A few times a year (15%)
- Never (4%)

Pray – "How often, if ever, do you do the following things: have personal or family prayer?"
- Daily (72%)
- A few times a week (14%)
- A few times a month (5%)
- A few times a year (7%)
- Never (3%)

Totals may not equal 100 because of rounding.
Cronbach's Alpha: 0.91

TABLE 3A.2. *Authority Index Items and Responses*

Sabbath – "Which comes closer to your view: 1) The Church has specific standards for obeying the Sabbath 4) obeying the Sabbath means deciding for yourself what is appropriate?"
- 1 (33%)
- 2 (30%)
- 3 (24%)
- 4 (13%)

Obey – "Which comes closer to your view: 1) A good Latter-day Saint should obey the counsel of priesthood leaders without necessarily knowing why 4) a good Latter-day Saint should first seek his or her own personal revelation as the motivation to obey?"
- 1 (11%)
- 2 (29%)
- 3 (29%)
- 4 (31%)

Teaching – "Which comes closer to your view: 1) Some teachings of the LDS Church are hard for me to believe 4) I believe wholeheartedly in all the teachings of the LDS Church?"
- 1 (8%)
- 2 (10%)
- 3 (19%)
- 4 (63%)

Say – "Women do not have enough say in the LDS Church."
- Strongly agree (5%)
- Agree (11%)
- Disagree (35%)
- Strongly disagree (49%)

Bother – "The fact that women do not hold the priesthood sometimes bothers me."
- Strongly agree (3%)
- Agree (11%)
- Disagree (24%)
- Strongly disagree (63%)

Totals may not equal 100 because of rounding.
Cronbach's Alpha: 0.72

TABLE 3A.3. *Insularity Index Items and Responses*

---

LDS Friend – "Thinking about your five closest friends, how many of them are LDS?"
• 0 (16%)
• 1 (5%)
• 2 (10%)
• 3 (15%)
• 4 (18%)
• 5 (35%)

Neighbor – "Thinking about your neighbors, how many of them are LDS?"
• All (1%)
• Most (30%)
• Some (38%)
• None (31%)

Family – "Thinking about your extended family, how many of them are LDS?"
• All (20%)
• Most (48%)
• Some (25%)
• None (7%)

Convert – "Are you a convert to the LDS Church (baptized when you were older than eight years old)?"
• Yes (33%)
• No (67%)

Spouse Active – "What is your current marital status?" Then, if married, "Is your spouse LDS?" and "How would you describe your spouse's activity in the LDS Church?" Recoded:
• No spouse (26%)
• Non-LDS spouse (7%)
• Not at all active (4%)
• Not too active (4%)
• Somewhat active (9%)
• Very active (50%)

---

Totals may not equal 100 because of rounding.
Cronbach's Alpha: 0.67

TABLE 3A.4. *Identity Index Items and Responses*

We – "When I talk about Mormons, I usually say 'we' rather than 'they.'"
• Strongly agree (55%)
• Agree (35%)
• Disagree (9%)
• Strongly disagree (1%)

Who – "Being a Mormon is an essential part of who I am."
• Strongly agree (64%)
• Agree (25%)
• Disagree (11%)
• Strongly disagree (1%)

Like – "I'm like other Mormons in many ways."
• Strongly agree (35%)
• Agree (50%)
• Disagree (13%)
• Strongly disagree (2%)

Proud – "If a Mormon were elected president, I would feel proud."
• Strongly agree (29%)
• Agree (55%)
• Disagree (15%)
• Strongly disagree (1%)

Insult – "When someone criticizes Mormons, it feels like a personal insult."
• Strongly agree (32%)
• Agree (40%)
• Disagree (25%)
• Strongly disagree (4%)

Totals may not equal 100 because of rounding.
Cronbach's Alpha: 0.78

TABLE 3A.5. *OLS Models of Each Index Regressed on the Other Three Indices*

| VARIABLES | Activity | Authority | Identity | Insularity |
|---|---|---|---|---|
| Authority | 0.453***(0.059) | – | 0.239***(0.047) | 0.0872(0.060) |
| Identity | 0.480***(0.068) | 0.306***(0.061) | – | 0.0235(0.069) |
| Insularity | 0.340***(0.044) | 0.0502(0.034) | 0.0106(0.031) | – |
| Activity | – | 0.277***(0.041) | 0.229***(0.034) | 0.361***(0.044) |
| Constant | -0.337(0.244) | 0.984***(0.191) | 2.023***(0.158) | 0.971***(0.221) |
| Observations | 483 | 483 | 483 | 483 |
| R-squared | 0.475 | 0.366 | 0.338 | 0.229 |

Robust standard errors in parentheses
*** $p < 0.01$, ** $p < 0.05$, * $p < 0.1$

PART II

POLITICAL BEHAVIOR OF MORMONS

# 4

# Mormon Political Views

## *Cohesive, Republican, and Conservative*

Like voters in the rest of the nation, Utahns of the 1870s had a choice between two political parties. Yet unlike elsewhere, the two parties were not the Democrats and the Republicans. Instead, they were the People's Party and the Liberal Party, both indigenous only to the Beehive state. While in the rest of the United States, Democrats and Republicans debated the merits of Reconstruction and the state of the post-Civil War union, the Utah parties were divided by religion. The People's Party was the Mormon party, organized under the auspices of the LDS Church; the Liberal Party was the non-Mormon, or "gentile," party.

This was not the first time that Mormons banded together at the polls. In the infant days of the Church, Mormons in Missouri voted as a bloc, causing friction with their non-Mormon neighbors. Likewise, when they fled Missouri at gunpoint and settled in Illinois, church founder Joseph Smith was regularly courted by prominent politicians seeking the sizeable Mormon vote in the thriving city of Nauvoo. By the 1840s, Mormons had become "swing voters," alternating between the Whigs and Democrats (Bowman 2012a). And in 1844, Joseph Smith ran for president as an independent candidate (see Chapter 8 for details).

Mormons were thus a politically peculiar people, voting as a bloc, bringing out bloc voting in others, challenging the two-party system, and experimenting with alternative political parties. This pattern was in keeping with the ethno-religious politics of the nineteenth and twentieth centuries. Although ethno-religious politics has declined overall in recent times, it still applies to Mormons. In recent times, the sacred tabernacle has resulted in a strong alignment with the Republican Party. Ethno-religious politics may be endangered, but the Mormon case affirms that it is not extinct.

Mormons are cohesive because of two clear boundaries around their community; they are fighting a "two-front war" in politics as well as society. On the one hand, Mormons are distinct from American society writ large. They are religious traditionalists who share much common ground with other cultural conservatives, particularly evangelicals. If Mormons, like evangelicals, only defined themselves in opposition to "the world" (the first front) then we would not expect them to differ much from evangelicals. On the other hand, Mormons also explicitly define themselves in contrast to other religions, including but not limited to evangelical Protestants (the second front). Consequently, Mormons do not occupy the same subcultural niche as any other group. They have some characteristics in common with evangelicals, but in other ways more closely resemble Jews, Catholics, and black Protestants.

Today Mormons are cohesive, Republican, and conservative – but also complex. This chapter focuses on Mormons' cohesiveness and conservatism, and the next highlights their complexity. If there is one message to come out of this chapter, it is that the current near-monolithic state of Mormon politics has not always been the case. The central message of Chapter 5 is that while Mormons are cohesive and conservative, they are also politically distinct, even from other cultural conservatives.

This chapter begins by examining Mormons' political cohesiveness, both now and in the past. It then moves on to an analysis of why so many Mormons today are Republicans – sharper boundaries foster a greater attachment to the GOP. We will see that Mormons receive very little political stimuli through formal Church channels, as their worship meetings are mostly devoid of any partisan content. Instead, their partisan cohesiveness is reinforced through the social networks formed within the sacred tabernacle.

## COHESIVELY REPUBLICAN

Mormons are one of the most politically cohesive religious groups in the nation. In fact, they are one of the most cohesive of any kind of group, whether defined in terms of race, ethnicity, or just about any other demographic characteristic (Fox 2006).

As shown in Figure 4.1, according to the Pew U.S. Religious Landscape Survey, 65 percent of Mormons identify as, or lean toward, the Republican Party. As a benchmark for comparison, that is substantially more than the half of evangelical Protestants – the oft-described base of the GOP – who identify as Republicans. Further underscoring Mormons' political cohesiveness, just 22 percent identify as Democrats. The only group with a lower percentage of Democrats is Jehovah's Witnesses, and that is because very few identify with either party (75 percent of them identify as political independents). The two groups that rank with Mormons for support of one party are to be found on the other end of the partisan spectrum, namely Jews and black Protestants. The proportion of Mormons who identify with the Republican Party is roughly comparable to the percentage of Jews who identify with the Democrats (66 percent). Among the major religious traditions in the United States, only black Protestants are more supportive of one party, as 77 percent

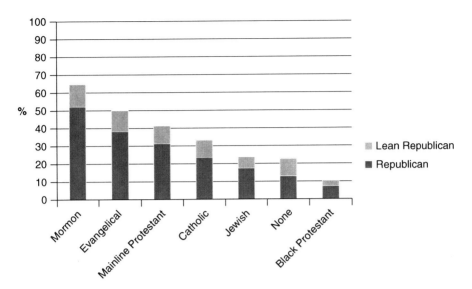

FIGURE 4.1. Mormons Are the Most Republican Religious Group
*Source:* Pew U.S. Religious Landscape Survey, 2007

are Democrats.[1] It is telling that the two groups who rival Mormons for political cohesiveness both have an ethno-religious character – one more sign that Mormons are such a group as well.

As would be expected, Mormons' strong attachment to the Republican Party translates into strong support for Republican candidates at the polls. According to the Peculiar People Survey, 75 percent of Mormons voted for John McCain in 2008 and 79 percent voted for a Republican congressional candidate in the 2010 midterm elections. By way of comparison, Mormons are about as politically cohesive as white evangelicals. National exit polls indicate that in 2012, 78 percent of Mormons voted for fellow Mormon Mitt Romney, compared to 79 percent of evangelical voters. In 2004, 79 percent of white evangelical voters pulled the lever for fellow evangelical George W. Bush, compared to 80 percent of Mormons.[2] Note, however, that neither Mormons nor evangelicals are the most politically cohesive religious group. That distinction belongs to black Protestants, as 95 percent voted for Barack Obama in 2012 and 94 percent voted for him in 2008 (Pew Forum on Religion & Public Life 2012c).

[1] These figures all come from the Pew U.S. Religious Landscape Survey; see Data Appendix for details regarding this survey.
[2] Owing to the margin of error, the differences between these numbers are inconsequential and should be treated as effectively identical.

Mormons' political cohesiveness is even more apparent when it comes to ideological self-identification. Sixty percent of Mormons identify as conservative, while only 6 percent describe themselves as liberal (the remainder are moderates). No other group has a higher proportion who identify with an ideological label, either conservative or liberal. For example, "only" 53 percent of evangelicals identify as conservative and, on the other side of the spectrum, 38 percent of Jews call themselves liberals. Among black Protestants, the most heavily Democratic group, more actually identify as conservative (35 percent) than liberal (21 percent).[3]

Mormons' conservatism is further illustrated by their support of the Tea Party, the conservative movement that emerged in the wake of President Obama's election. Even though the Mormon health code prohibits the consumption of tea, Mormons nonetheless heavily favor the Tea Party. Of the Mormons we interviewed in the Peculiar People Survey, two-thirds have a favorable view of the Tea Party. Given the general unpopularity of the Tea Party among voters as a whole, this is a notably high level of support (Putnam and Campbell 2010).

## MORMONS' PARTISANSHIP OVER TIME

The current period of Republican dominance is not the first time that Mormons have overwhelmingly favored one party. In the nineteenth century, Mormons regularly voted as a bloc. Indeed, their political cohesiveness was often a source of tension with the non-Mormons in their surrounding environment. In the debate over Utah's statehood, opponents pointed to the "Mormon party" as important evidence that the Latter-day Saints were not integrated into the national political system – just as polygamy and Brigham Young's encouragement that Mormons do business only with other Mormons demonstrated that they were not integrated into the nation's legal and economic systems. Going back further in history, in 1838 a riot broke out in Gallatin, Missouri when a group of Mormons attempted to vote as a bloc, and were met by a mob determined to prevent them from doing do. That conflagration was an impetus for Missouri's governor to issue his infamous extermination order, which called for all Mormons to leave Missouri or be killed (Arrington and Bitton 1992).

Prior to Utah's statehood, Mormons literally removed themselves from the rest of American society in search of their promised land. In the 1800s, the boundaries Mormons drew were not merely symbolic and subtle, but geographic and tangible. Today, the LDS Church emphasizes the symbolic boundaries demarcating Mormons' group identity; one consequence has been a return to the political homogeneity of an earlier era. Mormon political behavior today is a vestige of the ethno-religious politics of the past. While they no longer have their own political party and LDS leaders do not promise to deliver the Mormon vote, they nonetheless are a highly – albeit not entirely – uniform

[3] These figures are also from the Pew U.S. Religious Landscape Survey.

group. In contrast, during the early part of the twentieth century, Mormons placed less emphasis on those boundaries and more on integrating into American society. In this period the Mormon vote was not so heavily tilted in favor of one party.

In the absence of a single data source to track Mormons' voting over time, we can triangulate by drawing on information from multiple sources. For analysis of the present, we can rely on public opinion surveys for data on individuals. As we have seen already, there is a wealth of data available from surveys of Mormons, or samples of Mormons extracted from surveys of the general population. However, we have far less data from the past, before there were polls.

In previous research, voting trends in Utah have been used as a rough approximation of trends among Mormons, since a majority of Utahns are LDS (Campbell, Karpowitz, and Monson forthcoming). Although analysis of this kind can suggest broad trends, it is an approximation at best, since not all Utahns are Mormons, and not all Mormons live in Utah.[4] Nonetheless, the data are still informative as a reflection of how a large portion of Mormons have voted since 1896, using the only available data stretching back that far. For 1896 to 1980, we use a statistical method known as ecological inference, which enables us to exploit the variation in the LDS share of each Utah county's population to infer how Mormons voted (G. King 1997).[5] From 1984 to 2012, however, we use individual-level data from the Utah Colleges Exit Poll conducted by Brigham Young University.

Both Figures 4.2 and 4.3 display the results of our analysis by graphing presidential voting from 1896 (the year Utah became a state) to 2012. Since results from each election are driven by idiosyncratic factors such as the personal appeal of the candidates, current economic conditions, and whether the nation is at peace or war, it is most illuminating to compare Utah Mormons with the national popular vote. This way, we can essentially "control" for the vagaries of

[4] In interpreting these results, remember that they are for only the subset of Mormons who live in Utah. Early in the time series, this represented a relatively large proportion of all Mormons, but that share declined throughout the twentieth century. In 1890, 81 percent of Mormons in America lived in Utah. By 1952 that had fallen to 53 percent, and by 2010 it was 31 percent. Also, recall from Chapter 3 that Utah Mormons do not differ substantially from other Mormons except in their social networks. The 1890 data come from *Statistics of Churches in the United States, 1890* (U.S. Census Bureau), 1952 from *Churches and Church Membership in the United States, 1952* (National Council of Churches), and 2010 from *U.S. Religion Census: Religious Congregations and Membership Study, 2010* (Association of Statisticians of American Religious Bodies). These data can be found on the website of the American Religion Data Archive: http://www.thearda.com/Archive/ChState.asp (accessed October 7, 2013).

[5] We can validate these ecological inference (EI) results from 1984 to 2012 with the statewide Utah Colleges Exit Polls. The exit poll is a survey taken of a representative sample of voters as they leave their polling place, and thus can be treated as an accurate snapshot of Utah voters. For the years in which we have both EI and exit poll results, they are a close match – well within the respective estimates' margin of error. On average, the two estimates differ by only 4 percentage points.

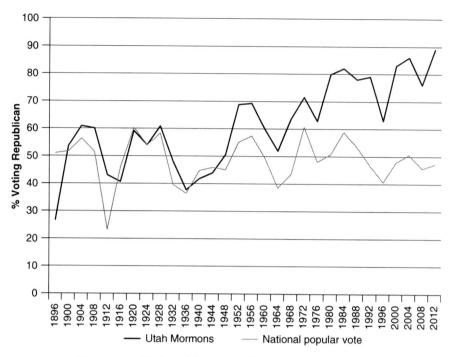

FIGURE 4.2. Mormons in Utah and the National Popular Vote
*Sources:* National popular vote: David Leip's Atlas of U.S. Presidential Elections; Utah Mormons, 1896–1980: ecological inference; Utah Mormons, 1984–2012: Utah Colleges Exit Polls

any one election. We present the same data in two different figures, as each one provides a different perspective. To enable comparison with national voting trends, Figure 4.2 displays both the percentage of Utah Mormons voting Republican and the nationwide Republican vote – accentuating the rising support for Republican presidential candidates since 1896. Figure 4.3 plots the difference between the percentage of Utah Mormons voting Republican and the popular vote.

These figures highlight the fact that *Mormons in Utah in the twentieth-first century are more politically distinctive than Utah Mormons in 1896.* Today, they heavily favor Republicans; then, they threw their support behind a Democrat. In the presidential election of 1896, an overwhelming 73 percent of Utah Mormons voted for the Democrat, William Jennings Bryan. Even though Mormons would have disliked Bryan's Protestant fundamentalism, they disliked the Republican Party even more. This anti-Republican sentiment no doubt reflected that, from the party's founding, the GOP had made an issue of anti-Mormonism. The party's original 1856 platform put polygamy next to slavery

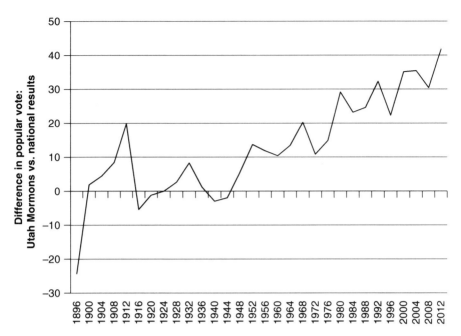

FIGURE 4.3. Utah Mormons Have Become Increasingly More Likely to Vote Republican Than the Rest of the United States
*Note:* Difference in popular vote = % of Utah Mormons voting Republican – % of all Americans voting Republican

as one of "those twin relics of barbarism."[6] Nonetheless, we must be careful not to exaggerate Mormons' peculiarity. Although they diverged dramatically from the national popular vote, Utah as a whole voted much like other Western states, where Bryan had strong support. His agrarian economic populism – including the coinage of silver – won the day in the rural West.

The 1896 election was the last gasp of Mormons' strong affinity for the Democratic Party, as by 1900 many Mormons were willing to bury the political hatchet and vote Republican. A new century brought a new political era for Mormons. Polygamy was ending and Mormons sought cultural, economic, and political accommodation with the rest of America. While only 27 percent of Utah Mormons voted for Republican William McKinley in 1896, 54 percent did when he ran for reelection (in a rematch with Bryan) in 1900.

[6] "Republican Party Platform of 1856," June 18, 1856. Online by Gerhard Peters and John T. Woolley, *The American Presidency Project.* http://www.presidency.ucsb.edu/ws/?pid=29619 (accessed February 3, 2014).

In 1900, Utah Mormons closely matched the national popular vote. From that point on, the two lines generally stick together through the first half of the twentieth century (with the exception of 1912, an unusual election because of the three-way race among Wilson, Taft, and former Republican president Teddy Roosevelt). Note that in Franklin Roosevelt's three reelection bids (1936, 1940, 1944), Utah Mormons aligned with the popular vote almost perfectly – favoring Roosevelt over his Republican opponents in each contest.

Utah Mormons' support for Republican candidates grew after World War II, averaging a thirteen-point gap with the national popular vote between 1948 and 1976 – with the exception of 1968, but that is largely because Richard Nixon, the Republican, had to compete with third-party candidate George Wallace for conservative voters in many other states. However, Wallace had little appeal in Utah, so Nixon did especially well there relative to his performance nationwide. Sociologist Armand Mauss likewise concludes, based on surveys of Mormons he conducted in the 1960s, that at that time, "Mormons (especially those outside Utah) tended to be about equally divided between Democrats and Republicans" (1994, 49).

Although the general trend is toward ever-greater Republican support, Ronald Reagan's election in 1980 is noteworthy. While the increase in Republican support does not represent a statistically significant structural break in the trend,[7] 1980 marks the beginning of Republican dominance, as Mormon voting patterns begin to diverge more sharply from the national average. From 1980 to 2008, the gap between Mormons and the national popular vote averaged 30 points.[8]

To ensure that Utah Mormons are a reasonable proxy for Mormons nationwide, Figure 4.4 displays the party identification of Mormons in the American National Election Studies (ANES), nationwide surveys done each election year.[9] Party identification is not the same as the presidential vote, but they are nonetheless highly correlated. Because the number of Mormons in any given year of the ANES is relatively small, we group Mormons together by decades: the 1960s, 1970s, 1980s, 1990s, and 2000s. These data match the general trend in Utah, which shows a sharp jump in the percentage of Mormon Republicans from the

---

[7] A Chow test was employed on the data in Figure 4.2 to see if there are any statistically significant structural breaks in the trend of Utah Mormons. This was done by fitting a model to the overall trend and then again fitting the model before and after the hypothesized break. The Chow test compares the fit of the two trends with the break to the overall trend to see if one model or two is more efficient. We checked for breaks at several points in the trend, but especially looked for significant breaks in the 1976 and 1980 presidential elections, when Utah Mormons deviated from national voting patterns and became especially distinctive in their Republican support. However, the Chow tests uncover no statistically significant breaks. In other words, even as Mormons became more and more distinctive – sharply so beginning with Reagan in 1980 – the overall trend among Mormons shows a steady increase in Republican support over time. For more discussion see Monson, Reed, and Smith (2013).

[8] Note that in 1992 we show the percentage of Mormons voting for George H. W. Bush and Ross Perot combined, as Perot picked up considerable support in Utah (the only state where Bill Clinton placed third).

[9] See Data Appendix for more details on the ANES surveys.

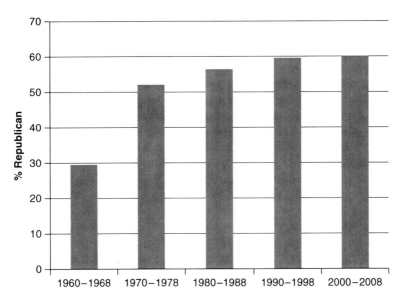

FIGURE 4.4. Mormons' Party Identification, Nationwide
*Source:* American National Election Studies

1960s to the 1970s, after which the percentage climbs a bit but basically holds high and steady through the 2000s.

There have been similar trends in the party affiliation of LDS members of Congress and state governors. In the early days of the twentieth century, there were only three such Mormons and all were Republicans. But as the number of Mormons elected grew, the partisan split became more balanced. From 1924 to 1930 Mormon officeholders were divided evenly between Democrats and Republicans. Between 1932 and 1944 – the Franklin Roosevelt years – there were either five or six Mormons serving in Congress or as governors, and all were Democrats. In the 1950s, there were between four and nine Mormons serving in these offices, most of whom were Republicans. Partisan balance then returned between 1962 and 1978. During this period, there were between ten and twelve Mormons serving in Congress. Of those, half or fewer were Republicans. But beginning in the 1980s the number of LDS Representatives and Senators grew, hitting a high of eighteen from 2002 to 2004. The year 1980 also marks the beginning of a Republican surge. The proportion of Republicans among the Mormon delegation increased from seven out of twelve (58 percent) in 1980 to fourteen out of seventeen (82 percent) in 2012.[10]

---

[10] These data on Mormon officeholders were collected at the University of Akron from a wide variety of biographic, historical, and journalistic sources. King and King (2000) provide the data for members of Congress and we used their criteria in our data collection.

It was also in the post-World War II period that the number of Mormons elected outside of Utah grew. From 1962 to the present, half or more of the Mormons elected as members of the House, Senate, or state governors have come from outside Utah, ranging from exactly half in some years (1974, 1988–90) to a high of 67 percent in others (1998, 2002–4). Given the success of Mormon politicians outside of Utah beginning in the 1960s, it is understandable that one of those officeholders, Governor George Romney of Michigan, would perceive the national political landscape as congenial toward a Mormon running for national office. (We elaborate on George Romney's 1968 bid for the presidency in Chapter 8.)

These data all point toward the same conclusion: over the course of the twentieth century, Mormons have gone through roughly three political periods. The days before Utah's statehood in 1896 were a period of *exclusion* from the national political system, as even the state's party system differed from the nation as a whole. Then, through much of the twentieth century, Mormons were in the era of *reinvolvement* with national politics. In the 1930s, Mormons (at least in Utah) went heavily for Roosevelt's Democrats but then began to shift toward the Republicans. Nonetheless, through the 1960s and 1970s there were still plenty of Mormon Democrats. More recently, since roughly the election of Ronald Reagan in 1980, Mormons have been in a *partisan* period, where they have overwhelmingly supported the Republican Party.

## WHO ARE THE MORMON DEMOCRATS?

Although Mormons today lean – heavily – toward the Republican Party, their support for the GOP is not universal. There is some variance, albeit small, to explain. We can thus ask what predicts identification with the GOP among Mormons or, put another way, who are the Mormon Democrats? While volumes have been written on what leads Americans to favor one party over another, here we focus on the known demographic correlates with party affiliation.

Figure 4.5 shows us how five demographic characteristics – age, income, gender, ethnicity, and attendance at religious services – are related to party preference for both Mormons and the non-Mormon population. In each case, Mormons are more likely to identify as Republicans than the rest of the population, but our focus is on the change in party preference across these demographic characteristics. Take age, for example. In general, as age increases so does the probability of identifying as a Republican. Strikingly, we see the opposite trend for Mormons. Older Mormons (over sixty-five) are less likely to favor the Republican Party (51 percent) than Mormons under thirty (69 percent), presumably reflecting the fact that during their formative political years, these Mormons were more likely to identify with the Democratic Party than they are today.

Even among evangelicals, another culturally conservative group that has undergone a partisan realignment over the last generation, Republicans do not have the same sort of advantage among the young that they do among older voters. In the Pew U.S. Religious Landscape Survey, 49 percent of evangelicals

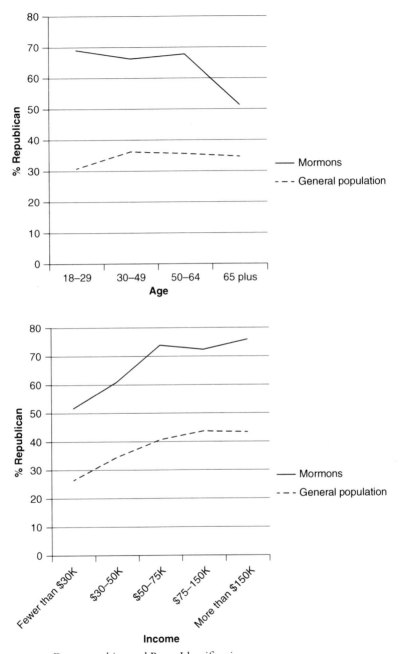

FIGURE 4.5. Demographics and Party Identification
*Source:* Pew U.S. Religious Landscape Survey, 2007

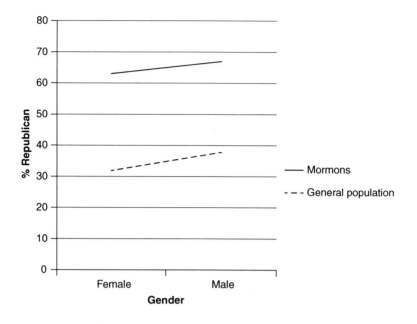

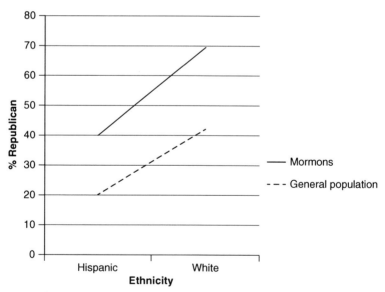

FIGURE 4.5. (cont.)

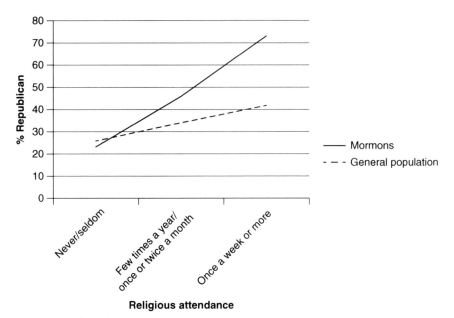

FIGURE 4.5. (cont.)

under thirty identified as Republicans, scarcely different from the 47 percent of evangelicals over age sixty-five who do. Because young people skew toward the Democrats more generally, the absence of a generation gap among evangelicals is remarkable. But it is even more remarkable that the Republicans have an eighteen-point *advantage* among young Mormons.

In contrast to age, the patterns for income, gender, and ethnicity are the same for Mormons and the rest of the population. Among both Mormons and non-Mormons, high-income earners, men, and whites are more likely to identify as Republicans. However, attendance at religious services reveals a sharp and highly illuminating contrast between Mormons and the general population. Roughly the same percentage of Mormons and non-Mormons who never or seldom attend religious services identify as Republicans – the only instance where Mormons are not overwhelmingly more Republican. In both cases we see that as religious attendance goes up, so does the likelihood of favoring the Republicans. Mormons, however, have a much steeper gradient: 73 percent of Mormons who attend church weekly or more are Republicans, compared to 42 percent of everyone else.

So who are the Mormon Democrats? They are a little more likely to be women than men (59 percent versus 55 percent), and less likely to be white (76 percent versus 91 percent). Using some rough back-of-the-envelope calculations, we also estimate that the average age of an adult Mormon Democrat is forty-eight, compared to forty-three for Mormon Republicans. Mormon Republicans have an average annual household income of $63,000, while Mormon Democrats earn an average of $41,000 per year. Among Latter-day Saints, Republicans also go to church meetings more than Democrats, although both have a relatively high rate of attendance compared to Americans as a whole – sixty-five times per year for Republicans, forty-one times for Democrats.

## SOURCES OF MORMON PARTISANSHIP

Although not all Mormons are Republicans, clearly most are. Why? And why have Mormons become increasingly likely to identify as Republicans? What changed: the parties or Mormons themselves? The answer is that both changed, in mutually reinforcing ways, to produce the current period of Republican ascendance among Latter-day Saints.

Mormons changed because, as a faith-based subculture, Mormonism shifted from a stance of assimilation – seeking to reduce tension with American society – in the first half of the twentieth century to one of high tension in the second half. As the Latter-day Saints' subculture became increasingly distinct from the broader culture, Mormons became more internally homogeneous, including in politics. To draw on Armand Mauss's felicitous dual metaphors, the low-tension period can be represented with the Mormon symbol of a beehive, reflecting business, industry, and "a sense of accommodation and comfort with the ways of the world" (1994, 3), while high tension can be represented with an angel, reflecting Mormons' distinctive beliefs and practices. Mormonism, he argues, swung from the beehive to the angel in the later decades of the twentieth century. It was during the angel era that Mormons became overwhelmingly Republican. By sharpening the dual boundaries of the sacred tabernacle with broader society, Mormon voters returned to the political cohesion of the nineteenth century, another period of clearly defined borders.

Although the swing from the beehive to the angel period explains why Mormons returned to a state of political cohesiveness, it does not necessarily explain why they gravitated to the Republican rather than Democratic Party. Lest one think it is obvious that Mormons would be Republicans, it is useful to recall that, historically, the Republican Party had been explicitly anti-Mormon. Furthermore, the Democratic Party has traditionally been the party of minority groups perceived as outsiders – like Mormons. Why, then, did the LDS swing to the GOP? While Mormons were changing, the Republican and Democratic parties were changing, too. Cultural conservatives of all stripes have come to identify as Republicans because, alongside the perennial debates over guns and butter, America's two parties also began to be divided over God and country. Increasingly, American politics were defined by differences in culture. Leege and colleagues detail the nature of such cultural politics, including a description of subcultures that fits Mormonism to a tee.

Political conflicts warrant the label of culture conflicts when they involve disagreements about what the society should or does prescribe as the appropriate way of life. It is not just about preference ordering; it deals with what is perceived as right and wrong, us versus them. This approach also entails an emphasis on subcultures, groups that persist within the larger society but maintain their own parochial views of the ordered life. While they may recognize that the claims of society as a whole are legitimate in a pragmatic sense – how else could the subculture persist if the society did not allow it leeway to practice and propound its values – the subculture may still feel that its way of life is superior, ordained of God or "natural" and may either maintain it in a separatistic manner or propound it in hopes of transforming the larger society. (Leege et al. 2002, 26)

The cultural politics that arose in postwar America, and especially in the 1960s and 1970s, have been defined by a cluster of issues, including patriotism, gender roles, sex, abortion, marriage, religion, and race. On each one, Mormons hold conservative attitudes that over time have come to align much more closely with the Republican Party. Mormons predominantly believe that the U.S. Constitution is divinely inspired, that men and women should maintain traditional roles, that sex should be limited to marriage (between one man and one woman), that abortion is rarely acceptable, and that religion should have a prominent place in the public square.

Given the racially restrictive policies of the LDS Church in the past (see Chapter 3), Mormons' attitudes toward race perhaps warrant special attention as a primary factor pulling them toward the Republican Party. There can be no doubt that, when compared to the general population, Mormons are racial conservatives (or, as many social scientists would put it, hold racially resentful views), generally disagreeing that slavery created conditions that have made it difficult for African Americans to succeed and endorsing the view that blacks can overcome prejudice like "the Irish, Italians, Jews, and many other minorities."[11]

---

[11] The 2012 Cooperative Congressional Election Study included two agree/disagree statements to measure "racial resentment." 1) "Generations of slavery and discrimination have created conditions that make it difficult for blacks to work their way out of the lower class," and 2) "The Irish, Italians, Jews and many other minorities overcame prejudice and worked their way up. Blacks should do the same without any special favors." An index created from these two questions shows that white Mormons exhibit higher levels of racial resentment than white Catholics, but slightly lower levels than white evangelicals (and much lower than Southern Baptists). The table below presents the percentage of each group that is above the median on the index. A simple chi-square goodness of fit test comparing the distribution of Mormons to each of the others demonstrates that in each case the differences are statistically significant. The results are the same with a simple regression analysis.

*Racial Resentment Index, Percent above the Median*

| | |
|---|---|
| Mormons (N = 759) | 67 |
| Non-Mormons (N = 39,576) | 58* |
| Catholics (N = 8,180) | 62* |
| Southern Baptists (N = 2,212) | 76* |
| Evangelicals (N = 10,709) | 70† |

\* = $p < 0.05$,† = $p < 0.10$ compared to Mormons
*Note:* Restricted to white respondents

However, Mormons are not as racially conservative (aka resentful) as evangelicals, another stalwart Republican constituency. Nor did Mormons suddenly embrace the Republican Party in the wake of the Democratic Party's endorsement of civil rights in the 1960s, as was the case for many Southern whites (Carmines and Stimson 1990). Instead, as shown in Figure 4.2, Mormons steadily became increasingly Republican throughout the second half of the twentieth century. Thus, race is only a small part of the story for Mormons' nearly monolithic support for the GOP and should be seen as only one among many factors. Given that Mormons were largely found in the Mountain West, not the South, it is not surprising that civil rights was not their top issue. Furthermore, even though the LDS Church had its internally restrictive policy on blacks, some Church leaders spoke out in support of the civil rights movement. This fact may help explain why Armand Mauss (1994) found that, when compared to members of other religious traditions, Mormons were relatively liberal on questions about race and civil rights during the 1960s.

Arguably more important than race is the divide between Democrats and Republicans on women's rights, abortion, and gay rights, which today comprise well-entrenched, even fundamental, differences between the two parties. In response to this deep cultural divide, the GOP became the home for moral traditionalists of many stripes, including evangelicals, conservative Catholics, and Mormons. Thus began the current era of the "God gap" – in which, among white voters, greater religiosity corresponds to greater support for the Republican Party. And Mormons are among the most religious, and the most white, of all religious groups in America.

The fact that over roughly the last thirty years, Mormons' partisan preferences mirrored those of regular churchgoers in other religious traditions reflects the successful assimilation of the earlier period. In the nineteenth century, Mormons voted as a bloc because Mormonism itself was a political issue. The Republican Party specifically decried Mormonism; the People's Party was quite explicitly the *Mormon* party. Mormons were politically cohesive as a reaction to partisan cleavages defined by explicitly ethno-religious conflict. Today, Mormons have not gravitated toward the Republican Party because the GOP advocates explicitly for "Mormon issues" and/or because Democrats take an overtly anti-Mormon position. Instead, they have found a home in the party of cultural conservatism defined broadly – the party that endorses American exceptionalism and is skeptical of civil rights. They are also moral traditionalists, wary of feminism, critical of the sexual revolution, and opposed to abortion and same-sex marriage (Leege et al. 2002; Layman 2001; Wolbrecht 2000). Not coincidentally, the very same moral traditionalism that attracts Mormons to the GOP also defines the tension Mormons have with secular society. The boundaries that define both their church and party are mutually reinforcing.

This mutual reinforcement is not unique to Mormons. Recall from Chapter 2 that evangelicals and Mormons share a sense of embattlement with "the world."

Or, more specifically, cultural conservatives feel threatened by the changing values of American society, particularly on matters relating to sex and family, and therefore flock to the party that speaks of upholding traditional morals. One implication of mutually reinforcing cultural and political attitudes is that Republican affiliation should be most common among voters with the strongest connection to their own religion. Specifically, religious commitment should differentiate Mormons' political preferences – more commitment to the faith should mean more commitment to the GOP. We have already seen some evidence of this in the tight link between church attendance – a common proxy for overall religious commitment – and Republican Party identification. Considering both the Republican Party's embrace of moral traditionalism and subcultural identity theory as applied to Mormonism leads us to hypothesize that this link between religiosity and the GOP has grown stronger over the same period that Mormons have become so predominantly Republican.

Because national surveys have too few Mormons to subdivide them by level of religious commitment, we again turn to data on Utah Mormons. Respondents to the Utah Colleges Exit Poll were asked their level of church "activity" – the term commonly used within Mormonism to distinguish those Church members who are more or less committed to the faith. We separate Utah Mormons between those who describe themselves as active, somewhat active, or inactive in the Church, while also controlling for other factors known to influence partisanship (including education, age, gender, and race).[12]

Figure 4.6 shows that, across this time span, higher activity consistently corresponds to a greater likelihood of identifying as a Republican – but the gap between the most and least active has grown wider over time. At all three levels of church activity, the percentage of Mormon voters in Utah identifying as Republicans has decreased, but that decline has been slight among the most highly active LDS Church members. The drop-off has been most pronounced among those who describe themselves as "somewhat active," with greater fluctuation among the least active. As a result, the partisan gap between active and somewhat active Mormon voters in Utah has grown considerably over the last three decades. In 1982, it was 9 percentage points. Through the 2000s, it has averaged 22 percentage points.[13]

We do not have comparable data on Mormons outside of Utah over this same span of time, but we can refer to the national Peculiar People Survey to compare Mormons by their level of activity in the present. We find precisely the same pattern as among Utah voters. Seventy-nine percent of "very active" Mormons identify as Republicans, compared to 65 percent of "somewhat active"

[12] "Inactive" also includes respondents who describe themselves as "not very active." Empirically, the two groups are indistinguishable. Note that in 1982, there was no "inactive" category, only "not very active."

[13] We are indebted to Zachary Smith for his excellent work analyzing the exit poll data.

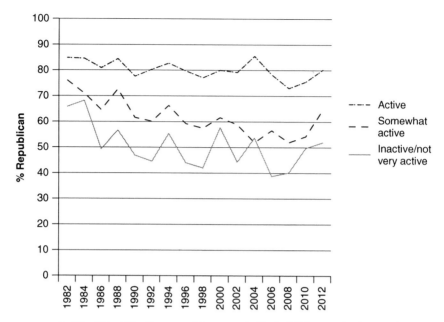

FIGURE 4.6. The "God Gap" among Mormons in Utah. With statistical controls; results from logistic regression. All control variables set to their mean or modal values
*Source:* Utah Colleges Exit Polls

Mormons and 57 percent of Mormons who describe themselves as not too active or not at all active.

There is irony in the growing partisan distinctions within Mormonism among those who are more or less active in the faith. This intra-Mormon pattern mirrors the trend in the general electorate, whereby religious commitment has become a stronger predictor of identification with the Republican Party. Thus, within Mormonism we see evidence of the same "religious restructuring" that has occurred among other religions. And yet, as we discuss at length in Chapters 7–9, devout Mormons have never been fully welcomed alongside members of other highly orthodox, strongly Republican religious groups – still another example of the Mormon paradox.

## THE SACRED TABERNACLE AND PARTISANSHIP

The relationship between Latter-day Saints' level of activity and their attachment to the Republican Party supports our argument that Mormons' Republicanism results from their subcultural identity. But we can conduct a more thorough test. A further implication of the subcultural identity theory is that Mormons' political distinctiveness – specifically, their strength of attachment to the Republican

Party – results from their integration within the Mormon subculture and the sharpness of the boundaries they draw around Mormonism. Sharper boundaries should mean a stronger attachment to the Republican Party, the party of moral traditionalism.

As introduced in Chapter 3, we have four measures of Mormons' boundary drawing: one behavioral (Activity), one psychological (Identity), one sociological (Insularity), and one theological (Authority). We have put these four measures into a statistical horse race, pitting them against each other as predictors of party identification among Mormons. To guard against finding any spurious relationships, our statistical model also controls for the other demographic characteristics we used earlier to predict partisan allegiances.[14] This statistical model enables us to determine the influence of each factor, independent of the others.

When we do this test, just two of the four dimensions of "Mormon-ness" turn out to be predictors of party identification. Authority and Identity have an independent influence on partisanship; Activity and Insularity do not. Thus, while measures of Mormons' religious activity – specifically, attendance – and in-group social bonds are correlated with their partisanship, this more detailed analysis reveals that it is actually attitudes toward Church authority and the strength of their Mormon identity that drive the relationship. Activity and Insularity serve as a proxy for Authority and Identity.

Attitudes toward Authority and the strength of voters' Mormon Identity have a substantial impact on partisanship, as displayed in Figures 4.7A and 4.7B. They show the change in the percentage of Mormons in each of five gradations of party identification as the Authority and Identity Indices vary from low (minimum) to high (maximum), with the other variables set to their means. As an example, let us take the percentage of self-described strong Republicans in Figure 4.7A. Among Mormons who score the highest on the Authority Index (darker bars), 55 percent identify as strong Republicans – by far the largest category. Among those who score at the bottom of the Authority Index (lighter bars), there is a roughly even distribution across the three middle categories of weak Democrats, independents, and weak Republicans.[15]

The same basic pattern repeats for Identity. Mormons who weigh adherence to Church authority over personal inspiration and exhibit a strong sense of Mormon identity are most likely to be Republicans, and "strong" Republicans at that. But even those Mormons who have a low score on the Authority Index

[14] Specifically, income, gender, race/ethnicity, and age. See Table 4A.1 in the appendix to this chapter for the full results of the model.
[15] "Weak" Democrats or Republicans include those who either say they have a "not so strong" attachment to their preferred party or those who initially say they are politically independent but, in a follow-up question, admit to leaning toward one or the other. Independents are respondents who initially describe themselves as politically independent and hold firm when asked if they lean toward either party. For details on how "weak" and "leaning" partisans are functionally equivalent, at least for the purposes of predicting how they vote, see Keith et al. (1992).

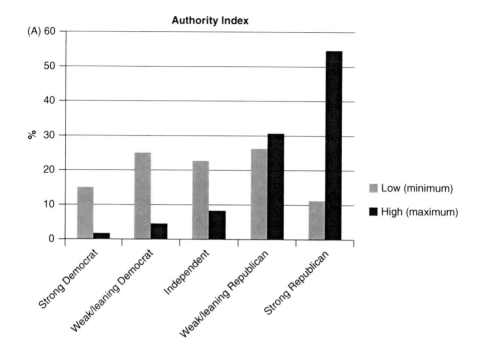

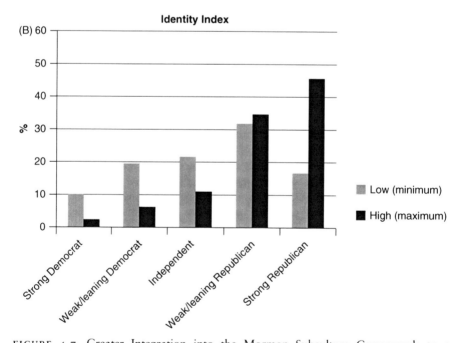

FIGURE 4.7. Greater Integration into the Mormon Subculture Corresponds to a Stronger Republican Identity. With statistical controls; results from ordered logistic regression. All control variables set to their mean or modal values

*Source:* Peculiar People Survey, 2012

and have a weaker sense of Mormon Identity still tilt rightward. It is just that rather than being strong Republicans, they are more likely to consider themselves weak Republicans or, perhaps, independents. Very few Mormons of any stripe identify as Democrats, and a vanishingly small percentage describe themselves as having a strong attachment to the Democratic Party.

The results are supportive of the subcultural identity theory, as both attitudes toward authority and strength of Mormon identity are boundary markers. Because these measures overlap considerably – one might have thought they were measuring the same thing – it is remarkable that each has an independent influence on partisanship. Like many ethnic groups, Latter-day Saints are predominantly of one party. But as an ethno-*religious* group, the strength of their attachment to that party is a function of the sharpness of the boundaries they draw around their Mormonism.

PARTISAN PEP RALLIES?

This degree of political cohesiveness calls for an explanation of the process by which Mormons end up as Republicans. One potential explanation could be that Mormons experience from-the-pulpit politicking, whereby LDS leaders issue partisan directives. Are Mormon meetings political pep rallies by another name? To the contrary: LDS meetings seldom contain overt political messaging. There are exceptions, as discussed further in Chapter 6, but they are rare – and thus highly potent when they happen.

As nonprofits, all religious organizations are constrained from making partisan endorsements at the risk of losing their tax-exempt status, although this does not restrict their freedom to comment on political matters (and some religious leaders make endorsements anyway). In the case of the LDS, the Church regularly reminds its members that Church buildings, meetings, membership directories, and the like are not to be used for any political purposes. Prior to each election, a letter from the Church's First Presidency is read from every LDS pulpit, reaffirming the Church's political neutrality and reinforcing that no politicking is to take place in Church facilities or using its resources.

Mormons appear to have gotten the message that they are to keep partisan politics out of church. They have the lowest reported rate of politicking at church of all American religious traditions. As shown in Figure 4.8, Mormons are the least likely to hear sermons on "social or political issues." LDS congregations are also the least likely to have voter registration drives or voter guides at church, or to organize marches or rallies.[16]

---

[16] These data are from the 2011 Faith Matters survey, as detailed in Putnam and Campbell (2010). The specific questions are:

(referring to the respondent's own congregation)
*How often, if at all, are social or political issues discussed from the pulpit in this congregation – several times a month, once every month or two, a few times a year or*

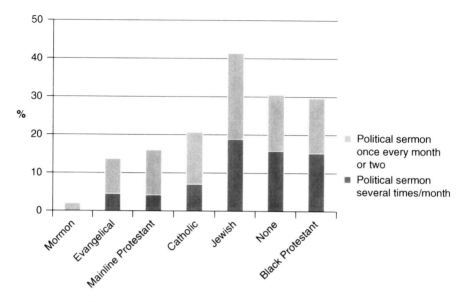

FIGURE 4.8. Mormons Are the Least Likely to Get Politics from the Pulpit
*Source:* Faith Matters Survey, 2011

The rarity of overt politicking during LDS worship meetings is confirmed in the Peculiar People Survey. To gauge the extent to which politics is discussed at church, we asked our respondents, "Thinking of your ward or branch, how often have you heard political issues or public affairs discussed in the following situations?" The survey then listed sacrament meetings (meetings for general worship and communion), classes at church, conversations among church members while at church, and conversations among church members outside of church.

As shown in Figure 4.9, fewer than 1 percent of Mormons report hearing about politics or public affairs in sacrament meeting talks (Mormon lingo for sermons in their Sunday worship services) "several times a month," while only 3.6 percent report hearing politics in their sacrament meetings "once every month or two." Half report that they *never* hear political issues discussed in their worship meetings.

Nor is there much political talk in the lessons taught during classes held in LDS churches. In addition to the weekly seventy-minute sacrament meeting for group worship, Mormons have other classes they are expected to attend each Sunday: a Sunday School (for both genders) and then separate meetings for men

*less often, or never?*
*Does this congregation ever:*
*Organize demonstrations or marches*
*Sponsor voter registration or distribute voter guides?*

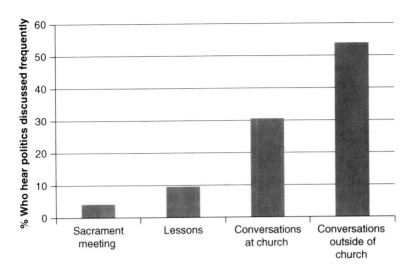

FIGURE 4.9. Mormons Get Little Politics from the Pulpit, but Talk about Politics a Lot with Fellow Mormons

"Frequently" is defined as several times a month or once every month or two.

*Source:* Peculiar People Survey, 2012

("priesthood") and women ("Relief Society"). We wondered whether there is more political talk in the lessons taught outside of formal worship, especially since the typical class includes a lot of discussion. Compared to sacrament meetings, political discussion is in fact more common in LDS classes, but only slightly: 1.5 percent say this happens several times a month, while 8 percent report that it occurs once every month or two. Almost a third (34 percent) indicate that politics comes up "a few times a year or less often," while 41 percent say politics is never discussed in their classes at church. We also asked about conversations at church outside of worship or classes, where political conversation is more likely, but still relatively uncommon. Just over 30 percent of Mormons report discussing politics among fellow church members "once every month or two" or more.

However, Mormons do talk about politics – a lot – with fellow Mormons outside of church. As we would expect of a tight-knit, politically cohesive group, political conversations among Mormons are relatively common. Twenty-eight percent of Mormons say that they discuss politics with fellow ward members (parishioners) outside of church several times a month, while another 26 percent report such conversations once a month or so. This means that over half of Mormons report having political conversations with fellow Mormons multiple times a year. Only 6 percent report never having such conversations. With a statistical model that predicts the frequency of talking about politics with fellow

Church members outside of Church meetings, we find that political talk is most common among Mormons who are highly active in the Church and have the most in-group social relationships (i.e., they bond more). Both effects are likely because of greater exposure to other Mormons, and thus more opportunities to discuss politics, although for some Mormons it might also be that sharing a worldview with their fellow Mormons – including politics – leads them to be more deeply embedded within the LDS subculture.

Mormons' political cohesion, then, is not a matter of receiving marching orders from Church authorities during sermons or lessons. Instead, the cohesion is reinforced within Mormons' social networks, comprised of fellow believers – for whom the boundaries demarcating them as a peculiar people are highly salient. Mormons who might be unsure of their political views, or how their faith might be applied to politics, can pick up cues from conversations within these tight-knit social networks.

There is a debate among political scientists over the extent to which churches foster conversations among people with differing political views, or what is often called "cross-talk" (Sokhey and Mockabee 2012; Djupe and Gilbert 2009; Mutz 2006). While our data do not enable us to say for certain what Mormons are discussing with their coreligionists, the degree of social, religious, and political cohesion among Mormons makes it unlikely that they engage in much political "cross-talk" with fellow Church members.

Latter-day Saints who are not as deeply embedded within the subculture are less likely to follow Mormon norms. We see this pattern most clearly with former Mormons, those who were raised as Mormon but do not now identify as LDS (see Chapter 3). While 65 percent of current Mormons identity as Republican, only 34 percent of former Mormons do. Among the general public, nearly the same share – 35 percent – identify as Republicans, reinforcing the point that, having left the sacred tabernacle, former Mormons are not politically distinctive. However, it is not clear whether these former Mormons' political views have weakened their attachment to the LDS Church or whether the weak attachment affects their political views.

In reporting the frequency with which people hear about politics at church, it is important to note that these questions only ask about overt political appeals or discussion. This query is different than asking whether religious teachings have a political application, at least in the eye of the beholder. Many LDS teachings undoubtedly have the effect of nudging Mormons toward the GOP, even if no one at an LDS meeting ever says, "Vote Republican" outright. The direction of the nudging, however, is dependent on both the political context and the individual's own interpretation of LDS doctrine. LDS teachings can be interpreted in different ways, thus leading to diverse political conclusions. While most Mormons interpret their doctrine in a Republican light, some see it as a reason to vote Democratic. Senator Harry Reid, the majority leader of the U.S. Senate and a practicing Mormon, made this point in a speech at BYU, when he said that "I am a Democrat because I am a Mormon, not in spite of it"

(Walch 2007). Yet while there is potential for a Democratic interpretation of Mormonism, only a small minority of Mormons share the views of Senator Reid. That most Mormons end up on the right end of the political spectrum is a further reflection of their subculture's cohesiveness, reinforced within the sacred tabernacle – all of the church-based meetings, projects, and social activities that occupy much of a Mormon's time.

CONCLUSION

In sum, we have seen that Mormons are staunchly Republican, to the point of peculiarity. Furthermore, the boundaries Mormons draw to distinguish themselves from secular society reinforce their attachment to the GOP. The sharper those boundaries, the stronger the partisan attachment. Yet it is important that the historical data also show that Mormons' current affinity for the Republican Party has not always been the case. To assume that Mormons are "natural" Republicans would be a case of historical amnesia. Mormons once overwhelmingly favored the Democrats and, for a considerable stretch of the twentieth century, gave support to both parties.

Today, Mormons' cohesiveness extends to the conservatism of their political views. However, Chapter 5 shows that this conservatism comes with nuance. As befitting an ethno-*religious* group, religion shapes their politics. While they are cohesive and conservative, they are also politically distinct, even from other cultural conservatives. On some issues their distinctiveness is subtle; for others it is clearer. Far from inexplicable divergences from the orthodoxy of political conservatism, the nuances of their views can be explained by their Mormonism.

CHAPTER 4 APPENDIX

TABLE 4A.1. *Ordered Logistic Regression Model of*
*"Mormon-ness" Indices Regressed on Party Identification*

| VARIABLES | Party identification |
|---|---|
| Authority | 0.465*** |
| | (0.110) |
| Identity | 0.309*** |
| | (0.122) |
| Insularity | 0.114 |
| | (0.123) |
| Activity | -0.019 |
| | (0.085) |
| Income | 0.129** |
| | (0.055) |
| Gender | 0.175 |
| | (0.181) |
| Age | 0.005 |
| | (0.006) |
| Black | -0.082 |
| | (0.561) |
| Hispanic | -0.289 |
| | (0.479) |
| Cut 1 | 0.3200 |
| | (0.804) |
| Cut 2 | 1.700 |
| | (0.791) |
| Cut 3 | 2.652 |
| | (0.797) |
| Cut 4 | 4.250 |
| | (0.814) |
| Observations | 452 |
| Pseudo R-squared | 0.054 |

Standard errors in parentheses
*** $p < 0.01$, ** $p < 0.05$, <* $p < 0.1$
Source: Peculiar People Survey, 2012

# 5

# A Politically Peculiar People

On March 8, 2013, Dieter F. Uchtdorf, Second Counselor in the First Presidency of the LDS Church, joined a group of religious leaders in a meeting with President Barack Obama to discuss immigration reform. Upon leaving the meeting, Uchtdorf said that what the president said "was totally in line with our values." While not endorsing any specific proposal, the LDS Church also issued a statement supportive of immigration reform that sounded a lot more like the platform of the Democratic than the Republican Party. "Public officials should create and administer laws that reflect the best of our aspiration as a just and caring society. Such laws will properly balance love for neighbors, family cohesion, and the observance of just and enforceable laws" (Canham 2013).

Some observers might be surprised at the common ground between LDS leaders and the Obama administration on immigration. As we have seen in Chapter 4, Mormons are more heavily Republican than any other religious group. Furthermore, Mitt Romney, President Obama's opponent in the 2012 election, is a devout Mormon who took a hard line on immigration, even endorsing a policy of "self-deportation" for undocumented immigrants. Yet Uchtdorf, and the LDS leadership more generally, are more in step with Mormons' attitudes on immigration than Romney – notwithstanding Mormons' overall conservatism and support of the Republican Party.

We have argued that because they have a strong subcultural identity, Mormons can be characterized as an ethno-religious group. Fundamental to our argument is that Mormons are distinctive, not just religiously but also politically. In the previous chapter we saw that when it comes to partisanship, today's Mormons are peculiar if only for their heavy support of one party. In this chapter, we examine Mormons' political opinions beyond their party preference, to see where they stand on a wide variety of issues. Not surprisingly, given their Republican leanings, Mormons are – generally speaking – cohesive and conservative. However, this chapter will demonstrate that their conservatism is also nuanced and thus distinctive, and that their political distinctiveness arises

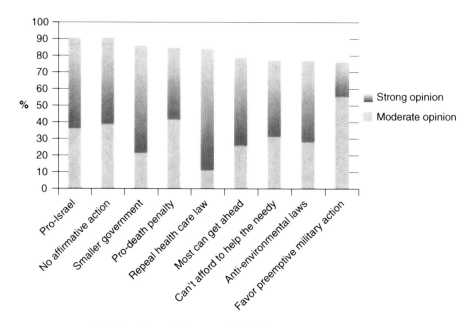

FIGURE 5.1. On Many Issues, Mormons Hold Conservative Opinions
*Source:* Peculiar People Survey, 2012

from the LDS religion, whether from the top-down instruction of LDS leaders or individual Mormons' personal experience (or both). Immigration is one, but not the only, example where Mormons' attitudes diverge from the Republican Party line.

We begin with Mormons' conservatism, which comes through clearly in the Peculiar People Survey. In the survey, we asked our nationally representative group of Mormons their opinions on a series of political issues. In each case, we gave them a choice among four responses. For some questions, they had to place their opinion on a four-point scale between two opposing positions, and on other questions they could indicate whether they strongly agree, agree, disagree, or strongly disagree with the statement. Figure 5.1 reports the percentage of Mormons who hold conservative views on each issue (including the percentage who take the most conservative position). This list includes a wide range of bread-and-butter issues in contemporary politics, and on each one, Mormons are both consistently conservative and consistently cohesive:

- 91 percent favor the Israelis over the Palestinians (55 percent "strongly")
- 91 percent oppose affirmative action for African Americans (52 percent "strongly")
- 86 percent would prefer a smaller government that offers fewer services over a bigger government and more services (65 percent "strongly")

- 85 percent favor the death penalty for convicted murderers (44 percent "strongly")
- 84 percent want the Obama administration's health care reform act to be repealed (73 percent "strongly")
- 79 percent agree that most people can get ahead if they work hard enough (53 percent "strongly")
- 77 percent say government cannot afford to do any more to help those in need (46 percent "strongly")
- 77 percent oppose stricter environmental laws (49 percent "strongly")
- 76 percent believe that the United States sometimes must take preemptive military action (21 percent "strongly")

Mormons' conservatism is underscored when they are compared to members of other religious traditions. The Pew U. S. Religious Landscape Survey contains many of the same questions as the Peculiar People Survey, enabling a comparison across religious traditions. Note, however, that Pew only presented respondents with two choices, which produces a different distribution of responses than the four-response items we asked on the Peculiar People Survey. With just two responses to choose from – homosexuality should be discouraged or encouraged by society – 68 percent of Mormons chose "discouraged," just edging out evangelicals (64 percent). No other religious group comes close. Compared to members of other religious traditions, Mormons are also the most likely to say that most people who want to get ahead can make it (77 percent), that government should be smaller and offer fewer services (56 percent), and that the government cannot afford to do more to help the needy (42 percent). Mormons and evangelicals are equally likely to believe that military strength is the best way to ensure peace (37 and 38 percent, respectively) – far more so than members of any other religious tradition. However, it is Mormons and Jews who share a similar outlook on whether the United States should be active in world affairs. Fifty percent of Jews agree, compared to 51 percent of Mormons. Both are much higher than any other group. (For example, only 36 percent of evangelicals support global engagement for the United States)

Mormons endorse a conventional conservatism blending cultural, economic, and foreign policy issues. In some respects their views have a libertarian bent, as seen in their belief that government should be smaller and their reluctance to see government do more to help the needy. Yet they are not consistently libertarian, as they also take issue with homosexuality (which "pure" libertarians would consider a matter of personal choice). Nor – unlike most libertarians – are they isolationists on foreign policy, as they believe in military strength as the means to keep peace and favor America's intervention in world affairs. Altogether, these views put them in the mainstream of the current Republican Party.

The conservative bent of Mormons can easily leave the impression that their views simply mirror the views held by other conservatives, particularly evangelicals, only with greater intensity and cohesion. It is tempting, therefore, to conclude that Mormons are "just like evangelicals, even more so." However, a close look reveals that Mormons have distinctive political opinions, even when compared to other conservative religious groups, including evangelicals. We argue that Mormons' distinctive political views result from their religion. For that to be true, the burden is on us to demonstrate the connections between the LDS religion and Mormons' politics. We have already seen that Mormons have distinctive religious beliefs and that the sacred tabernacle – the social networks of believing, active Mormons organized through the infrastructure of the LDS Church – serves to reinforce Mormons' political views. In this chapter, we present evidence that Latter-day Saints' political views are often tied to their peculiar religious beliefs.

To understand how Mormons' political views are shaped by both their political and religious environment, we turn to the seminal work of political scientist John Zaller, who has developed a compelling theory of how people form political opinions (1992). Zaller builds on the well-known observation that most of the time most people do not have firm opinions on most political issues. Instead, people first receive and then accept "considerations" – "any reason that might induce an individual to decide a political issue one way or another" – on various issues from their surrounding information environment (40). When people are called upon to express a political opinion, they sample across the relevant considerations they have "accepted." The opinion they express depends on the mix of considerations they have deposited in their memory bank account. For individuals, the more considerations in the bank that support a given opinion, the more likely they are to withdraw that opinion when they go to their mental ATM.

This process also means that when a group is collectively exposed to consistent considerations, its members will express cohesive opinions; conversely, a flow of ambiguous or inconsistent arguments will lead a group to express diverse opinions. Key to Zaller's theory is that not everyone is exposed to the same amount of politically relevant information, and that not all information is equally impactful. People who are politically disengaged are less likely to receive political messages, while those who are engaged but ideological are resistant to information from those on the other side of the political fence.

While Zaller does not mention religion as a source of political information, the logic of his theory suggests that considerations from one's own religion are especially likely to be both received and accepted, perhaps especially so within Mormonism's sacred tabernacle. Mormons are highly engaged in their religion, which means that they are likely to be exposed to the politically relevant information found within their subculture. And because of their strong identification with their religion, they are likely to accept whatever information they receive. Mormons thus place considerable weight on information from religious channels, while not being immune to considerations from secular sources on "their" side of the political spectrum. Where the two disagree, we should see diversity of opinion instead of cohesion.

## POLITICALLY INFLECTED RELIGIOUS VIEWS

In making the link between Mormons' religious beliefs and positions on political issues, we stress that, as with perhaps all religious traditions, the political implications of Mormon theology are open to interpretation, and indeed have been understood differently throughout Mormon history. Take the example of the strong communitarian ethos found within Mormonism – a reflection of the strong bonds formed within the sacred tabernacle. As detailed in Chapter 3, Mormons devote considerable time and energy to their callings (local congregational responsibilities). These Church assignments often involve providing for the temporal needs of others. The LDS Church operates a massive welfare program, complete with farms, ranches, canneries, and storehouses, all of which are connected through a Church-run distribution system. Latter-day Saints in need can ask for assistance from their bishop, who can draw on the resources of the Church welfare system. Twenty-first-century Mormonism's Tocquevillian spirit of volunteerism has the same motivation as the Latter-day Saints' communitarian economic system in the nineteenth century, when Brigham Young encouraged – one could say ordered – Mormons to avoid truck and trade with "gentiles," and was openly critical of eastern capitalists (Turner 2012; Arrington, Fox, and May 1992). Then and now, Mormons have always believed in taking care of their own, and put their money – and their time – where their mouths are. In the past, however, many Mormons viewed their communitarian ways as an alternative to the individual focus of laissez-faire capitalism. But today, Latter-day Saints are staunch supporters of an unfettered free market. They see their communitarian impulse as a complement to, not a critique of, a capitalistic economy.

Our point is that the political implications of any given LDS belief depend on how it is framed. The communitarianism dimension of Mormonism has been a constant; what changed (and what could change again in the future) was the understanding of its political implications. Many Mormons probably see a limited role for government in providing for the poor because, in their experience, the Church-run welfare program demonstrates the effectiveness of private charity.

The framing of an issue may or may not have a religious origin, however. In the opinions displayed in Figure 5.1, it is often difficult – if not impossible – to sort out the relative weight of considerations from either religious or secular sources. For example, Mormons are hardly alone in their dislike of the dole. Many other conservatives have the same view, obscuring whether Mormons' views are uniquely shaped by their religion. Skepticism toward state-provided welfare could just as easily result from reading Ayn Rand as Joseph Smith (indeed, it is more likely to come from the former than the latter). Similarly, Mormons' pro-Israel perspective could be tied to a belief that the modern state of Israel fulfills biblical prophecy and is a precursor to the last days. In this they are not alone, as other conservatives, particularly evangelical Protestants, are also philo-Semitic and take a hawkish position on Israel.

The real test of whether Mormons' religious beliefs and experiences connect to their political opinions lies in identifying distinctive Mormon religious beliefs that have a plausible connection to political views. The beliefs we highlight fall into two categories. First we discuss *politically inflected religious views*. These are LDS beliefs that do not automatically lead to a specific position on public policy, but nonetheless can – and often do – intertwine with political attitudes. Then we turn to describing *religiously inflected political views*. These are political opinions with a clear antecedent in LDS doctrine, policy, or culture.

The first two politically inflected religious views we describe are attitudes toward the U.S. Constitution and gender roles. For both, it is easy to draw a line from LDS teachings to Mormons' attitudes. Latter-day Saints' belief that the Constitution was written under God's direction resonates with Americans' general reverence for the document, but nonetheless has a particular theological dimension within Mormonism. In the case of gender roles, Mormons are sharply distinct from other Americans, including other conservatives, in their idealization of two-parent homes with breadwinning dads and homemaking moms. Yet like polygamy and race (see Chapter 3), this is another area where Mormons' attitudes are slowly changing, as LDS Church members increasingly approve of mothers who work outside the home.

## Constitution

The first of these distinctive doctrines pertains to the historical significance of the United States, the divine origins of the U.S. Constitution, and the future role of Mormons as protectors of the Constitution. Like many Americans, most Mormons subscribe to American exceptionalism. While the specifics vary, American exceptionalism holds that the United States stands apart from all other nations culturally and economically (Hartz 1955; Huntington 1981). It is not just a belief that "America is number one," as patriotic citizens from all nations routinely cheer on their compatriots. American exceptionalism often includes a divine element, namely that God had a hand in the country's creation. In believing that the United States is unique, Mormons are hardly alone. This view is widely, if vaguely, held among many Americans. In particular, many evangelical Protestants believe in a special, divinely sanctioned role for the United States – another example of a belief shared by Mormons and evangelicals. However, this is also an example of how both groups can share a common sentiment and even rhetoric, even though the beliefs underpinning that sentiment differ.

God's role in the founding of the United States is a critical element of Mormon theology. Mormons, you will recall, believe that their church is a restoration of Christianity as established by Jesus himself. Furthermore, LDS doctrine holds that God prepared the United States as the nation where the restoration could take place and the new church could flourish. The *Book of Mormon* speaks of the Americas as a promised land. In the *Doctrine and Covenants*, a canonized book of revelations received by Joseph Smith, God is recorded as saying, "And for this purpose have I established the Constitution of this land [i.e. the United States], by the hands of wise men whom I raised up unto this very purpose, and redeemed the land by the shedding of blood."[1]

Nor is this view an obscure bit of doctrinal arcana. LDS leaders have long taught that the Continental Army was divinely protected while fighting the Revolution, and that America's Founders were divinely inspired while writing the Constitution (Benson 1987; Oaks 1992). The United States also figures into the LDS understanding of both the beginning and the end of the world. Joseph Smith taught that the Garden of Eden was located in Missouri, and that the same site will be a gathering place for faithful Latter-day Saints in the last days. Even when facing the lawlessness of mob violence, early Mormons maintained their belief that America's Constitution had a heavenly mandate – to them, the document was inspired, even if its application was anything but (S. B. Gordon 2002). In other words, Mormons do not merely hold to American exceptionalism as a philosophical abstraction or an expression of intense patriotism. Within LDS theology, God has designated the United States to play a critical role in the grand sweep of history.

Mormons' attitudes about America's place in the world reflect their theology. A recent national survey demonstrates that Mormons are the "most exceptionalist" of any religious tradition in the country. Seventy-two percent of Mormons believe that "the United States has a special role to play in world affairs and should behave differently than other nations" – higher than any other religious group (Guth 2012, 78). Mormons even top evangelicals, of whom 60 percent agree that the United States has a special role in the world.

The Peculiar People Survey enables us to get more specific about LDS beliefs regarding American exceptionalism. The results are shown in Figure 5.2. In the survey, we asked Mormons whether they agree that "the U.S. Constitution and Bill of Rights are divinely inspired." Ninety-four percent agree with this statement; of those, 69 percent say they "strongly agree."[2] As a point of comparison, recall that 96 percent of Mormons agree that the *Book of Mormon* is a record of real people and events, arguably their faith's defining belief.

The divine inspiration of the U.S. Constitution is authoritative LDS doctrine. Less formally, another "folk doctrine" within Mormonism has also long held that the United States' constitutionally guaranteed freedoms will one day be in

---

[1] *Doctrine and Covenants* 101:80.

[2] Dallin H. Oaks, a current member of the Quorum of the Twelve Apostles and former law professor, laments that many Latter-day Saints who express this belief cannot express what it means. His view places the Constitution on a different plane from scripture. "Reverence for the United States Constitution is so great that sometimes individuals speak as if its every word and phrase had the same standing as scripture. Personally, I have never considered it necessary to defend every line of the Constitution as scriptural. For example, I find nothing scriptural in the compromise on slavery or the minimum age or years of citizenship for congressmen, senators, or the president." He goes on to define the divine inspiration of the Constitution in terms of "great fundamentals" such as the separation of powers and a written bill of rights (1992, 70–1).

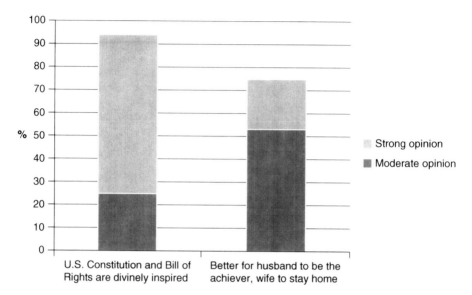

FIGURE 5.2. Two Ways That Mormons Are Peculiar: Gender Roles and the Divine Origins of the U.S. Constitution
*Source:* Peculiar People Survey, 2012

jeopardy, and that a Mormon, or group of Mormons, will somehow preserve them. More precisely, the folklore is that the Constitution will "hang by a thread," only to be saved by "the elders of Zion" (a fusty term referring to holders of the LDS priesthood, which includes virtually all LDS men). This wording has circulated within LDS culture for decades, although many LDS Church members are probably unaware of its origins. The phrase stems from a purported prophecy given by Joseph Smith but never published in an official Church document. The prophecy has long been dismissed by LDS authorities as inauthentic, but the key point that the "constitution will hang by a thread" has nonetheless been repeated by numerous LDS authorities over many years and has seeped into the LDS vernacular (Bringhurst and Foster 2011).[3]

As seen in Figure 5.3, when asked if they have ever heard that "there will come a day when the U.S. Constitution will hang by a thread and that it will be

---

[3] Joseph Smith clearly spoke about the U.S. Constitution being besieged (Jesse 1979), but the folk doctrine uses the "hang by a thread" language along with other associated events and has been referred to by some Mormons as the "White Horse Prophecy." As recently as 2010, the Church issued a public statement saying, "The so-called 'White Horse Prophecy' is based on accounts that have not been substantiated by historical research and is not embraced as Church doctrine" (Church of Jesus Christ of Latter-day Saints 2010a).

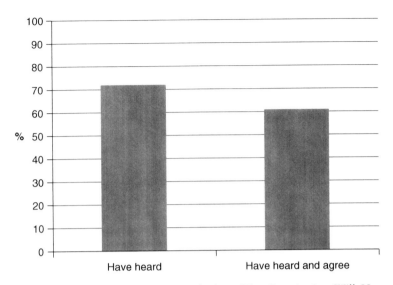

FIGURE 5.3. Most Mormons Have Heard That "The Constitution Will Hang by a Thread"; of Those Who Have Heard It, Most Believe It
*Source:* Peculiar People Survey, 2012

preserved by members of the LDS Church," 72 percent of Mormons today say they have. We then asked those who said they have heard this phrase if they agreed with it. Eighty-six percent of those who have heard it, agree with it. Combining the two parts of the question reveals that 61 percent of Mormons have both heard and agree that Mormons will somehow be instrumental one day in protecting the Constitution. In other words, many Mormons have put the twin pieces of information that the Constitution is divinely inspired and that Mormons will one day save it into their memory banks. When asked about either one, these considerations are readily retrieved.

While to our knowledge no one has ever asked the non-Mormon general population whether they think that Mormons will one day save the country from constitutional peril, it seems safe to assume that this is not a widely held belief outside of Mormonism. On this, Mormons are distinctive – even peculiar.

Importantly, the specifics of Mormons' beliefs about the Constitution are open to interpretation, as in recent years LDS leaders have generally refrained from offering any particular application of these beliefs to current events. One Mormon might point to warrantless wiretapping in the name of national security as an example of threadbare Constitutional rights, while another might point to the Supreme Court decision upholding the Affordable Care Act. Given the rightward tilt of today's Mormons, the divine origin of the U.S. Constitution seems most likely to be interpreted from a conservative perspective – that the document will dangle because of threats from the left, not the right. It is only a short step from Mormons' reverence for the Constitution and the related belief that God directed the founding of the United States to an originalist interpretation of the Constitution and a belief that America has a special role to play in world affairs – both of which are articles of faith among many political conservatives. It is also a small step from a God-given Constitution to a belief that "America has been strong because of its faith in God," a statement endorsed by 95 percent of Mormons in the Peculiar People Survey.

## Gender Roles

Attitudes toward gender roles are another example of Mormons' distinctiveness. In this case, their religious considerations appear to outweigh any from secular sources. That men and women have different, if complementary, roles is fundamental to LDS theology. Because the LDS priesthood is limited to males, only men can serve as general Church leaders and bishops (local clergy), perform baptisms, officiate at weddings, give blessings to the sick, and so on. While there are some positions of responsibility held by women within the Church, Mormonism clearly has a gendered division of labor, where men are given exclusive ecclesiastical authority.

With few exceptions, Mormon women do not appear to object to this state of affairs. We base that conclusion on the Peculiar People Survey, where we gauged attitudes on women's role in the Church. In designing questions on this topic, we had to tread carefully. We feared that asking outright whether women should hold the LDS priesthood would be tantamount to asking Mormons whether they believe in their religion (which, as we have seen, they overwhelmingly do). Instead, we designed a question meant to "provide cover" for Latter-day Saints, of both genders, who might sometimes be frustrated by the role played by women in the Church, even if they are devout, believing, and active Church members. Accordingly, our respondents were asked to respond to this statement: "The fact that women do not hold the priesthood sometimes bothers me." Nearly all men said that they were not bothered by the male-only priesthood – an overwhelming 92 percent. Most women also say that they are not bothered, but by a slightly less overwhelming margin: 86 percent.

The Pew Mormons in America survey found a similarly high rate of acceptance for a male-only priesthood. When asked, "Should women who are dedicated members of the LDS Church be ordained to the priesthood?" Eighty-seven percent said no. This survey also finds a slight gender gap but, on this question, men are slightly more likely to approve of women receiving the priesthood. While 90 percent of women say no to women's ordination, "only" 84 percent of men do (Pew Forum on Religion & Public Life 2012a).

In the Peculiar People Survey, we also asked our respondents whether women do not have enough say in the LDS Church. Again, our wording was chosen carefully to leave space for highly active Mormons to express a desire for something other than the status quo. Respondents were asked for their reaction to the statement that "Women do not have enough say in the LDS Church." In recent years, there has been a movement of sorts within the Church to gently increase the role of women in decision-making at the local level,[4] and so our thought was that devout Mormons might be willing to express a desire for women to have more voice without feeling like they are questioning the Church. Even with this tepid statement we found that, by a substantial margin, Mormons are comfortable with the role of women in the Church. In combining those who "disagree" and "strongly disagree," we find that, overall, 84 percent of Mormons – 86 percent of men and 83 percent of women – are fine with the role women play. While the gender gap does not reach the level of statistical significance, to the extent there is any gender difference it is women who are most likely to *strongly* disagree that women do not have enough say (46 percent vs. 55 percent). The double negative can be confusing, so for clarity's sake let us restate that. It means that women are *more* likely than men to believe – strongly – that women have enough voice in the Church.[5]

In short, Mormons have highly cohesive views on gender roles within the Church. Furthermore, their perspective straddles both Church and society, as many Mormons believe in a similar division of labor between men and women beyond the Church as well. For example, LDS leaders regularly cite a document known as the *Proclamation on the Family*, an official statement from LDS leaders which has near-canonical status among Church members. The *Proclamation* is frequently quoted, widely disseminated, and even displayed in many Mormons' homes. It reads, in part:

By divine design, fathers are to preside over their families in love and righteousness and are responsible to provide the necessities of life and protection for their families. Mothers are primarily responsible for the nurture of their children. (Church of Jesus Christ of Latter-day Saints 1995)

This is only one example of how traditional gender roles – husband as bread-winner, wife as homemaker – are reinforced within LDS culture. More subtly, Church publications and curricular materials for religious education classes

---

[4] The current handbook for LDS leaders includes the following instructions for what are known as "ward council" meetings, which include those Church members who run the various programs within a congregation. Note the stress on including women's voices.

"Council members are encouraged to speak honestly, both from their personal experience and from their positions as organization leaders. Both men and women should feel that their comments are valued as full participants. The bishop seeks input from Relief Society, Young Women, and Primary leaders in all matters considered by the ward council. *The viewpoint of women is sometimes different from that of men, and it adds essential perspective to understanding and responding to members' needs*" (Church of Jesus Christ of Latter-day Saints 2012c, section 4.6.1, emphasis added).

[5] Again, we remind readers that these data only reflect the opinions of self-identified Mormons, and thus not former Church members who may have left the faith.

often portray men and women in traditional gender roles. Notably, the curriculum for the Church's standardized program for teenagers teaches LDS girls to prepare themselves for marriage and motherhood.

This emphasis on gender roles does not fall on deaf ears, as no other religious tradition comes anywhere close to the gender traditionalism of Mormons. As seen in Figure 5.2, in the Peculiar People Survey, 73 percent of Mormons agree that "It is much better for everyone involved if the man is the achiever outside the home and the woman takes care of the home and family." By way of comparison, less than half as many of the general population – only 30 percent – agree that men should be the sole breadwinner. After Mormons, the two religious groups with the most traditional views on gender roles are black Protestants and evangelicals, but they are well behind Mormons: respectively, 43 and 39 percent think men ought to be the breadwinner. Furthermore, on this question, Mormons are again both distinctive and cohesive, as there is not much of a gender gap on gender roles. Mormon women and men differ only slightly, and not enough to be considered statistically significant (74 percent of men and 72 percent of women agree).

Interestingly, the Pew Mormons in America survey found similar results, even though it asked a different question about gender roles. This survey asked about the marital arrangement respondents would find most satisfying: "One where the husband provides for the family and the wife takes care of the house and children or one where the husband and wife both have jobs and both take care of the house and children." Fifty-eight percent of Mormons said having the husband as the provider would be more satisfying, nearly twice as many as the general population (30 percent). Yet again, LDS men and women have faintly different views on this question: 59 percent of men prefer a one-income family compared to 56 percent of women (Pew Forum on Religion & Public Life 2012a).

Earlier, we noted that LDS leaders have not made an explicit connection between Church doctrine about the Constitution and a given political position. In sharp contrast, Mormon authorities have, in the recent past, given an explicitly political interpretation to LDS attitudes on gender roles. Indeed, attitudes regarding gender roles are the emblematic case of a religious belief that can be made politically salient. In the 1970s, the LDS Church engaged in a successful effort to mobilize Mormons to oppose the Equal Rights Amendment, even in states where Mormons were a small share of the population. In the words of Elizabeth Ellen Gordon and William L. Gillespie (2012, 345), "In fighting ERA ratification, the Church mobilized members by convincing them that the amendment posed a threat to the faith's foundation of male leadership and traditional family structure." This case was a classic example of strong, persuasive political information coming from a trusted source.

While in comparison to the rest of the population Latter-day Saints are most likely to believe in a traditional division of labor within the home, in recent years, Mormons' attitudes on gender roles, and working mothers especially, have been changing. According to the General Social Survey,[6] in the 1980s, 69 percent of Mormons believed that preschool children suffered when their mother worked outside the home, compared to 51 percent of the general (i.e. non-Mormon) population. In the 1990s, that fell to 60 percent of Mormons, falling even further in the 2000s to 55 percent. Meanwhile, the percentage of the general population who saw harm in working moms dropped from 44 to 40 percent over the same period. Extrapolating from the trend, we would expect Mormon attitudes toward working mothers in 2020 to be roughly the same as what the rest of the population thought in the 1980s.

In Chapter 3 we discussed polygamy and race, two cases where LDS practices changed abruptly. In contrast, the LDS Church has not issued a single statement changing course on gender roles. Instead, a combination of both bottom-up and top-down factors explain Mormons' changing attitudes on gender. From the bottom up, more Mormon women are actually working outside the home (Heaton and Jacobson forthcoming) while, at the top, some LDS leaders have delivered addresses in which they have legitimized working mothers (Hinckley 1996; Cook 2011), two developments that are no doubt related to one another. Indeed, this softening of attitudes on gender roles was detected as far back as the 1980s by Laurence Iannaccone and Carrie Miles (1990, 1241–2) who wrote that "Over time . . . the Church began accommodating changed roles for women." In other words, the signal on gender roles coming from the Mormon subculture became more nuanced. Accordingly, Mormons' considerations regarding the roles of men and women are more diverse today than in the past. While believing Mormons may be largely immune to the strong endorsement of the women's revolution within secular American society, inside the sacred tabernacle the rhetoric of gender traditionalism has begun to be tempered by statements and signals supportive of women who work outside the home.

The cases of the Constitution and gender illustrate the internal workings of Mormonism as a subculture undergoing both stasis and change. The widespread belief that Mormons will somehow be instrumental in preserving the Constitution reveals a strong sense of in-group identity, pride, and perhaps even chauvinism. Attitudes regarding gender roles demonstrate that Mormons can hold firm to beliefs that have been largely discarded by other Americans, including other political conservatives, and that those religious beliefs can be effective for political mobilization. Nonetheless, their attitudes regarding gender roles also remind us that Mormons' views are not frozen in amber. They can change, albeit slowly in this case.

RELIGIOUSLY INFLECTED POLITICAL VIEWS

We have seen that Mormons are strongly conservative, including two examples of conservative Mormon beliefs that either could have (the Constitution) or have

---

[6] See Data Appendix for details of the General Social Survey.

had (gender roles) a particular political application. However, the claim that Mormons are politically distinctive rests on their having views on public policies that do not align with other political conservatives. Our argument, at which we have already hinted, is that when the LDS Church takes a public policy position, LDS Church members take heed. LDS doctrine plays an extremely important part in shaping Mormons' opinions – not just on matters pertaining to church but also to affairs of state. We shall see that the specifics of Mormons' beliefs align with the teachings and policies of the LDS Church, even when they diverge from the positions taken by other politically conservative groups. Republican Mormons thus have dual reference groups for their political views: their party and their church. When they diverge, Mormons are likely to follow their church. Dual reference theory suggests that membership groups (like churches) exert more influence on political attitudes than identity groups (like political parties) (M. R. Welch and Leege 1991).

## Abortion

Abortion is a prime, if subtle, example of the divergence between Mormons and other conservative religious groups. While Mormons are generally opposed to abortion, that opposition comes with some nuance. LDS theology does not hold that abortion is murder, and so LDS policy permits it in some circumstances, specifically in cases of rape, incest, and when the life of the mother is in jeopardy. Thus, Mormon attitudes on abortion are sharply bimodal – strong opposition to abortion under most circumstances, but equally strong approval for some exceptions.

Because the sensitivity of the issue makes polling on abortion fraught with complications, the most informative survey questions on the subject are both specific and detailed. An excellent example of such a question has been asked for decades by the General Social Survey, where respondents are presented with the following series of circumstances and asked whether women should be able to obtain a legal abortion in each one:

- If the woman's own health is seriously endangered by the pregnancy
- If she became pregnant as a result of rape
- If there is a strong chance of serious defect in the baby
- If the family has a very low income and cannot afford any more children
- If she is not married and does not want to marry the man
- The woman wants it for any reason

The list is presented in a random order, in order to avoid any bias that might result from asking about one particular situation ahead of another.

As displayed in Figure 5.4, Mormons are more likely to approve of abortion in the cases of serious risk to the woman and rape than the general population, but less likely to approve of abortion in the other circumstances. They are also less likely to approve of abortion for other reasons than Catholics and evangelicals,

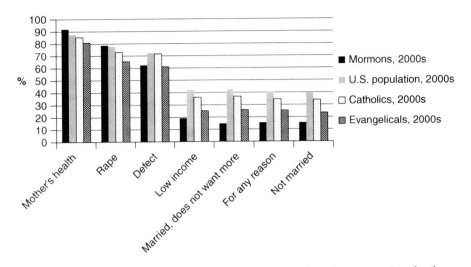

FIGURE 5.4. Nearly All Mormons Favor Abortion When Pregnancy Results from Rape or Risks the Health of the Woman; Very Few Mormons Favor It in Other Situations
*Source:* General Social Survey, 2000s

two other groups known for their position against abortion. Strikingly, 92 percent of Mormons approve of abortion when the mother's health is in jeopardy, compared to 88 percent of the general population, 85 percent of Catholics, and 81 percent of evangelicals. In contrast, only 15 percent of Mormons approve of abortion when the woman wants one for any reason, a far smaller percentage than the general population (40 percent), Catholics (34 percent), and evangelicals (23 percent).

Abortion is one of the best examples of how Mormons' attitudes align with the LDS Church. As defined by the authoritative handbook of instructions used by all local LDS leaders, Church policy permits abortion only when:

1. Pregnancy resulted from forcible rape or incest.
2. A competent physician determines that the life or health of the mother is in serious jeopardy.
3. A competent physician determines that the fetus has severe defects that will not allow the baby to survive beyond birth.[7]

As reflected in Figure 5.4, these are the three situations where Mormons are most likely to approve of abortion, particularly rape or incest and when the mother's

[7] See section 21.4.1 of the LDS Handbook 2 ("Administering the Church") used by local church leaders (Church of Jesus Christ of Latter-day Saints 2012c).

health is at risk. The strong opposition to abortion in other situations reflects the LDS position that, again quoting the leaders' handbook, "the Church opposes elective abortion for personal or social convenience." Furthermore, even in the situations where abortion might be justified, it is still considered an option of last resort. Again, in the words of the handbook, the "persons responsible" are to consult with their local ecclesiastical leader first and seek "divine confirmation through prayer" of their weighty decision to terminate a pregnancy.

Is the LDS adherence to the stated policies of their church really all that remarkable? It is when compared to other religious traditions. Catholics are perhaps the best benchmark for comparison, as the Catholic Church's opposition to abortion is absolute and well known. Contrary to Catholic teachings, 73 percent of Catholics approve of abortion in the case of rape. Admittedly, that is a hard case, so perhaps it is more informative to note that 35 percent of all Catholics favor abortion when the woman wants one for any reason – the most unequivocally pro-choice position possible.

The case of abortion illustrates how many Mormons place considerable weight on the considerations that circulate within their subculture, resulting in their unique opinion profile on the issue – nearly universal opposition to abortion in most cases coupled with widespread willingness to allow it in those situations where it is deemed permissible by the LDS Church.

## Same-Sex Marriage

In recent years, Mormons have become known, and in some circles notorious, for their energetic opposition to same-sex marriage. Like abortion, Mormons have distinctive views on marriage, but not in the way that many readers might expect. Mormons' disapproval of same-sex marriage is well known because of their mobilization on behalf of a 2008 California ballot initiative to write a ban on same-sex marriages into the state constitution. As with abortion, however, Mormon attitudes on same-sex marriage have some nuance. The Peculiar People Survey asked respondents whether they think same-sex couples should be allowed to marry, form civil unions but not marry, or have no legal standing whatsoever. Since this exact question was asked on Faith Matters 2011, a nationally representative survey of all Americans, we can compare Mormons to members of other religious traditions.

As Figure 5.5 shows, while very few Mormons support same-sex marriage outright (only 12 percent), when given a choice between civil unions for same-sex couples and no legal recognition whatsoever for same-sex relationships, more Mormons favor civil unions (49 percent) than nothing (40 percent). More Mormons favor some sort of legal status for same-sex couples – whether marriage or civil unions – than oppose it. Also, *Mormons are more likely to choose the "middle ground" option of civil unions than members of any other religious tradition in America* (although, of course, members of many other traditions are more likely to favor gay marriage outright). A comparison with evangelicals and

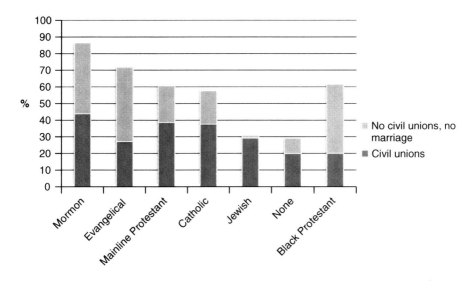

FIGURE 5.5. Nearly All Mormons Oppose Gay Marriage but Many Approve of Civil Unions for Same-Sex Couples
*Source:* Peculiar People Survey, 2012/Faith Matters Survey, 2011

black Protestants, two other groups known for their opposition to gay marriage, best illuminates Mormons' distinctiveness. All three groups have similar levels of opposition to any legal standing for same-sex couples; 45 percent of evangelicals and 42 percent of black Protestants object to marriage and civil unions. But only 27 percent of evangelicals and 20 percent of black Protestants approve of civil unions. Consequently, when compared to Mormons, opinion on same-sex marriage is more polarized among evangelicals and black Protestants – more of them either oppose or support it than take the middle road of civil unions.

Mormons' opinions on same-sex marriage again reflect the emphasis of LDS leaders. While the LDS Church considers homosexual sexual activity to be sinful, the Church's opposition to same-sex marriage has focused more on the definition of marriage than criticism of homosexuality per se. Church statements on the subject of same-sex marriage are generally framed as a defense of traditional (i.e., heterosexual) marriage and include language encouraging Church members to show love and respect for everyone, regardless of sexual orientation. For example, a document published by the LDS Church on its official webpage in August of 2008 – as the Proposition 8 campaign was heating up – includes the following language affirming some rights for homosexual couples:

The focus of the Church's involvement is specifically same-sex marriage and its consequences. The Church does not object to rights (already established in California) regarding hospitalization and medical care, fair housing and employment rights, or probate rights, so long as these do not infringe on the integrity of the family or the constitutional rights of churches and their adherents to administer and practice their religion free from government interference. (Church of Jesus Christ of Latter-day Saints 2008b)

As we will detail in the next chapter, the Church has even explicitly endorsed a statute in Salt Lake City banning discrimination toward homosexuals in housing and employment. We suggest that the reason roughly half of Mormons are willing to go along with civil unions for gay couples lies in the LDS Church's approval of some rights for same-sex couples. The information that circulates through the sacred tabernacle blends strong opposition to same-sex *marriage* with a quieter willingness to accept other rights for same-sex couples. Mormons' views on same-sex relationships reflect this mix of considerations.

### Young Mormons and Attitudes toward Homosexuality

Recall from Chapter 4 that Mormons are unusual in that the young are more Republican than their elders. Similarly, on many issues – including health care, what it takes to get ahead, government assistance for the needy, preemptive military action, and gender roles – young and old Mormons do not differ.[8] The link between age and attitudes toward homosexuality, however, is different among Latter-day Saints: young Mormons are more conservative in their attitudes toward gays and lesbians than other young Americans, but they are more liberal than older Mormons.

To illustrate the age-based differences in attitudes toward homosexuality among Mormons, Figure 5.6 displays the relationship between age and attitudes toward same-sex marriage and adoption by gay and lesbian couples. To ensure that age is not confounded with other factors affecting attitudes toward gay marriage and adoption, these figures are based on a statistical model that controls for gender, education, and the four indices of Mormon-ness introduced in Chapter 3 (Activity, Authority, Insularity, and Identity).[9]

When these other influences are accounted for, our statistical model estimates that among Mormons age twenty-five, roughly 12 percent approve of gay marriage – much lower than the 61 percent of their peers nationally who support it.[10] But 12 percent is higher than the 10 percent of fifty-year-old Mormons who think that same-sex marriages should be recognized by

---

[8]  This statement is based on analysis of the Peculiar People Survey.

[9]  To estimate the values in Figures 5.6 and 5.7, we use ordered logistic regression. All of the control variables have been set to their means except for gender, which as a categorical variable has instead been set to its mode (female). We then estimate the probability of approval of gay marriage homosexuality in general when age is set to twenty-five, fifty, and seventy-five. See Table 5A.1 and 5A.2 in the appendix at the end of this chapter for the details of the full models.

[10] This number is based on the 2011 Faith Matters survey, which included exactly the same question about gay marriage as the Peculiar People survey. More precisely, 61 percent of non-Mormons between the ages of eighteen and thirty support gay marriage.

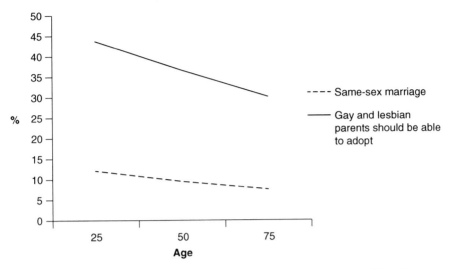

FIGURE 5.6. Younger Mormons are Slightly More Likely to Approve of Gay Marriage and Adoption. With statistical controls. With statistical controls; results from ordered logistic regression. All control variables set to their mean or modal values
*Source:* Peculiar People Survey, 2012

the law, and higher still than the 7 percent of seventy-five-year-old Mormons with this view. And the contrast between young and old is starker for attitudes toward adoption of children by gay and lesbian couples. This issue has a much lower profile within Mormonism, as it has not been the subject of political activity by the LDS Church. Almost half (44 percent) of twenty-five-year-old Mormons think that gays and lesbians should be allowed to adopt, compared to 37 percent of fifty-year-olds and 30 percent of seventy-five-year-olds.

Attitudes toward homosexuality among Mormons closely resemble those of evangelicals. In Figure 5.7, we draw on the Pew U.S. Religious Landscape Survey to compare the relationship between age and the belief that "homosexuality is a way of life that should be accepted by society" among Mormons, evangelical Protestants, and everyone else in the population. Again, we use a statistical model to control for potentially confounding factors.[11] For all three groups, twenty-five-year-olds are more likely to think that homosexuality should be accepted by society than fifty-year-olds, and fifty-year-olds more likely than seventy-five-year-olds. But regardless of their age, Mormons and evangelicals are far less likely to agree with societal acceptance of homosexuality than the rest

---

[11] Specifically, we control for gender, education, and frequency of religious attendance. See note 9 for more methodological details.

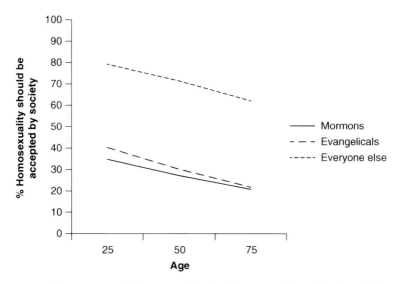

FIGURE 5.7. Acceptance of Homosexuality by Mormons, Evangelicals, and Everyone Else. With statistical controls; results from ordered logistic regression. All control variables set to their mean or modal values
*Source:* Pew U.S. Religious Landscape Survey, 2007

of the population. Their views are nearly identical – another example where Mormons and evangelicals share common ground.

The greater acceptance of homosexuality among young Mormons likely reflects that they are exposed to a different mix of considerations than their elders. Through formal church channels, Mormons of all ages hear that gay marriage is wrong and that homosexual activity is sinful. It seems highly probable, however, that young Mormons are more likely than their elders to receive counterbalancing messaging in favor of gay rights from secular sources, including popular culture and personal contact with gays and lesbians – a reminder that the walls of the sacred tabernacle are permeable.

### Immigration

On all the previously discussed issues, Mormons clearly lean to the political right. But what about an LDS position on the political left? Because of Mormons' overall political conservatism, this is the real test of the Church's influence on political views.

As indicated by the opening anecdote for this chapter, one such issue is immigration. As the debate over immigration has heated up across the United States, including in the Mormon heartland of the Mountain West, the LDS Church has publicly supported immigration policies that put compassion over enforcement. As with the Catholic Church, the LDS position on immigration is likely motivated by both theology and institutional self-interest. Theologically, the Church's position blends a general sense of compassion with the salvific primacy of the family, as deportations often break families up. Practically speaking, the Church has a large number of undocumented members, as immigration status is not used as a qualification for conversion to the Church nor for remaining in good standing within it. Indeed, there are many LDS templegoers, missionaries, and local ecclesiastical leaders who are in the United States illegally (Stack 2011). One might say that the LDS Church has a "don't ask, don't tell" policy regarding immigration status. Furthermore, the Church has been a voice of moderation on immigration, particularly in the state of Utah. As we detail further in the next chapter, LDS leaders have spoken out in support of immigration policies that prioritize keeping families intact and that open a path to citizenship for undocumented residents.

Cutting against the LDS Church's position on immigration policy is the increasingly hard line taken by Republicans on the issue. Indeed, some of the politicians advocating punitive immigration policies in states like Arizona and Utah have been Mormons (Stuart 2011). Immigration thus presents a dilemma for most Mormons, who are generally in the conservative wing of the Republican Party. Does Church prevail over party? Or, in other terms, how do Mormons balance the competing, even conflicting, considerations coming to them through political and religious channels?

As suggested by Zaller's theory of public opinion formation, Mormons can be said to split the difference. In the Peculiar People Survey, we asked respondents to indicate where their opinion falls between these two positions:

*Immigrants today strengthen our country because of their hard work and talents*
and
*Immigrants today are a burden on our country because they take our jobs, housing, and health care*

They could choose either option, or one of two positions in between.

As we see in Figure 5.8, Mormons are divided almost evenly on this question. Fifty-two percent fall on the "strengthen our country" side of the scale, while the remaining 48 say that immigrants "are a burden on our country." When the Pew Mormons in American survey asked the same question with only the two polar options and an in-between category of "neither or both," they found nearly the same: 45 percent said immigrants strengthen the country, 41 percent said they are a burden, and 9 percent said neither or both (6 percent said they did not know).

Mormons are not alone in their ambivalence on immigration, as their opinions match those of the general public almost exactly. Forty-five percent of all Americans say immigrants strengthen the country, while 44 percent believe them to be a burden.

If Mormons' attitudes on immigration so closely track the rest of the public, why suggest that this is a sign of their distinctiveness? As a group that is so

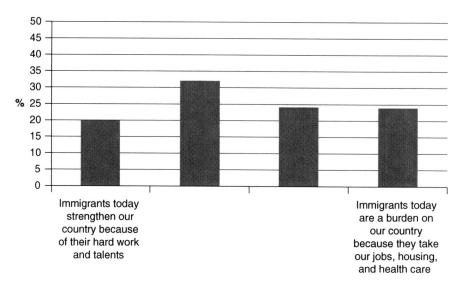

FIGURE 5.8. Mormons Are Conflicted on Immigration
*Source:* Peculiar People Survey, 2012

strongly conservative on virtually every other issue, Mormon moderation on immigration stands out, particularly when compared to other conservative religious groups. Consider that 56 percent of evangelical Protestants, 47 percent of mainline Protestants, 55 percent of black Protestants, and 49 percent of white Catholics say that immigrants burden the country – all higher than the percentage of Mormons who say the same. Perhaps even more telling is to limit our comparison to white Republicans. Of all white Republicans in the country, 58 percent believe that immigrants are a burden, compared to 44 percent of white *Mormon* Republicans.[12] When we narrow the scope even further to look only at white Republicans in states with a high percentage of undocumented immigrants, Mormons are still more moderate – although the gap is a little narrower. Fifty-eight percent of all Republicans in such states believe immigrants are a burden, compared to 49 percent of Mormons.[13]

[12] In this paragraph, "white" refers to "white, non-Hispanic." The source for the data on evangelical Protestants, mainline Protestants, black Protestants, and white Catholics is the Pew Political Typology Survey and for Mormons the data comes from the Pew Mormons in America survey (see survey details in Data Appendix). Both surveys were conducted in 2011 using identical questions. Note that Republicans include respondents who report "leaning" toward the Republican Party.

[13] States with a high percentage of undocumented immigrants are defined as those above the national average of 3.7 percent of the population (not including Utah, which has .1 percent more than the national average). These include Arkansas, Arizona, California, the District of Columbia, Florida, Georgia, Illinois, Maryland, Nevada, New Jersey, New Mexico, Oregon, and Texas (Passel and Cohn 2011).

If Mormons' primary source of information on immigration came from politically conservative opinion leaders, we would expect their views on immigration to be cohesively conservative, just like their views on most other issues. And, as we show in the next chapter, when Mormons are reminded of the LDS Church's statements on immigration, most (but, importantly, not all) Mormons' attitudes shift toward a pro-immigration position. If the Church amplified its voice on immigration through Church channels, attitudes would shift even further.

## Missionaries

The LDS Church's moderate position on immigration is not the only reason for Mormons' positive view of immigrants. Another peculiar element of Mormon culture also shapes their opinions – missionary service. Many Latter-day Saints serve either two years or eighteen months as full-time missionaries for the Church, proselytizing in an effort to bring converts into the Church. Most often, this missionary service is done in early adulthood, although some retired couples serve as missionaries as well. Missions are typically self-financed and require total commitment for the duration of the service; for the young missionaries, communication with home is limited to one letter per week and only two phone calls per year.[14] Missionaries serve wherever the Church sends them, often a foreign country. Whether they serve in the United States or abroad, many missionaries learn to speak another language. Within the United States, LDS missionaries might be assigned to serve a population where a language other than English is most common – often Spanish, but perhaps Portuguese or even languages like Laotian or Hmong. Wherever they serve and whatever language they speak, LDS missionaries almost invariably spend considerable time with people who are economically disadvantaged. Upon returning home, many former missionaries maintain ties with the culture and people where they served.

We hypothesize that missionary service fosters empathy for people of other cultures, particularly those on the lower rungs of the socioeconomic ladder. Not all considerations on a given issue are created equal. Those borne of personal experience, particularly during the formative period of one's life, are likely to carry a lot of weight. Consequently, we postulate that former missionaries will be especially compassionate to the plight of immigrants to the United States, whether documented or not. The fact that many LDS missionaries are sent to Latin America, the primary origin of immigration to the United States, should only strengthen the connection between missionary service and sympathy for immigrants.

To test our hypothesis, we examined whether Mormons who have served as missionaries are more likely to have a positive opinion of immigration. Even more specifically, we looked at the opinion of those Mormons who learned a new language while serving. Our focus is on learning a foreign language rather than serving in another country, since U.S.-based missionaries who learn a new

---

[14] The rules are less stringent for missionaries who serve later in life.

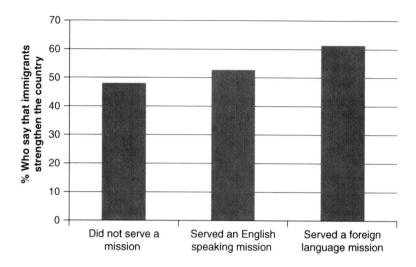

FIGURE 5.9. Mormons Who Learn a Foreign Language as a Missionary Are More Positive toward Immigrants. With statistical controls; results from ordered logistic regression. All control variables set to their mean or modal values
*Source:* Peculiar People Survey, 2012

language are likely to have first-hand experience with the struggles facing immigrants within the nation's borders.

Our test entails a statistical model that also accounts for other factors with a plausible impact on one's attitude toward immigrants.[15] As hypothesized, Mormons who learned a new language as a missionary are significantly more likely to say that immigrants strengthen the United States than LDS Church members who have not served a mission at all. Compared to those who have not spent time as missionaries, Mormons who serve in their own language are slightly more likely to have a positive regard for immigrants, but the difference falls short of statistical significance. As Figure 5.9 shows, 48 percent of Mormons who have not served a mission believe immigrants strengthen the United States, about the same as the general population. That rises to 56 percent of Mormons who have served a mission but did not learn a new language, and 61 percent among former missionaries who did.[16]

---

[15] These models include age, education, party identification, and the four indices of Mormon-ness (Activity, Authority, Identity, and Insularity). See Table 5A.3 in the appendix at the end of this chapter for the details of the full model.
[16] We employ ordered logistic regression for this analysis. To estimate these predicted values, all control variables were set to their means.

Note that these results are not easily explained by the preexisting opinions on immigration by those who serve LDS missions. If Mormons could choose where they serve a mission, these results might simply reflect selection bias, with potential missionaries already sympathetic to other cultures choosing a foreign-language mission. However, prospective missionaries do not choose their area of service, nor whether they are to learn a new language. Their mission is assigned to them by the Church (or, as believing Latter-day Saints would typically put it, the call comes from God).[17]

CONCLUSION

We have seen that notwithstanding their overwhelming support for the Republican Party and strongly conservative views, Mormons do not march in lockstep with other Republicans nor toe the line of ideological orthodoxy. Their religious beliefs and culture shape their political opinions, even if this means that they are slightly out of step with other politically conservative groups. For some issues, this consists of a slightly different, and thus moderate, shade of conservatism – opposition to gay marriage but approval of civil unions; opposition to abortion but with exceptions for pregnancies resulting from rape and/or that pose a risk to the health of the mother. As we have also seen, the one issue where Mormons stand most clearly apart from other conservative groups is their relatively positive sentiment toward immigrants, which stems in part from the peculiar Mormon practice of lengthy full-time missionary service as a young adult.

The distinctiveness of Mormon opinion illustrates how religion shapes politics, reinforcing our theoretical point that Mormons are accurately characterized as an ethno-religious group. It is not just that Mormons are distinctive; it is that their distinctiveness is borne of their religion and reinforced within the sacred tabernacle. These religiously inflected political views demonstrate that LDS teachings can, and do, have political significance.

However, whatever the nuances of Mormon opinion, they are generally lost on Election Day, when the choices are much less nuanced. Mormons are predominantly Republican and vote accordingly. For students of history this situation is highly ironic, given that the Republican Party was initially the nemesis of the LDS Church.

In spite – and likely because – of the nearly monolithic support of the GOP among Mormons, the top leadership of the LDS Church has recently reiterated through official channels that Latter-day Saints are free to belong to the party of

---

[17] We concede that we cannot completely rule out some degree of selection bias, as the application form does include space for a potential missionary's local bishop (pastor) to indicate whether he recommends a foreign language mission for the applicant. Bishops are presumably more likely to check that box if the missionary-to-be already has language training (suggesting a predisposition to appreciating other cultures) or generally appears to be amenable to a new cultural experience. On balance, it seems credible to claim that this process avoids the worst of selection bias.

their choice. In 2012, the First Presidency sent a letter to be read from the pulpit of all Utah congregations, encouraging Church members to attend the upcoming party caucuses. The letter stated: "Principles compatible with the gospel may be found in the platforms of the various political parties."[18] To facilitate members' participation, Church meetings were also canceled on the evenings of the caucuses, freeing up time for busy Mormons. While attendance was up at both the Republican and Democratic caucuses, it is difficult to isolate the effect of the letter per se, since candidates were also working to boost attendance. On the Republican side especially, Senator Orrin Hatch invested heavily in mobilization efforts for the caucus to defend his seat against an insurgent Tea Party-backed candidate. Although we cannot be sure that the letter, and the cancellation of LDS meetings to make time for the caucuses, had a direct, causal effect on attendance at the caucuses, we do know that many Mormon party activists heard the message. In a survey of delegates to the Utah state conventions of both the Democratic and Republican parties, Mormons were essentially the only Utahns who reported, "I was urged to attend the caucus by my church." Among Democratic convention delegates, 47 percent of Mormons said that they were, compared to no Protestants or Catholics (precisely zero percent of both groups). Among Republican delegates, 50 percent reported being encouraged to attend by their church – again, no Protestants or Catholics said the same.[19]

While Mormon Democrats would no doubt welcome a letter from the LDS First Presidency explicitly encouraging more Mormons to affiliate with the Democratic Party, obviously this is not going to happen. Nonetheless, the very suggestion brings us back to the story of the People's Party, the Church's political party in the days prior to Utah's statehood (see Chapter 4). Recall that the party's very existence suggested that Mormons were not politically independent of the LDS hierarchy. To assuage such concerns, the Church dissolved the party. Somewhat paradoxically, LDS leaders sought to demonstrate Mormons' independence from the Church by "encouraging" – some accounts say commanding – Mormons to affiliate with either the Democrats or Republicans. It is difficult to know how much of this is fact versus folklore, but the very perpetuation of the story raises the interesting question of how Mormons respond to political cues from LDS leaders (Barrus 1992; Lyman 1986). Here we have made the argument that when LDS leaders make explicit the connection between Mormon teachings and political views, Mormons generally follow their leaders' cues. But thus far, we concede that the evidence is only circumstantial. The next chapter looks to other evidence to cinch the case.

---

[18]  The full text of the letter can be found at http://www.sltrib.com/sltrib/politics/53504504-90/utah-letter-lds-caucus.html.csp (accessed October 7, 2013).

[19]  These figures come from surveys of state convention delegates conducted by the Center for the Study of Elections and Democracy at Brigham Young University. For complete reports on both surveys see http://csed.byu.edu/Research/2012UtahDelegateSurveys.html (accessed October 7, 2013).

CHAPTER 5 APPENDIX

TABLE 5A.1. *Ordered Logistic Models of Age Regressed on Attitudes toward Same-Sex Marriage and Gay Adoption (Mormons Only)*

| VARIABLES | Same-sex marriage | Gay adoption |
|---|---|---|
| Age | 0.011* | 0.012** |
| | (0.006) | (0.006) |
| Authority | 0.464*** | 0.638*** |
| | (0.113) | (0.109) |
| Identity | 0.414*** | 0.316*** |
| | (0.125) | (0.118) |
| Insularity | 0.269** | 0.305** |
| | (0.129) | (0.120) |
| Activity | 0.108 | 0.026 |
| | (0.242) | (0.085) |
| Gender | 0.124 | 0.384** |
| | (0.187) | (0.177) |
| Education | −0.106 | 0.041 |
| | 0.069 | (0.065) |
| Cut 1 | 2.170 | 2.447 |
| | (0.598) | (0.559) |
| Cut 2 | 4.989 | 4.113 |
| | (0.643) | (0.581) |
| Cut 3 | | 5.695 |
| | | (0.606) |
| Observations | 481 | 480 |
| Pseudo R-squared | 0.106 | 0.103 |

Standard errors in parentheses. Both dependent variables are coded so that a higher number corresponds to greater opposition to either gay marriage or adoption.

*** $p < 0.01$, ** $p < 0.05$, * $p < 0.1$

*Source:* Peculiar People Survey, 2012

TABLE 5A.2. *Ordered Logistic Models of Age Regressed on Attitudes toward Homosexuality*

| VARIABLES | Should homosexuality be accepted by society? | | |
|---|---|---|---|
| | Mormons | Evangelicals | Everyone else |
| Age | −0.015*** | −0.018*** | −0.017*** |
| | (0.006) | (0.001) | (0.001) |
| Education | −0.036 | 0.077*** | 0.210*** |
| | (0.065) | (0.015) | (0.008) |
| Gender | 0.713*** | 0.548*** | 0.788*** |
| | (0.202) | (0.048) | (0.029) |
| Religious attendance | −0.517*** | −0.427*** | 0.351*** |
| | (0.081) | (0.016) | (0.009) |
| Cut 1 | −1.247 | −0.821 | −0.746 |
| | (0.569) | (0.126) | (0.067) |
| Cut 2 | −0.965 | −0.549 | −0.462 |
| | (0.568) | (0.126) | (0.067) |
| Observations | 558 | 9003 | 23924 |
| Pseudo R-squared | 0.08 | 0.07 | 0.08 |

Standard errors in parentheses
*** $p < 0.01$, ** $p < 0.05$, * $p < 0.1$
*Source:* Pew U.S. Religious Landscape Survey, 2007

TABLE 5A.3. *Ordered Logistic Model of Missionary Service Regressed on Attitude toward Immigrants (Mormons Only)*

| VARIABLES | Immigrants strengthen the country |
|---|---|
| Served an English-speaking mission | 0.186 |
| | (0.262) |
| Served a foreign-language mission | 0.542** |
| | (0.257) |
| Age | −0.015*** |
| | (0.006) |
| Education | 0.230*** |
| | (0.068) |
| Party identification | −0.107** |
| | (0.052) |
| Authority | −0.111 |
| | (0.108) |
| Activity | 0.360*** |
| | (0.087) |
| Insularity | −0.049 |
| | (0.119) |

TABLE 5A.3 (*continued*)

| VARIABLES | Immigrants strengthen the country |
|---|---|
| Identity | −0.220* |
|  | (0.120) |
| Cut 1 | −1.599 |
|  | (0.584) |
| Cut 2 | −0.335 |
|  | (0.580) |
| Cut 3 | 1.317 |
|  | (0.582) |
| Observations | 468 |
| Pseudo R-squared | 0.06 |

Standard errors in parentheses
*** $p < 0.01$, ** $p < 0.05$, * $p < 0.1$
*Source:* Peculiar People Survey, 2012

# 6

## Following the Leader

### Mormons' Responsiveness to Church Leaders

In the fall of 2012, Hurricane Sandy devastated parts of New York and surrounding areas. Within a few days of the hurricane, Mormon volunteers donned yellow vests with a "Mormon Helping Hands" logo and divided into small teams to help local residents begin to clean up. For the next several months, they spent weekends in "chainsaw brigades," clearing fallen trees, removing mud and debris from homes, tearing out damaged walls and carpet, and disinfecting what remained (Trapasso 2012). The LDS Church estimates that 28,000 Mormons logged more than 275,000 hours of labor – a remarkable figure given that Mormons make up a very small share of the population in the region (Church of Jesus Christ of Latter-day Saints 2012a).[1]

This vast volunteer effort was led and coordinated by the regional and local LDS leadership. Recall that in Chapter 1 we described the importance of religious authority within Mormonism. With authority comes hierarchy, which means a clear "chain of command" for activating Church members. For example, volunteers from the Princeton First Ward responded to a call from their stake president that was delivered through the ward's bishop and other ward-level leaders such as the "Elders Quorum President" (the leader of a ward's priesthood organization for men). Within a week of the hurricane, ward members were asked to attend or participate via conference call in an "all hands" training session to learn the basics of participating in the Mormon Helping Hands program. As part of ten- to twelve-person teams, the typical active ward member spent two or three weekends working from late October to late

---

[1] Mormons are 0.4 percent of the population in both New Jersey and New York (Grammich 2012). Since the Church formally began its "Mormon Helping Hands" efforts in 1998 (Church of Jesus Christ of Latter-day Saints 2009a) there have been many similar volunteer efforts, such as when hurricanes Katrina and Rita devastated New Orleans and the Gulf Coast area in 2005 (Hart 2005; N. C. Hill and Romney 2007). But such efforts predate this program. A notable example prior to the creation of "Mormon Helping Hands" was the massive cleanup after the Teton Dam broke in southern Idaho in 1976 (Blumell 1980).

December. Nor was the volunteer effort limited to Mormons in storm-ravaged communities. Mormons from less-affected areas traveled to New York and the New Jersey shore, camping at LDS ward buildings while they worked for the weekend (Snell 2013).

In sum, Mormons were *mobilized* on a large scale for disaster relief, a non-controversial cause among Mormons (as well as other Americans). However, the mobilization potential of the Latter-day Saints is not limited to community service. It also extends to political causes – which are not always as popular among Mormons or others. The LDS Church's opposition to the proposed Equal Rights Amendment (ERA) to the U.S. Constitution provides an illuminating example.

After Congress passed the ERA in 1972, it appeared that ratification would occur quickly, with thirty state legislatures approving it within a year (Wolbrecht 2000). However, as the 1982 ratification deadline approached, a late-blooming coalition of opponents emerged, including conservative Catholics, evangelicals, and Mormons, that worked to prevent ratification in the remaining states and for repeal in states that had already approved the ERA.[2]

In early 1975, LDS leaders came out strongly against the ERA. The *LDS Church News* – widely recognized as reflecting the official view of the Church – editorialized against the amendment, quoting leading LDS women who called it "dangerous" and "a confused step backward in time" ("Equal Rights Amendment" 1975). The Church's First Presidency issued official statements against the ERA in 1976 and 1978, which were compiled into a single booklet in 1980 and inserted in the Church's flagship magazine, the *Ensign* (Church of Jesus Christ of Latter-day Saints 1980a). Church leaders issued a call for Mormons to lobby state legislators, write letters, and raise funds for anti-ERA political action committees and candidates. Rank-and-file Mormons responded enthusiastically. Together, these efforts contributed to the defeat of the ERA in the "Mormon corridor" of Utah, Idaho, and Nevada. Mormon volunteers also played a crucial role in defeating the amendment in states like Florida, Virginia, Maryland, and Georgia, where Latter-day Saints made up less than 1 percent of the population (E. E. Gordon and Gillespie 2012; Quinn 2005; Mansbridge 1986; White 1989).

LDS leaders did not just mobilize Mormon activity against the ERA, they also *persuaded* Mormons to oppose it. A November 1974 poll of Utah residents found that 63 percent of Mormons favored passage of the ERA (Knight and Jones 1974).[3] But a 1980 *Salt Lake Tribune* poll found that 76 percent of Utah Mormons opposed its passage (Bardsley 1980).[4] The same poll asked

---

[2] When Congress passed the ERA in 1972, it was given a seven-year deadline for ratification that was later extended until June 30, 1982.

[3] The question was, "Are you in favor or not in favor of passage of the Equal Rights Amendment?" Non-Mormons were marginally more in favor, at 73 percent.

[4] Similar to the Utah Mormon data, at first the ERA enjoyed support nationally among people who held to more traditional positions on women's roles. The shift in opinion among Utah Mormons reflects broader national trends in which support for the ERA eroded as the debate shifted "away

respondents about the actual language of the proposed amendment without identifying it as the ERA: "Equality of rights shall not be denied or abridged by the United States or by a state on account of sex." Only 38 percent of Utah Mormons were against this statement and 51 percent were in favor. This discrepancy suggests that LDS leaders successfully persuaded Mormons to oppose the amendment itself, notwithstanding their general support for women's rights (Bardsley 1980; Mansbridge 1986, 26; White 1989, 261).

Both Hurricane Sandy and the ERA illustrate the ability of LDS Church leaders to mobilize and persuade church members. By "mobilize" we mean increasing the participation of Mormons on behalf of a Church-supported cause; by "persuade" we mean shifting the attitudes of Mormons in favor of a Church-supported cause.[5] Hurricane Sandy is an example of extensive mobilization on a nonpolitical cause that required no persuasion; the ERA is an example of extensive mobilization but also strong persuasion in favor of a political position.

This chapter discusses in detail how the LDS Church engages in mobilization and persuasion on behalf of political causes. We find that Mormons are like "dry kindling" that can be ignited by a "spark" from their Church leaders. We begin by reviewing the features of the sacred tabernacle that create the kindling and then the character of Church leadership that generates the spark to ignite it. Next we turn to case studies of Church-led efforts at mobilization and persuasion, finding that such efforts are often effective but infrequent, occurring only under particular conditions. The case studies also suggest, as we found in Chapter 5, that when faced with a choice between their Church and their politics, Mormons tend to follow their Church. We conclude with experimental evidence that many Mormons align their views with the Church's position *even when it runs counter to their ideological inclinations.*

This evidence contradicts a common stereotype of the Latter-day Saints as blindly obedient to their Church leaders. As a historian (and former Mormon) claims: "From the late 1960s onward, LDS headquarters reestablished political obedience, so that Mormons now act like army ants when given instructions about political matters" (Quinn 2005, 131–2). The truth is far more nuanced: Mormons listen to their leaders when their leaders speak efficaciously within the sacred tabernacle. Church leaders must work hard to mobilize church members, even for a popular cause like disaster relief. And they also must work to persuade church members on potentially less popular political causes. If Mormons do not blindly follow their Church leaders, neither are Church leaders captives to their members, as they are willing to raise a prophetic voice contrary to prevailing opinion.

---

from equal rights and focused it on the possibility that the ERA might bring substantive changes in women's roles and behavior" (Mansbridge 1986, 20–1).

[5]  The definition of mobilization is consistent with how Rosenstone and Hansen (2009, 24–5) discuss direct and indirect mobilization. The definition of persuasion is consistent with the influence of elites on attitudes as discussed by Zaller (1992; 1994).

## THE KINDLING

Four features of the sacred tabernacle help explain how Mormons are like dry kindling when it comes to mobilization and persuasion by Church leaders: tight-knit social networks, extensive civic skills, strong attitudinal cohesion, and a deep respect for religious authority. These topics were discussed in Chapters 3, 4, and 5, and we review them in a political context here. At their root, these features all reflect the internal solidarity of the sacred tabernacle.

Tight-knit social networks have been shown to be a powerful factor in both mobilization and persuasion (Mutz 2006). Recall from Chapter 3 that, when compared to members of other religious groups, Mormons have a high rate of "bonding" with one another rather than "bridging" to members of other faiths. That is, they are more likely to have family members, friends, and neighbors of the same religion than most other Americans (Putnam and Campbell 2010, 525). Mormons regularly experience the kind of close, interpersonal relationships that generate social capital – social networks that foster a sense of trust and reciprocity. By building within-group ties, they are especially high in "bonding social capital," which produces high levels of in-group trust that "mobilize solidarity" (Putnam 2001, 22).

A good example of such experiences is that members of a ward are regularly asked to help load or unload a moving truck or take a meal to a family that has experienced childbirth. A recent survey conducted among the members of a Mormon stake of married college students in Salt Lake City included a question about a list of "ways in which members of a ward can serve each other." Respondents were asked if they had been personally involved in any of the activities within the "current semester." Forty-nine percent had personally helped someone move, 51 percent had provided a meal to another family, 53 percent had provided child care, 48 percent had interacted socially (an "outing or date with another couple"), and 19 percent had helped with car or home repairs.[6] A young student congregation may have an unusual number of moving vans and births, although their mobility also means that many ward members do not have the long-term relationships with one another that are typically associated with lending a hand.

As noted in Chapter 3, Mormons' religious voluntarism extends beyond informal neighborliness to formal callings within their ward. Such congregational service builds civic skills, the verbal and organizational experiences that transfer over to other forms of voluntarism. As Sidney Verba, Kay Schlozman, and Henry Brady (1995, 304) succinctly put it, "Citizens who can speak or write well or who are comfortable organizing and taking part in meetings are likely to be more effective when they get involved in politics." Mormons' congregational

---

[6] The survey was of the Salt Lake Married Student 2nd Stake during November and December 2012. The responses were obtained via an Internet survey and had a response rate of about 70 percent. Kelly Patterson, a professor of political science at Brigham Young University who was serving in a Church assignment within the stake, conducted the survey and provided the data.

activity leads them to develop many civic skills. And additional skills are developed by Mormons who have served as missionaries, including initiating conversations with complete strangers, door-to-door contacting, and public speaking outside of church settings.

Does the high degree of congregational activity among Mormons dampen their nonreligious voluntarism, limiting the use of civic skills in community service or political activity? Some previous research has shown that more religious activity leads to more volunteering – both for religious and secular causes – but few religious groups have a level of religious activity to match that of Mormons (Putnam and Campbell 2010; Campbell and Yonish 2003; Wuthnow and Hodgkinson 1990). Other research has found that political engagement drops off at the high end of religious volunteering, suggesting that Mormons' faith-based activity may keep them from being engaged outside of the LDS Church (Campbell 2004).

To answer this question, we examine the degree to which Mormons engage in nonreligious civic activity with a national survey of all Americans, which enables a comparison between Mormons and the rest of the American population. Because engagement comes in different forms, we look at three types of activity: voting, political activity (besides voting), and community activity.[7] We have also created a simulation of what Americans' engagement would look like if everyone had the same demographic characteristics – most importantly, the same level of religiosity – as Mormons.

Figure 6.1 shows how Mormons compare to the rest of the population on each measure of engagement. In every case, Mormons show a higher level of

---

[7] This analysis draws on data from the Faith Matters surveys (described in Data Appendix), while Figure 6.2 uses data from the Peculiar People Survey. The indices created in the two data sets are very similar:

Voting Index: Voted in 2010 congressional election; voted in 2008 presidential election; frequency of voting in local elections (in the Peculiar People Survey, this also includes whether the respondent is registered to vote).

Political Engagement Index: Frequency of political discussion; contacted government official in the past year; attended political rally in the last year; participated in a march in the last year; boycotted a business for a political purpose in the last year.

Community Engagement Index: Worked on a community project; served as an officer of an organization; served as a volunteer for any of the following organizations: health care, school or youth, poor or elderly, arts and culture, or a neighborhood or civic group.

Each index was created using principal components factor analysis. Note that in the Faith Matters Survey, the variables for the Voting and Community Engagement Indices are from 2011, while those for the Political Engagement Index are from 2006 (because they were not all asked on the 2011 survey).

The regression models for Figures 6.1 and 6.2 include the following control variables: race (white), ethnicity (Hispanic), income, gender, education, and age. The Faith Matters models also include an index of religiosity, which includes frequency of religious attendance, frequency of prayer, importance of religion, strength of religious identity, strong belief in one's religion, and certainty of belief in God. (See Putnam and Campbell 2010 for more details on this index.)

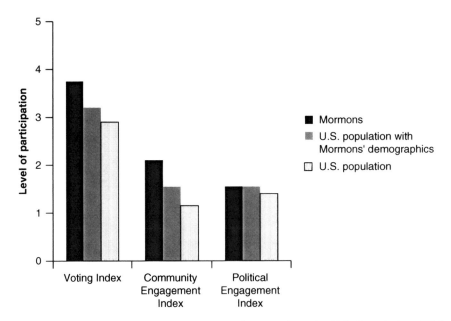

FIGURE 6.1. Mormons' Civic Engagement Compared to the U.S. Population. With statistical controls; results from OLS regression
*Source:* Faith Matters Surveys, 2006 and 2011. For Mormons and U.S. Population, all control variables set to their mean or modal values. For U.S. population with Mormons' demographics, all control variables set to the mean or modal values of the Mormon population

engagement than the population in general, but about the same level as other highly religious Americans. Indeed, in this comparison the gap between Mormons and other religious Americans substantially shrinks for both community engagement and voting – the form of political activity that shares the same civic motivations as volunteering (Campbell 2006). In other words, Mormons' high level of religious activity does not appear to dampen their civic engagement. Importantly, however, note that Mormons' level of *political* activity (other than voting) is no higher or lower than that of the rest of the population, even when we account for Mormons' high religiosity. Thus, while Mormons may be primed for intense political mobilization, this fact does not mean that their "natural state" is an unusually high degree of involvement in political activity.

Comparisons between Mormons and non-Mormons raise another question: is their engagement *in spite of* their religious activity or *because of* it? Does more time in congregational service mean less time in community service? Drawing on data from our Peculiar People Survey, we use a statistical model to test the relationship between time spent in Church service and each type of activity, while controlling

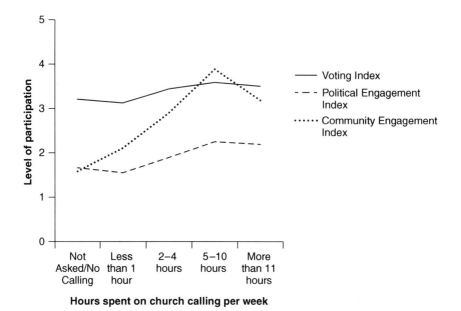

FIGURE 6.2. Time Spent on Church Callings and Civic Engagement. With statistical controls; results from OLS regression
*Source:* Peculiar People Survey, 2012. All control variables set to their mean or modal values

for an array of demographic characteristics also known to affect civic engagement. Figure 6.2 presents the results.[8]

For the most part, Mormons' congregational activity leads to more engagement. For each type of activity, the relationship between time spent on a church calling and participation starts off positive, peaks for the group spending between five to ten hours a week on church work, and then either levels off (voting, political engagement) or drops off slightly (community engagement). Thus, Mormons who are more involved in church work are more involved in politics and in the community, but only to a point. Eventually the clock runs out.

We have further evidence that Mormons' congregational voluntarism and the social networks formed through their service can lead to voluntarism beyond their congregations. In the Peculiar People Survey, we asked our respondents whether they had volunteered in their community over the past year. The

---

[8] These OLS regression models include the control variables described in note 7. The calling time variable was split into a set of dummy variables with no calling as the baseline. Because only ten respondents (2 percent of the sample) spent more than twenty hours a week on a calling, the top two categories were collapsed together. See Table 6A.1 in the appendix at the end of this chapter for the details of the models.

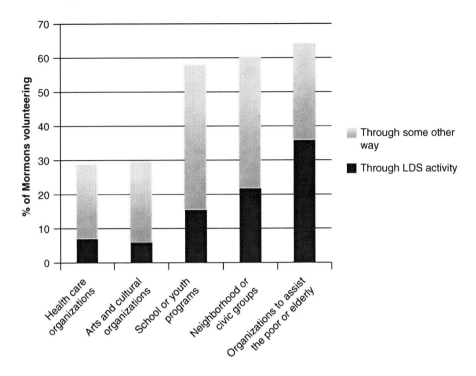

FIGURE 6.3. Mormon Volunteering Outside of Church
*Source:* Peculiar People Survey, 2012

question makes clear that we were interested in activity apart from a Church assignment:

*Besides from a church calling, in the past twelve months have you volunteered for any of the following kinds of organizations that are not associated with the LDS Church?*

*School or youth programs, organizations to assist the poor or elderly, neighborhood or civic groups, arts and cultural organizations, and health care organizations.*

*If yes, did you get involved through a LDS-sponsored activity, or through some other way?*

Seventy-two percent of Mormons report engaging in volunteer activity apart from their calling or congregation. As shown in Figure 6.3, many Mormons report becoming civically engaged through the LDS Church, although it is more common for some forms of voluntarism than others. For example, 36 percent of Mormons volunteer for an organization to help the poor and needy because they became involved through an LDS-sponsored activity (compared to 28 percent who volunteer for such an organization but got involved some other way). On the other hand, only 6 percent of Mormons volunteer for an arts or cultural organization because of an LDS-sponsored activity.

In sum, Mormons participate extensively in their congregations, but that voluntarism does not appear to put a brake on their civic engagement. If anything, it is an accelerator. Religious and civic activity reinforce one another. Congregational volunteering develops civic skills that can be put to use when volunteering in the community; civic engagement, in turn, teaches skills that can be employed when serving within the congregation. And the skills developed through community and congregational activities are ideal for political activity: running meetings, speaking in public, talking to neighbors, and so on.

Mormon civic and political engagement does not occur in an attitudinal vacuum, however. As we showed in Chapters 4 and 5, the Latter-day Saints are highly cohesive in terms of political attitudes, including partisanship, ideology, and especially positions on cultural issues, such as same-sex marriage. Indeed, on such issues a traditional (that is, conservative) position is "baked into" LDS Church teachings. Such cohesion facilitates mobilization because it can draw on commonly held values and goals, and in many cases, reduce the need for persuasion. But it is important to remember that Mormons are not monolithic when it comes to their political views.

As Chapter 3 showed, this peculiar pattern of opinion is rooted in the religious beliefs widely held among Mormons, particularly their deep respect for religious authority. This perspective can facilitate the mobilization and persuasion of Church members by LDS leaders. As described in Chapter 1, the LDS Church has a hierarchical leadership structure. At its apex is "the prophet" (Church president) who, Mormons believe, is the successor to Church founder Joseph Smith, carrying the same mantle as biblical prophets. Mormons often speak of "following the prophet." A popular LDS children's song even has it as its catchy refrain: "Follow the prophet, don't go astray; follow the prophet, he knows the way."

The idea of following the prophet also extends down through the hierarchy of Church leaders to the local level. Church members are periodically asked to "sustain" their ward leaders by a formal show of hands. This sustaining vote includes a commitment to follow and support their leaders. Typically, "following the prophet" translates into "living LDS teachings" within the tradition of continuing revelation. However, recall that Mormon theology contains within it a natural tension between following priesthood leaders and receiving personal revelation. Individual Mormons strike the balance between these competing priorities in different ways, potentially complicating the effort required to mobilize and persuade the laity.

THE SPARK

To return to our metaphor of dry kindling, Mormons' tight social networks, extensive civic skills, strong attitudinal cohesion, and deep respect for religious authority make them highly combustible when it comes to political activism. But for mobilization and persuasion to occur, the kindling must be ignited. Such a spark occurs when LDS leaders speak out on a political cause and encourage Church members to become involved.

While the prophet and other LDS leaders typically focus their sermons on the fundamentals of the faith, they have also explicitly said that political affairs are not off limits (Benson 1980; Hinckley 1999). For example, Ezra Taft Benson, Church President during the 1980s, spoke to this point directly:[9]

[T]he living prophet gets at what we need to know now, and the world prefers that prophets either be dead or worry about their own affairs. Some so-called experts of political science want the prophet to keep still on politics.... How we respond to the words of a living prophet when he tells us what we need to know, but would rather not hear, is a test of our faithfulness. (1980)

Although the norm in modern times is for LDS Church leaders to stay away from politics in their day-to-day activities and the formal policy is to steer clear of partisan politics completely, Church leaders occasionally speak out on what they describe as "moral issues." Such issues are typically cultural, such as gambling, abortion, gay marriage, pornography, drug use, and alcohol policy. During the heat of the Church's involvement in Proposition 22, the first California initiative on gay marriage in 2000, Church President Gordon B. Hinckley underscored that Church leaders consider it their responsibility to speak out when they see moral threats. "We regard it as not only our right but our duty to oppose those forces which we feel undermine the moral fiber of society" (Hinckley 1999).

Over the course of Mormon history, Mormons have been most likely to follow the prophet in politics when two conditions are met.[10] Condition 1 is public internal agreement among the leadership. On this matter, we build on John Zaller's theory of opinion formation discussed in Chapter 5, in which attitudes are a function of the "considerations" that individuals receive and accept, and thus have available to them when making political choices (1992; 1994). Considerations come from many sources, but those from religious leaders are likely to be impactful – especially when, as Mormons believe, their leaders speak for God. If LDS leaders at the highest levels send mixed signals about their preferred course on a political question, collectively, Mormons are not likely to follow. Some will absorb conflicting information, while others will pick and choose among the leaders to justify their own political perspective. Conversely, when Church leaders are unified, Mormons are much more likely to respond.

Note that there was once a time when LDS leaders disagreed publicly with one another, both on theology (Bergera 2002) and politics (Prince and Wright 2005). However, since the move in the 1960s to coordinate, unify, and simplify Church doctrine and materials (known as "correlation"), disagreements have occurred behind closed doors. The strong norm in the modern LDS Church is for the

---

[9] Note that Benson was not the prophet at the time that he delivered these remarks. He was, however, next in line to become the Church's President.
[10] This section draws upon Campbell and Monson (2003).

leaders to speak with a unified voice (Alexander 1996). Thus, exceptions to Condition 1 are to be found only in the past.

Condition 2 is that Church leaders offer an official endorsement of a political issue. Such endorsements are most commonly done via an official policy statement in the form of a letter from the Church's First Presidency that is sent to all local leaders and read to members during Sunday worship meetings. Other avenues, in roughly descending order of significance, might include a statement by the prophet in the official proceedings of the semiannual worldwide general conference of the Church, a press release invoking the First Presidency, speeches by other general authorities in general conference, an official Church press release from the public affairs office that does not reference Church leaders by name, a speech by a Church leader in another setting (a regional conference, Church satellite broadcast, or speech at Brigham Young University), and so on. As the message moves further down this rough ladder of "official-ness," the potential exists for individual Mormons to resist Church leaders by rationalizing that the Church does not really have an official position that they must follow.[11]

We can see how these two conditions work in tandem in Table 6.1, which displays the percentage of Mormons voting for a series of ballot propositions in

TABLE 6.1. *Percentage Voting for the LDS Church Position on Utah Ballot Propositions*

| Year | Issue | Official public endorsement | Consensus Among Leaders | Mormon vote, EI estimate | Standard error |
|------|-------|------------------------------|--------------------------|---------------------------|----------------|
| 1933 | Prohibition | Yes | No | 55.0 | 3.0 |
| 1968 | "Liquor-by-the-drink" | Yes | Yes | 71.4 | 3.3 |
| 1984 | Cable TV programming | No | No | 49.8 | 4.6 |
| 1992 | Off-track betting | Yes | Yes | 76.3 | 3.4 |

*Notes:* Results shown are the estimated percentages voting in favor of the "Mormon" position In 1933 this was against repealing Prohibition (a "no" vote on the referendum). In 1968 this was against the relaxation of Utah's liquor laws (a "no" vote on the referendum). In 1984 this was in favor of limiting content of cable TV broadcasts (a "yes" vote on the referendum). In 1992 this was against the legalization of pari-mutuel wagering (a "no" vote on the referendum).
*Source:* Adapted from Campbell and Monson (2003)

---

[11] In addition to the message source, the frequency of the message is also important. In a recent explanation of how Church doctrine is promulgated, D. Todd Christofferson, a current member of the Church's Quorum of the Twelve Apostles, emphasizes the centrality of the Church President or prophet to official Church doctrine. Then he says, "At the same time it should be remembered that not every statement made by a Church leader, past or present, necessarily constitutes doctrine. It is commonly understood in the Church that a statement made by one leader on a single occasion often represents a personal, though well-considered, opinion, not meant to be official or binding for the whole Church" (2012, 88).

Utah from 1933 to 1992. The analysis uses county-level data for voting and religion in Utah, using the statistical method of ecological inference (EI) to estimate the proportion of Mormons who supported the Church's position (see Chapter 4 for a similar analysis of partisan voting).[12]

The first example is a 1933 vote on the 21st Amendment to the U.S. Constitution – the repeal of Prohibition. While Church President Heber J. Grant spoke out publicly against repeal, other Church authorities held contrary and changing positions. So while repeal had the prophet's endorsement, there was no consensus among LDS leaders. Without a unified leadership, only an estimated 55 percent of Mormons voted against repeal, producing the unusual outcome of Utah – a state full of teetotalers – becoming the decisive thirty-sixth state to repeal Prohibition.[13]

The politics of alcohol control appeared in a 1968 referendum vote to allow bars and restaurants to sell "liquor by the drink." This time the Church both took an official position – opposing the proposal – *and* Church leaders were unified. As Table 6.1 shows, an estimated 71 percent of Mormons voted with the Church.

In 1984, we see an example where Church leaders had a unified position, but there was no official endorsement of a particular ballot initiative. Had it passed, this initiative would have restricted certain kinds of cable television programming. The LDS Church is staunchly opposed to salacious media, but without a clear official endorsement, the initiative only received the support of an estimated 50 percent of Mormons.[14]

The opposite conditions held on a 1992 initiative to legalize some forms of horse-race gambling in Utah.[15] LDS Church leaders were unified against the measure and there was an official endorsement to that effect. This time, an estimated 76 percent of Mormons voted in line with the Church's position against the initiative.[16]

---

[12] Gary King (1997) provides an overview of the EI technique. Analysis of the full results from Table 6.1 is available in Campbell and Monson (2003).

[13] Technically, the popular vote in Utah elected delegates to a state ratifying convention that then voted to ratify the 21st Amendment.

[14] This is a tough test of Condition 2, because Church leaders did speak out during the campaign in general terms about lewdness in the media, even making specific references to cable television. However, these statements did not reference the ballot initiative in particular (Haight 1984).

[15] Unlike in 1968, the Church's opposition was not part of the official campaign materials. Instead, the Church issued an official statement opposing gambling just before the 1992 state legislative session where a similar gambling proposal was considered (Harrie 1992). Once the proposal made it to the ballot, local LDS leaders from across the state attended meetings on May 31, 1992, where Church leaders emphasized their opposition to gambling and asked for help in mobilizing opposition to the initiative (Harrie and Stack 1992).

[16] There are still other examples of LDS political mobilization, including ballot initiative endorsements on state lotteries in Idaho (1986 and 1988) and Arizona (1998) (Campbell and Monson 2003), a 2004 gay marriage constitutional amendment vote in Utah (Monson et al. 2006), and the

CASE STUDIES OF LDS CHURCH-LED ACTIVISM

Three case studies of political activism led by LDS Church leaders illustrate the spark that ignites the dry kindling. These cases show a mix of mobilization and persuasion. First, Mormons' support in 2008 for Proposition 8 to ban same-sex marriage in California shows the capacity of church leaders to mobilize on behalf of a conservative issue position, with only modest efforts at persuasion. Second, the opposition to the MX Missile in the 1980s shows the capacity of Church leaders to persuade Mormons contrary to a conservative issue position. Third, support for immigration reform in 2010–11 shows the capacity of Church leaders to persuade Mormons in favor of a liberal issue position.

### Case 1: Support for Proposition 8

California's Proposition 8 was a ballot initiative to enact a state constitutional amendment to ban gay marriage, which would overturn a decision by the California Supreme Court to allow same-sex unions. That decision negated a previous ballot initiative, Proposition 22, which created a statutory ban on gay marriage. In 2000, Mormons were also heavily involved in the campaign to pass Proposition 22 (Campbell and Monson 2007).

In June of 2008, the large-scale mobilization of Mormons began with a letter from the First Presidency, read in the worship services of every LDS congregation in California. The letter clearly defined the doctrinal rationale for the Church's position – the traditional family – and then included this call to political action:

> We ask that you do all you can to support the proposed constitutional amendment by donating of your means and time to assure that marriage in California is legally defined as being between a man and a woman. Our best efforts are required to preserve the sacred institution of marriage. (Church of Jesus Christ of Latter-day Saints 2008a)

Thus, the letter included some persuasion but, given that most Mormons were already opposed to gay marriage, was focused on mobilization. LDS leaders in California, spurred into action by the First Presidency letter and by additional encouragement from Church headquarters, urged local members to get heavily involved in the campaign.[17] The request to do "all you can," combined with opposition to gay marriage by most Mormons led to a vigorous response by many rank-and-file Church members.

Details from the three-phase plan drawn up by the "State LDS Grassroots Director" and campaign pollster Gary Lawrence illustrate the breadth of the

---

International Women's Year Conference held in Salt Lake City in 1977 (Huefner 1978). In each case, Mormons responded energetically to an official unified call to action.

[17] For example, a satellite broadcast with Church leaders from Salt Lake City was held on October 8, 2008, for all California Mormons, to encourage their participation in the campaign.

LDS mobilization efforts. The plans included a sophisticated database to identify every California voter as a supporter or opponent, telephone calls, and Saturday neighborhood walks. Undecided voters and soft "no" voters were then targeted for persuasion efforts. (The full text of the Gary Lawrence memo is included in the appendix to this chapter).[18]

Mormon volunteers formed the backbone of a grassroots campaign that closely resembled the organizational structure of the LDS Church in California. There were seventeen "area coordinators," covering areas that roughly corresponded with the geographically defined LDS missions in the state. Below them, there were "regional coordinators," recruited to align with Mormon stakes, and "zip code coordinators" in areas that approximately matched the geographic boundaries of Mormon wards (Lawrence 2008). This ensured that the entire state of California had grassroots leadership in rough proportion to the distribution of Mormons throughout the state. In his memo to volunteers, Lawrence makes several references to LDS leaders or terminology, including asking the "zip code coordinators" to "find someone in your ward or stake who could help out," a sign that he was speaking to a largely Mormon audience of volunteers, at least in early August. These efforts reveal the extensive social networks and civic skills of rank-and-file Mormons. Note that the kind of "shoe leather" politicking used by the campaign for Proposition 8 closely resembles the experience of LDS missionaries – face-to-face contact on the doorsteps of strangers.

Jeff Flint, a co–campaign manager for Protect Marriage (the pro–Proposition 8 organization) estimated that Mormons constituted 80 to 90 percent of the volunteers who did the early door-to-door canvassing (McKinley and Johnson 2008), even though they are only 2 percent of the state's population (Grammich 2012). Elsewhere he estimated that more than 30,000 volunteers turned out on the first weekend of canvassing in August 2008, a much higher turnout than campaign officials expected. On Election Day, there were 100,000 volunteers staffing precinct-level get-out-the-vote efforts, a large portion of whom were LDS. While members of other religious groups, including Catholics and evangelicals, also campaigned on behalf of Proposition 8, Mormons became a critical component of the coalition by participating in a substantial and sustained way over a sophisticated three-month campaign (McKinley and Johnson 2008; Schubert and Flint 2009a; Schubert and Flint 2009b).

Mormons in and out of California also responded to the call from Church leaders to give of their means. The Protect Marriage campaign estimated that Mormons gave about half of the nearly $40 million raised to support Proposition 8 (McKinley and Johnson 2008; Schubert and Flint 2009b).

---

[18] The memo was obtained from http://yesonprop8.blogspot.com in June 2009. At the time, the blog was open to the public, but it has since been taken down. For full text, see the appendix at the end of this chapter.

Mormon leaders tracked donations by Mormons by bundling them and then sending them to the "Protect Marriage" campaign in batches (Schoofs 2008).[19]

Proposition 8 was close, but it passed with 52 percent of the vote. LDS involvement in the campaign caused a firestorm of controversy, more so than any previous case of Mormon mobilization. The high level of national attention was no doubt due to the fact that it was a close contest regarding a high-profile issue on which attitudes are rapidly changing. In the wake of Proposition 8, there were boycotts of businesses owned by Mormons, protests at LDS temples, and "shunning" of Mormons by their neighbors (Gehrke 2008; Kuruvila 2008; Riccardi 2008; Stack and Ravitz 2008).

However, the Church's Proposition 8 campaign did not persuade or mobilize every Mormon. The Church's public opposition to gay marriage has caused much anguish among some Latter-day Saints, who are torn between loyalty to their faith and their personal support for gay rights. Some Mormons have been unable to reconcile this conflict and have left the Church because of Proposition 8 (Brooks 2012; C. Martin et al. 2008). Their anguish was no doubt magnified by the infrequency of such political mobilization by the Church. As we will discuss further below, the rarity of the Church's mobilization efforts accentuates their effectiveness among many Mormons, while also alienating others.

## Case 2: Opposition to the MX Missile

In the midst of the Cold War nuclear arms race, the MX Missile system offered a way to conceal missiles from the Soviet Union by hiding a few hundred missiles in a few thousand shelters connected through a series of tracks built throughout the desert of western Utah and eastern Nevada. The idea was that shuttling the missiles around the desert would keep the Soviets from knowing which shelters actually contained a missile and thus preserving some from a first strike. Early on, Utah residents, including Mormons, expressed opposition to the proposal. As Table 6.2 indicates, in an April 1980 poll, 64 percent of Utah Mormons opposed deploying the MX Missile in the state.

Then Utah Mormons' opinions began to shift, probably nudged by President Ronald Reagan's support for placing the MX Missile in Utah,[20] as well as the fact that Utah's all-Republican congressional delegation was in favor. By March

---

[19] During the campaign an effort was widely reported by a group named "Mormons for 8" to sift through the California campaign-finance disclosure documents and use a myriad of online and other sources to publicly identify Mormon donors to the Proposition 8 campaign. The group's website no longer exists and the effort was limited to donations more than $1000, but the proportion of total campaign funds that "Mormons for 8" estimated came from Mormons is roughly consistent with the nearly 50 percent reported publicly by campaign officials. The LDS Church itself donated about $190,000, mostly through in-kind contributions, and was fined after the campaign by the state of California because a portion of the filings were late (California Fair Political Practices Commission 2010; Church of Jesus Christ of Latter-day Saints 2009b).

[20] Eighty percent of Mormons in Utah voted for Reagan in 1980 (see Chapter 4).

TABLE 6.2. *MX Missile Polls of Utah Mormons*

|  | Favor | Oppose | No opinion |
|---|---|---|---|
| April 1980 (n = 400) | 32% | 61% | 7% |
| March 1981 (n = 600) | 44% | 46% | 9% |
| September 1981 (n = 600) | 25% | 67% | 7% |

*Note:* Does not total to 100 percent due to rounding
Question wording: "From what you know or have heard, do you favor or oppose the Air Force plan for deployment of the MX missile project in the desert area of Utah and Nevada?"
*Source: Deseret News* polls conducted by Dan Jones and Associates (*Deseret News* 1980; Wade 1981a; Wade 1981b)

1981, statewide polling showed opinion among Mormons split about evenly (see Table 6.2). The LDS Church remained publicly silent on the issue, but the movement in public opinion could have contributed to a Christmas message from the Church's First Presidency that decried nuclear weapons and the nuclear arms race more generally and called "upon heads of government . . . to sit down and reason together to resolve their concerns" (Church of Jesus Christ of Latter-day Saints 1980c).[21] The 1981 First Presidency Easter message likewise condemned nuclear arms in general terms, but without mentioning the MX Missile specifically (Church of Jesus Christ of Latter-day Saints 1980b; Firmage 1983).

With momentum building toward building the MX in Utah, the First Presidency upped the ante, releasing a statement on May 5, 1981, that went beyond the general statements in previous messages. This time, they specifically opposed the MX Missile (Church of Jesus Christ of Latter-day Saints 1981). Their statement appears to have had the intended effect. By September 1981, opposition to the MX among Utah Mormons had surged back to 67 percent. However, it is difficult to isolate the impact of Church leaders on this issue because in the months between the statement and the poll, some Utah political leaders also came out against the MX Missile (Hildreth 1984).

The case of the MX missile represents a good test of LDS leaders' ability to persuade Church members, by shifting Mormons' opinion against the grain of their conservatism on foreign policy questions. However, one could argue that the MX Missile case is not a pure case for leftward movement in opinion because there was also a strong dose of self-interest: Mormons support a hawkish foreign policy in the abstract, but the very concrete prospect of living close to a mobile system of nuclear weaponry is another matter.

---

[21] An excerpt from the Christmas message reads, "We are dismayed by the growing tensions among the nations, and the unrestricted building of arsenals of war, including huge and threatening nuclear weaponry. Nuclear war, when unleashed on a scale for which the nations are preparing, spares no living thing within the perimeter of its initial destructive force, and sears and maims and kills wherever its pervasive cloud reaches."

## Case 3: Support for Immigration Reform

In early 2010, the Arizona legislature enacted a law – sponsored by an LDS legislator – that was at the time the country's strictest effort at immigration enforcement. Soon after, a Mormon state representative in Utah proposed a similar bill, to be taken up by the state legislature in early 2011. Around the same time, a group of religious and business leaders released a statement on immigration called the "Utah Compact."[22] In sharp contrast to the hard line on enforcement enacted in Arizona and proposed in Utah, the Utah Compact articulates a moderate set of principles designed to find common ground in the contentious debate over immigration. It refers to the need for "reasonable policies," opposes "policies that unnecessarily separate families," and says, "Utah should always be a place that welcomes people of goodwill." The LDS Church did not sign the Utah Compact, but did release a statement the same day endorsing its principles (Church of Jesus Christ of Latter-day Saints 2010b).

Between October 2010 and January 2011 – precisely the time period of Utah's immigration debate – a panel survey of Utah voters showed that Utahns' attitudes on immigration softened. In particular, "active" Mormons shifted toward a more moderate opinion on immigration – a half point on a five-point scale.[23] The case of immigration reform is a good test of LDS leaders' ability to persuade Church members, in that it shifts Mormons' opinion against a conservative issue position. One could argue that immigration is a better case for gauging leftward movement in opinion than the MX Missile because self-interest may go the other way: Mormons support immigrants in the abstract, but the costs of illegal immigrants in the Mountain West are another matter. Of course, it is difficult to separate the effects of the various endorsers of the Utah Compact from each other. Prominent political, business, and religious leaders either signed or endorsed the moderate stance, making it difficult to isolate the effect of the LDS Church on voters.[24]

### A CLOSER LOOK AT CHURCH-LED PERSUASION

The case studies of Church-led political efforts reveal strong evidence for the mobilization of rank-and-file Mormons, but less conclusive evidence for the

---

[22] See http://www.theutahcompact.com/ for the full text (accessed October 7, 2013).

[23] This analysis is from the October 2010 and January 2011 Utah Voter Polls; see http://utahvoter poll.org (accessed October 7, 2013). This result controls for other possible influences, such as partisan identification, ideology, gender, age, income, and education. For a complete analysis see Monson and Stauss (2011).

[24] Two important epilogues are worth noting here. First, the Church made increasingly supportive statements of a moderate stance on immigration in the Utah Legislature during the 2011 legislative session. Eventually, statements named a particular bill number as being consistent with the Church's principles and the Church's "Presiding Bishop" was a prominent figure at the bill signing ceremony after the session in the spring of 2011. Second, Arizona state senator Russell Pearce (the original sponsor of Arizona's strict law) was eventually defeated in a recall election by another, more moderate, Mormon Republican.

persuasion of Church members. To further explore the persuasive capacity of LDS leaders, we designed a survey experiment as part of the Peculiar People Survey. The experiment tests the effect of LDS leaders' views on the political opinions of rank-and-file Mormons (Mutz 2011). (Recall that this survey included only Mormons among the respondents.) Specifically, our experiment answers three questions:

## On what type of issue are LDS leaders most persuasive?

Which has the greatest effect on Mormons' opinions: when the Church takes a conservative position or a liberal one? On the one hand, perhaps the general conservatism of Mormons means that a conservative stance by the Church reinforces their predispositions and moves them further to the right. Or maybe Mormons are already so conservative that there is no more room to move. On the other hand, just as "man bites dog" makes news, a liberal position by LDS leaders is likely to catch Mormons' attention, perhaps leading to persuasion. It could also be that Mormons' conservatism runs so deep that they disregard the Church's position, instead choosing their ideology over their religion.

In our experiment, we test how Mormons respond to actual statements made by the LDS Church on three issues. On one issue – opposition to gambling – the LDS position is conservative. But on the other two issues – immigration and nondiscrimination toward gays and lesbians – the Church has taken a more liberal stance. The Church supports a relatively permissive immigration policy, buttressed by the pro-immigration sentiment of many Mormons, owing to their missionary service (see Chapter 5). Thus, a more liberal Church position on immigration would presumably not come as a total surprise, at least to attentive Church members. More unexpected, perhaps, is the Church's support of an antidiscrimination law to protect gays and lesbians. In 2009, with the bruises from the Proposition 8 campaign still fresh, Salt Lake City proposed an ordinance banning discrimination in housing and employment against gays and lesbians. In a move that surprised many, the LDS Church publicly endorsed the proposed law by sending a spokesperson to the city council meeting to read a statement in support (Canham, Jensen, and Winters 2009).

## What type of message is most persuasive?

Given that LDS leaders are sometimes more specific, and sometimes less so, how much specificity is required to move Mormons' opinions? Recall that in the case of the MX missile, the historical record suggests that only when the First Presidency spoke directly did Mormon opinion appear to move. Similarly, we have also seen that Mormons are most likely to follow their leaders when the Church provides an official endorsement of a political position. Accordingly, we test the limits of that condition by varying the Church statements. Some statements endorse general principles while others endorse a particular political position.

Importantly, we devised the "treatments" for the experiment using actual language taken from LDS publications or statements on the issues. This enhances the realism and external validity of the treatments.[25] The control group was given a question where no LDS position was mentioned; the general treatment consisted of an LDS position phrased in broad terms; and the specific treatment made explicit reference to a policy position taken by the Church.[26] Table 6.3 contains the full question wording for the three conditions for each issue.

## What type of Mormon is most persuadable by Church leaders?

Recall from Chapter 3 that Mormons vary in their view of authority within the Church. For some, "following the prophet" takes precedence over personal inspiration. Therefore, we might expect that authority-minded Mormons would be the most likely to heed political statements from the Church. But this is a tough test, as Mormons high on the Authority Index are often highly conservative as well – the hardest case for the Church's political persuasion. Does following the prophet mean overriding personal political predispositions?

The design of the experiment was straightforward. Respondents were assigned to receive either the control, general, or specific Church statements. After being presented with the statement, they were asked to express their opinion on a 100-point scale.[27]

---

[25] It also avoids any ethical issues. Because all of the information we provided was taken from actual statements from the LDS Church, there was no deception and thus no need for debriefing.

[26] Each respondent received all three issues, but was randomly assigned to receive either the control, general, or specific version for all three. In addition, respondents received the three issues in random order.

[27] Because our concern here is primarily internal validity (or unpacking the causation between Church statements and attitudes) we include all of the cases available in the Peculiar People Survey (n = 609) rather than limiting ourselves to the 500 cases that were demographically "matched" to the LDS population. The methodology employed by YouGov/Polimetrix, the firm that conducted the Peculiar People Survey, entails deliberately drawing an oversample of the relevant population and then using an algorithm to match the demographic profile of the sample to the population, which means that some respondents end up omitted from the final sample (see Data Appendix for more on the matching procedure). Importantly, our main findings are unchanged if we limit the analysis to the 500 matched cases. We also included a validation check to see if respondents in the treatment condition were more likely to perceive the Church's position on each issue. After receiving the three issues in random order and expressing their own attitudes, respondents were asked to choose a position for the LDS Church on each issue on a 100-point scale with endpoints labeled as opposite sides of the issue debate. For example, given the language used for the Church position on immigration, we would expect respondents in either treatment condition to rate the Church's position closer to "Should be allowed to work in the U.S. without necessarily becoming U.S. citizens" than "Should be sent back to their home countries." Likewise, those in the treatment conditions should rate the Church's position on gays and lesbians as closer to "Should be legally protected from discrimination in housing and employment" than "Should not...." And for gambling, respondents in either treatment condition should rate the church closer to "Should not be legally permitted" than "Should...." Both the general and specific treatments produce a statistically significant effect in the desired direction for all three issues. In other words, our treatments are strong enough to shift perceptions about the LDS position on each issue.

TABLE 6.3. *Experimental Treatments and Control Question Wording*

**Gambling**
*Control Group*
"Some state and local governments have proposed laws to legalize slot machines and other forms of casino gambling. Some people oppose this idea because they believe it would increase crime."
*General Treatment*
Control intro language + "In response to the debate on the issue, the Church of Jesus Christ of Latter-day Saints issued the following:
'Experience has clearly shown gambling to be harmful to the human spirit, financially destructive of individuals and families, and detrimental to the moral climate of communities.'"
*Specific Treatment*
Control intro language + "In response to the debate on the issue, the Church of Jesus Christ of Latter-day Saints issued the following:
'The Church of Jesus Christ of Latter-day Saints opposes gambling in its various forms. We regard efforts to legalize gambling as a moral issue and unalterably oppose such proposals on grounds of private and public morality, as well as a threat to the cultivation and maintenance of strong family and community values.'"
*Asked of All:*
"To what extent do you favor or oppose legalized slot machines and other forms of casino gambling?"

**Immigration**
*Control Group*
"An important issue facing the country is immigration. One proposal would allow illegal immigrants to obtain a guest worker permit after paying a fine and passing a background check. Some people oppose this idea because it would only encourage illegal immigration."
*Immigration: General Treatment*
Control intro language + "In response to the debate on the issue, the Church of Jesus Christ of Latter-day Saints issued the following:
'What to do with the estimated 12 million undocumented immigrants now residing in various states within the United States is the biggest challenge in the immigration debate. The bedrock moral issue for The Church of Jesus Christ of Latter-day Saints is how we treat each other as children of God.'"
*Immigration: Specific Treatment*
Control intro language + "In response to the debate on the issue, the Church of Jesus Christ of Latter-day Saints issued the following:
'The Church of Jesus Christ of Latter-day Saints is concerned that any state legislation that only contains enforcement provisions is likely to fall short of the high moral standard of treating each other as children of God.... The Church supports an approach where undocumented immigrants are allowed to square themselves with the law and continue to work without this necessarily leading to citizenship.'"
*Asked of All:*
"To what extent do you favor or oppose a law that would allow illegal immigrants to obtain a guest worker permit after paying a fine and passing a background check?"

*(continued)*

TABLE 6.3 (*continued*)

---

**Nondiscrimination toward Gays and Lesbians**
*Control Group*
"Some state and local governments have proposed laws to prohibit discrimination in
    housing and employment based on sexual orientation. Some people oppose this idea
    because they believe it would show approval of homosexuality."
*General Treatment*
Control language + "In response to the debate on the issue, the Church of Jesus Christ of
    Latter-day Saints issued the following:
'The Church believes in human dignity, in treating others with respect even when we
    disagree – in fact, especially when we disagree.'"
*Specific Treatment*
Control intro language + "In response to the debate on the issue, the Church of Jesus
    Christ of Latter-day Saints issued the following:
'The Church believes in human dignity, in treating others with respect, and in the right of
    people to have a roof over their heads and the right to work without being
    discriminated against.'"
*Asked of All:*
"To what extent do you favor or oppose a law to prohibit discrimination in housing and
    employment based on sexual orientation?"

---

*Note:* In each case, the favor/oppose question was answered on a 1 to 100-point sliding scale
with "strongly oppose" at 1 and "strongly favor" at 100. For immigration and nondiscrimination,
answers closer to "strongly favor" are more consistent with the Church's statements. To be
consistent in our analysis we reversed the coding on the gambling question so that higher values
were also more consistent with the Church's gambling statements

Figure 6.4 presents the results as an average on the 100-point favor/oppose
scale for each of the three issues presented to the control and two treatment
groups. We have coded the responses consistently, so that the LDS position is at
the higher end of the scale.

Mormons are more likely to oppose gambling upon receiving the general
Church statement, moving 7 points on the 100-point scale (a statistically significant effect), but there is no effect for the specific statement. On immigration
we see movement – statistically significant, but still relatively modest – toward
the Church position on both the general and specific statements. Each produces
an effect of roughly the same size (8–10 points).[28] Last, but certainly not least, on
the nondiscrimination statement we again see a modest effect for the general
treatment, but this time the specific treatment has a much larger effect, moving
attitudes about 20 points on the 100-point scale toward the Church's position.

[28] A look back to the wording of the general and specific treatments in Table 6.3 suggests that despite
    our best efforts to find general and specific treatments on immigration, the two may be more
    similar than different. Both make references to treating each other "as children of God."

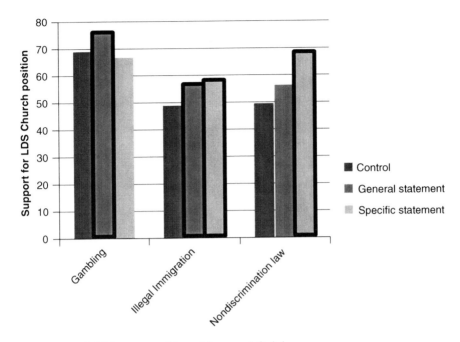

FIGURE 6.4. LDS Statements Move Mormons' Opinions
*Source:* Peculiar People Survey, 2012. A black border represents a statistically significant effect compared to the control ($p < 0.05$, one-tailed test)

This is the clearest evidence that a specific position, using language from actual Church statements, has a powerful effect on Mormons' opinions.

The next step is to plumb the results to see if Church statements have a greater effect on more authority-minded Mormons.[29] Figures 6.5 and 6.6 show how Mormons in the highest and lowest quartiles of the Authority Index (introduced in Chapter 3) react to the antidiscrimination and immigration statements. First, note that those in the lowest quartile start off about 10 points higher in the control group. In other words, those lower on the Authority scale start with significantly more liberal attitudes about discrimination (and thus less room for movement on the issue). Those highest on the Authority Index begin with more conservative views, and respond more strongly to the treatment. When low-authority Mormons hear the specific treatment, they move about 14 points toward the Church's position on nondiscrimination – that is, in a liberal direction. However, high-authority Mormons move a whopping 24 points. On

---

[29] Recall that the Authority Index measures Mormons' degree of obedience to the institutional Church using two related constructs: the tension between reliance on Church authority versus personal revelation and the degree to which Mormons are willing to question Church teachings.

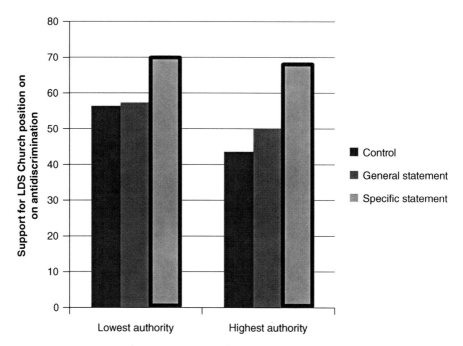

FIGURE 6.5. On Antidiscrimination, High-Authority Mormons End Up in the Same Place as Low-Authority Mormons
*Source:* Peculiar People Survey, 2012. A black border represents a statistically significant effect compared to the control ($p < 0.05$, one-tailed test)

immigration, low-authority Mormons move slightly toward the Church position upon receiving the general statement and modestly away if given the specific statement – in other words, the effect is essentially a wash. However, high-authority Mormons move toward the Church position.

But what about highly conservative Mormons?[30] Figures 6.7 and 6.8 display how self-identified political conservatives respond to both the immigration and antidiscrimination statements. Note that the low-authority Mormon conservatives are not persuaded by any information to modify their immigration views. For the specific treatment, the direction even appears to reverse, although the movement is not statistically significant from the control. Notably, high-authority conservatives do significantly modify their views in favor of the Church's position on immigration. In Figure 6.6 we see that among all high-authority Mormons the

[30] Conservatives are identified using the following question: "Thinking politically and socially, how would you describe your own general outlook?" Conservatives include those who answer "very conservative" or "moderately conservative."

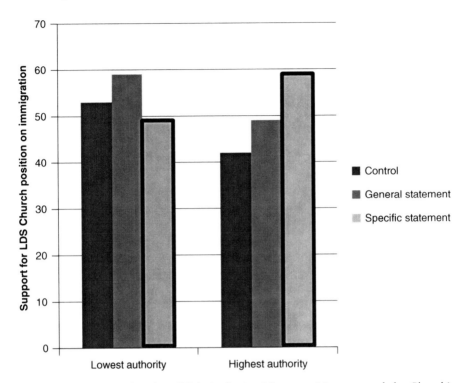

FIGURE 6.6. On Immigration, High-Authority Mormons Move toward the Church's Position

*Source:* Peculiar People Survey, 2012. A black border represents a statistically significant effect compared to the control ($p < 0.05$, one-tailed test)

effect is about 17 points from the control to the specific treatment; among conservative high-authority Mormons, the effect is still 14 points. Conservative Mormons who rank high on the Authority Index place Church authority above political ideology, but for those who are less authority-minded, ideology seems to trump authority.

In contrast, the resistance on the immigration issue among conservatives does not hold on antidiscrimination. When the same conservatives are examined on the nondiscrimination treatments, the high-authority and low-authority Mormons move in tandem. Apparently, strongly held prior beliefs do not inhibit adjustment on the issue of nondiscrimination toward gays and lesbians the way they do for undocumented immigrants.

With these results, we can answer our three questions about Mormon persuasion. We have seen that LDS leaders are most persuasive when they take a liberal position, given the conservatism of Mormons. Statements that mention a specific political position by the Church are typically more persuasive than

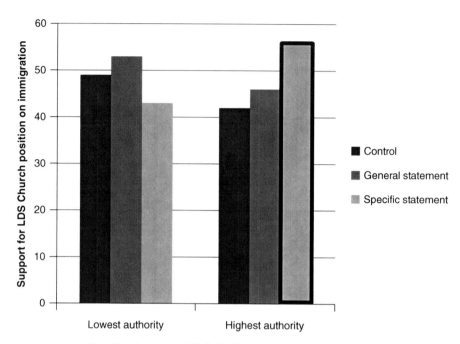

FIGURE 6.7. On Immigration, High-Authority Conservatives Move toward the Church's Position (Conservatives Only)
*Source:* Peculiar People Survey, 2012. A black border represents a statistically significant effect compared to the control ($p < 0.05$, one-tailed test)

general statements of principles. Finally, Mormons who have the strongest adherence to authority are most consistently persuaded by the Church.

These results also suggest that the combination of LDS leaders' capacity for both mobilization and persuasion could channel Mormon political activism in unexpected directions – to the left rather than the right. For example, what would happen if the LDS Church mustered its members on behalf of immigration reform, as it has in opposition to gay marriage? For now, however, such a scenario remains speculative, as there is no real-world example of full-throated Mormon mobilization on anything but a politically conservative issue.

CONCLUSION

This chapter has demonstrated that under the right conditions, Mormons follow their leaders. Within the sacred tabernacle, Mormons are like dry kindling, able to be ignited by the spark from Church leaders. Their tight-knit social networks, extensive civic skills, high issue cohesion, and deep respect for religious authority make for a highly combustible mix. When LDS leaders speak with one voice,

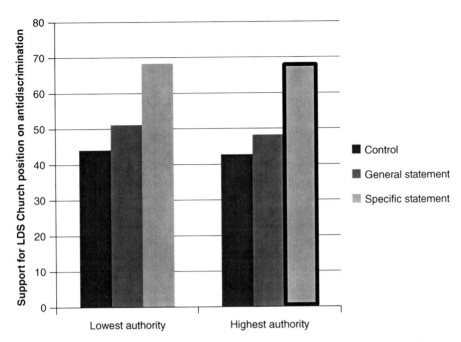

FIGURE 6.8. On Antidiscrimination, Both High- and Low-Authority-Minded Conservatives Move toward the Church Position (Conservatives Only)
*Source:* Peculiar People Survey, 2012. A black border represents a statistically significant effect compared to the control ($p < 0.05$, one-tailed test)

operate through official channels, and give specific directions on political issues, Mormons respond – with alacrity. This response can include a high level of political mobilization as well as significant persuasion. Indeed, LDS leaders can persuade their members to take a political position that runs counter to their ideological inclinations. This effect is the largest for Mormons with the strongest belief in adhering to religious authority.

However, the metaphor of dry kindling is meant to connote one other essential component of Mormon political mobilization – its infrequency. In Chapter 4, we saw that Mormons hear very few political statements from the pulpit, fewer than any other religious group. While this chapter has detailed cases of mobilization and persuasion by LDS leaders, these examples warrant attention precisely because they are unusual. The rarity of calls to political action means that when Mormons do receive political direction from Church leaders, it gets their attention. Local Church leaders likely put more energy into building support because the sheer novelty heightens its perceived importance. Many Church members respond to the call, but others are alienated.

In other words, just as kindling ignites easily because it has not yet been exposed to fire, Mormon mobilization is intense because the Church does not often call for political activity. In this regard, it is worth noting that intensive mobilization for community service – such as disaster relief – is also relatively rare among Mormons. Burning kindling quickly extinguishes; repeated appeals by LDS leaders bring diminishing returns. For Mormons high on the Authority Index, frequent mobilization could exhaust the ready supply of fuel to burn. For Mormons low on the Authority Index, recurring political action could have the dampening effect of a good steady rainstorm.

Thus far, we have seen how Mormons are distinctive (Part I) and what that distinctiveness means for their political behavior (Part II). In Part III, we change the perspective by looking at how Mormons are perceived by other Americans, and how such perceptions matter politically.

## CHAPTER 6 APPENDIX

TABLE 6.A.1. *OLS Models for Engagement Indices*

| VARIABLES | Voting Index | Political Index | Community Index |
|---|---|---|---|
| Calling (< 1 hour/week) | −0.08 | −0.11 | 0.53 |
| | (0.15) | (0.21) | (0.37) |
| Calling (1–4 hours/week) | 0.23** | 0.23 | 1.31*** |
| | (0.10) | (0.15) | (0.26) |
| Calling (5–10 hours/week) | 0.38*** | 0.59*** | 2.29*** |
| | (0.13) | (0.18) | (0.33) |
| Calling (>11 hours/week) | 0.28* | 0.52** | 1.62*** |
| | (0.17) | (0.24) | (0.43) |
| Income | 0.10*** | 0.11*** | 0.22*** |
| | (0.03) | (0.04) | (0.07) |
| Gender (Female) | −0.27*** | −0.37*** | −0.07 |
| | (0.08) | (0.12) | (0.21) |
| Education | 0.09*** | 0.09* | 0.17*** |
| | (0.03) | (0.05) | (0.08) |
| Age | 0.02*** | 0.01** | −0.01 |
| | (0.00) | (0.00) | (0.01) |
| Hispanic | 0.07 | −0.35 | 0.18 |
| | (0.21) | (0.30) | (0.54) |
| White | 0.45* | 0.40 | −0.12 |
| | (0.24) | (0.33) | (0.59) |
| Constant | 0.99*** | 0.01 | 0.52 |
| | (0.31) | (0.43) | (0.77) |
| Observations | 475 | 474 | 473 |

Standard errors in parentheses
*** $p < 0.01$, ** $p < 0.05$, * $p < 0.1$
*Source:* Peculiar People Survey, 2012

PROPOSITION 8 STRATEGY MEMO FROM GARY LAWRENCE

*This memo was obtained from http://yesonprop8.blogspot.com/2008/08/gary-lawrence-grassroots-coordinator.html (accessed June 16, 2009). At the time, the blog was open to the public.*

## UPDATE

TO: All Area Directors, Regional Coordinators and Zip Code Supervisors
  FROM: Gary Lawrence, State LDS Grassroots Director
  DATE: August 7, 2008 / 5:00p
  PLEASE FORWARD THIS UPDATE IMMEDIATELY TO ALL REGIONAL COORDINATORS AND TO ALL ZIP CODE SUPERVISORS
  Thanks to all of you for your great work as we organize our grassroots efforts in this critically important endeavor, one that Elder Lance Wickman has aptly called the "Gettysburg of the culture war." Thanks, too, for the questions you have asked. This update should address all those I'm aware of. Please send me others if these instructions and answers are not clear enough.

## SCHEDULE

Phase One – Identification. We have three "Walk Saturdays" planned for this phase: August 16, August 23, and September 6. This phase is designed to find our voters and our potential voters. The information will be used for the Get-Out-The-Vote (GOTV) effort both for those who will vote on election day itself (November 4) and those who are Vote-By-Mail voters (formerly known as absentee voters) who can begin voting on October 6.

Phase Two – Advocacy and Persuasion. In this phase we will re-contact (either by walking or phoning) those who are in the Mushy Middle – soft Yes, undecided, and Soft No voters. We will provide information and persuasive points for them to consider.

Phase Three – Get-Out-The-Vote. This will have two parts – an ongoing contacting effort to those who intend to vote by mail, and a big GOTV effort on election day itself.

ELECTION DAY: We will need 100,000 volunteers on November 4 – about 5 per voting location. One of the team will be posted at a polling place to monitor the voting list that election officials must post indicating who has and has not voted. The monitor will then contact the others on the team who will drive to the homes of our voters who have not yet voted and encourage them to do so. Please ask every volunteer to plan now to take a vacation day off of work, if at all possible, and help us on election day.

DISTRIBUTION OF MATERIALS: Where regions are relatively compact and ZCSs don't have to drive very far, we will ship materials to the Regional

Coordinator and ask Zip Code Supervisors to go there and pick up materials. For regions that are more spread out, would you Regional Coordinators please email my assistant [email omitted] the mailing addresses of ZCSs for whom driving to the RC is a burden and we will ship directly to them.

DEADLINE: To get materials and files to everyone in plenty of time to prepare for August 16, I need the contact information for all Zip Code Supervisors by 10:00am Monday morning August 11.

Regional Coordinators: Please fill out the Zip Code Supervisor Information Form (an Excel spreadsheet) that your Area Directors forwarded to you. If some zip code supervisors cannot be assigned by that time, please list those zip codes and the number of voter households so we can determine how much material to send to you so that you can then distribute it later in the week when a supervisor is appointed. When you send those forms to me, make sure they remain in the .xls extension.

REIMBURSEMENT: We are asking ZCSs, with the help of RCs, to bear the price of printing various materials. If this becomes too much of a burden for anyone, would you Regional Coordinators please find someone in your ward or stake who could help out?

LANGUAGES: The campaign is translating and printing materials in Spanish. I will let you know when these are ready for distribution. For other languages, local leadership is free to get materials translated and then distribute as they deem appropriate.

SCHEDULERS: Each Zip Code Supervisor should ask one or two people to be schedulers. This must be done quickly. These schedulers should work from their homes, call people in the ward and ask them to participate. Even if we could pass around a sign-up list in Priesthood or Relief Society, we wouldn't do it. People respond best when directly asked by someone they know, while a sign-up list only causes them to study their shoelaces.

CHURCH ANNOUNCEMENT: Elder John Dalton, the Area Authority responsible for all aspects of our LDS effort to assist the coalition, is asking stake presidents and bishops to announce our Walk Saturday program in Church this Sunday. We cannot organize volunteers or hold training meetings on Church property, but we can provide information concerning the who, where, when and what of our effort, the same as we do for a Red Cross blood drive. Bishoprics are being asked to provide that information as part of their regular ward announcements.

BRING A FRIEND: Many religious leaders are asking their congregations to participate as volunteers, but we should also use our own friendship circles to invite neighbors and friends to help. Please ask every LDS volunteer to bring a friend to our "Walk Saturdays."

TRAINING OF VOLUNTEERS: A better term may be orientation because it is short and easy. Zip Code Supervisors will hand out to each volunteer: walk lists, badge, walk or phone script, handouts for walkers, and the background materials (Facts, FAQ, and Myths & Facts) they can read before the start.

They will show the volunteers how to mark the walk sheets and pass out examples. Other than that, it's a matter of answering whatever questions they may have.

Each ZCS will receive two pdf files for each zip code, one for even-numbered addresses and one for odd-numbered addresses. Each file lists the streets of a zip code in alphabetical order. Where two people want to work together as a team, distribute the even-numbered address sheets of a street to one and the odd-numbered address sheets to the other so they will be working across the street from each other. Of course, volunteers are free to work alone if they desire.

We need more walkers than phoners, so encourage volunteers to give walking a try. Give walkers the streets they'd feel most comfortable working. If they do not have a preference, give them walk sheets in neighborhoods where they're most likely to meet people who support Prop 8. Then as their confidence grows, they can walk the less receptive neighborhoods. If there is any doubt about the advisability of walking a neighborhood, turn it over to the phoners. Safety of our walkers is paramount.

As a logistical matter, ZCSs should record who is given what sheets (they will be numbered). Whatever sheets are not completed can be returned to the stack for the next week.

VOLUNTEERS FROM THE WEBSITE: Every day, several dozen people use the ProtectMarriage.com website to volunteer to help. Their contact information is being organized by zip codes and will be sent to the appropriate ZCSs next Tuesday or Wednesday.

REGISTERING ON THE PM WEBSITE: Our volunteers should not register as volunteers on the ProtectMarriage.com website. It will only lead to duplication and confusion.

OTHER WORK TIMES: Volunteers are free to walk and phone at any time, but no one should walk after dark. The three Walk Saturdays are a focused effort and we know that not everyone is available on Saturday mornings. Those wishing to work at other times should contact the ZCS and receive the necessary materials. We prefer that people take only those sheets that they are ready to work on within the next day or so. We do not want anyone taking walk sheets home to work on when they get around to it. Those tend to be turned in blank on November 3rd.

AGE REQUIREMENTS: We would prefer that all walkers and phoners be at least 16 years of age. They do not have to be registered to vote to participate, but if they are 18 or over, make sure they register as soon as they can.

RESOURCES: Please indicate on the ZCS information form whether the resources available for a particular zip code are strong, medium, or weak to get the job done. After we see how things go on August 16, we may ask some phoners in strong zips to phone voters in other areas of the state.

RECORDERS: After each walk/phone session, the ZCSs should turn the walk lists over to the Recorders for data entry into our statewide data base. I will have further information about this – access, procedures – in a few days when the setup is complete.

VOTER REGISTRATION: We will not take voter registration materials with us on our Walk Saturdays. The details of what our registration program will be are still being worked out.

FUNDRAISING: Similarly, we will not take fundraising materials with us while walking. One of the questions we will ask of our voters is whether they would like to help, and we have a place for walkers/phoners to check whether the voter will place a yard sign or make calls. Once our voters are identified, those willing to help will later be asked if they'd like to contribute. But we do not include that question on our walking or phoning scripts.

MAJORITY VOTE: To clarify: Proposition does not need a 2/3 majority. One vote more than 50% means victory. But let's not call it that close, if you don't mind.

# PART III

# THE CONSEQUENCES OF DISTINCTIVENESS

# 7

## Assessing the Saints

### How Americans View Mormons

Reed Smoot represented Utah in the United States Senate from 1903 to 1933. During his tenure, he became the most senior member of the powerful Senate Appropriations Committee and the head of the equally important Senate Finance Committee. Within his party, Smoot was instrumental in seeing that Warren G. Harding secured the 1920 Republican presidential nomination, and was also a close confidant of presidents Teddy Roosevelt and William Howard Taft (Flake 2004).

Smoot's career, however, had an inauspicious start. Upon arriving in the nation's capital, there was vehement opposition to his seating in the Senate. The question of whether his religion disqualified him from service in the U.S Congress was debated in the Senate, and around the country, for years. That Smoot was a Mormon was controversial enough. But Smoot was also a member of the Mormon hierarchy – a "prophet, seer, and revelator" – and, as a member of the Quorum of the Twelve Apostles, one of a small number of men in line to become the Church's president. At the time that Smoot was elected by the Utah State Legislature,[1] Mormonism still met with widespread disapproval nationwide. Polygamy – which had not yet been fully extinguished – remained controversial, but that did not exhaust the concerns raised about Mormonism. What did Mormons do in their temples, out of public view? Did they place loyalty to their Church over fealty to flag, country, and constitution? Would Smoot be a puppet controlled by the president of the LDS Church?

The battle was joined. Was Smoot fit to serve? The Senate lived up to its reputation as a deliberative body, taking from 1903 to 1907 to decide Smoot's fate. In the words of Kathleen Flake, who has written the definitive book on Smoot's struggle to be seated:

[1] U.S. Senators were not directly elected until 1912.

The four-year Senate proceeding created a 3,500 page record of testimony by 100 witnesses on every peculiarity of Mormonism, especially its polygamous family structure, ritual worship practices, "secret oaths," open canon, economic communalism, and theocratic politics. The public participated actively in the proceedings. In the Capitol, spectators lined the halls, waiting for limited seats in the committee room, and filled the galleries to hear floor debates. For those who could not see for themselves, journalists and cartoonists depicted each day's admission and outrage. At the height of the hearing some senators were receiving a thousand letters a day from angry constituents. What remains of these public petitions fills eleven feet of shelf space, the largest such collection in the National Archives. (2004, 5)

Unlike B. H. Roberts, another LDS leader elected to the House of Representatives in 1898 but denied his seat after a similar debate, Smoot had never been a polygamist. Thus, the rancorous proceedings did not center on Smoot's personal conduct, but on the bigger question of how a pluralistic nation accommodates religious differences (S. B. Gordon 2002). Although the disagreement was ostensibly over whether Smoot could take his seat in the Senate, the real issue was the status of Mormonism within the nation. Could such a peculiar people be wholly American?

Smoot was eventually seated, on a vote that was largely along party lines.[2] Once the dust settled from the exhausting debate he never looked back and went on to have a distinguished senatorial career.

Reed Smoot's story provides yet another example of the Mormon paradox. Smoot's opponents portrayed his religion as so peculiar that it disqualified him from service as a representative of his state. Yet once safely ensconced in his seat, he was a conventional Republican senator. His Mormonism was initially a liability but, over time, it apparently did not impede him from winning the respect of his peers. The tale of Reed Smoot is a microcosm of how Mormons in general are perceived, even today. Many of the concerns Smoot faced continue to be raised about Mormonism – sometimes quietly, sometimes less so. However, as suggested by Smoot's successful career, Mormonism is not always an impediment to social acceptance. In some circles it can even be an asset, not a liability.

This chapter first discusses our expectations, derived from theory, for the factors shaping perceptions of Mormons. Next, we examine different perspectives on how Mormons are perceived. By bringing a variety of data to bear, we plumb the depths of attitudes toward Latter-day Saints, both complimentary and critical. From description we move to analysis, asking why Americans view Mormons as they do. To answer that question, we start with religious factors, including both individuals' religious tradition (or lack thereof) and their intensity of religious

---

[2] The resolution was whether to unseat Smoot, who had been serving in office while his final status was debated. Forty-seven senators voted to keep Smoot in the Senate; twenty-eight voted to remove him. Nine Republicans crossed party lines to vote against Smoot. Three Democrats did likewise to vote for him (Flake 2004, 145).

commitment (or lack thereof). We then examine other factors beyond religion that also affect attitudes toward Mormons: knowledge of and contact with Latter-day Saints.

## PERCEPTIONS OF PECULIARITY

In previous chapters we examined whether Mormons meet the internal criteria to be considered an ethno-religious group. As we have seen, they do. However, to be considered an ethno-religious group, its members must also be recognized externally as distinctive, mirroring what we observe internally within the sacred tabernacle. Just as Mormons consider themselves to be a peculiar people, others must also recognize them as peculiar. And just as Mormons themselves do not necessarily see peculiarity as a negative, we should not assume that the perception of peculiarity is all bad. While there are unquestionably negative Mormon stereotypes, for some people Mormons are peculiar in a good way. In having a mixture of positive and negative perceptions, Mormons resemble other ethno-religious groups. In the nineteenth and early twentieth centuries, ethno-religious coalitions formed among many different groups – some were foes, but others were friends. Just as ethno-religious identities led to affinities as well as antagonisms then, Mormons now are likewise subject to a mix of both negative and positive perceptions.

The balance of opinions about Mormons can be understood by returning to the concept of information flow, and how that flow brings us the "considerations" we store in our mental hard drives (see Chapter 4). Competing considerations lead to uncertainty, inconsistency, and ambivalence; a preponderance of considerations on one side of an issue results in a clear opinion favoring that perspective (Zaller 1992). While developed to explain the nature and origins of political opinions, this stylized model also works to explain perceptions of a social group, especially a distinctive ethno-religious group like Mormons. If people are exposed to – and accept – a stream of positive information about Mormons, we should expect the perception of Mormons to be primarily positive. Thus, Mormons themselves have high self-regard because, within the sacred tabernacle, positive information about Mormonism is powerfully reinforced.

Outside the sacred tabernacle, far more variegated information circulates about Mormonism and from a wide variety of sources. In 2007, the Pew Forum on Religion & Public Life asked a nationally representative sample of Americans what, if anything, had had the biggest influence on their view of Mormons.[3] The responses were varied, and included a personal experience with a Mormon (29 percent), the media (20 percent), their education (14 percent), religious beliefs (11 percent), and the views of their family and friends (10 percent) (Pew Forum on Religion & Public Life 2007). And the nature of this information is also highly variable. Americans inevitably have both positive and

---

[3] See Data Appendix on the details of the Pew Forum 2007 survey.

negative experiences with their Mormon neighbors, coworkers, friends, and family members. In the media, some stories featuring Mormonism are positive, some negative, and some are a mix of both. Furthermore, negativity is in the eye of the beholder, as two people can come to opposite conclusions about the very same set of facts. For example, when Brigham Young University suspended a star basketball player for breaking the university's code of conduct by having (consensual) sex with his girlfriend, most commentators lauded the school – and, by implication, the LDS Church – for upholding its own rules regulating sexual behavior. Others, however, were critical of the school for enforcing that very same rule.[4] Our point is simply that Americans are exposed to a range of data about the LDS Church and Mormon culture. We should thus expect their attitudes about Mormons to reflect that diversity of information.

However, not everyone is exposed to the same mix of information about Mormons, as some groups will be exposed to far more negative information than others. Groups that have the sharpest boundaries with Mormons are more likely to be exposed to negative than positive information – the inverse of the overwhelmingly positive information within the sacred tabernacle. Within the evangelical subculture, for example, there is a thriving industry of anti-Mormon literature and movies. Christian bookstores typically stock literature about Mormons under the category of "cults." While perhaps less organized and systematic, many highly secular Americans are also in a social environment where criticism or even ridicule of Mormonism is acceptable. In the words of a non-Mormon academic in an essay about anti-Mormon sentiment being "the acceptable prejudice":

I've attended numerous scholarly conferences . . . where Mormonism has been discussed, and it is amazing to confront snide and disdainful comments and even overt prejudice from intellectually sophisticated academics. And it seems perfectly acceptable to express this bias. (Terry 2012)

Social networks characterized by such negative information flows are not likely to have a social norm inhibiting critical comments about the group in question. It was once perfectly acceptable to repeat negative opinions about blacks and gays in nearly all corners of American society. Today, norms have changed. Although racism and homophobia have not disappeared, they now meet with opprobrium in most social circles. In contrast, we suggest that there are still many contexts in which there is no norm against expressing prejudice against Mormons.

We thus expect three basic patterns from our examination of how Mormons are perceived. First, attitudes toward Mormons will be mixed – some negative, some positive. Second, the groups with the sharpest boundaries, and thus the greatest tension, with Mormons, will be most likely to view them negatively. Third, exposure to positive – or, at least, accurate – information about Mormons leads to a more positive assessment of them.

---

[4] For representative examples of each opinion, see Gregory (2011) and Samuel (2011).

## General Perceptions

How are Mormons perceived by their fellow Americans? How does that perception compare to that of other religious groups? Recall that no major religious group has a higher regard for its own members than Mormons – evidence, we have argued, for the ethnic-like nature of Mormonism (see Chapter 2, Figure 2.1). We now review the analog of that same data, namely how members of religious groups perceive other religious groups – how non-Catholics feel about Catholics and non-Jews about Jews and so on. As before, these perceptions are measured on a 0 to 100 scale known as a feeling thermometer, with higher numbers showing a more positive assessment and 50 being neutral.[5]

As shown in Figure 7.1, the perception of Mormons by others is nearly the inverse of how they perceive themselves: while Mormons rate other Mormons very highly, non-Mormons give Mormons a relatively low rating. Mormons are

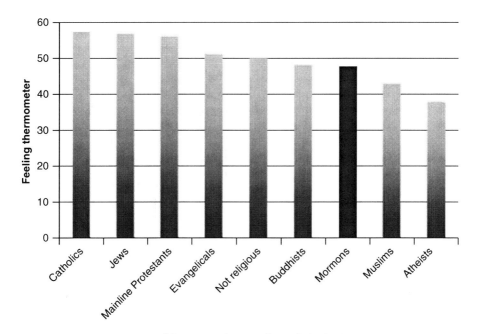

FIGURE 7.1. Mormons' Public Perception Ranks Relatively Low. Perceptions are a "feeling thermometer," ranging from 0 to 100. Each bar represents how everyone else feels about each group (e.g. how non-Catholics feel about Catholics)
*Source:* Faith Matters Survey, 2011

[5] These data are from the 2011 Faith Matters survey. See Data Appendix for details.

not at the bottom of this "popularity contest" – both Muslims and atheists are ranked lower – but they are much nearer to the bottom than the top.[6]

## Favorability

A single number on a 100-point scale can only tell us so much. We have seen that, compared to most other religious groups, Mormons have a relatively low rating, but this blunt measure obscures the full distribution of opinion. The variation in attitudes toward Latter-day Saints is revealed with a question that asks respondents to select among a range of opinions: very favorable, mostly favorable, mostly unfavorable, very unfavorable. We asked a representative sample of Americans this question in January of 2008.[7] The timing is important because, at the time of our survey, Mitt Romney had only just emerged on the national scene. As Chapter 9 discusses in depth, in the wake of Romney's candidacy attitudes toward Mormons have become polarized along partisan lines. While we will have much more to say about that trend later, for now we note that at the time of this survey, Republicans and Democrats had very similar assessments of Mormons.

As we see in Figure 7.2, a slight majority of Americans say that they have a favorable opinion of Mormons – 49 percent say that they are "mostly favorable" and another 7 percent say that they are "very favorable."[8] In a follow-up question, respondents indicated why they feel the way they do. For those with a favorable opinion, the survey provided three possibilities: respect for Mormon beliefs, shared values with Mormons, and having had a good personal experience with Mormons. Respondents could select as many of the options as they wished and list their own reasons as well.

Among non-Mormons with a favorable impression, the most common reason for their opinion is their respect for Mormon beliefs (45 percent), followed closely by a good personal experience with a Mormon (39 percent). Rounding out the list were volunteered, open-ended responses on the theme of "live and let live": a statement that all religions deserve respect (7 percent), shared values with Mormons (12 percent), and proffered statements that indicate respect for Mormons' family values or similar beliefs (7 percent). See Figure 7.3 for details.

Tolstoy wrote that all happy families are alike, but each unhappy family is unhappy in its own way.[9] Similarly, while people favorable toward Mormons provide a small number of reasons for their opinion, those who are unfavorable are more likely to offer a personalized explanation for their disfavor. As with the

---

[6] For more on how members of different religions perceive each other, see Putnam and Campbell (2010).

[7] These data are from the 2008 Cooperative Campaign Analysis Project; see Data Appendix for details.

[8] Note that Mormons themselves have been omitted from this analysis, a practice we will follow throughout this chapter.

[9] Paraphrased from the opening sentence of *Anna Karenina*.

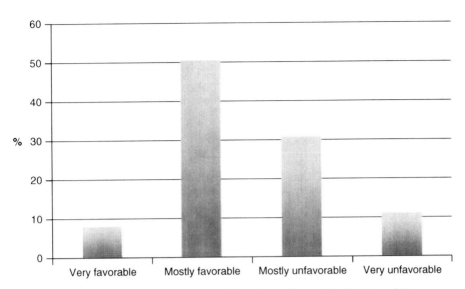

FIGURE 7.2. While Most Americans Say They Have a Favorable Opinion of Mormons, a Sizeable Fraction Do Not
*Source:* Cooperative Campaign Analysis Project, 2008

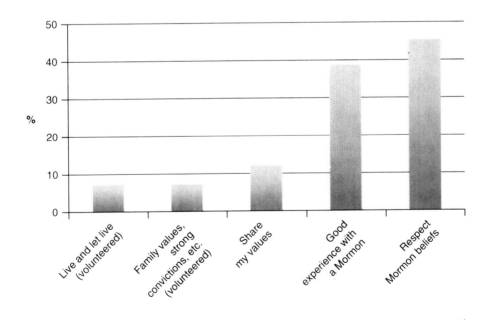

FIGURE 7.3. Why Do You Have a Favorable Opinion of Mormons? (Of those who said they have a favorable opinion)
*Source:* Cooperative Campaign Analysis Project, 2008

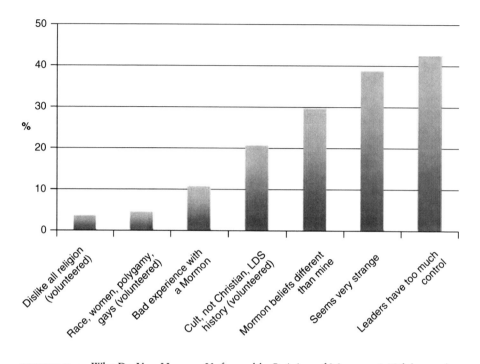

FIGURE 7.4. Why Do You Have an Unfavorable Opinion of Mormons? (Of those who said they have an unfavorable opinion.)
*Source:* Cooperative Campaign Analysis Project, 2008

reasons for a favorable opinion, on this survey those who had a negative view could provide their own and/or select from a list we provided: Mormon leaders have too much control over Church members, the Mormon religion seems very strange, Mormons have beliefs that are "different than mine," or a bad personal experience with a Mormon. Here, too, respondents could choose as many options as they wished and add their own reasons, producing a vast array of responses that often included multiple objections in a single response.

Of non-Mormons with an unfavorable impression of Mormons, two out of five (43 percent) said that Mormon leaders have too much control over LDS Church members – an issue that has political relevance given the longstanding concern that the LDS hierarchy will issue marching orders to Mormon elected officials. This accusation was leveled at Reed Smoot in the early 1900s (Flake 2004) and Mitt Romney a century later (Linker 2006). Next on the list of reasons for an unfavorable impression is the perception that Mormons have very strange beliefs (39 percent), followed by the opinion that Mormon beliefs differ from the respondent's (30 percent), which for some is probably another way of saying that Mormons are not Christians – more on that below. Roughly 20 percent described the LDS Church as a "cult," explicitly stating that Mormons are not Christian, or indicated disagreement with specific doctrinal and/or historical claims of Mormonism. Eleven percent said that they had a negative experience with a Mormon (notably, a smaller percentage than indicated a positive experience). Roughly 4 percent gave a response that mentioned LDS policies, practices, or beliefs regarding race, women, polygamy, homosexuality, or some combination. Finally, 3 percent indicated their disapproval of all religions.

## One-Word Impressions

We see further evidence that perceptions of Mormons are a mixture of positive and negative from an interesting question asked in the Pew Forum 2007 survey. In a form of free association, respondents were asked to verbalize what comes to mind when they hear the word "Mormon." Importantly, 30 percent said nothing came to mind – reminding us that for a significant share of the population, their attitudes about Mormons have yet to form.

Even though our earlier question about Americans' overall perception of Mormons showed that a majority gives them a positive rating, this word-association elicits more negative than positive responses. On the negative side, the most frequent terms were (in order of frequency):

- Cult
- Polygamy
- Strict/restrictive
- Strange, misguided, false, crazy, or odd

While slightly less common than derogatory terms, many respondents also mentioned positive associations, such as:

- Family and/or family values
- Good or good people
- Dedicated
- Christian
- Devout, faithful
- Honest
- Interesting
- OK
- Friendly

Still other words are best described as neutral, or at least ambiguous.

- Different
- Conservative
- Utah
- Religion

All in all, 24 percent of the one-word responses were negative, 27 percent were neutral, and 18 percent were positive (as noted, 30 percent had no opinion).

## Stereotypes

The mixture of positive and negative perceptions comes into sharper focus when we compare the perceptions of Mormons to those of other religious groups.[10] In the Mormon Perceptions Study our team conducted in the fall of 2012, we asked a representative sample of Americans if a series of potential stereotypes – both critical and complimentary – applied to Mormons. Depending on the stereotype, we compared Mormons to Catholics, Jews, or Muslims or, in some cases, to all three groups. We did not make these stereotypes out of whole cloth, but drew on terms that are plausibly associated with each group within the public consciousness. For example, on the positive side we have seen that many Americans associate Mormons with strong families, an idea that could be associated with Muslims and Catholics as well. As a negative example, Mormons are also thought by some to have strange beliefs, which, in a predominantly Christian nation, might also be the case for Jews and Muslims. Figure 7.5 displays results for all of the stereotype items.[11]

Our survey included four positive stereotypes: members of the group in question are patriotic, caring, friendly, and have strong families. Of these

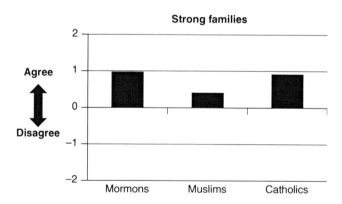

FIGURE 7.5. Stereotypes
*Source:* Mormon Perceptions Study, 2012

[10] For a similar, and enlightening, discussion on Catholic stereotypes, see Greeley and Hout (2006, chapter 12).
[11] Each stereotype item had five response categories, from which we created Figure 7.5 using the following values for each response: strongly agree (+2), agree (+1), neither agree nor disagree (0), disagree (−1), or strongly disagree (−2). The figure displays the mean value for each stereotype. Thus, a number below 0 means that the average respondent disagrees with the stereotype, while one above 0 indicates agreement.

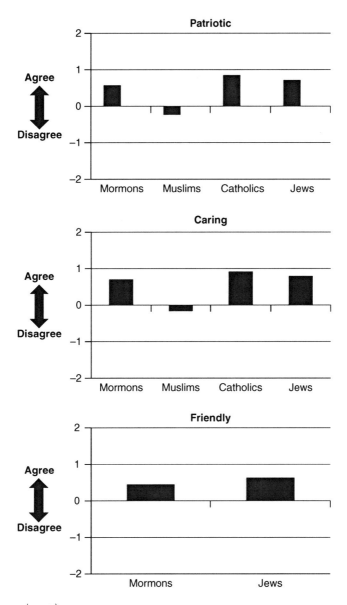

FIGURE 7.5. (cont.)

four, Mormons score highest on strong families, more so than Muslims and just edging out Catholics. They also receive relatively high marks for being patriotic, caring, and friendly – about the same as Jews or Catholics.

The list includes one ambiguous stereotype, namely that Mormons are rich. Since this perception is also sometimes repeated as a stereotype for Jews

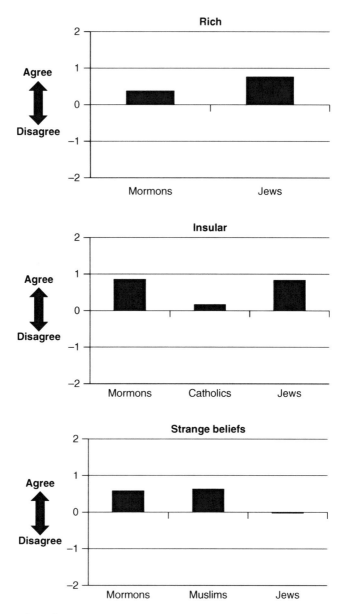

FIGURE 7.5. (cont.)

as well, they are the group we use as a benchmark. We classify this stereotype as ambiguous because, in the context of contemporary America, viewing a group as rich could be either a compliment or criticism. When applied to Jews, the stereotype of being "rich" has often had a negative connotation, as it might

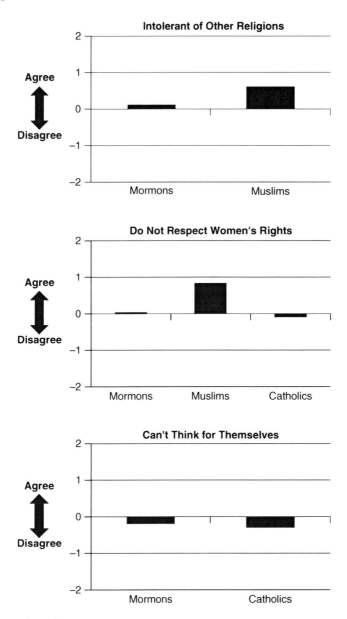

FIGURE 7.5. (cont.)

invoke such anti-Semitic imagery as Shylockian moneylenders. Outside of any specific anti-Semitic tropes, in some circles deriding "the rich" is a populist rallying cry. On the other hand, for many Americans being rich is a matter of aspiration, not derogation – whoever is being described. Whatever its valence, Americans are more likely than not to describe both Jews and Mormons as rich.

Our negative stereotypes include being insular, having strange beliefs, being intolerant of other religions, having disrespect for women's rights, and not thinking for themselves. Mormons are perceived as being about as insular as Jews (again, a longstanding anti-Semitic stereotype), but less so than Catholics. Mormons and Muslims are equally likely to be perceived as having strange beliefs, while Jews are not thought to have strange beliefs by comparison. Mormons are also less likely than Muslims to be described as intolerant of other religions. Mormons are not seen as especially disrespectful of women – compared to Muslims, who are, and Catholics who are not by a slight margin. The average American disagrees, slightly, that Mormons "can't think for themselves," and also disagrees that this phrase describes Catholics.

Thus each of these religious groups faces a blend of positive, negative, and neutral reactions; some tilt more to the positive, others to the negative. Here, too, Mormons are viewed less positively than Catholics and Jews, but more positively than Muslims.

Just as the ethno-religious groups of the past had both allies and antagonists, these multiple sources of data demonstrate that Mormons' distinctiveness as a peculiar people works both for and against their popular perception. One should not facilely assume that Mormonism elicits universally negative reactions. Rather, the received wisdom about Mormons includes both good and bad although, on balance, the scale tips toward the negative.

PREDICTING PERCEPTIONS

Given the variation in how Mormons are perceived, what predicts whether someone views them with disdain or esteem? For guidance, we can turn to our explanation of the dual boundaries Mormons have drawn to mark themselves as a peculiar people by distinguishing themselves both from secular society and from other religions. Those same boundaries also shape perceptions of Mormons. Just as we have spoken of dual boundaries, we can speak of dual tensions – both with people who hold to a secular worldview and those who have different religious beliefs. It is within these groups that we would expect the information environment to tilt toward negative perceptions of Mormons.

We have tested what predicts how Mormons are perceived using a statistical model that simultaneously accounts for multiple potential factors, enabling us to compare the relative impact of each one. Our model includes a wide array of variables: religious tradition, race, marital status, age, education, and partisan identification.[12] Results are displayed in Figure 7.6, which only includes those factors that are statistically significant. Even when accounting for a variety of

---

[12] These same control variables are used in each of the statistical models we present in this chapter. See Table 7A.1 in the appendix to this chapter for a more detailed presentation of these models.

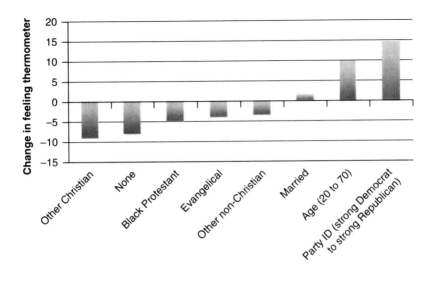

FIGURE 7.6. What Affects Perceptions of Mormons? With statistical controls; results from OLS regression
*Source:* Cooperative Congressional Election Study, 2010

characteristics that might influence attitudes toward Mormons, negativity toward them is greatest among people who are themselves distinctive – reflecting tension with secularists and religionists alike. Mormons are viewed unfavorably by religiously unaffiliated Americans, whose lack of religion marks them as distinctive in the context of a highly religious nation like the United States (Norris and Inglehart 2011). On the opposite side of the religious spectrum, this negative view is shared by evangelicals and black Protestants. Evangelical Protestants have been among the most vocal of Mormonism's critics, taking issue with many points of LDS theology. Many black Protestants concur with the evangelicals' theological critique of LDS beliefs, but likely also have particular concerns about the LDS Church's history of racial exclusion.

Interestingly, people in two categories often omitted from the analysis of American religion have comparatively negative perceptions of Mormons: "other Christians" and "other non-Christians." Each category combines groups that are too small to be broken out for reliable analysis. "Other Christians" include members of religions, such as Jehovah's Witnesses, who are distinctive enough that they are not accurately grouped with evangelical Protestants. "Other non-Christians" primarily includes adherents of eastern religions such as Islam, Buddhism, and Hinduism – each of which is obviously distinctive but, though growing, have only a small share of the overall population. While these are catchall categories that, by necessity, meld a number of disparate groups together, they nonetheless share the common characteristic of having a high degree of distinctiveness from both "mainstream" American culture *and* Mormonism.

As important as the groups that have a negative view of Mormons are those that do not: mainline Protestants, Catholics, and Jews. As implied by their name, mainline Protestants are the epitome of conventional American society as, historically, the faiths grouped in this tradition are the closest thing to an "establishment" religion the United States has ever had. Jews and Catholics were once much more distinctive – to the point of negative and even hostile reactions – but the sharp edges separating them from the rest of America have today been dulled (Putnam and Campbell 2010). We suspect their experience as ethno-religious groups that have historically faced hostility from a Protestant majority leads to sympathy for Mormons, or at least a lack of discomfort with Mormons' distinctiveness.

The dual tensions resulting from the boundaries Mormons have drawn to distinguish themselves are even clearer when we examine the degree of commitment to one's religion and not just nominal affiliation. To gauge the impact of religious commitment we use a composite index of "religiosity" that includes the frequency of religious attendance (behavioral commitment in a formal institutional setting), frequency of prayer outside of worship services (behavioral commitment outside of an institutional channel), and the degree to which one's life is guided by religion (a nonbehavioral, noninstitutional measure of religious salience). Using such a composite measure is like investing in a mutual fund instead of a single stock; the performance of the index is not dominated by the vagaries of one measure. If the dual tensions hypothesis holds, the greatest concern about Mormons should be expressed by those farthest from the religious median – both above and below.

As expected, Mormons are indeed viewed most negatively by people at the two poles of personal religiosity, with a more positive assessment by those in the middle (see Figure 7.7). In fact, the relationship is almost perfectly symmetrical, such that highly secular and highly religious Americans rate Mormons very nearly the same. Furthermore, religiosity turns out to matter more than religious tradition. Put another way, once we account for differences in personal religiosity, the boundaries between religious traditions blur to the point of being indistinguishable. Whatever their specific religious background, two Americans of equal religious commitment are likely to share a common assessment of Mormons.

Let us distill the most important conclusion from our analysis of what predicts how Mormons are perceived. Their dual boundaries produce a dual set of tensions. Mormons see themselves as distinct from secular society, and in response, the most secular Americans have a comparatively negative perception of Mormons. And just as Mormons believe that their religion is distinct from other faiths, so too do many other highly religious Americans view Mormons with disfavor.

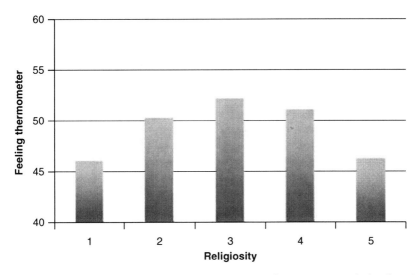

FIGURE 7.7. The Dual Tensions: Mormons Are Viewed Most Negatively by the Most Secular and the Most Religious. With statistical controls; results from OLS regression
*Source:* Cooperative Congressional Election Study, 2010

## ARE MORMONS CHRISTIANS?

Among the many concerns raised about Mormons, one question in particular stands out for the controversy it provokes. Are Mormons Christians? Various surveys have consistently shown that roughly 30 percent of the U.S. population believes that Mormons are not Christians (Pew Forum on Religion & Public Life 2012b). Mormons, it is important to note, are not alone in facing this question. Historically, some Protestants have similarly labeled other denominations like Catholics and Jehovah's Witnesses as non-Christians.

If "Christian" simply means someone who professes Jesus Christ as the Son of God, Mormons certainly qualify. Mormons often testify of their belief that Christ has atoned for the sins of mankind, was literally resurrected, and will return again – all bedrock Christian beliefs. Most any Mormon will readily point out that the full name of their church is the Church of *Jesus Christ* of Latter-day Saints.

Likewise, if being Christian is a matter of self-definition, Mormons clearly count. As noted previously, 97 percent of Mormons agree that theirs is a Christian religion in the Pew Mormons in America Survey (Pew Forum on Religion & Public Life 2012a). To most Mormons, the whole debate is puzzling. From inside the faith, it seems self-evident that they are Christians.

So why the debate? The theological disagreement rests on what it means to be a "Christian" – or perhaps "really Christian." Is it enough to believe in Christ or does one have to believe particular things about Christ? As Mormons readily acknowledge, their beliefs differ from those of other Christian traditions. The central narrative in Mormonism's founding is that Joseph Smith restored the only legitimate form of Christianity – the true Church – because all other churches are false. Mormons do not recognize baptisms performed in other faiths; to our knowledge, no other religion accepts LDS baptisms as valid. Accordingly, Latter-day Saints do not believe in some of the fundamentals found in mainstream Christian denominations, including the trinity, salvation by faith alone, or in any of the creeds from the early days of Christianity. Mormons' belief in the *Book of Mormon* as scripture and in an open canon – that is, further additions to scripture – also causes some others to question their place within Christianity. (For evangelical Protestants who take the Bible as God's final word, the doctrine of an open canon is particularly problematic.[13]) If these beliefs define who counts as Christian, then Mormons will be left off the list.

The debate over whether Mormonism falls within the family of Christianity is more than a matter of theology. It has also become a matter of sociology, as in recent years "Christian" has evolved into a shorthand term for the evangelical wing of Protestantism. Ask yourself what comes to mind when you hear a bookstore, school, or television channel described as "Christian." We suspect that it connotes evangelicalism, not the mainline wing of Protestantism or Catholicism. Mormons clearly do not meet this informal definition of Christian. Consequently, when evangelicals say that Mormons are not Christians, they are really making a statement about religious boundaries and, perhaps, tensions. Mormons, they are saying, are not like us – at least in religious terms.

Above, we saw the dual boundaries that lead to tensions that shape general perceptions of Mormons. On the specific matter of whether Mormons should be considered Christians, however, we would expect it to matter much more to people who consider themselves to be Christians.[14] Accordingly, the "Christian

---

[13] Similarly, some biblical-literalist evangelicals take issue with Pentecostals who believe that speaking in tongues consists of revelation from God, a reason that in the early days of the Christian Right, fundamentalists who supported Jerry Falwell (a Baptist) were in tension with Pentecostals allied with Pat Robertson (a Pentecostal) (Wilcox and Robinson 2010; Layman 2001).

[14] These results are from questions we included on the 2010 Cooperative Congressional Election Study. To be sure that we have isolated the impact of each religious tradition, we have used a logistic regression model with the same control variables mentioned above, setting each to its mean value. See Table 7A.2 in the appendix to this chapter for a more detailed presentation of these models. The results without statistical controls are similar. The percentage of each group saying that Mormons are not Christians is as follows: Jews, 9 percent; "other non-Christians," 19 percent; mainline Protestants, 32 percent; Catholics, 42 percent; "nones," 45 percent; black Protestants, 47 percent; evangelical Protestants, 47 percent. Adding the controls has the biggest effect on the percentage of Catholics, nones, and Jews who say that Mormons are not Christians.

or not?" question has little resonance with Jews and members of other non-Christian faiths. When we adjust for demographic differences to isolate the impact of religious tradition, just 21 percent of Jews and other non-Christians, respectively, say that Mormons are not Christians, well below the rate for the general population. People with no religious affiliation are right on the national average, at 31 percent.

In contrast, evangelical Protestants have the greatest stake in the debate as, like Mormons, they have drawn clear boundaries around their identity as Christians. Over half (54 percent) of evangelicals say that Mormons are not Christians. Similarly, 49 percent of black Protestants, a religious tradition that shares many beliefs with evangelicalism, do not include Mormonism within Christianity. Among mainline Protestants it is only 25 percent; Catholics are right on the national average, at 30 percent. We would not expect most Catholics to be concerned about whether Mormonism falls inside of Christianity or out, as the bulk of theological criticism leveled at Mormons has come from Protestantism. Catholics may also be wary of saying that others are not true Christians, because they, too, are sometimes defined out of Christianity. Interestingly, Catholics seem willing to accept Mormons as Christians even while recognizing the distinctions between their two faiths. In a 2011 Pew survey, white Catholics (68 percent) were about as likely as evangelicals (70 percent) to say that their religion is "very different from the Mormon religion" (Pew Forum on Religion & Public Life 2012d).[15] The Catholic case suggests that recognizing differences does not preclude accepting Mormons as fellow Christians, which is essentially the point LDS leaders and scholars have attempted to make in an ongoing dialogue with prominent evangelical Protestants.

Using our statistical model, we also find that the tensions resulting from either high or low religious commitment matter for the perception of whether Mormons are Christians – at least among Protestants. While among Catholics religiosity has no bearing on whether Mormons are thought to be Christians, for evangelical Protestants it matters a lot. Three-quarters of the most highly religious evangelicals say that Mormons are not Christians, compared to only 18 percent of the least religious evangelicals.[16]

SOCIAL CONTACT AND FACTUAL KNOWLEDGE

The dual boundaries shape the general contours of opinion toward Mormons, but other factors can intervene to ameliorate negative attitudes toward Latter-day

---

[15] See Data Appendix for details of the Pew Forum 2011 survey.
[16] These results are from a statistical model with the same controls as in the earlier one, but with religiosity included. At the low end of religiosity, mainline Protestants look a lot like evangelicals – 11 percent of mainliners at a low level of religiosity say that Mormons are not Christians. Yet at the high end of religiosity, mainline Protestants are less likely than evangelicals to deny Mormons the label of Christians; about half say that they are.

Saints, or even foster a positive impression. Positive personal experiences and factual information can supplant negative stereotypes and sensational inaccuracies.

The case of Senator Reed Smoot illustrates that attitudes toward Mormons can change through interpersonal contact and accurate information. When Smoot first arrived in Washington, most of the available information about Mormons would have been mere caricature. In both the press and pulp fiction, they were portrayed as lecherous, avaricious polygamists bent on theocratic domination of both government and the economy. They were "vipers on the hearth" (Givens 1997). Because Mormons were almost entirely ensconced in their refuge in the Mountain West in that era, very few members of the Washington establishment would have ever met a Mormon, let alone become acquaintances or even friends with one. Over time, however, Smoot came to be accepted by his colleagues as a trusted member of the Senate. Those disparaging caricatures were supplanted by the sort of information that can only be gleaned from personal relationships. Smoot went from "viper" to "valued colleague."

## Social Contact

Smoot's experience illustrates one of the most venerable theories in social science about overcoming intolerance – social contact with members of an otherwise unfamiliar group can change hearts and minds, negating prejudice about that group. Social contact theory is more nuanced than how it is often portrayed, as it does not claim that throwing people together pell-mell magically produces harmony. As originally articulated by Gordon Allport (1979), the contact in question must meet a series of conditions. The relationship must be predicated on equal status, common goals, cooperation between groups, and the support of law or custom. Friendship meets all of these conditions and, next to familial ties, is the quintessential type of relationship capable of reducing or even reversing prejudice.

Although most research into social contact has focused on racial prejudice (Pettigrew and Tropp 2000), Robert Putnam and David Campbell (2010) have also applied it to religious differences. Their evidence indicates that the United States maintains its relatively high level of religious tolerance – in the face of considerable religious diversity and a political system riven by religious disputes – because most Americans have neighbors, friends, family members, and even spouses of a different religion.

The role of interfaith relationships in fostering goodwill across religious lines presents Mormons with a problem. For all of the religious vitality fostered within Mormons' tight-knit communities, the strong intrareligious bonds of the sacred tabernacle mean fewer inter-religious bridges. Consequently, Mormons are viewed with greater suspicion than members of most other religious traditions. The comparison between Jews and Mormons is instructive. There are about as many Mormons as Jews in America, but while Jews are viewed very positively, Mormons rank near the bottom of public perception. It is no coincidence that Jews are the religious group most likely to bridge to people of other faiths, while Mormons are among the least likely to do so (Putnam and Campbell 2010).[17]

Earlier we described how attitudes toward Mormons are affected by any given individual's own supply of information about the LDS Church, people, and culture. Personal relationships cause a dramatic change in the information that is readily accessible. Instead of sensationalism in the news media or passing references in popular culture, friends and family provide a quieter but more powerful exposure to lived Mormonism.

Keep in mind that although greater contact with Mormons can foster a more positive assessment of Latter-day Saints, more exposure could also lead to a negative assessment – sometimes familiarity breeds contempt. Even though, on balance, we find that contact and/or knowledge corresponds to a higher regard for Mormons, remember that for some people the relationship may go the other way.

Social contact comes in different degrees, so we divide the non-Mormon population into three categories of increasing personal familiarity with Mormons. First, there are those who do not know any Mormons personally, comprising just over half of the U.S. population (55 percent). Next, one-third of Americans know a Mormon, but only in passing (an acquaintance, neighbor, or coworker). Finally, roughly one-eighth of Americans have at least one Mormon among their close friends or family members.[18] Even when we account for other factors known to influence attitudes toward Mormons – most notably, strength of religious commitment – the degree of social contact affects how Mormons are rated on the same 0 to 100 scale introduced earlier. Figure 7.8 has the details: a close personal relationship with a Mormon (and not just knowing a Mormon in passing) is associated with a more positive assessment of Mormons. (This pattern will be explored in Chapter 9.)

We acknowledge that, with these data, it is impossible to know whether a close personal relationship with a Mormon leads to higher regard for Mormons, or if the reverse is true. But previous research leads us to be reasonably confident that contact fosters the goodwill rather than the other way around. In their work, Putnam and Campbell (2010) bring evidence to bear on the direction of causality that applies here. By drawing on repeated interviews with the same people over time, they find that adding friends of a new faith leads to greater warmth toward that faith, rather than warmth leading to friendships.

Social contact has a complex relationship to the belief that Mormons are Christians. Instead of a linear pattern, it is curvilinear. People with only

[17] Religious groups that are defined in explicitly ethnic terms, namely black Protestants and Latino Catholics, are the least likely to bridge to people of other faiths.
[18] These data come from the 2010 Cooperative Congressional Election Study; see Data Appendix for details.

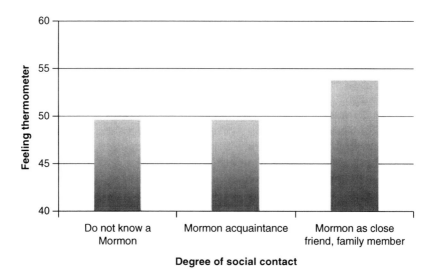

FIGURE 7.8. A Close Relationship with a Mormon Corresponds to a More Positive Perception of Mormons. With statistical controls; results from OLS regression
*Source:* Cooperative Congressional Election Study, 2010

moderate contact with Mormons (passing acquaintances) are the least likely to consider them Christians. But those who either have no contact or a close relationship are more, and equally, apt to think so. As shown in Figure 7.9, the differences are not enormous, but they are on the cusp of conventional statistical significance.[19] Holding everything else constant, 63 percent of people who know a Mormon in passing believe Mormons are Christian, compared to 67 percent of those who do not know a Mormon and 66 percent who have a close relationship with one. We might be tempted to dismiss this curvilinear relationship as a statistical fluke, except that the very same pattern also appears in Chapter 9's analysis of how contact with Mormons affected voters' perceptions of presidential candidate Mitt Romney.

Why would people with a passing familiarity with Mormons be the least likely to believe they are Christians? We suspect that this is another consequence of Mormons' distinctiveness. Knowing a Mormon in passing produces awareness of the distinctive aspects of Mormonism, without the kind of personal relationship that might assuage suspicions raised by these peculiar people. They know just enough to be suspicious. In Chapter 9, we discuss this idea in more depth.

---

[19] The difference between no contact and a passing acquaintance has a *p* value of .08 (two-tailed test).

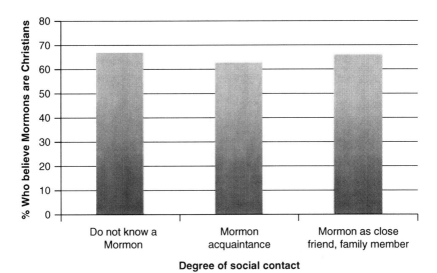

FIGURE 7.9. The People Least Likely to Think Mormons are Christians? Those Who Have a Passing Acquaintance with a Mormon. With statistical controls; results from OLS regression
*Source:* Cooperative Congressional Election Study, 2010

### Factual Knowledge

For all its importance, social contact is only one factor that softens negative attitudes toward Mormons. A second is factual knowledge, the product of exposure to a particularly important type of information. Just as greater cognitive knowledge about politics results from greater engagement in the political process (Delli Carpini and Keeter 1996; Zaller 1992), more factual knowledge about the LDS faith reflects greater engagement with Mormonism. People who know more about the LDS religion will base their view of Mormons on more accurate information.

We measure factual knowledge with four questions about Mormonism, each of which has an objectively right answer (unlike, say, the contested question of whether Mormons are Christians). The correct answer has been bolded, with the percentage selecting the correct answer in parentheses.[20]

- *Which statement is currently true about practicing Mormons and polygamy (having more than one wife)?*
  Mormons have never practiced polygamy
  **Mormons used to practice polygamy but don't anymore (46 percent correct)**

[20] These data come from the 2008 Cooperative Campaign Analysis Project Survey; see Data Appendix for details.

Mormons say they don't practice polygamy but they really do
Mormons openly practice polygamy today

- *Who is the person responsible for founding the Mormon Church in the 1800s?*
  Brigham Young
  Joseph Young
  **Joseph Smith (49 percent correct)**
  Gordon Hinckley

- *Practicing Mormons generally abstain from which of the following?*
  **Alcohol and coffee (51 percent correct)**
  Alcohol only
  Coffee only
  Neither; they are allowed to drink both

- *Which statement is the most accurate about what Mormons believe about scripture?*
  Mormons do not believe in the Bible at all
  **Mormons believe in the Bible, and in other scripture as well (62 percent correct)**
  Mormons believe only in the Bible but not in other scripture
  Mormons only believe in the Old Testament of the Bible

All told, our quiz produced a reasonably smooth distribution of correct answers. (See Table 7.1.) Only 16 percent of the population received a zero; likewise, 16 percent received a perfect score.[21]

Like social contact, greater factual knowledge predicts a more positive assessment of Mormons, as shown in Figure 7.10. Unlike contact, however, the relationship with knowledge is linear, resembling a staircase – each increment of factual knowledge corresponds to a higher score. Similarly, greater factual

TABLE 7.1. *Mormon Knowledge Quiz*

| Number correct on quiz | Percentage of population receiving that score |
|---|---|
| 0 | 16 |
| 1 | 23 |
| 2 | 23 |
| 3 | 21 |
| 4 | 16 |

*Note*: Total does not equal 100 because of rounding
*Source*: 2010 Cooperative Congressional Election Study

---

[21] Skipping the question was coded as an incorrect answer.

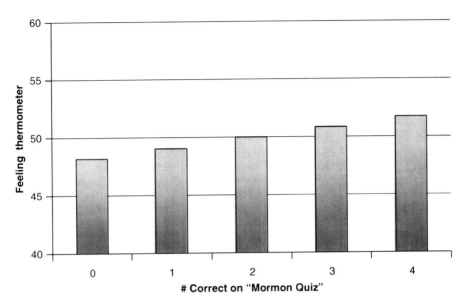

FIGURE 7.10. More Knowledge about Mormons Leads to a More Positive Perception. With statistical controls; results from OLS regression
*Source:* Cooperative Congressional Election Study, 2010

knowledge about Mormonism corresponds to a higher probability of including Mormons within Christianity. Holding everything else constant, among those who score a zero on the knowledge quiz, only about half (52 percent) think Mormons are Christians, compared to the three-quarters (74 percent) of those who received a perfect score on the quiz. (See Figure 7.11.)

As suggested by the fact that they have different effects on attitudes toward Mormons, contact and knowledge are not substitutes for one another. They have a correlation of only 0.44, indicating that there are many people who have a lot of knowledge and no contact, and others who have a lot of contact but little knowledge. When both are paired as predictors in the same model – thus "competing" against each other in a statistical horse race – they both continue to have an impact on how Mormons are perceived. This is not surprising, as different types of exposure to Mormonism elicit different types of information. A friendship may impart some objective knowledge, but is just as likely to foster a subjective sort of learning, whereby people develop impressions rather than learn facts per se.

Importantly, this analysis also teaches us that social contact and factual knowledge are not the only factors influencing perceptions of Mormons. In our statistical models we find that even when we account for knowledge and contact, both religiosity and religious affiliation still have a statistically significant impact – whether we are looking at Mormons' favorability or the belief

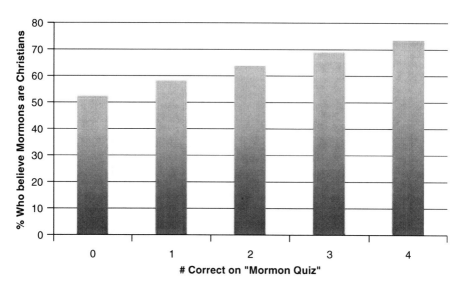

FIGURE 7.11. More Knowledge about Mormons Leads to a Belief That They Are Christians. With statistical controls; results from OLS regression
*Source:* Cooperative Congressional Election Study, 2010

that Mormons are Christians. In other words, the negative perception of Mormons found among the groups in greatest tension with Mormons is not fully explained by either a lack of knowledge about or a lack of contact with them. In fact, when compared to the rest of the population, evangelicals actually have a slightly higher level of knowledge about Mormonism and are slightly less likely to report that they do not know a Mormon. People without a religious affiliation have no more or less factual knowledge about the LDS faith than other Americans but are less likely to know a Mormon. While we have pointed to the tensions these groups have with Mormons as a proximate cause of their negative attitudes, further research should examine their information environments in more detail to better understand the origins of their views toward Latter-day Saints.

CONCLUSION

Throughout this chapter we have seen the consequences of being a peculiar people. Mormons are widely recognized as distinctive, which turns out to be a mixed blessing. For every American who has a positive impression of Mormons – associating them, say, with strong families or patriotism – a few more Americans have a negative impression, linking them to polygamy or strange beliefs. More knowledge about Mormonism softens, or even reverses, such negative impressions, as do close personal relationships with Mormons themselves (but not passing acquaintances).

But do the public's attitudes have *political* consequences? For Reed Smoot they certainly did. Today, the irony of Mormonism's place in the American political sphere is that their closest political allies, evangelical Protestants, are also their religious antagonists. Evangelicals, and highly religious Americans more generally, often share Mormons' positions on political issues and partisan identity, but also have a generally negative perception of Latter-day Saints. Their level of suspicion toward Mormons rivals that of secularists, who are political opponents of Mormons. If religion was irrelevant in American politics, then perhaps none of this would matter. However, religion is highly relevant, as our current political environment encourages candidates – particularly for the presidency – to wear their religion on their sleeves. How, then, have Mormon presidential candidates navigated their way through these waters? We take up that question in the next chapter.

CHAPTER 7 APPENDIX

TABLE 7A.1. *OLS Models of Perceptions of Mormon*

| VARIABLES | Perceptions of Mormons | |
|---|---|---|
| Evangelical Protestant | −4.104*** | −3.469** |
| | (1.118) | (1.564) |
| Black Protestant | −5.167** | −2.856 |
| | (2.568) | (3.647) |
| Catholic | −0.437 | 1.054 |
| | (1.140) | (1.518) |
| Liberal faith | −6.111 | −0.586 |
| | (4.121) | (6.686) |
| Jew | −2.580 | −1.690 |
| | (5.473) | (7.022) |
| Other non-Christian | −3.600* | 0.922 |
| | (2.126) | (2.993) |
| Other Christian | −9.020*** | −5.578 |
| | (2.979) | (4.158) |
| No religion | −8.185*** | −3.848** |
| | (1.244) | (1.873) |
| Age | 0.193*** | 0.205*** |
| | (0.026) | (0.036) |
| Married | 1.637** | 1.813* |
| | (0.749) | (0.995) |
| Education | −0.182 | −0.282 |
| | (0.370) | (0.529) |
| Party identification | 2.439*** | 2.436*** |
| | (0.179) | (0.243) |

*(continued)*

TABLE 7A.1 *(continued)*

| VARIABLES | Perceptions of Mormons | |
|---|---|---|
| Black | 5.594*** | 6.191** |
| | (2.133) | (3.095) |
| Hispanic | -0.552 | -0.796 |
| | (1.525) | (2.140) |
| Religiosity, 1st quintile | | -6.260*** |
| | | (1.753) |
| Religiosity, 2nd quintile | | -2.031 |
| | | (1.534) |
| Religiosity, 4th quintile | | -1.110 |
| | | (1.433) |
| Religiosity, 5th quintile | | -5.943*** |
| | | (1.885) |
| Mormon acquaintance | | -0.008 |
| | | (1.129) |
| Mormon as close friend, family member | | 4.281*** |
| | | (1.556) |
| Mormon knowledge | | 0.915** |
| | | (0.440) |
| Constant | 43.629*** | 40.331*** |
| | (2.139) | (3.081) |
| Observations Adjusted R-squared | 4073 0.10 | 2227 0.11 |

Standard errors in parentheses
*** $p < 0.01$, ** $p < 0.05$, * $p < 0.1$
*Note:* The model with the contact and knowledge questions has a smaller N
because these items were asked of a subset (randomly selected) of respondents
*Source:* Cooperative Congressional Election Study, 2010

TABLE 7A.2. *Logit Models of "Are Mormons Christians?"*

| VARIABLES | Mormons are Christians | |
|---|---|---|
| Evangelical Protestant | -1.262*** | -1.249*** |
| | (0.109) | (0.150) |
| Black Protestant | -0.408* | -0.252 |
| | (0.232) | (0.323) |
| Catholic | -0.253** | -0.371** |
| | (0.114) | (0.153) |
| Liberal faith | -0.389 | -0.063 |
| | (0.382) | (0.647) |
| Jew | 0.326 | 0.084 |
| | (0.542) | (0.702) |
| Other non-Christian | 0.273 | 0.177 |
| | (0.237) | (0.350) |

TABLE 7A.2 (*continued*)

| VARIABLES | Mormons are Christians | |
|---|---|---|
| Other Christian | −0.442* | −0.670* |
| | (0.268) | (0.380) |
| No religion | 0.288** | −0.527*** |
| | (0.122) | (0.187) |
| Age | 0.015*** | 0.017*** |
| | (0.002) | (0.003) |
| Married | 0.038 | 0.216** |
| | (0.071) | (0.098) |
| Education | 0.098*** | 0.075 |
| | (0.035) | (0.051) |
| Party identification | 0.017 | 0.022 |
| | (0.017) | (0.023) |
| Black | −0.645*** | −0.413 |
| | (0.190) | (0.270) |
| Hispanic | −0.195 | −0.033 |
| | (0.137) | (0.194) |
| Religiosity, 1st quintile | | −0.217 |
| | | (0.175) |
| Religiosity, 2nd quintile | | −0.071 |
| | | (0.153) |
| Religiosity, 4th quintile | | −0.616*** |
| | | (0.137) |
| Religiosity, 5th quintile | | −1.259*** |
| | | (0.175) |
| Mormon acquaintance | | −0.199* |
| | | (0.109) |
| Mormon as close friend, family member | | −0.05 |
| | | (0.148) |
| Mormon knowledge | | 0.235*** |
| | | (0.042) |
| Constant | −0.039 | −0.173 |
| | (0.202) | (0.293) |
| Observations | 4119 | 2335 |
| Pseudo R-squared | 0.060 | 0.099 |

Standard errors in parentheses
*** $p < 0.01$, ** $p < 0.05$, * $p < 0.1$
*Source:* Cooperative Congressional Election Study, 2010.

# 8

## A Stained-Glass Ceiling?

## Mormon Candidates and Presidential Campaigns

On January 29, 1844, Joseph Smith launched an independent campaign for the White House (Garr 2007). The first member of the clergy to run for president, Smith was described as a "prophet, priest, and king." These titles reflected Smith's concept of "theo-democracy" and his combined roles as mayor and general of the militia in the Mormon settlement of Nauvoo, Illinois (Wicks and Foister 2005, 105–7). The Church was central to the operation of the campaign: his vice-presidential running mate, Sidney Rigdon, was also a Mormon leader; the effort was managed by a newly founded "Council of Fifty"; and nearly 600 missionaries, elders, and apostles were dispatched across the country to campaign (Robertson 2000). These activities, plus the possibility of a Mormon "bloc vote" determining the outcome in Illinois, gave the campaign potential influence in the close presidential contest.

Styled as "General" Smith in his campaign, the candidate was described as "an independent man with American principles," in contrast to his major party rivals, Democrat James K. Polk and Whig Henry Clay (Wicks and Foister 2005, 127). In this regard, Smith offered a broad agenda of reform that cut across major party lines, including western territorial expansion, the abolition of slavery, founding a national bank, and the end of penitentiaries. One of his most controversial proposals was the use of the federal army to protect religious minorities. The campaign argued that Mormons could no longer be "oppressed and mobbed under a tyrannical government" and compared their mistreatment to that of Catholics, abolitionists, and African Americans (Bringhurst and Foster 2011, 43).[1]

The sacred tabernacle was on full display in Smith's candidacy, including the external secular and religious tensions associated with it. On the secular front, a widely published letter raised the fear of a "Mormon king," and warned: "Let no man sneer at these people or deem them of little consequence, either for good or

---

[1] For the text of Smith's platform, "General Smith's Views," see Bringhurst and Foster (2011, 325–37). This chapter is indebted to the fine scholarship in that book.

evil. . . . What will be the end of things?" (Wicks and Foister 2005, 109). On the religious front, the *Weekly American Eagle* of Memphis, Tennessee wrote that Smith's "ideas of matters temporal are as expansive as his opinions of things spiritual. He would grasp territory as he would eternity – by a process peculiarly his own – regardless of the claims of others or his own conscience" (Bringhurst and Foster 2011, 31).

Smith's candidacy attracted wide attention, but it was cut short when an Illinois mob murdered him on June 27, 1844.[2] Most Mormons soon migrated to Utah, inaugurating their period of exclusion from presidential politics. After Utah became a state, Mormon candidates returned to presidential politics during their period of reinvolvement, and eventually two candidates broke new ground by seeking major party presidential nominations: Michigan Governor George Romney (Republican Party, 1968) and Arizona Congressman Morris Udall (Democratic Party, 1976). Then, during the recent period of partisan politics, three Mormon candidates sought the Republican presidential nomination: Utah Senator Orrin Hatch (2000), former Utah Governor Jon Huntsman, Jr. (2012), and former Massachusetts Governor Mitt Romney (2008 and 2012).[3]

As with presidential candidacies in general, many of these campaigns had limited success. Three campaigns ended with the initial nomination contest: George Romney (1968), Orrin Hatch (2000), and Jon Huntsman, Jr. (2012). Two campaigns were competitive – Morris Udall (1976) and Mitt Romney (2008) – while the most successful campaigns were in 2012, when Mitt Romney won the GOP presidential nomination and then lost a close general election to Barack Obama.

Thus, over the course of nearly two centuries, Mormon candidates have gone from the margins to the center of presidential campaigns. All these candidates faced a "stained-glass ceiling" because of their faith, but the more recent candidates came closer to shattering this barrier. This chapter investigates these major party campaigns, seeking to understand the electoral impact of Mormonism.

A key factor affecting the role of Mormonism within a campaign is the degree to which a Mormon candidate's religion was politicized, linking voter attitudes toward Mormons in general with support of particular Mormon candidates. The degree of politicization depended on the flow of information to voters about the candidate's faith, including the level, novelty, and framing. And the flow of such information was influenced, in turn, by how Mormon candidates chose to address their religion.

After a brief discussion of the campaigns politics and the sacred tabernacle, we review general measures of the politicization of Mormonism in presidential

---

[2] Most scholars see Smith's murder as a product of local anti-Mormon vigilantes – see Bushman (2005) – but a few have argued that it was part of a larger political conspiracy (Wicks and Foister 2005, chapter 20).
[3] Several candidates with Mormon connections also ran on minor party tickets; see Bringhurst and Foster (2011) for details.

campaigns from 1967 to 2012 and then consider the specific cases of recent Mormon presidential campaigns. While our focus here is on Mormon presidential candidates, it is worth noting that this process could apply in principle to candidates from any ethno-religious group, in the past and the future (see Chapter 10 for a fuller discussion).

## CAMPAIGN POLITICS AND THE SACRED TABERNACLE

The fundamental task of any presidential campaign is seeking votes. In this regard, a candidate's religion can either help or hurt. Joseph Smith's 1844 campaign was no exception, illustrating the electoral advantages and disadvantages of the sacred tabernacle. On the first count, Smith's campaign was based on the high internal solidarity found among Mormons (as reported in Chapter 3), which provided useful means for seeking votes, both in terms of campaign themes and resources as well as public sympathy toward the faith. On the second count, Smith's campaign faced external religious and secular tensions (as discussed in Chapter 7), providing opponents with the opportunity to dampen his support. In 1844, both Smith and his opponents sought to provide information that would encourage the desired response among voters. These two features – campaign information and voter response – are worth discussing in more detail.

Campaign information about a Mormon candidate depends in part on the candidate's own personal degree of religiosity. A useful distinction was discussed in Chapter 3, between a Mormon who is *active* in the faith (with a strong and public connection to the LDS Church) and a Mormon who is *inactive* (with a weak or private connection to the LDS Church). All else being equal, active Mormon candidates are likely to enjoy the electoral advantages of the sacred tabernacle, but also to suffer its disadvantages – and contrariwise, inactive Mormon candidates may lose the former but avoid the latter. Joseph Smith was the very definition of an active Mormon; since then, both active and inactive Mormons have sought the White House.

Of course, things are not always equal in campaigns, and another key factor is the context of the election. We can distinguish between a *congenial* context (where the advantages of the sacred tabernacle are greater than the disadvantages) and a *non-congenial* context (where the disadvantages are greater than the advantages). Joseph Smith certainly faced a non-congenial electoral context, but since then other Mormon candidates have encountered both congenial and non-congenial contexts when seeking the White House.

Public attitudes toward Mormons are a basic determinant of congeniality, but for such views to matter at the ballot box they must be linked to a specific Mormon candidate. That is to say, the electoral context influences the extent to which a candidate's Mormonism is politicized. Because presidential campaigns are a series of state-level contests, geography is an important context. For example, states in the Mountain West are likely to be congenial for an active

TABLE 8.1. *Approaches to Mormonism in Presidential Campaigns: Candidate Religiosity and Electoral Context*

|  | ELECTORAL CONTEXT | |
|---|---|---|
|  | Congenial | Non-congenial |
| CANDIDATE RELIGIOSITY | | |
| Active | *Affirmation* | *Alliance* |
| Inactive | *Avoidance* | *Aloofness* |

Mormon candidate, while other states are likely to be non-congenial. For an inactive Mormon, the reverse may be true.

Other aspects of context can also influence how Mormonism is politicized, including the election rules, party coalitions, and the activity of opponents. While such details vary by election, there have been some long-term trends. After 1968, the presidential nomination system became more open and participatory. At the same time, the restructuring of American religion altered the faith-based constituencies of the Republican and Democratic coalitions. These two changes were often linked together by competition among rival candidates in the open nomination process for the support of religious voters (Layman et al. 2010). Taken together, these contextual factors influenced the flow of the information to voters about a Mormon candidate's religion. (Chapter 9 covers such information effects in more detail for the 2008 and 2012 campaigns.)

Thus, within the context of a particular campaign, a Mormon presidential campaign must decide how best to provide – and respond to – information about its candidate's religion so as to attract voters. Ultimately, such campaign judgments rest on perceptions of the relationship between the candidate's religious activity and electoral congeniality. Table 8.1 illustrates four ideal-type approaches to such judgments: affirmation, aloofness, alliance, and avoidance.

The first two approaches involve consistency between religious activity and electoral congeniality. *Affirmation* occurs when a Mormon candidate is religiously active *and* perceives an electoral context that is congenial to the faith (top left-hand quadrant of Table 8.1). Because information about the candidate's active religiosity is a potential means of attracting votes, it makes strategic sense for the campaign to highlight the distinctiveness of the sacred tabernacle. In analogous fashion, *aloofness* occurs when a Mormon candidate is religiously inactive *and* perceives an electoral context that is non-congenial to the faith (bottom right-hand quadrant of Table 8.1). Because information about the candidate's inactive religiosity is a potential means of attracting votes, it makes strategic sense to highlight departures from the sacred tabernacle's distinctiveness.

The remaining two approaches involve inconsistency between the two factors. *Alliance* occurs when a Mormon candidate is religiously active *and* perceives an electoral context that is non-congenial to the faith (top right-hand quadrant of Table 8.1). Because information about the candidate's active religiosity can repel votes, it makes strategic sense to downplay the distinctiveness of the sacred tabernacle and play up its nondistinctive features. And in a similar way, *avoidance* occurs when a Mormon candidate is religiously inactive *and* perceives an electoral context that is congenial to the faith (bottom left-hand quadrant of Table 8.1). Because information about the candidate's inactive religiosity can repel voters, it makes strategic sense to ignore the sacred tabernacle altogether.

Of course, actual campaigns are unlikely to fit these ideal types perfectly. In fact, candidates might use all of these approaches at specific moments in a given campaign. Candidates and other observers are often incorrect in their perceptions of electoral congeniality. And even if correct, the execution of an approach may be flawed or meet unexpected obstacles. Nonetheless, these categories are useful in discussing how Mormon presidential campaigns have approached the flow of information about their candidates' religion. Before we turn to the details of specific campaigns, a general assessment of the information environment and public attitudes toward Mormons is in order.

### INFORMATION AND PUBLIC ATTITUDES, 1967–2012

A first step is to assess the relative level of information about the Mormon presidential candidates between 1967 and 2012. Figure 8.1 reports the number of mentions in the *New York Times* of the Mormon candidates, along with the mentions that also included the candidates' religion (calculated as a percentage of the total candidate mentions). All these figures come from the period of active campaigning of each candidacy.[4]

In part, the volume of candidate mentions reflects the relative success of these campaigns, with less successful ones having fewer mentions (George Romney 1968, Hatch 2000, and Huntsman 2012), more successful ones having more mentions (Udall 1976, Mitt Romney 2008 and 2012), and the 2012 general election generating the most mentions. This increase may also reflect the expanded salience of presidential politics in the post-1968 open nomination process, including information provided by the Mormon candidates, their rivals, other participants, and observers. Given that these data rely on only one news source, they likely underestimate the level and expansion of information about Mormon presidential candidates.

---

[4] These data come from the search engine provided on the *New York Times Article Archive*. The campaign dates were: George Romney (November 18, 1967 to August 15, 1968); Morris Udall (October 24, 1974 to June 17, 1976); Orrin Hatch (July 2, 1999 to February 3, 2000); Mitt Romney (February 13, 2007 to February 14, 2008); Jon Huntsman, Jr. (June 14, 2011 to January 23, 2012); Mitt Romney (June 2, 2011 to June 6, 2012); and Mitt Romney (general election campaign; June 7, 2012 to November 13, 2012).

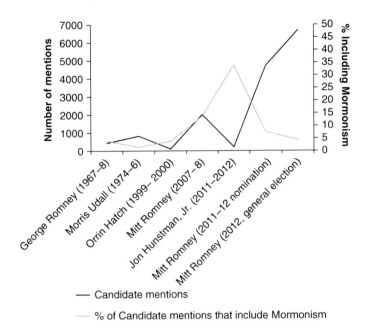

— Candidate mentions

········· % of Candidate mentions that include Mormonism

FIGURE 8.1. Overall News Coverage and Mentions of Mormonism (*New York Times*)
Source: *New York Times Article Archive*

There was considerable variation in the percentage of the mentions that involved a reference to Mormons. For the first three candidacies (George Romney 1968, Udall 1976, Hatch 2000), the proportion of Mormon mentions was relatively low, while it was much higher for the fourth and fifth candidacies (Mitt Romney 2007–8, Huntsman 2012). However, mentions of Mitt Romney's religion declined in the 2012 primaries and fell again in the 2012 general election. By this measure, the attention to George Romney's religion in the 1967 nomination campaign was roughly the same in relative terms as for Mitt Romney's religion in the 2012 general election.

Indeed, the spike in mentions of Mitt Romney's religion in the 2008 campaign suggests increased attention to Mormonism compared to the previous candidacies. These data also suggest that the novelty of Mormon candidates also mattered – especially for first-time candidates: Mitt Romney in 2008 and Huntsman in 2012 (and the fact that there were two Mormon candidates in 2012). Once the candidate's religion was no longer novel, there were fewer mentions of his religion, such as with Mitt Romney in the 2012 campaigns. It is likely that in 1967 George Romney's religion was novel as well, but there is no previous Mormon candidate for comparison.

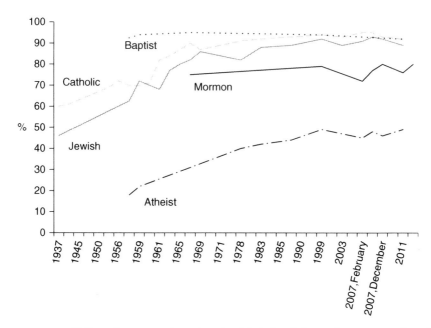

FIGURE 8.2. If Your Party Nominated a Qualified Candidate Who Happened to be
a _____, Would You Vote for that Person?
*Source:* Gallup Polls

It is worth noting that before 2008, Mormonism was mentioned more in
news stories that were not about presidential candidates than in stories that
were. This pattern suggests that attention to Mormons candidates was less a
product of greater attention to the LDS Church specifically than of the greater
salience of religion in presidential politics.[5] In sum, information about
Mormon candidates' religion expanded between 1967 and 2012, and this
expansion appears to have been driven by the changing nature of presidential
campaigns.

A second step is to assess public attitudes toward Mormon candidates
between 1967 and 2012. Figure 8.2 reports Gallup survey data on religion and
presidential candidates drawn from this question:

*Between now and the [year] political conventions, there will be discussion about the
qualifications of presidential candidates – their education, age, religion, race, and so on. If
your party nominated a generally well-qualified person for president who happened to be
[religion], would you vote for that person?*

[5] These data were collected from the *New York Times Article Archive* for 1967, 1999, 2007, 2011,
and 2012.

Starting in 1937, this question included generic Catholic and Jewish candidates, with generic Baptist and atheist candidates added in the late 1950s; a generic Mormon candidate was included in 1967, 1999, 2007, 2011, and 2012.[6]

Overall, these data show the decline of ethno-religious politics during the restructuring of American religion (see Chapter 2): the willingness to vote for generic Catholic and Jewish candidates steadily increased over time, while willingness to vote for a generic Baptist presidential candidate remained relatively high (all three showed modest declines toward 2012). Support for a generic atheist candidate also increased, but remained relatively low.

There was a different pattern for Mormons. In 1967 (75 percent) and again in 1999 (79 percent), willingness to vote for a generic Mormon candidate was lower than for generic Baptist, Catholic, and Jewish candidates (but remained above an atheist candidate). In 2007, support for a Mormon candidate declined (bottoming out at 72 percent of the public in February 2007). After some fluctuation, willingness to vote for a Mormon returned to roughly its 1967 in June 2011 (76 percent), when the presidential campaign was underway, and then rose modestly by June 2012 (80 percent), as the general election campaign was just beginning. Thus, opposition to a generic Mormon candidate was about the same in the initial stages of George Romney's 1967 nomination campaign against Richard Nixon and Mitt Romney's 2012 general election campaign against Barack Obama.

The basic Gallup question probably understates public opposition to a Mormon presidential candidate. At the low point in the series, respondents were asked a follow-up query on how comfortable they were in voting for a Mormon candidate. In these data, just 58 percent of respondents say they would vote for a Mormon candidate "without reservations" and another 14 percent said they would do so "with reservations." If the latter were added to the 28 percent openly opposed to a Mormon candidate, the level of opposition is 42 percent.[7]

A variety of other surveys at the time found a similar level of opposition to a generic Mormon candidate (see Bringhurst and Foster 2011, 248–9). For example, a 2007 Pew survey found that 25 percent of Americans were "less likely" to vote for a Mormon presidential candidate (with 6 percent "more likely" and 68 percent reporting no difference). As Figure 8.3 shows, opposition to a generic Mormon candidate was more common among respondents with unfavorable views toward Mormons, a belief that Mormons are not Christians, and the perception that their faith differed from the LDS Church.[8] This pattern suggests that opposition to a generic Mormon candidate was rooted in negative perceptions of the faith, as described in Chapter 7.

---

[6] See Data Appendix for details of the Gallup 1967; Gallup 1999; Gallup 2007a, b, and c; Gallup 2011; and Gallup 2012 surveys.

[7] See Data Appendix for the details of the Gallup 2007a survey.

[8] See Data Appendix for the details of the Pew 2007 survey.

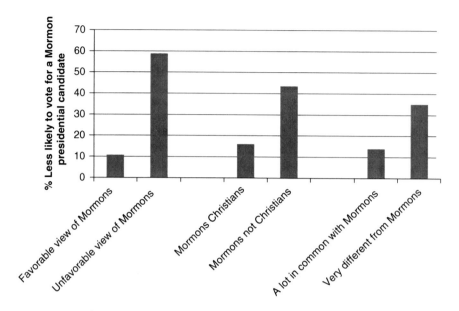

FIGURE 8.3. Who Is Less Likely to Vote for a Mormon Candidate?
Source: Pew Forum on Religion & Public Life, 2007

Figure 8.4 plots both the mentions of Mormon candidates' religion and the opposition to a generic Mormon candidate. The two series rise to a peak in 2007 and then decline afterwards. These dual high points coincide with the 2008 Republican nomination contest. After 2008, the level of mentions and generic opposition both decline. This pattern suggests that the information received by the public about Mormon candidates had a negative frame – and such information evoked a negative reaction. In turn, this suggestion points to the role of presidential campaigns in the flow of such information.

Although opposition to a generic Mormon candidate was basically constant between 1967 and 2012, there were substantial shifts in the partisan location of the opposition – just as one might expect if presidential campaigns were a major cause. As shown in Figure 8.5, Democrats were more opposed to a generic Mormon candidate than Republicans in 1967 and 1999. In 2007, however, Democrats and Republicans were nearly evenly matched in their opposition to a generic Mormon candidate. By 2012 – after a Mormon candidate became the presumptive GOP presidential nominee – Democratic opposition remained high and Republican opposition declined substantially.

Shifts among religious groups were an important feature of this partisan change. Figures 8.6A and 8.6B report opposition to a generic Mormon candidate by key Democratic and Republican religious constituencies, some associated with

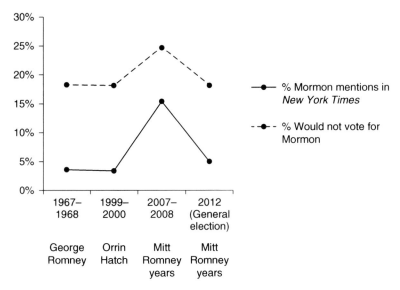

FIGURE 8.4. Media Coverage and Opposition to a Mormon Candidate
*Source: New York Times Article Archive*, Gallup Polls

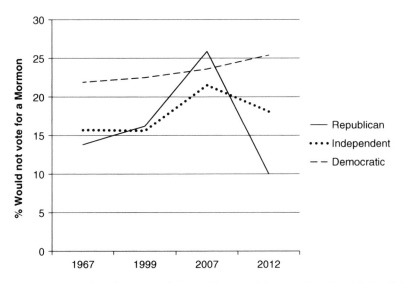

FIGURE 8.5. Party Identification and Opposition to a Mormon Presidential Candidate
*Source:* Gallup Polls

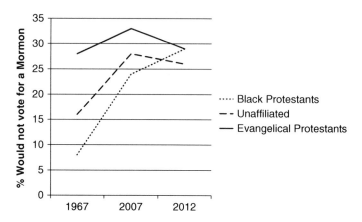

FIGURE 8.6A. Among Democrats, Black Protestants and the Religiously Unaffiliated Became More Likely to Oppose a Mormon Candidate (Democrats Only)
*Source:* Gallup Polls

secular tensions (the unaffiliated) and some with religious tensions (evangelical and black Protestants).

As Figure 8.6A shows, evangelical Democrats were the most opposed to a Mormon presidential candidate in 1967 and were still the most opposed in 2012. Meanwhile, black Protestant Democrats went from being the least opposed in 1967 to nearly as opposed as evangelical Democrats in 2012. Unaffiliated Democrats also became more opposed over time. As Figure 8.6B shows, evangelical Republicans were more opposed to a generic Mormon candidate than mainline Republicans in 1967 (but less than their Democratic coreligionists), but by 2012, they were less opposed, nearly matching mainline Republicans.

All these religious groups showed an increase in opposition to a generic Mormon candidate in 2007, with evangelical Republicans roughly tying with evangelical Democrats in this regard. Except for black Protestant Democrats, all the groups showed some decline in opposition to a generic Mormon candidate in 2012.

In part, these religious shifts reflect the restructuring of American religion, with the rise of the "religious right" and the "secular left." In 2012, opposition to a generic Mormon candidate was concentrated among *both* regular worship attenders and nonattenders.[9] Figure 8.7 highlights that the combination of

---

[9] Overall, there was a modest increase in opposition among regular worship attenders between 1967 and 2012 using the Gallup measure of whether the respondent reported attending worship in the previous seven days.

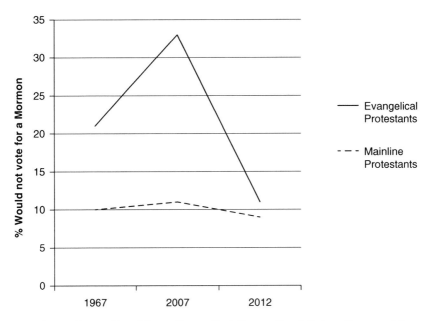

FIGURE 8.6B.   Among Republicans, Evangelicals Became Less Likely to Oppose a Mormon
Candidate (Republicans Only)
*Source:* Gallup Polls

religious and secular tensions associated with the sacred tabernacle shown in
Chapter 7 have a political manifestation as well.

These patterns are bolstered by individual-level data from Gallup surveys
on the relationship between public opposition to a generic Mormon candidate
and opposition to particular Mormon candidates (George Romney in 1967;
Mitt Romney in 2009 and 2012).[10] As Figure 8.8 shows, the percentage of
Democrats who had unfavorable views of the particular Mormon candidates
rose steadily between 1967 and 2012. A different pattern obtains for
Republicans: those opposed to a generic candidate became more unfavorable
toward the particular candidates between 1967 and 2007, but then became less
so between 2007 and 2012. Thus, it appears that negative public attitudes
toward Mormon candidates were linked to negative views of particular candidates in parallel with the extent, novelty, and framing of information about the
Mormon candidates.

---

[10]   See Data Appendix for the details of the Gallup 1967, Gallup 2007a, and Gallup 2012 surveys.
Although the measures of candidate favorability differed in these surveys, each was coded into a
three-point scale with approximately one-third of the samples in each category.

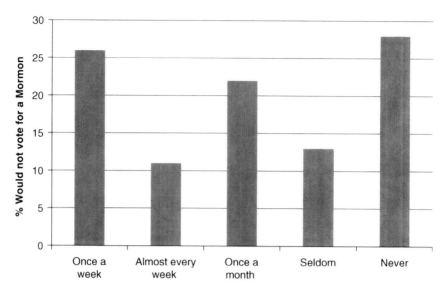

FIGURE 8.7. More Evidence of the Dual Tensions: Worship Attendance and Opposition to a Mormon Candidate, 2012
*Source:* Gallup Poll, 2012

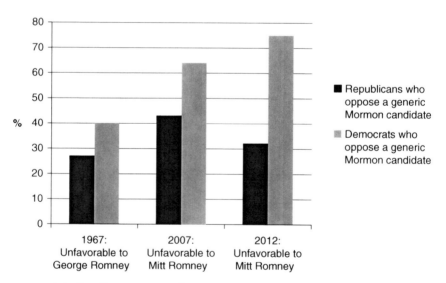

FIGURE 8.8. For Democrats, a Growing Connection between Opposing a Generic Mormon and Unfavorability toward a Specific Candidate
*Source:* Gallup Polls

Taken together, this evidence reveals a changing electoral context for Mormon presidential candidates: a relatively congenial context in 1967 and 2012, and a relatively non-congenial context in 2007. This shift appears to have had less to do with the level of underlying public opposition to generic Mormon candidates than with an expansion of information about particular Mormon candidates, and how that information was framed politically. Put another way, the degree of politicization of Mormon candidates' religion varied over this period.

## MORMON PRESIDENTIAL CAMPAIGNS, 1967–2012

A review of the major-party Mormon presidential candidates between 1967 and 2012 reveals the details of the politicization of their religion. The extent, novelty, and framing of information about the candidates' religion affected each race – including both the campaigns' approaches and the reactions of observers and critics.

The seven cases of Mormon presidential candidacies illustrate different combinations of candidate religiosity and electoral context. Four of the cases involve the Romneys: George Romney (1967 nomination campaign) or his son Mitt Romney (2008 and 2012 nomination campaigns, 2012 general election). Both were active Mormons and Republicans, but their campaigns occurred in different contexts: a nomination campaign in two different time frames, and a contrast between nomination and general election campaigns. In terms of Table 8.1, George Romney took an affirmation approach to his faith and Mitt Romney an alliance approach.

The three remaining Mormon candidacies offer contrasts with the Romneys' campaigns across both parties and time: Morris Udall, an inactive Mormon and a Democrat (1976 nomination campaign); Orrin Hatch, an active Mormon and Republican (2000 nomination campaign); and Jon Huntsman, Jr., an inactive Mormon and a Republican (2012 nomination campaign against fellow Mormon Mitt Romney). In terms of Table 8.1, Udall took an avoidance approach, Hatch an affirmation approach, and Huntsman an aloofness approach.

The level of politicization was modest for George Romney in 1968 and Morris Udall in 1976, and much stronger for Orrin Hatch in 2000, Jon Huntsman, Jr. in 2012, and Mitt Romney in 2008 and 2012.

### George Romney, 1968

On November 18, 1967, George W. Romney announced his candidacy for the 1968 Republican presidential nomination. An active Mormon, he perceived an electoral context congenial to his faith, taking an affirmation approach to religion and making it a prominent feature of his campaign. Due to other political problems, Romney suspended his candidacy two weeks before the New Hampshire primary on February 28, 1968.[11]

George Romney displayed many of the markers of an active Mormon. Having descended from Mormon pioneers, he was born in a polygamous community in Mexico in 1907, although by 1911, his monogamous parents had resettled in Salt Lake City. He graduated from the Latter-day Saint High School, spent two years as a missionary, and married a fellow Mormon in the Salt Lake Temple in 1931. Devout as an adult, he held various Church offices, eventually serving as president of the Detroit stake.

Romney's political path was unusual for a Mormon officeholder of his generation. After a successful career as an automobile executive, he became the first Mormon elected governor outside of the Mountain West. In an era when Mormons were elected from both parties, Romney was the only statewide GOP candidate to win in solidly Democratic Michigan. Although his faith was an issue in his initial 1962 gubernatorial campaign, it was not when he won reelection in 1964 and 1966.[12] In 1968, Romney was the first Mormon to seek a major party nomination for the White House.

Based on his record in Michigan, Romney offered himself as a progressive alternative to other GOP contenders. His 1968 nomination strategy was common in the era of a closed nomination: demonstrate electoral viability to party leaders by winning the New Hampshire primary. Yet unlike Republican contenders at the time, Romney made his religion a prominent part of his campaign.

Romney discussed his faith to illustrate his personal values, including "belief in individual responsibility, moral order, God and brotherhood" (Coit 1968, 28).[13] Like John F. Kennedy in 1960, he strongly defended the separation of church and state, but unlike Kennedy, he asserted a crucial role for religion in politics, drawing on his 1966 speech, "Most Important is Faith."[14] Romney saw the greatest threats to the country as "the decline of religious conviction, moral character, and family life" (Shannon 1967, 56), arguing that America needed "leadership worthy of God's blessing" (*Newsweek* 1967b). His religion was highlighted by a well-publicized trip to Utah and he had enthusiastic support from prominent Mormons, such as hotel executive J. Willard Marriott, who headed Romney's fundraising. LDS Church President David O. McKay

---

[11]  This section relies on Mollenhoff (1968) and also Bringhurst and Foster (2011, 62–77).

[12]  In the 1962 gubernatorial election, Romney was criticized for the LDS Church's ban on the ordination of African Americans (Mollenhoff 1968, 186). Interestingly, his Democratic opponent also had a similar religious background, having been raised in the Reorganized Church of Jesus Christ of Latter Day Saints, the primary offshoot of the LDS Church that formed after Joseph Smith's death.

[13]  See *Dialogue* (1967) for an interview with Romney in a publication geared toward an LDS audience.

[14]  For the full text of this speech, see Bringhurst and Foster (2011, 349–352).

also offered positive comments about Romney's candidacy (Mollenhoff 1968, 257–60).[15]

Thus the Romney campaign was a source of extensive and novel information about the candidate's religion. Some observers had positive responses to this information (Brower 1967), but it also provoked negative reactions, revealing the secular and religious tensions associated with the sacred tabernacle. Secular criticism centered on Romney's personal piety, which was emblematic of Mormons generally (see Chapter 3). Student protestors at Dartmouth College in New Hampshire proclaimed that "God is alive and thinks he is George Romney" (Weaver 1967, 45); others described Romney as a "latter-day Puritan" (Shannon 1967, 60) and "the most avowedly religious candidate since the fundamentalist Bryan last ran in 1908" (Kilpatrick 1967, 1374). Here the campaign had no effective response because "Romney's politics and his piety were inseparable" (Lythgoe 1971, 240). Religious criticism focused on the LDS Church's restriction of African Americans from the priesthood, a policy that was increasingly unusual among American churches by the late 1960s (see Chapter 3). Romney refused to criticize the Church publicly, but took pains to distinguish his personal views from LDS policy (*Newsweek* 1967a).

However, there is little evidence that rival Republican candidates criticized his religion openly – campaign activity that would naturally attract media attention. It could be that his rivals were unsure of how to respond to the novelty of the Romney campaign in this regard, especially in light of the impact of religion in the 1960 presidential election (when Kennedy's Catholicism was an issue). And there may have been little to be gained by mobilizing religious opposition when the dominant religious group in the GOP coalition, mainline Protestants, had generally positive views of Mormons (Figure 8.6B). Besides, Romney's poorly managed campaign offered other effective avenues for attack.

What impact did Romney's religion have on the nomination campaign? On balance, his affirmation approach was probably beneficial. Romney's religion attracted relatively modest media attention, despite the campaign's open discussion of Mormonism and the novelty of a Mormon presidential candidate (see Figure 8.1). Although public opposition to a generic Mormon candidate was relatively high (see Figure 8.2), this opposition was not strongly linked to unfavorable views of Romney (see Figure 8.8). Religious and secular criticism of Romney's faith had only a modest impact because evangelical and secular voters were not a major factor in the 1968 GOP nomination contest. However, Romney's religion could have been a larger issue if the nomination campaign had gone on longer or into a general election (Lythgoe 1971).

---

[15] Not all of the LDS leaders backed Romney, including Ezra Taft Benson, a future president of the Church. In 1967, Benson was actively considering an independent presidential campaign and in 1968 he turned down an invitation to be George Wallace's vice-presidential running mate (Bringhurst and Foster 2011, 133–61).

In sum, Romney's Mormonism was only modestly politicized during the 1968 nomination campaign, but the campaign reveals the dimensions of the stained-glass ceiling that would be problematic for future Mormon candidates – including his own son a generation later.

## Morris Udall, 1976

On October 24, 1974, Morris K. Udall announced his candidacy for the 1976 Democratic presidential nomination. An inactive Mormon, he perceived the electoral context to be congenial to religion, taking an avoidance approach and discussing his religious background as little as possible. Udall finished second in the nomination contests, suspending his candidacy at the end of the season on June 12, 1976.[16]

Udall displayed few markers of an active Mormon. Like George Romney, his ancestors were Mormon pioneers – in fact, their grandfathers had done Church work together in Arizona, where Udall was born in 1922. But Udall became religiously inactive as a child. He graduated from public high school, attended the University of Arizona, married a lapsed Episcopalian in a civil ceremony in 1949, divorced in 1966, and married two more times. Udall later said, "I have not found a need for organized religion in my life," but expressed support for many Christian values in public policy (Carson and Johnson 2001, 146).

Udall's political path was not unusual for a Mormon officeholder of his generation: he was from the Mountain West, with Mormon roots and low levels of activity, and elected as a Democrat. After practicing law, Udall won a special election for the congressional seat vacated when his brother, Stewart Udall, was appointed U.S. Secretary of the Interior in 1961. He won a very close race over a conservative Republican and active Mormon, but religion did not appear to have been a factor in his subsequent congressional campaigns.[17] Throughout his career, Udall identified as a Mormon, despite his strong disagreement with LDS Church policies, especially the exclusion of African-American men from the priesthood.

Based on his congressional record, Udall offered himself as a liberal alternative to other Democratic contenders. Like George Romney, his 1976 nomination strategy was to win the New Hampshire primary. But changes in party rules had created a more open nomination process, where campaigning for the support of primary voters played a larger role than courting the favor of party leaders. Unlike the Republican coalition in 1968, the Democrats had diverse religious constituencies that candidates could mobilize to win nomination contests. The Udall campaign chose to ignore religion altogether, providing little

---

[16] This section relies on Carson and Johnson (2001) and Bringhurst and Foster (2011, 78–97).

[17] Udall's well-known Republican opponent was associated with the John Birch Society, like Ezra Taft Benson (who opposed George Romney in 1968), and campaigned on opposition to big government and civil rights (Carson and Johnson 2001, 58).

information on the subject and receiving little criticism on this score – with one notable exception.

Former Georgia Governor Jimmy Carter took the opposite approach, making his evangelical Protestant faith a prominent part of his campaign. He gained attention in the largely uncontested Iowa caucuses and rode the momentum to a victory over Udall in New Hampshire, and subsequently defeated him in a very close Wisconsin primary.

Then, during the hard-fought Michigan primary, the Carter campaign raised the issue of the LDS Church's policy on race. Speaking to an audience of black Baptist ministers, Detroit Mayor Coleman Young, an African American and Carter ally, said: "I am asking you to make a choice between a man from Georgia who fights to let you in his church, and a man from Arizona whose church won't even let you in the back door" (Witcover 1977, 338). Udall strongly objected to this attack, pointing to his break with the Church over this policy – and thus highlighting both his Mormon background and religious inactivity. Carter went on to win the Michigan primary by about 2,200 voters; Udall's religion was not raised in subsequent contests.

What impact did Udall's Mormon background have on the campaign? On balance, Udall's avoidance of his religious background was probably beneficial. The subject attracted the least media attention of all the Mormon campaigns (see Figure 8.1), largely because there was little to report except for the Carter campaign's attack. Evidence on the impact of this criticism is inconclusive. On the one hand, Carter did no better among all black voters in Michigan than he had done previously in Wisconsin,[18] and black Protestants were among the religious groups least opposed to a Mormon candidate (see Figure 8.6A). On the other hand, the black Protestant vote in Michigan split almost evenly between the two candidates, with Carter having a very slight edge – perhaps just enough to win.

However, there was potential opposition to a Mormon candidate among evangelical Democrats in 1976. Among the 62 percent of the Michigan primary voters who preferred a candidate "who stresses the need to restore honesty and other moral values in our government," Carter won a large majority – and he did especially well with evangelicals. But among the 38 percent of voters who preferred a candidate "who proposes specific programs to deal with pressing national problems," Udall won a large majority – except for evangelicals. In a contest over "moral values," an active evangelical who talked openly about his faith was likely more competitive than an inactive Mormon who avoided the subject. A positive note for Udall was his success among unaffiliated voters, where his response to Carter may have been an asset.

As with George Romney in 1968, Udall's religious background was only modestly politicized during the 1976 nomination campaign, but it reveals

---

[18] See Data Appendix for details on the 1976 Wisconsin and Michigan exit polls.

the dimensions of the stained-glass ceiling that would vex future Mormon candidates.

## Orrin Hatch, 2000

On July 2, 1999, Orrin G. Hatch announced his candidacy for the 2000 Republican presidential nomination. An active Mormon, he perceived the electoral context to be congenial to his faith, taking an affirmation approach to religion and making it a building block of his campaign. Hatch suspended his candidacy after finishing last in the Iowa caucuses on February 3, 2000.[19]

Like George Romney, Hatch displayed many markers of an active Mormon. His ancestors were Mormon pioneers, but he was born in Pittsburgh, Pennsylvania in 1934. He attended Brigham Young University, did two years of service as a missionary, and married a Utah Mormon in the Salt Lake Temple in 1957. Devout as an adult, Hatch moved his family and legal career to Salt Lake City in 1969.

Like Udall, Hatch's political path was not unusual for Mormon officeholders of his generation: he was elected from the Mountain West, with strong Mormon roots and active faith, and elected as a Republican. In 1976, Hatch ran as a long-shot candidate for a U.S. Senate seat in Utah, where he won a four-way Republican primary and then defeated incumbent Democratic Senator Frank Moss. His success resulted from staunch conservatism and vigorous grassroots campaigning. His Mormon credentials were an issue in 1976, but not in his subsequent senate campaigns.[20]

Based on his senate record, Hatch offered himself as a conservative alternative to other GOP contenders. His 2000 nomination strategy was to establish credibility by doing well in the Iowa caucuses, now a key part of the open nomination process. But much had changed since Democrat Jimmy Carter pioneered this strategy in 1976. In contrast to 1968, it had become common for Republican presidential contenders to talk openly about their faith to win nomination contests, responding to the shift of evangelicals and other social conservatives into the GOP coalition.

Drawing on the experience of his 1976 senate campaign, Hatch set out to build an organization to deliver his staunchly conservative message. He identified his coreligionists as "a natural constituency" (Bernick, Jr. 1999a), targeting Iowa's 16,000 Mormons for grassroots activities and LDS Church members nationwide for fundraising (Bernick, Jr. 1999b; Davidson 1999). Hatch further publicized his faith with comments concerning the "White Horse Prophecy" (see

---

[19] This section relies on Roderick (2000) and Bringhurst and Foster (2011, 98–118).
[20] In the 1976 campaign, opponents accused Hatch of being a carpetbagger and Hatch responded by identifying his Mormon ancestors and defending his Church activity (Bringhurst and Foster 2011, 105).

Chapter 5),[21] suggesting that he may have seen himself as fulfilling the prophecy about "the elders of Zion" rescuing the U.S. Constitution as it "hangs by a thread" (Heilprin 1999).

Thus the Hatch campaign provided extensive and novel information about his religion. However, most of the reaction was negative, especially among evangelicals and other social conservative activists in Iowa. Some campaigned against Hatch because of his Mormonism, while others supported conservative candidates with more congenial faiths, such as Baptist Gary Bauer, Catholic Alan Keyes, or Methodist George W. Bush. Hatch complained that "Bigotry has raised its ugly head in Iowa," accusing rival candidates of exploiting religious prejudice and the news media of an anti-Mormon bias (Spangler and Bernick, Jr. 1999). This religious criticism was coupled with regular and pointed dismissal of Hatch's prospects by commentators from across the political spectrum.

What impact did Hatch's Mormonism have in the 2000 campaign? Hatch's affirmation approach to his faith was problematic. Although the religious aspects of his campaign attracted about as much attention from the media as Romney's 1968 campaign (see Figure 8.1) and public opposition to a Mormon candidate was the same (see Figure 8.2), Hatch's religion mattered a great deal in Iowa. As Bringhurst and Foster conclude: "With Hatch, the Mormon issue also emerged more prominently as a direct consequence of the greater attention given the religious beliefs of the various candidates running for president" (2011, 118).

Unlike 1968 and 1976, Hatch's religion was strongly politicized in 2000, further revealing the dimensions of the stained-glass ceiling.

### Jon Huntsman, Jr. 2012

On June 14, 2011, Jon M. Huntsman, Jr. announced his candidacy for the 2012 Republican presidential nomination. An inactive Mormon, he perceived the electoral context to be non-congenial to his faith, taking an aloofness approach to his religious background and actively distancing himself from it. After losing the New Hampshire primary to fellow Mormon Mitt Romney, he suspended his candidacy on January 23, 2012.[22]

Huntsman showed some of the markers of an active Mormon. Like Romney, Udall, and Hatch, his ancestors were Mormon pioneers (he shares a common ancestor with the Romneys). He was born into a devout family in Palo Alto, California in 1960. He served two years as a missionary, earned a G.E.D., and graduated from the University of Pennsylvania. In 1984, he married a convert to the LDS Church. But as an adult, Huntsman became a less active Mormon.

---

[21] For the text of the prophecy see Bringhurst and Foster (2011, 338–48). It surfaces in political discussion enough that the Church has formally distanced itself from it (Church of Jesus Christ of Latter-day Saints 2010a).

[22] This section relies on Bringhurst and Foster (2011, 293–318).

Huntsman's political path differed somewhat from other Mormon office-holders of his generation. He held a series of high-level foreign policy appointments under Republican presidents before being elected governor of Utah in 2004 and reelected in 2008. Many observers were surprised by the differences between the conservative policies of his first term – which fit well with the views of most Mormons – and the moderate policies of his second term. However, a bigger surprise came in 2009, when Huntsman was appointed U.S. Ambassador to China by President Barack Obama. He resigned his ambassadorship in 2011 to seek the 2012 Republican presidential nomination.

Based on his government experience, Huntsman offered himself as a moderate alternative to other Republican contenders. Like George Romney and Morris Udall, his strategy was to win the New Hampshire primary. However, Huntsman's model was John McCain, whose presidential campaign he had endorsed in 2008. McCain had successfully navigated the open nomination system and faith-based politics in part by skipping the Iowa caucuses and winning the New Hampshire primary. In 2008, McCain defeated Mitt Romney in New Hampshire – a feat Huntsman hoped to duplicate in 2012, setting up a much-discussed "Mormon primary" in the Granite State (Ball and Martin 2011).

After he left Utah, Huntsman began distancing himself from his Mormon background. In 2010, he told an interviewer, "I can't say that I am overly religious. . . . I get satisfaction from many different types of religions and philosophies" (Ball and Martin 2011). Later he described himself as more "spiritual than religious," and equivocated on whether he still belonged to the LDS Church, saying, "That's tough to define. . . . There are varying degrees [of Mormons]. I come from a long line of saloon keepers and proselytizers, and I draw from both sides" (Henneberger 2011, 30). But unlike George Romney and Orrin Hatch, and perhaps like Morris Udall, Huntsman saw no public role for faith: "I believe in a strict separation of religion and politics."[23]

Thus, the Huntsman campaign provided extensive and novel information about the current state of the candidate's religion. Although Huntsman received some political praise from observers, he drew criticism in LDS circles and little support from other religious or secular sources (Bringhurst and Foster 2011, 312–3). Mitt Romney won the "Mormon primary" handily, 39 to 17 percent.

What impact did Huntsman's religion have on the election? His aloofness approach to his religious background was problematic. He attracted a high level of media attention in the early stage of his campaign (see Figure 8.1) and the level of opposition to a Mormon candidate was relatively high (see Figure 8.2). Yet in New Hampshire, Huntsman did not do especially well with unaffiliated voters,

---

[23] Personal interview with John Green, November 15, 2012, University of Akron.

garnering just 21 percent compared to 47 percent for Ron Paul. Meanwhile, he received just 9 percent of the evangelical vote, compared to 31 percent for Romney.[24] It is hard to see how Huntsman would have done much better in South Carolina, the next contest of the season, where evangelicals are a much larger share of Republican primary voters.

In sum, Mormonism was already highly politicized in 2012 and the Huntsman campaign could not remain aloof from it – a case study that reveals an additional dimension of the stained-glass ceiling.

### Mitt Romney, 2008–2012

On February 13, 2007, Willard "Mitt" Romney announced his candidacy for the 2008 Republican presidential nomination and, after disappointing results in the Super Tuesday contests, he suspended campaigning on February 7, 2008. A little more than four years later, Mitt Romney announced his second nomination bid on June 2, 2011, this time securing the Republican presidential nomination by June 6, 2012. Romney then shifted to the general election campaign, losing a close contest to Barack Obama on November 8, 2012. An active Mormon, Romney perceived the electoral context to be non-congenial to his faith in all three campaigns, taking an alliance approach to religion, discussing his faith cautiously, and stressing its commonalities with other religions.[25]

Mitt Romney displayed many of the markers of an active Mormon. The youngest son of George Romney and hence a fifth-generation Mormon, he was born in 1947 in Detroit, Michigan. Like Huntsman, he attended public and private schools and did two years of missionary service, and then in 1968 married a convert to Mormonism in the Salt Lake Temple. Like Hatch, Romney graduated from Brigham Young University, and then earned a graduate degree from Harvard University. Like his father, Romney was devout as an adult, eventually serving as both a bishop and then a stake president in Boston.

Mitt Romney's political path also resembled his father's. After a successful business career, Mitt Romney ran for the U.S. Senate in Massachusetts in 1994 against Ted Kennedy – a context perhaps as non-congenial to a Republican Mormon as Michigan had been in 1962 for his father George Romney. As with Morris Udall in 1976, the hard-fought contest provoked an attack from the Kennedy campaign on the LDS Church's past policy on race (which had been changed in 1978, see Chapter 3). Romney responded vigorously to this criticism, raising the ironic example of John F. Kennedy's defense of religious tolerance in 1960. Although the impact of this issue was inconclusive, Romney ended up losing to Ted Kennedy (Rimer 1994).

---

[24] For the 2012 New Hampshire exit poll, see http://www.cnn.com/election/2012/primaries/epolls/nh (accessed October 7, 2013).
[25] This section relies on Kranish and Helman (2012) and Bringhurst and Foster (2011, 229–92).

After successfully rescuing the troubled Salt Lake City 2002 Winter Olympics, Romney ran for governor of Massachusetts in 2002. This race was close and hard fought, but Romney's Mormonism did not feature prominently in the campaign. In fact, Romney's religion received only about half as many media mentions as in 1994 (Paulson 2002) – a pattern similar to his later 2008 and 2012 presidential nomination campaigns (and analogous to his father's experience in Michigan). Romney became only the second Mormon elected governor outside of the Mountain West.

Based on his management record, Romney offered himself as a moderate conservative alternative to other GOP contenders, adjusting his message to shifts in the electoral context. In 2008, he stressed his conservative credentials in a field of rivals that included more moderate candidates (such as John McCain). In 2012, he was viewed as the front-runner, and he stressed his moderate credentials in a field dominated by more conservative rivals (such as Rick Santorum). In both years, Romney followed a well-tested plan for securing the nomination: win the Iowa caucuses, use the momentum to win the New Hampshire primary, and then secure the nomination in the later primaries. This approach recognized the open nature of the nomination process, the religious diversity of the GOP coalition, and the likelihood of faith-based attacks by rivals.

As befitting a CEO, Romney planned his campaigns methodically (Levenson 2007a), developing cautious themes that could appeal to a broad range of Republican voters and seeking to promote the themes with great discipline. With regard to religion, his alliance approach fell in between his father's affirmation and Morris Udall's avoidance. Rather than address his Mormonism directly, Romney chose to respond to the issue as it arose, in a minimal fashion and using the following tactics:

1. *Deflection.* If asked about distinctive Mormon beliefs and practices, Romney sought to deflect the query, noting that he was running for "commander-in-chief" and not "pastor-in-chief." If necessary, the campaign directed the questioner to the LDS Church for answers, arguing that Romney could not speak for the Church (Stephanopoulos 2007).
2. *Parallels to Other Faiths.* If deflection was unsuccessful, the campaign downplayed Mormon distinctiveness, drawing parallels to other faiths. If necessary, Romney distanced himself from well-known aspects of Mormon distinctiveness, such as the long-discontinued practice of polygamy and the past LDS policy on race (Reilly 2006).
3. *Demands for Tolerance.* When attacked on the religion issue, Romney responded with John F. Kennedy's defense of religious tolerance. If necessary, Romney responded directly to such attacks but without discussing the details of his faith (Hamby 2011).
4. *Appeals to Common Values.* When pressed on his faith, Romney made appeals to religious values common to Mormons and other faiths. If necessary, Romney would discuss his religious commitment and volunteer service to reinforce such connections (Memoli 2012).

Romney felt this approach would be effective and proclaimed that "America is ready for people of almost any faith to lead the country" (Bringhurst and Foster 2011, 248).

This strategy was adjusted over the course of the 2008 and 2012 campaigns. But the largest adjustment came in December 2007, when campaign events led Romney to discuss his faith directly – something he had hoped to avoid (Levenson 2007b). The result was "Faith in America," a well-covered speech that fit the alliance approach of the campaign.[26]

Although Romney acknowledged "differences in theology" between Mormons and other Americans, the speech did not discuss the details of his faith, as George Romney had done in various venues. The speech also deployed John F. Kennedy's religious tolerance argument: "A person should not be elected because of his faith nor should he be rejected because of his faith." But the major theme of the speech was religion as a source of common moral convictions in public life, a role protected by religious liberty and threatened by a "religion of secularism." The concern with secular tensions resembled his father's "Most Important is Faith" speech in 1966, but the emphasis on reducing religious tensions was novel.

The most novel aspect of the speech was a dramatic effort to draw a parallel between Mormons and other Christians, especially evangelicals, when Romney proclaimed: "I believe that Jesus Christ is the Son of God and the Savior of mankind." Romney would repeat these themes – including the last one – numerous times in the 2012 campaigns. (In Chapter 9, we examine how voters reacted to the themes of Romney's speech.)

In addition to campaign themes, Romney cautiously mobilized financial and campaign support from coreligionists (Rutenberg 2012) and also sought support from leaders of the Christian Right (Bacon, Jr. 2007). The Romney campaign adjusted its tactics in light of campaign experience. For example, in the 2008 Iowa caucuses, the campaign said little about the candidate's religion while spending heavily on television touting the candidate's conservative record and seeking to mobilize conservative caucus participants (Burr 2008). By way of contrast, in 2012 Romney used television – and even a passing reference to his religious commitment – to distinguish himself from a conservative opponent (Shahid 2011) and shifted to micro-targeting technology both to mobilize voters likely to support him and to avoid contact with those likely to oppose him based on religion (Issenberg 2012).

The Romney campaign thus provided limited and largely conventional information on the candidate's religion. This information generated some positive responses, especially with regard to the "Faith in America" speech. But it also generated intense criticism on secular and religious grounds. On the first count, the left-leaning *New Republic* ran a cover story arguing that the hierarchical nature of the LDS Church raised legitimate doubts about a Mormon president

---

[26] For the full text of this speech, see Bringhurst and Foster (2011, 353–60).

(Linker 2006). Other critics objected to the supernatural beliefs of Mormons (Weisberg 2006), while still others attacked the social issue positions of the LDS Church (Hewitt 2007, Chapter 10).

On religious grounds, Romney received some pushback from fellow Mormons for his cautious approach to discussing his faith (Patashnick 2007), while many social conservatives were skeptical of Romney's "flip-flops" on abortion (Bringhurst and Foster 2011, 251–2) and evangelicals opposed his religion on theological grounds. A good example of the latter criticism came in 2011, when evangelical Pastor Robert Jeffress introduced a rival candidate, Texas Governor Rick Perry, as "a genuine follower of Jesus Christ" at the "Values Voters Summit" in Washington, DC. Jeffress later said that Romney was "not a Christian" and that Mormons were a "cult." Jeffress then noted that Romney's faith was a political problem for Republicans:

I think it is going to be a major factor among evangelical voters.... Most people don't want to admit – even evangelical Christians – that they have a problem with Mormonism. They think it is bigoted to say so. But what voters say to a pollster sometimes is different than what they do when they go into the privacy of a voting booth. (Oppel and Eckholm 2011)

This kind of criticism was common on the campaign trail (Spencer 2007), which enabled some rival Republicans to take advantage of it in both the 2008 and 2012 nomination campaigns. The best example was Mike Huckabee in 2007. Like Democrat Jimmy Carter in 1976, he was a former Southern governor (of Arkansas) and a Southern Baptist (a former pastor), who made his evangelical faith a campaign theme. He rallied Christian Right leaders, evangelical pastors, and "Huck's Army" of grassroots volunteers. He also raised the Mormon issue. In a *New York Times* profile, Huckabee asked rhetorically, "Don't Mormons believe that Jesus and the devil are brothers?" repeating a common evangelical criticism of LDS theology (Chafets 2007). Although he never mentioned Mormonism per se in 2012, former Pennsylvania Senator Rick Santorum, a Catholic, used a strident defense of traditional Christianity to emerge as Romney's chief rival.

As is common in many presidential nomination contests, Romney faced a roller-coaster ride of failures and successes. Like Hatch, he lost the Iowa caucuses decisively, to Mike Huckabee in 2008, and then lost the New Hampshire primary to John McCain. In 2012, Romney appeared to win the Iowa caucuses by eight ballots over Rick Santorum and took this "momentum" on to defeat fellow Mormon Jon Huntsman, Jr. in New Hampshire (but a recount later showed Santorum had actually won Iowa by thirty-four ballots). In both 2008 and 2012, Romney lost the South Carolina primary. In 2008, his losing streak extended to Florida and many Super Tuesday primaries, effectively ending his campaign, but in 2012, Romney won Florida and then traded victories with Rick Santorum, until he eventually emerged as the presumptive nominee.

## The 2012 General Election Campaign

Once Romney secured the Republican presidential nomination, he faced a strikingly different electoral context than the nomination contests. For one thing, the Democratic nominee, Barack Obama, was already disliked by most Republicans, and the campaign needed to appeal to independent voters. Also, the state-by-state calculus changed in a general election: some states that had been problematic for Romney, such as South Carolina, became solid wins, while others, like Iowa, became swing states.

In a time-honored fashion, Romney sought to unify the Republicans, shift his issue position to the center, and organize an effective general election campaign. Romney sought the endorsement of his rivals, especially Rick Santorum, to appeal to social conservatives, and he spoke at Liberty University, a fundamentalist Protestant school, to appeal to evangelicals. At the same time, social conservative and evangelical leaders worked hard on Romney's behalf. Former critics endorsed him, such as Pastor Robert Jeffress (Camia 2012). Notably, so did evangelical icon Billy Graham (Zaimov 2012).

The campaign also recalibrated its approach to religion, putting greater emphasis on Romney's piety and religious service. He talked about these topics in media interviews (Georgetown/On Faith 2012), in his acceptance speech at the Republican National Convention, and in the fall presidential debates. A good example appeared in *Cathedral Age*, a magazine of the Washington National Cathedral, which published interviews with both Obama and Romney. When asked, "How does faith play a role in your life?" Romney said:

Faith is integral to my life. I have served as a lay pastor in my church. I faithfully follow its precepts. I was taught in my home to honor God and love my neighbor. My father was committed to Martin Luther King, Jr.'s cause of equality, and I saw my parents provide compassionate care to others, in personal ways to people nearby and in leading national volunteer movements. My faith is grounded in the conviction that a consequence of our common humanity is our responsibility to one another – to our fellow Americans foremost, but also to every child of God.

The interviewer asked, "How do you respond to those who have questioned the sincerity of your faith and your Christianity?" Romney answered with a verbatim quote from his "Faith in America" speech:

I am often asked about my faith and my beliefs about Jesus Christ. I believe that Jesus Christ is the Son of God and the Savior of mankind. Every religion has its own unique doctrines and history. These should not be bases for criticism but rather a test of our tolerance. Religious tolerance would be a shallow principle indeed if it were reserved only for faiths with which we agree.

The interviewer went on to ask, "And what does a political leader's faith tell you about him/her as a person?"

A political leader's faith can tell us a great deal or nothing. So much depends on what lies behind that faith. And so much depends on deeds, not words. Perhaps the most important question to ask a person of faith who seeks a political office is whether he or she shares these American values: the equality of humankind, the obligation to serve one another, and a steadfast commitment to liberty. They are not unique to any one denomination. They belong to the great moral inheritance we hold in common. They are the firm ground on which Americans of different faiths meet and stand as a nation, united. ("Faith in America: Interviews with President Barack Obama and Governor Mitt Romney" 2012)

Romney was aided in this approach by the lack of faith-based criticisms from the Obama campaign – a surprise to some observers, including Orrin Hatch (Catanese 2012). But like Romney, Obama had little incentive to raise religion as an issue. After all, polls showed that a large minority of Americans believed Obama was a Muslim – an ethno-religious group even less popular than Mormons – and a larger group was unsure of Obama's religious affiliation (Pew Forum on Religion & Public Life 2012b). For the most part, the faith-based allies of each campaign followed a similar route, fiercely contesting the "Republican war on women" and the "Democratic war on religion," but with little reference to the candidate's faith. One exception was Harry Reid, the Democratic leader of the U.S. Senate, a fellow Mormon and a fierce Romney critic. In an interview, Reid argued that Romney had "sullied" the LDS faith and was "not the face of Mormonism" (Burr 2012b). By Election Day, religion had largely disappeared from the campaign as an issue. And the election results closely resembled 2008, when Obama defeated John McCain.

What impact did Romney's religion have on these elections? On balance, his alliance approach was successful, allowing him to be competitive in the 2008 nomination, win the 2012 nomination, and run a close race in the 2012 general election. Romney's religion attracted a great deal of attention in the 2008 nomination contests, despite the cautious approach by the campaign. However, the attention declined in the 2012 nomination contests, so that by the 2012 general election, the level of attention resembled the attention his father received in 1968 (see Figure 8.2). The increased attention in 2007 was associated with opposition to a generic Mormon candidate (see Figure 8.4); this shift occurred among most religious groups, but particularly evangelical Protestants (see Figure 8.6B). Then in 2012, such opposition declined back to its 1967 level – but with the Republican groups less opposed and opposition remaining high among Democratic groups, especially black Protestants. And as Figure 8.8 indicates, the linkage of such opposition with unfavorable views of Mitt Romney increased in 2008, but declined in 2012.

CONCLUSION

In sum, Romney's religion was strongly politicized in the 2008 and 2012 Republican nomination contests – much more so than for his father in 1968 and Udall in 1976, and perhaps about the same as for Hatch in 2000 and Huntsman in

2012. This politicization clearly hurt the Romney effort in key states at crucial moments. In 2008, the primary exit polls showed that he lost the "born-again or evangelical Christian" vote to Huckabee in the Iowa caucuses (46 percent to 19 percent) and South Carolina primary (43 percent to 11 percent); in 2012, he lost the evangelical vote to Santorum in Iowa (32 percent to 14 percent) and to Gingrich in South Carolina (44 percent to 22 percent).[27] Although Romney failed to overcome these setbacks in 2008, he did so in 2012.

Romney's religion was less politicized in the 2012 general election, in part because it was subsumed under partisanship (see Figure 8.5). The exit polls showed that Romney received 79 percent of the evangelical vote nationally, the same margin as George W. Bush in 2004, and evangelicals made up a larger portion of the electorate in 2012 than in 2004 (26 to 23 percent). Indeed, the 2012 faith-based vote looked much like the previous two elections.

The conventional wisdom on Election Night was that the religion issue had not been important to the final outcome. At the same time, Romney did not break the stained-glass ceiling that was first evident with Joseph Smith in 1844. In the next chapter, we further explore the impact of Mormonism on Romney's campaigns, and also examine the impact of Romney's campaigns on the public perception of Mormonism.

[27] For the 2008 primary exit poll data, see http://www.cnn.com/ELECTION/2008/primaries/results/scorecard/#R (accessed October 7, 2013) for each of the states. For the 2012 primary exit polls, see http://www.cnn.com/election/2012/primaries.html (accessed October 7, 2013) for each of the states.

# 9

## How Mormonism Affected Mitt; How Mitt Affected Mormonism

Chapter 8 provided an overview of Mitt Romney's political career and the role Mormonism has played within it. In this chapter, we dig deeper into voters' reactions to Romney's LDS faith. To do so, we begin with two incidents from his first and last campaigns that illustrate the Mormon paradox: peculiar people or quintessential Americans?

Romney's religion was first used against him during his unsuccessful 1994 U.S. Senate campaign against Ted Kennedy. With Romney and Kennedy tied in the polls and the campaign heating up, Joseph Kennedy, Ted's nephew and a member of the House of Representatives, played the religion card. He told reporters:

I believe very strongly in the separation between church and state. But I think that if a particular church has a belief that blacks are second-class citizens, and that's the stated belief of the church, or that women are second-class citizens, I mean you ought to take a look at those issues. (quoted in Allot 2012)

Kennedy later apologized, saying that he was unaware that the LDS Church had ended its racial restrictions in 1978 but, in doing so, nonetheless again reminded voters of the Church's controversial history regarding race. Notwithstanding his nephew's apology, Ted Kennedy himself entered the fray by once again raising the issue of the LDS Church and its pre-1978 racial policies. The Kennedy campaign was only picking up where Romney's opponent in the Republican primary, John Lakian, had left off. He too had broached the issue of Romney's religion, even referring to Romney as "Mr. Mormon" during a televised debate (R. L. Welch and Jensen 2007).

The second incident occurred in the fall of 2012, as Romney was in the midst of his tight presidential race against Barack Obama. Although buoyed by his strong performance in the first presidential debate, Romney faced continued criticism for comments he had made at a private fundraiser in which he dismissed 47 percent of Americans as "dependent upon government, who believe that they are victims … and so my job is not to worry about those people. I'll never convince them that they should take personal responsibility for their lives" (*New York Times* 2012). At the end of the second presidential debate, the two candidates were asked the following question by an audience member:

What do you believe is the biggest misperception that the American people have about you as a man and a candidate? Using specific examples, can you take this opportunity to debunk that misperception and set us straight?

Romney went first. In seeking to defuse criticism for his "47 percent" comment, he began by saying, "I care about 100 percent of the American people." After underscoring that point, he went on to say,

[M]y passion probably flows from the fact that I believe in God. And I believe we're all children of the same God. I believe we have a responsibility to care for one another. I–I served as a missionary for my church. I served as a pastor in my congregation for about 10 years. I've sat across the table from people who were out of work and worked with them to try and find new work or to help them through tough times. (ABC News 2012)

Romney was referencing one of the most potentially controversial parts of his biography, his Mormonism, to rebut one of the most damaging charges leveled against him, that he was a callous elitist. In doing so, he employed an alliance strategy by emphasizing the universalistic aspects of his faith (see Chapter 8).

The contrast between these two incidents underscores the paradox of Mormonism. Joseph Kennedy cast Mormonism in a negative light by alluding to some of its more distinctive and controversial past policies. Mitt Romney portrayed his Mormonism in a positive light by stressing a belief common to virtually all of the world's religions.

This chapter begins by asking how attitudes toward Mormons affected support for Romney. Which side of Mormonism mattered more? Did its peculiarity scare voters off or did its common ground with other religions win voters over? That is, how do voters respond to the different ways that Mormonism can be framed? Furthermore, how do the factors known to affect attitudes toward Mormons – factual knowledge and social contact – affect support for Romney?

We then turn the question around and ask whether attitudes toward Mormons were affected by Mitt Romney's time in the presidential spotlight. Did perceptions of Mormons change because of the twin facts that the nation's most prominent Republican was a Mormon and the most prominent Mormon was a Republican? One might think that having a Mormon come close to the presidency burnished Mormons' public image. Or perhaps the fact that Romney was running in an inherently partisan contest during a highly polarized time divided perceptions of Mormons along partisan lines.

## HOW DID ATTITUDES TOWARD MORMONS AFFECT MITT ROMNEY?

We concluded Chapter 8 with the consensus among the pundits on Election Night in 2012 that Romney's religion did not appear to be an important factor at the polls. However, the conventional wisdom that forms after the instant analysis of Election Night is deepened, corrected, and sometimes even reversed by in-depth analysis of more detailed data available well after the election. In the case of the 2012 election, we have used a statistical model to weigh the impact of voters' attitudes toward Mormons on the presidential vote, including a measure of Mormon perceptions combining the positive and negative stereotypes into a single index (see Chapter 7).[1] The model also contains an extensive array of factors that have long been known to predict both voter turnout and vote choice in elections.[2]

When we include the measure of Mormon stereotypes in the model, it has a relatively large and statistically significant impact on the vote. Importantly, attitudes toward Mormons have an impact on the vote *even when accounting for party identification.* In other words, perceptions of Mormons are not just a proxy for partisanship, even though, as we will explain below, there is a growing connection between voters' party preference and their attitudes toward Mormons. Based only on this information, one might be tempted to conclude that the Election Night conventional wisdom was wrong and that Romney's religion actually did have a large impact on the vote. But the story is not so simple. Statistical significance is not the same as substantive significance. We need more information before concluding that Mormon stereotypes were a major factor on Election Day. As evidence that perhaps anti- or pro-Mormonism did not matter so much after all, consider that adding the Mormon stereotypes to our model does not increase its predictive accuracy, as it only rises negligibly from 94.86 percent to 95.41 percent.

So, which is it? Did attitudes toward Mormons matter a lot (as suggested by the statistical significance) or a little (as suggested by the nonimprovement in predictive accuracy)? We can reconcile these apparently mixed signals when we look carefully at who holds what attitudes toward Mormons and those attitudes' measurable effect on both voter turnout and the probability of voting for Mitt Romney once at the polls. We have thus used a statistical model that has three possible outcomes: did not vote, voted for Romney, voted for Obama. We

---

[1] Our measure of Mormon stereotypes is a single factor score of all the stereotypes described in Chapter 7 but one – whether Mormons are "rich." It does not load well on the factor, presumably because of its ambiguous valence. The eigenvalue for the factor is 3.72. The model described in this paragraph is a logistic regression (1 = vote for Romney, 0 = vote for Obama). We calculated the percentage correctly predicted by using the "estat" command in STATA.

[2] The variables are party identification, race, gender, age, socioeconomic status, geographic region, as well as measures of religion like religious tradition, intensity of religious commitment, and having a religious versus secular worldview.

include "did not vote" as an option, given the hypothesis that voters with a negative view of Mormons would stay home on Election Day.[3]

Figure 9.1 displays the results of this analysis. For illustration, we highlight results from "pure" independents, those people who claim no allegiance to either party, in contrast to those who identify themselves as either Democrats or Republicans. The first panel displays the results for independents, showing the connection between the Mormon stereotypes and (a) abstention and (b) a vote for Romney (obviously, the remainder is the Obama vote). Among independents, there is a substantial rise in the percentage voting for Romney as attitudes toward Mormons become more positive – from 10 percent among those in the lowest quartile of perceptions toward Mormons to 73 percent among those in the top quartile. Voter abstention falls (that is, turnout rises) among those with positive stereotypes, but to a much lesser degree. The figure also includes a third piece of information that is vital for making sense out of the election results. Each bar represents the percentage of political independents that fall into each quartile of the Mormon stereotype measure. Since attitudes toward Mormons are pretty evenly distributed among independents, each bar is right around 25 percent. In other words, the percentage of independents with a negative view of Mormons is nearly identical to the percentage of those with a positive view – suggesting that, roughly speaking, they cancel each other out.

The second panel of Figure 9.1 displays the same results for Democrats. Notice that among Democrats with a negative view of Mormons (bottom quartile) our model shows that only 2 percent voted for Romney. However, among Democrats with the most positive view of Mormons (top quartile), 19 percent voted for Romney. Nineteen percent may not sound like a lot, but it is considerably more than 2 percent. In fact, it is an increase of more than 850 percent – an interpretation that is both technically correct and highly misleading. Equally important is the fact that only 5 percent of strong Democrats have a positive view of Mormons (that is, are in the top quartile). We also see that voter abstention rises among Democrats with a positive view of Mormons, probably because they are cross-pressured (Mutz 2006). Unlike the independents – for whom attitudes toward Mormons are distributed evenly across the scale – Democrats are much more likely to have a negative perception. When we put this all together, it means that a small percentage of strong Democrats with a positive impression of Mormons voted for Romney, but they are a tiny sliver of the electorate.

The story is reversed for Republicans (Panel 3 of Figure 9.1). Of those Republicans who have a negative view of Mormons, 54 percent turned out and voted for Romney, compared to 95 percent of those with a positive perception. We see some evidence for the hypothesis that anti-Mormon Republicans (bottom quartile) chose to abstain, as they stayed home in larger numbers

---

[3] Because our dependent variable has three nominal (i.e. non-ordinal) categories, we employ multinomial logistic regression. All of the independent variables are the same as described in note 1. See Table 9A.1 in the appendix to this chapter for the full model.

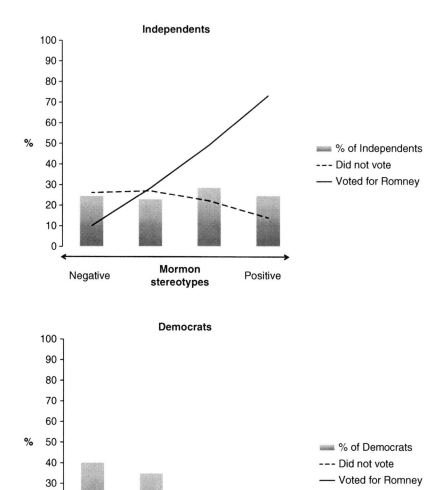

FIGURE 9.1. Mormon Stereotypes and the 2012 Presidential Vote
*Source:* Mormon Perceptions Study, 2012

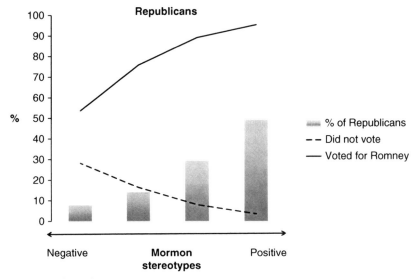

FIGURE 9.1. (cont.)

(28 percent) than those Republicans with the most positive perception (top quartile) of Mormons (4 percent). But in a mirror image of the Democrats, only 8 percent of Republicans have a negative view of Mormons.[4]

In sum, these results allow us to reconcile the statistical model with the election results. The former shows that attitudes toward Mormons mattered a lot; the latter suggests that they mattered little, if at all. While Mitt Romney's Mormonism mattered a lot to very few voters, it mattered little to most voters. The net result is that, on Election Day 2012, Mitt Romney's Mormonism turned out to be the dog that didn't bark.

## The 2008 Campaign

When Sherlock Holmes observed the dog that did not bark, it was a vital piece of information for cracking his case.[5] Likewise, the very minimal effect of either pro- or anti-Mormon attitudes on the presidential vote is vital for understanding the place of Mormonism within American politics. As Chapter 8 showed, voters' attitudes changed considerably between Romney's entrance onto the presidential stage in 2008 and his exit in 2012. In his debut performance during the 2008

---

[4] Our online survey, administered by YouGov/Polimetrix, has an inflated voter turnout rate of 85 percent, presumably owing to the fact that people who participate in online surveys are also likely to participate in elections. Thus, one should take the specific turnout numbers with a grain of salt. However, an inflated turnout rate does not mean we should dismiss the *relationship* between attitudes toward Mormons and either vote choice or turnout.

[5] For interested readers, the case is found in the Sherlock Holmes story, "The Silver Blaze."

Republican primaries, his Mormonism was a significant detriment to many voters.

Political science theory illuminates why voters would react strongly to the "peculiar" religious background of a relatively unknown candidate running in the primary process. Voters typically have little information about the candidates running. Not only are the candidates often unfamiliar, since they are all in the same party, primary voters cannot glean any information from their party label as in a general election. In such an environment, a little bit of information can have an outsized impact on how voters perceive a candidate. Political scientist Samuel Popkin has memorably described the "low information rationality" that characterizes voters' behavior during primaries (1994). We have earlier described the information that circulates on a given subject; the same holds true for candidates. Voters receive information – often limited – about candidates. If they accept the information as reliable, it is stored for retrieval until needed for a decision. At the decision point, people sample across the stored information in order to form an opinion (Zaller 1992). For candidates with a long track record in public life (e.g. Hillary Clinton), most voters will already have a lot of stored information. One more piece of information, like her religious affiliation, is not likely to make much difference – it's a small pebble in a large pond. But for lesser-known candidates, one piece of information, particularly novel information, will have a far greater impact, like a large rock in a small pond. And if that information is membership in a distinctive, even controversial, religion, it is likely to make a big splash.

As we saw in Chapter 8, information about a candidate, including his or her religious background, can be framed in different ways. For example, in 1976, Jimmy Carter was a relatively obscure governor with no national political experience. Running in the immediate aftermath of the Watergate scandal, he skillfully framed his religious piety as evidence of his moral rectitude and trustworthiness. Similarly, in 2000, George W. Bush framed his religious faith as an important element of his personal biography. It informed his social views, reinforced a cultural connection with many Republican primary voters, and provided a story of personal redemption to reassure voters worried about any youthful indiscretions.

During the 2008 primaries, we tested how voters responded to information about Mitt Romney's background in the LDS Church.[6] In particular, we examined how voters reacted to different ways of framing Mormonism. We did so while the primaries were underway, when Romney was still relatively unknown

---

[6] These data come from Cooperative Campaign Analysis Project 2008; see Data Appendix for details of this survey. Much (but not all) of what we report in this section has been previously published in our article "The Stained Glass Ceiling: Social Contact and Mitt Romney's 'Religion Problem,'" *Political Behavior* 34: 277–99 (Campbell, Green, and Monson 2012). Note, however, that the specific results vary slightly, since the results reported in the article are derived from a statistical model that controls for age, gender, and region. Substantively, the controls make no difference since this is a randomized experiment and so we report bivariate results here.

and a viable candidate for the Republican nomination.[7] This study was an experiment, complementing the information we gleaned from the Gallup question about voting for a generic Mormon candidate (see Chapter 8), by referring to Mitt Romney by name and providing more biographical information, more closely simulating the range of information to which voters were exposed during the course of the campaign.

We randomly assigned different groups of respondents (roughly 200 each) to read different descriptions of Mitt Romney. Everyone received this positive, boilerplate description of him:

*As you know, Mitt Romney is running for president. He is a successful businessman, a former governor of Massachusetts, and the head of the 2002 Winter Olympics. He has been married for thirty-nine years and raised five sons.*

Some respondents were randomly chosen to receive more information, which was added immediately following the information about his personal background. One group learned that Romney "has been a local leader in his church," while another learned that he has been a local leader of "the Church of Jesus Christ of Latter-day Saints, often called the Mormon Church." After reading the description of Romney, all respondents were asked whether the preceding information made them more or less likely to vote for him.

This method enables us to compare the reactions of voters who received only the boilerplate biography (control group) to those who received additional information about his religion. By comparing the two groups, we determine if adding information about Romney's religion made voters more or less likely to vote for him. Recall that, at this time, Romney was a newcomer on the national political scene, so for many voters our information would have made a large splash.

As shown in Figure 9.2, the information that Romney was a leader in the Mormon Church had a substantially negative effect on the likelihood of voting for him.[8] The figure compares the reaction of respondents in the control group – who, recall, read nothing about Romney's religion – to those who received information about his religion. As shown in the figure, when Romney's church is not identified, voters register no statistically significant reaction. But when his affiliation with the Mormon Church is explicitly mentioned, Romney's support drops by roughly 32 percentage points.

Figure 9.2 also displays the results for evangelicals and people with no religious affiliation (the "nones"). As we have discussed previously, these groups illustrate a source of tension: between Mormons and other religions (evangelicals), and between Mormons and secular society (nones). Both groups have a slightly more negative reaction to Romney's Mormonism than the general

---

[7] Specifically, the experiment ran from January 24 to February 4, although 90 percent of the surveys were completed by January 28. Romney dropped out of the race on February 7.

[8] As in Chapter 7, all of the results we report in this chapter omit Mormons.

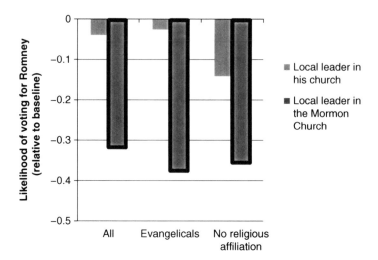

FIGURE 9.2. Reactions to Romney's Religion, January 2008
Note: A black border represents a statistically significant effect ($p < 0.05$, one-tailed test)
Source: Cooperative Campaign Analysis Project, 2008

population. Not surprisingly, evangelicals do not have a negative reaction upon reading that Romney has been a leader in "his church," when it remains unidentified, while nones have a more negative reaction to the unnamed church that approaches statistical significance.[9]

Romney was not the only candidate in the 2008 primary season to face questions about his religious background. Among his Republican opponents, Mike Huckabee was an ordained Southern Baptist pastor, which was potentially a problem for some voters. On the Democratic side, Barack Obama faced the double whammy of controversial comments made by the pastor of his Chicago church, Jeremiah Wright, and the rumor that he was actually a Muslim. To gauge the relative impact of concerns about Romney's LDS background compared to the concerns raised about other candidates, we conducted a parallel set of experiments during the primary season. Since Romney, Huckabee, and Obama were all relatively unknown to most voters, for contrast we also tested voters' reactions to information about the religious background of Hillary Clinton, as she was extremely well known.

In each case, members of the control group read a boilerplate description of the candidate while another randomly selected group read the same description with additional information about the candidate's religion. As with the Romney experiments, we limited our descriptions to information that was factually

---

[9] Results are similar for respondents with high versus low religiosity.

TABLE 9.1. *Descriptions of Candidates' Religious Backgrounds, 2008 Experiment*

| Candidate | Religious description |
|---|---|
| Hillary Clinton | "is an active layperson in the United Methodist Church" |
| Mike Huckabee | "has been an ordained Southern Baptist pastor" |
| Barack Obama (controversial church) | "Some people have said his church is hostile to whites and promotes black separatism." |
| Barack Obama (actually a Muslim) | "Some people have said that he must be a Muslim, because his paternal grandfather was a Muslim." |

correct, using language with a neutral tone. This undoubtedly limits the effects we observe, as far more incendiary, and often inaccurate, information circulates during a political campaign. Table 9.1 contains the descriptions of these candidates' religious backgrounds provided to the subjects in the respective experimental groups.[10]

Figure 9.3 displays how each description affected voters' likelihood of voting for the candidate in question. Not surprisingly, the effect for Clinton was small and statistically insignificant. Not only did most Americans already have their minds made up about her, Clinton's background as a United Methodist, a mainline Protestant denomination, was unlikely to cause voters as much concern as the other candidates' religions. Huckabee's background as a Southern Baptist minister triggered a significant negative reaction but, at 13 percentage points, was far less than the concern elicited by disclosure of Romney's Mormonism. Voters' reaction to information about Obama's alleged Muslim background and his pastor were highly negative – the former a little smaller and the latter a little larger, than the "Mormon effect" for Romney.[11] All told, in 2008 Romney's

---

[10] Here are the full descriptions of the candidates used in the experiments:

As you know, Hillary Clinton is running for president. She is a graduate of Yale Law School and the former First Lady. She is currently a U.S. Senator, representing the state of New York. She has been married for thirty-two years and raised a daughter. Hillary Clinton has also been an active layperson in the United Methodist church.

As you know, Mike Huckabee is running for president. He is a former governor of Arkansas. In 2003, he lost 110 pounds after being diagnosed with Type II diabetes and is a spokesman for living a healthy lifestyle. He has been married for thirty-three years and raised three sons. Mike Huckabee has also been an ordained Southern Baptist pastor.

As you know, Barack Obama is running for president. He is a former community organizer in Chicago and a best-selling author. He is currently a U.S. Senator, representing the state of Illinois. He has been married for sixteen years and has two daughters. Barack Obama is a member of the Trinity United Church of Christ. (1) Some people have said his church is hostile to Whites and promotes Black separatism. (2) Some people have said that he must be a Muslim, because his paternal grandfather was a Muslim.

[11] The survey was fielded from March 21 to April 9, 2008, after the controversy over Obama's pastor had become national news and Obama had delivered a very high-profile speech, on March 18, 2008, in response to the controversy.

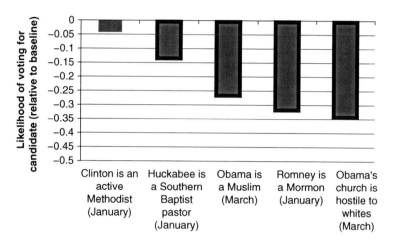

FIGURE 9.3. Reactions to Presidential Candidates' Religion, 2008
*Note:* A black border represents a statistically significant effect ($p < 0.05$, one-tailed test)
*Source:* Cooperative Campaign Analysis Project, 2008

Mormonism was as large a political liability for him as two of the most explosive charges leveled against Barack Obama.

Recall from Chapter 8 that, historically, Democrats have had a stronger aversion to Mormon presidential candidates than Republicans. That pattern is also borne out in our Romney experiment, as the Mormon effect for Republicans was a drop of 25 percentage points, compared to 36 points for Democrats.[12] Among Democrats there is also a negative and statistically significant reaction to describing Romney as a leader in his unnamed church, albeit smaller than the Mormon effect (13 percentage points).

## Contact and Knowledge

Even though this experiment shows that, on balance, voters' reaction to Romney's Mormonism was negative, recall from Chapter 7 that general impressions toward Mormons are a mixture of both positive and negative (and not every voter reacted negatively to Romney's religion). And as we also demonstrated in Chapter 7, two factors in particular foster a positive perception of Mormons: a close personal relationship with a Mormon and factual knowledge about Mormonism. We further find that both close contact and factual

---

[12] Likewise, we see virtually the same results for self-described voters in Republican versus Democratic primaries.

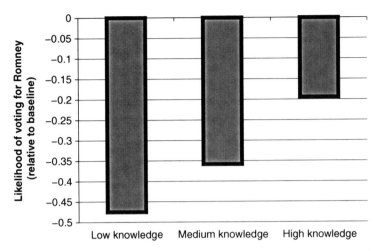

FIGURE 9.4. Factual Knowledge about Mormonism – "Romney was a local leader in the Mormon Church"
*Note:* A black border represents a statistically significant effect ($p < 0.05$, one-tailed test)
*Source:* Cooperative Campaign Analysis Project, 2008

knowledge also ameliorated, at least partially, the negative reaction to Romney's Mormonism when he first appeared on the political scene in 2008.

Figure 9.4 displays the reaction to the description of Romney as an active Mormon among voters with low, medium, and high factual knowledge about Mormonism.[13] Among those with low knowledge, describing Romney as a Mormon drops his support by 48 percentage points, compared to 36 points among those with a medium level of knowledge, and 20 points among those with high knowledge. Even though greater knowledge "buffers" a negative reaction to Romney's Mormonism – a 20-point drop is obviously less than a 48-point drop – it is still noteworthy that the reaction was negative across the board.

Figure 9.5 makes a similar comparison, but this time by the degree of reported social contact with a Mormon. In Chapter 7, we introduced the faint possibility of a curvilinear relationship between degree of contact and perceptions of

[13] The quiz of factual knowledge about Mormonism in 2008 differs from the one in 2010, discussed in Chapter 7. It consisted of four true-false questions, which provided little differentiation (in other words, the test was too easy). Specifically, the quiz was worded:

Of the following statements about practicing members of the Church of Jesus Christ of Latter-day Saints, indicate which are true:
    Practice polygamy (have more than one wife) [False]
    Do not drink alcohol [True]
    Give 10% of their income to their church [True]
    Do not believe in the Bible [False]

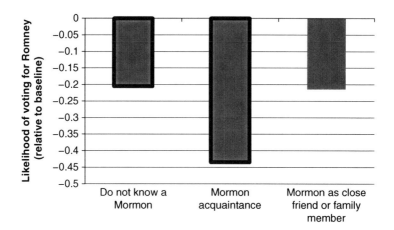

FIGURE 9.5. Contact with Mormons – "Romney was a local leader in the Mormon Church"
*Note:* A black border represents a statistically significant effect ($p < 0.05$, one-tailed test)
*Source:* Cooperative Campaign Analysis Project, 2008

Mormons. Now we see much stronger evidence that a moderate level of contact does more harm than good for attitudes about Romney. Among people with the least and most contact with Mormons, the negative reaction to Romney's Mormonism is about the same – a drop of roughly 20 percentage points in support. But among those in the middle (who know a Mormon but only as an acquaintance) the effect is twice as large: a decline of 43 percentage points.

These results reflect the reactions to Romney's Mormonism in the absence of any further information, thus providing a baseline in the absence of the back-and-forth in a political campaign. Of course, political campaigns are designed to increase what voters know about a candidate, whether positive or negative. Just as important is how such information is framed. Scholars of framing effects distinguish between "frames in thought" and "frames in communication" (Chong and Druckman 2007; Druckman 2001). The former refers to what we might think of as a preexisting condition – the attitudes or opinions that people hold on a given matter. The latter refers to the way information on a given matter is presented in public discourse by the media, politicians, and other opinion shapers. Framing effects result from the interaction of the two. Thus, in the 1976 Democratic primaries, Jimmy Carter could exploit the fact that many Americans had a preexisting frame in thought that religious people are trustworthy by introducing the frame in communication that being a Sunday school teacher signaled his integrity.

As shown by the way voters reacted upon reading of his involvement in the Mormon Church, Romney definitely faced negative frames in thought about

Mormonism. Among these, one of the most potent is the claim that Mormons are not Christians. As we saw in Chapter 7, evangelical Protestants, a key constituency in the Republican primaries, are especially likely to hold this belief. Labeling Mormons as non-Christians thus has potential political implications. A majority of Americans (and an even greater share of Republicans) believe the United States was founded as a "Christian nation," and thus may not want a non-Christian to lead it (Pew Forum on Religion & Public Life 2006). The presidency has quasi-religious trappings, as exemplified by the office's many public ceremonies and patriotic rituals with religious undercurrents – examples of what Robert Bellah (1967) has aptly described as America's civil religion. If, as we suggested in Chapter 7, saying that Mormons are not Christians is often another way of saying that "Mormons are not like us," voters may likewise be reluctant to have a president whose religious beliefs are not like theirs.

There are countercurrents within the collective American psyche that could dampen, perhaps negate, any potential concern that Mormons are not Christians. To address those potential concerns, Romney introduced two counter-frames in his December 2007 speech "Faith in America" (see Chapter 8). The first echoed John F. Kennedy's argument for religious tolerance in 1960, when he faced antagonism toward his Catholicism. Both Kennedy and Romney drew on the widespread frame in thought among Americans in favor of religious freedom, guaranteed by the separation of church and state. Romney consciously referenced Kennedy and argued that "a person should not be elected because of his faith nor should he be rejected because of his faith." In doing so, he was tapping the deeply held American value of religious freedom. Call this the "separationist" counter-frame.

As you will recall from Chapter 8, Romney did not stop with deploying Kennedy's argument about religious freedom. Unlike Kennedy, Romney felt he had to reassure religious conservatives that he shared their values, even if not the same theology, and that all religious communities supported a common moral perspective:

There is one fundamental question about which I often am asked. What do I believe about Jesus Christ? I believe that Jesus Christ is the Son of God and the Savior of mankind. My church's beliefs about Christ may not all be the same as those of other faiths.... It is important to recognize that while differences in theology exist between the churches in America, we share a common creed of moral convictions. And where the affairs of our nation are concerned, it's usually a sound rule to focus on the latter – on the great moral principles that urge us all on a common course. (Romney 2007)

Call this the "common values" counter-frame, a central feature of Romney's alliance strategy.

We designed our experiment to test reactions to the frame that Mormons are not Christians, thus taking what was a latent frame in thought among some voters and ensuring that it was a frame in communication for all of the respondents in this particular treatment group. Accordingly, a random selection of subjects not only received the boilerplate biography of Romney and the information that he was a local leader in the Mormon Church, but they also read that "some people believe Mormons are not Christians." Still another group of subjects received all of that information plus the separationist counter-frame:

*Others say that Mitt Romney's religion should not be an issue in the campaign, since a person's faith should be irrelevant to politics.*

Yet another group received the common values counter-frame:

*Others point out that Mormons believe in Jesus Christ, and that they have the same values as members of other faiths.*

Here, too, these statements would have been frames in thought for some of our respondents. By articulating them, they became frames in communication.

Figure 9.6 displays how voters reacted to the frame and counter-frames. As expected, telling – or reminding – voters that Mormons are sometimes described as non-Christians drove support down for Romney by roughly 30 percentage points. Interestingly, this impact is about the same size as the reaction elicited by simply mentioning that Romney is an active Mormon. The two counter-frames lessen the negative reaction, but do not neutralize it completely. In each case, hearing the "not Christian" frame followed by a counter-frame led to a drop in Romney's support of about 20 percentage points – roughly 10 points less than

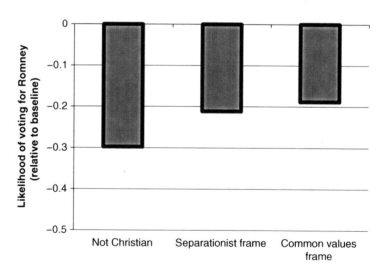

FIGURE 9.6. Reaction to "Not Christian" Frame and Counter-Frames
*Note:* A black border represents a statistically significant effect ($p < 0.05$, one-tailed test)
*Source:* Cooperative Campaign Analysis Project, 2008

the drop in support among those who were only exposed to the "not Christian" frame.

As we would expect, evangelical Protestants had a stronger reaction to the "not Christian" frame than the general public – their support for Romney dropped by roughly 40 points. Evangelicals were also largely not persuaded by the counter-frames. With the separationist counter-frame, Romney's support among evangelicals dropped 32 points. Evangelicals appeared to be a little more receptive to the common values counter-frame, as it led to a decline of "only" 27 points.

Political campaigns do not occur in a vacuum, as the information that circulates is filtered through voters' own opinions and experiences. The real test of a frame in communication is how it interacts with frames in thought. For some voters, especially evangelicals, George W. Bush's story of personal redemption echoed a familiar and no doubt inspiring narrative. To others, particularly people with little sympathy for evangelicals, it might have seemed naïve at best and cynical at worst. Similarly, we were interested in knowing how the impact of the "not Christian" frame and the two counter-frames varied according to the ameliorating factors of knowledge about Mormonism and personal contact with Mormons.

Figure 9.7 displays how voters reacted to the frame and two counter-frames according to their degree of factual knowledge about Mormonism. As expected, voters with the least information about Mormonism reacted most negatively upon reading the "not Christian" frame (64 percentage points!). The counter-frames were partly ameliorative, with the common values argument modestly more persuasive than the separationist one. Among voters with medium information about Mormons, the counter-frames were more effective – the common values frame weakens the negative reaction to the point that it no longer meets the threshold for statistical significance. For voters with a high level of knowledge, the counter-frames produce a muted response. While the differences are slight, there is even a hint that the counter-frames actually decrease support for Romney. The general pattern for the different levels of knowledge comports with our expectations. Less preexisting knowledge about Mormons means that the information introduced through the campaign was novel, thus making a bigger splash and having a bigger effect. More knowledge means that further information hardly makes a wave.

The pattern for social contact once again has a curvilinear pattern. As shown in Panel 1 of Figure 9.8, people who do not know a Mormon react quite negatively to the information that Mormons may not be Christians (a drop of 29 percentage points). But, upon hearing either counter-frame, their concerns are mostly assuaged, as the drop in support for Romney is slight and, in statistical terms, insignificant. (The counter-frames are equally effective.) Each frame and counter-frame has an effect as these respondents have little of the information gleaned from personal relationships. In contrast, people who have close contact with a Mormon (Panel 3, Figure 9.8) are hardly affected at all by

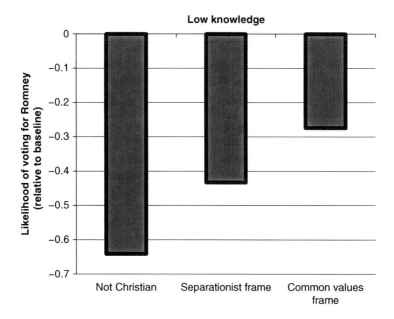

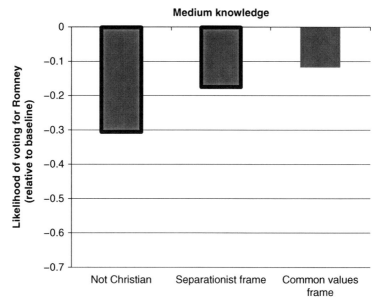

FIGURE 9.7. Reaction to "Not Christian" Frame and Counter-Frames, by Knowledge of Mormonism
*Note:* A black border represents a statistically significant effect ($p < 0.05$, one-tailed test)
*Source:* Cooperative Campaign Analysis Project, 2008

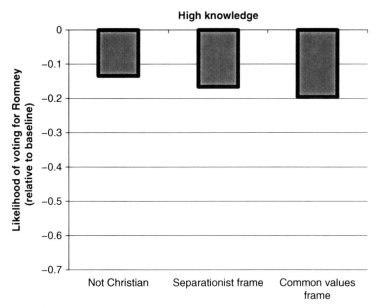

FIGURE 9.7. (cont.)

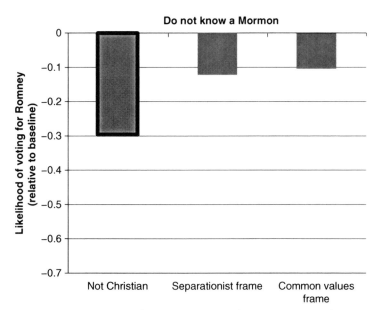

FIGURE 9.8. Reactions to "Not Christian" Frame and Counter-Frames, by Contact with Mormons
*Note:* A black border represents a statistically significant effect ($p < 0.05$, one-tailed test)
*Source:* Cooperative Campaign Analysis Project, 2008

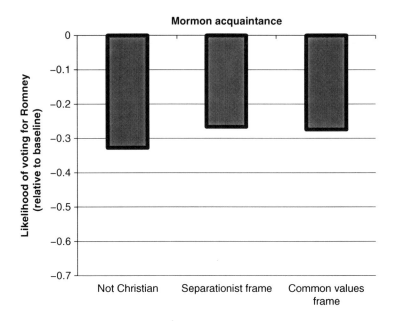

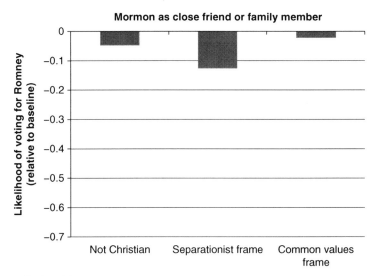

FIGURE 9.8. (cont.)

the frame or the counter-frames – the slight negative effects are substantively small and statistically insignificant.[14] These people have already made up their minds about Mormons, and so the information we presented in the experiment has little to no effect.

---

[14] The cell sizes are small, so statistical significance is not very informative.

We see a very different result for people who have a moderate amount of contact with a Mormon. They react negatively to the claim that Mormons are not Christians, but their likelihood of voting for Romney barely budges upon hearing either counter-frame. This non-effect is consistent with the earlier finding that it is also the people with moderate contact who have the strongest negative reaction to Romney's Mormonism.

Let us pause to summarize what we have learned thus far about voters' reactions to information about Mitt Romney's Mormonism, circa the 2008 primary season.

1. *Romney's Mormonism Mattered, and Not in a Good Way*
   Identifying Romney as an active Mormon, not just an active churchgoer, produced a substantial, negative drop in his support. In relative terms, the drop in Romney's support was comparable to the negative effect of Obama's association with Pastor Jeremiah Wright, an issue that threatened to derail Obama's 2008 nomination bid. Specifically, framing Mormonism as a non-Christian religion triggers a negative reaction among voters; counter-framing only partially ameliorates that negative reaction. Importantly, in 2008 the information that Romney is a Mormon was novel, as many voters would have been unaware of that fact. More generally, few Mormons had run for president. Not since the 1968 campaign of Mitt's father, George Romney, had voters been faced with a Mormon presidential candidate who was both devout and viable.[15]

2. *The More People Knew about Mormonism, the Less It Concerned Them*
   The "Mormon effect" was less among people with greater factual knowledge of Mormonism. Conversely, voters with the least factual information about Mormons have the strongest negative reaction to the frame that Mormons are not Christians.

3. *A Little Social Contact Leaves a Big Impression*
   People who have a moderate degree of contact with a Mormon – who know a Mormon in passing – had a stronger negative reaction to Romney's Mormonism than either people with no contact or close contact. Like people with no contact, they evince a strong negative reaction to the "not Christian" frame; like those with close contact, the counter-frames do not affect their opinion. We might call this a reverse Goldilocks effect. In the fairy tale, Goldilocks always finds the middle option to be "just right." For Romney, the people who had experienced middling contact with Mormons were his biggest problem.

---

[15] Recall from Chapter 8 that, since George Romney's abortive presidential bid in 1968, two more Mormons had run, but one was not devout (Morris Udall) while the other was never a serious contender (Orrin Hatch).

## The 2012 Campaign

With these results from 2008 in mind, it might seem as though Romney's Mormonism should have mattered a great deal to a great many voters in the 2012 general election. After all, the degree of factual knowledge did not increase in 2012. Between 2010 and 2012, the average score on our Mormon knowledge quiz did not change substantially; the average score was 2.02 in 2010 and 2.17 in 2012. Likewise, using different measures, a Pew survey also found that factual knowledge about Mormons did not increase in 2012 – in spite of countless media stories about the LDS Church and Mormon culture (Pew Forum on Religion & Public Life 2012d). Nor did we see an increase in self-reported contact with Mormons between 2008, 2010, and 2012. In 2008, 15 percent of people surveyed had a close relationship with a Mormon. It was 13 percent in 2010 and 14 percent in 2012 – fluctuations all within the margin of error.[16] With a steady level of knowledge of and contact with Mormons, it might have appeared that Romney's Mormonism would prove to be a big electoral liability. As noted in Chapter 8, many observers at the time expected as much.

And yet it was not. To underscore that point, Figure 9.9 displays what happened when we replicated our original Romney experiment in October 2012, as Romney was in the closing stage of a heated general election with President Obama.[17] Everything about the experiment was identical,[18] but while the direction of the results remained the same, the magnitude substantially decreased. In 2008, identifying Romney as a Mormon dropped his support by roughly 25 points for Republicans, 35 points for independents, and 36 points for Democrats. In 2012, the negative effect was about 12 percentage points for all three groups.

We see an even more dramatic decline in the effect of the "not Christian" frame. In particular, Figure 9.10 displays the change in effect for evangelical Protestants – a group that is both heavily Republican and most likely to consider Mormonism to be a non-Christian religion (see Chapter 7). In 2008, the "not Christian" frame caused a 40-point drop in Romney's support among evangelicals and a 27-point decline among non-evangelicals. By the 2012 general election, it had no statistically significant effect on either evangelicals or non-evangelicals.

In other words, our experiments reinforce the story told by our analysis of how attitudes toward Mormons affected the 2012 general election

---

[16] These figures come from the 2008 Cooperative Campaign Analysis Project and from the 2010 and 2012 Cooperative Congressional Election Studies. See Data Appendix for details.

[17] We ran our experiment on the 2012 Mormon Perceptions Study, which is described in Data Appendix.

[18] The biography was exactly the same, except that we updated the number of years that Mitt and Ann Romney have been married.

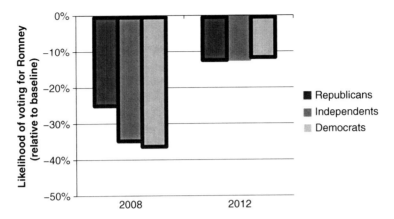

FIGURE 9.9. The Negative Effect of Romney's Mormonism Declined from 2008 to 2012 – "Romney was a local leader in the Mormon Church"
*Note:* A black border represents a statistically significant effect ($p < 0.05$, one-tailed test)
*Source:* Cooperative Campaign Analysis Project, 2008 and Mormon Perceptions Study, 2012

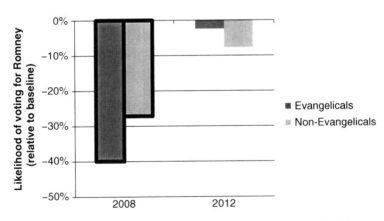

FIGURE 9.10. The Claim That Mormons Are Not Christians Ceased to Have an Effect Between 2008 and 2012, Even among Evangelicals – "Mormons are not Christians"
*Note:* A black border represents a statistically significant effect ($p < 0.05$, one-tailed test)
*Source:* Cooperative Campaign Analysis Project, 2008 and Mormon Perceptions Study, 2012

presidential vote. There may have been an effect, but it was small and likely inconsequential.

What explains the "case of the disappearing Mormon effect"? Actually, there is little mystery. In early 2008, voters were still forming an opinion about

Romney, as he was in his first national campaign. By late 2012, voters had been exposed to a lot of information about Romney – first as he ran the gauntlet of the Republican primaries, then as the GOP nominee. When we did our survey in October of 2012, only weeks before Election Day, most voters had learned enough about Romney to have made up their minds about him. For many voters, information about Romney's religion was no longer novel. As just one indication that voters had undergone a learning process, in 2008 about half of our respondents could correctly identify Romney's religion. By the fall of 2012, this had risen to 68 percent.[19] But it is worth noting that this still means that even when the presidential campaign had its greatest salience, roughly one in three Americans did not know that Romney is Mormon.

Thus, any bits of information we included in our vignettes were small pebbles, leaving barely a ripple. This is not to say that Romney's Mormonism had no effect on voters' attitudes toward him. Rather, by the time of the general election those voters who cared about his religious background had already incorporated that information into their assessment of him. By way of analogy, this is similar to the way that investors account for the available information about a firm when trading its stock. At any given point in time, the stock price reflects what investors know about that company. In the case of the 2012 election, most Republicans who may have been inclined toward a negative reaction to Romney's Mormonism were more concerned with ousting President Obama from the White House.

To summarize what we have learned from our analysis of the 2012 presidential election:

1. *Novelty Wears Off*
   In the 2008 Republican primaries, Romney was largely unknown. Thus, information about him – particularly his membership in an "exotic" religion – had a large effect on voters' perceptions. However, by the general election of 2012, Romney had become a household name. Accordingly, the novelty of learning about his background – including information about his religion – had worn off.

2. *Context Matters*
   In the 2012 general election, Romney was no longer one among many Republican hopefuls vying for the party's presidential nomination. He had become the party's standard-bearer against a Democratic president

---

[19] A December 2012 Pew survey found a nearly identical result: that 65 percent of Americans could identify Romney's religion. However, a November 2011 Pew survey found that only 39 percent of Americans could identify Romney's religion. We found a higher percentage in 2008. The difference could be that some voters could recall Romney's religion in the midst of the 2008 primary race but it slipped their mind by the fall of 2011. It could also be that the sample drawn for the online Cooperative Campaign Analysis Project 2008 was more politically knowledgeable than the sample drawn for the Pew telephone surveys. It could also be because we used different standards for determining a correct answer. Or it could be because of sampling variability.

with exceedingly low approval among Republicans. When people were given a choice between a dislike for Obama and a dislike of Mormonism, the former overwhelmed the latter.

We should not dismiss the significance of the diminishing impact of Romney's Mormonism the longer he was in the public eye. The dog that didn't bark – at least not much – suggests that many voters had no problem voting for a Mormon in the context of the 2012 election, even when those voters had theological concerns about Mormonism. Although a small majority of voters chose Obama over Romney in 2012, the vast majority of Obama's supporters did so for political, not theological, reasons. We find it especially telling that our 2012 experiment shows that Republicans, Democrats, and independents alike all had a similarly mild reaction to the description of Romney as a devout Mormon. While the decision to vote for Romney was largely determined by voters' partisanship, reactions to his Mormonism were the same regardless of party.

## DID MITT ROMNEY AFFECT ATTITUDES TOWARD MORMONS?

Throughout 2011 and 2012, Mormonism was subject to extensive public attention – so much so that pundits regularly began referring to the "Mormon Moment" (Bowman 2012c). In journalistic parlance, a "news hole" opened up for stories about all things Mormon. There were articles about fashion among LDS hipsters (Williams 2011), Mormon cuisine (Moskin 2012), and, of course, *The Book of Mormon* musical on Broadway (Zoglin 2011). In the course of reporting on Mitt Romney's biography, journalists introduced many Americans to numerous aspects of Romney's Mormonism, including his time as a missionary in France (Evans 2012), his temple marriage to Ann (Kantor 2012), his considerable financial contributions to the LDS Church (Podhoretz 2012), and his service as a bishop and stake president (Ertl 2012). Although we have already seen that this media attention did not lead to an increase in knowledge about Mormons, the media attention to all things LDS suggests that public attitudes toward Mormons might have changed.

At first blush, it would appear that they have not. In our 2008 survey, 49 percent of respondents had a very favorable opinion of Mormons and 7 percent had an opinion that was very favorable. In 2012, 51 percent had a favorable opinion while 8 percent were very favorable – increases so small as to fall within the surveys' margin of error. Likewise, between 2007 and 2012, the Pew Forum on Religion & Public Life found that the percentage of Americans who say that Mormons are not Christians had remained at 31 percent.[20]

---

[20] In the surveys we have conducted, we have actually found a slight increase in the percentage saying that Mormons are not Christians, from 36 percent in 2008 to 43 percent in 2010, and then a slight dip to 41 percent in 2012. Our results differ from Pew surveys in 2007, 2011, and 2012, at least in part because Pew uses telephone surveys while we have administered ours online. The Pew surveys have a sizeable fraction of "don't know" responses, because in a telephone survey respondents can easily volunteer that they do not know the answer, whereas our online survey did not have an

Similarly, the general perception of Mormons held steady. Panel 1 of Figure 9.11 displays the nearly flat line in general perceptions of Mormons, as measured on the 0 to 100 scale we have seen in earlier chapters (known as a feeling thermometer). Initially, we will focus on the period from 2006 – before Mitt Romney entered the political stage – to 2012, during and immediately after the presidential election.[21] In 2006, Mormons received an average score of roughly 48 on the 0 to 100 scale; in the fall of 2012 it was 49.

A closer look reveals that there has been a notable change in the distribution of opinions about Mormons. In the second panel of Figure 9.11, we break out how Republicans, Democrats, and independents have each perceived Mormons over the period from 2006 to 2012. In 2006, there are no partisan differences; Mormons receive the same rating across the party spectrum. By 2012, a wide party gap opened up. Republicans became much more favorable toward Mormons, independents became slightly more so, and Democrats became sharply less favorable. Like an object being acted on by equal and opposing forces, the net result is that the overall attitude toward Mormons did not move.

Similarly, the Pew Forum on Religion & Public Life found that between 2011 and 2012, Republicans became more likely to offer a positive one-word impression of Mormons, while Democrats became less likely.[22] Republicans also became more likely to say that their religion has "a lot in common" with Mormon beliefs, while Democrats did not change (Pew Forum on Religion & Public Life 2012d). In Chapter 8, we found a similar pattern with Gallup survey data on support for a generic Mormon candidate.

In our politically polarized times, perhaps we should not be surprised that attitudes toward the religion of the Republican presidential nominee would split along party lines. When so much in American society takes on political meaning, why not the perceptions of a religion, especially the religion of the Republican presidential nominee?

---

explicit "don't know" option. In 2012, 18 percent of Pew survey respondents said they did not know whether Mormons are Christians, compared to 16 percent in 2011 and 17 percent in 2007. When we put our results alongside Pew's we can either conclude that the percentage of Americans who think Mormons are not Christians stayed the same (Pew) or increased slightly (our data). Either way, the percentage did not decrease. See Data Appendix for details of the 2007, 2011, and 2012 Pew surveys.

[21] The flat line is especially noteworthy given that these data came from different surveys and are thus subject to the vagaries of what are known in the polling business as "house effects," or variations in sampling, question wording, weighting, and so on that produce systematic differences across survey research firms. Note that the "Secularism Study" referenced in Figure 9.11 is a nationally representative survey of the U.S. population (N = 1,412). See Data Appendix for more details.

[22] Specifically, in November 2011, 23 percent of Republicans offered a positive one-word response compared to 35 percent of Republicans in December 2012. Among Democrats, the percentage of positive responses dropped from 26 percent to 19 percent.

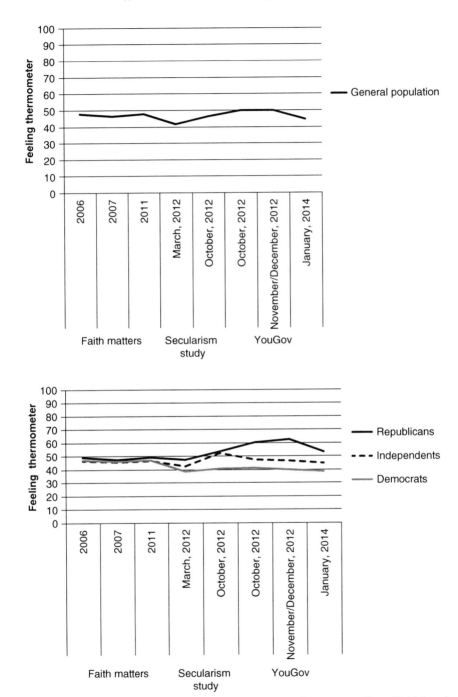

FIGURE 9.11. (Panel 1) Overall, General Perceptions of Mormons Have Held Steady
(Panel 2) General Perceptions of Mormons Have Become Politically Polarized

Whether a matter of surprise or not, the partisan inflection in attitudes toward Mormons complicates our assessment of the 2012 presidential election. For while Mitt Romney's Mormonism did not, in the end, have much of a direct effect on the presidential vote, this does not mean Mormonism has ceased to matter at the polls. Another experiment indicates that Mormon candidates for other offices risk a negative reaction to their religion. In the fall of 2012, we tested people's likelihood of voting for a mayoral and gubernatorial candidate when he was and was not identified as a Mormon.[23] As in the Romney experiment, we provided a baseline, boilerplate biography of a fictitious candidate, and then in the experimental group added that the candidate was "active in the Mormon Church."

Figure 9.12 contains the results, broken out by Republicans and Democrats. In both cases Democrats had a sharp aversion to the Mormon candidate, comparable to the negative effect that information about Romney's religion produced in early 2008, when he was relatively unknown. Among Democrats,

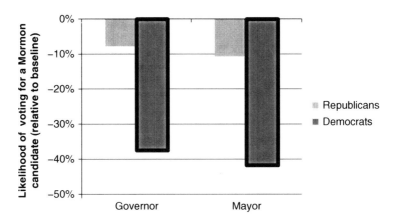

FIGURE 9.12. More Partisan Polarization: Democrats Are Much Less Likely to Vote for Mormon Candidates – Candidate is "an active member of the Mormon Church"
*Note:* A black border represents a statistically significant effect ($p < 0.05$, one-tailed test)
*Source:* Mormon Perceptions Study, 2012

[23] The full experimental treatments were worded as follows. Respondents were assigned to either the mayoral or gubernatorial experiment. The text in bold was not included in the description given to the control group.

Jim Anderson is running for mayor/governor of a mid-sized city/state close to yours. He is forty-two years old, married, and a father of three school-age children. He started a successful local real estate company. He has also been the president of the local Rotary Club **and is an active member of the Church of Jesus Christ of Latter-day Saints, also known as the Mormon Church.** Anderson was reelected twice to the state legislature.

support for this hypothetical candidate dropped by roughly 40 percentage points once he was identified as Mormon. Among Republicans, support dropped a little, but the effect is not statistically significant.

Is the "Mormon effect" among Democrats because of religious bigotry? Not necessarily. With limited information about these hypothetical candidates, including no party label, most Democrats likely inferred that this candidate was a Republican. After all, the Republicans' presidential nominee was Mormon. And as we showed in Chapters 4 and 5, Mormons *are* mostly Republicans and generally conservative. Similarly, Mormons' highly publicized and tightly organized movement to muster support for California's Proposition 8 has likely also contributed to the perception of Mormons as politically active social conservatives squarely under the Republican umbrella (see Chapter 6 for a full discussion).

These inferences are not merely hypothetical, as we have empirical confirmation that voters are largely aware of Mormons' Republican-ness. In the same 2012 survey, we asked our respondents whether members of different religious groups are Republicans, Democrats, or "an even mix of both." As many people describe Mormons as "mostly Republicans" (59 percent) as say the same about evangelicals (61 percent) – who are often referred to as the base of the Republican Party.

It is one thing to see partisan polarization in attitudes toward the Republican nominee's religion during the presidential election; it is quite another if that polarization persists once the contest is over. To find out if the partisan divide is frozen into place or has begun to thaw, we commissioned a brief survey in January of 2014, a little over a year past the election, to once again gauge Americans' attitudes toward Mormons using a feeling thermometer.[24] In early 2014, the average perception toward Mormons had dropped a little, to 44 (see Figure 9.11). We also still see sharp partisan polarization (Figure 9.12). However, Republicans' feelings toward Mormons have cooled a bit, from a score of 62 a month or so after the presidential election to 53 in January 2014. Among both independents and Democrats, perceptions of Mormons have also dropped slightly (2 points for independents and 1.5 for Democrats).

At this point, it is impossible to say whether we are seeing the start of one or both of two trends: increasing negativity toward Mormons and/or the end of the partisan gap in perceptions toward Mormons. Alternatively, it could be that the slight drop in perceptions of Mormons is only a statistical blip and/or that the partisan divide will persist, even if it is not as wide as at the apogee of the 2012 election.

Perhaps the most interesting shift in attitudes toward Mormons is among white, churchgoing Protestants (WCPs), a group that approximates white

---

[24] This question was included on a daily YouGov Omnibus Survey. See Data Appendix for details.

evangelical Protestants.[25] In the post-election survey of 2012, WCPs gave Mormons a score of 54; by 2014, the score had dropped to only 43. Even more dramatically, the gap among Republicans who are and are not WCPs grew between the post-election survey in 2012 and the one in early 2014. In the immediate wake of the election, WCP Republicans rated Mormons at 58, while all other Republicans rated them at 65 – a difference of 7 points. By 2014, that difference increased to 13 points: Republicans who are also white, Protestant, and frequent churchgoers gave Mormons a 44; all other Republicans gave them a 57.

In other words, partisanship seemed to lessen the longstanding religious tensions many Protestants, particularly evangelicals, felt with Mormons while Mitt Romney was the Republican nominee for president. But as memory of the election recedes, the old religious tensions appear to have reappeared – to a degree. This pattern suggests that dual tensions are still an element of Mormon politics.

CONCLUSION

Much is rightly made of John F. Kennedy's victory in the 1960 presidential election as a giant leap for religious tolerance in America. In winning that election, Kennedy demonstrated that the Constitution's promise that there shall be no religious test for office was true in fact as well as law, at least for Catholics. However, while Kennedy was the first Catholic to win, he was not the first to run. That distinction belongs to Al Smith, who ran as the Democratic presidential nominee in 1928. During the 1928 campaign, Smith faced virulent anti-Catholicism in a landslide loss to Herbert Hoover (Prendergrast 1999). There were many reasons for Smith's loss and so it would not be accurate to pin it all on his religion. But neither should we dismiss the hostility and even bigotry directed toward him because of his religion.

In assessing Romney's 2012 campaign, is he the Mormons' Kennedy or Smith? Superficially, he resembles Smith. After all, both Romney and Smith failed to break the stained-glass ceiling. The data we have presented in this chapter, however, suggests that Romney more closely resembles Kennedy – or, at least, his 2012 run for the White House was more like 1960 than 1928. During his first presidential run in 2008, Romney's Mormonism was definitely a drag on his political support. While Americans highly knowledgeable about Mormonism or who have a close relationship with a Mormon expressed little concern about his religion, such people were in relatively short supply. But in 2012, Romney's Mormonism faded as an issue. In not winning the presidency,

---

[25] "Churchgoing" is defined as self-reported religious attendance once a week or more. Note that in this survey we are unable to identify evangelicals more precisely, and so use white, churchgoing Protestants as an imperfect, but reasonable, approximation. We would expect a more refined measure of white evangelicals to show even more dramatic results.

he may not have broken through the stained-glass ceiling, but perhaps he made it more like an open window. Romney is a Mormon candidate who lost a presidential election, not a candidate who lost because he was Mormon.[26] The difference is significant.

While Romney's campaign represents a significant step toward the widespread acceptance of Mormons, suspicions remain. Specifically, our findings regarding social contact are worth noting. Recall that it is people who know a Mormon in passing who react most negatively to Mormonism and are the most impervious to changing their minds. We suspect that the explanation for the negative reaction among people with only moderate contact lies in Mormons' distinctiveness, which is apparent to those who have a Mormon acquaintance. Their distinctiveness apparently raises suspicions. Furthermore, Mormons' tendency to form strong bonds with fellow Mormons likely limits the sort of close relationships between Latter-day Saints and "gentiles" that would soften those suspicions. Mormons who are concerned with fostering a positive perception of their faith should take note of our findings. Warm feelings toward Mormons result from close relationships with people outside of the sacred tabernacle; just living and working alongside non-Mormons without forming tight connections is not enough. In fact, shallow relationships of this type may do more harm than good.

Throughout this book, we have argued that Mormons' relationship to politics is a vestige of the ethno-religious cleavages that once defined American politics. The strong identification of Mormons with the Republican Party in the public eye adds still another dimension to their ethno-religious nature. In the heyday of ethno-religious political alliances, denominations and parties were intertwined, just as Mormons today are tightly coupled with the Republican Party. Accordingly, it is entirely rational for a voter who leans Democratic to oppose a Mormon candidate, in the absence of little other information. Rational or not, however, the blurry lines in the public eye between their church and the Republican Party should give Mormons pause.

Mormonism did not cost Mitt Romney the presidency in 2012, but his presidential bid has shaped attitudes toward Mormonism. Although Romney's time on the national stage did not lead to greater knowledge of the LDS religion or to a change in whether Mormons are thought to be Christians, it did lead to a sharp partisan divide in how Mormons are perceived. They rose in favor among Republicans and fell in the eyes of Democrats. Romney leaves a legacy of intensifying partisan relevance for Mormonism; whether this legacy lasts remains to be seen. Should it last, Mormons may find the religious mission of the LDS Church hampered by its close association with one party. On this, we have more to say in Chapter 10.

---

[26] Our conclusions about Romney and Mormonism in 2012 are consistent with those of John Sides and Lynn Vavreck (2013), who offer a detailed analysis of the 2012 campaign, including discussion of factors beyond the scope of our book.

CHAPTER 9 APPENDIX

TABLE 9A.1. *Multinomial Logit Model of the 2012 Presidential Vote*

| VARIABLES | Vote for Romney | Vote for Obama |
|---|---|---|
| Party identification (3 categories) | 1.642*** | −1.359 |
| | (0.210) | (0.198) |
| Mormon stereotypes (quartiles) | −0.889*** | 0.324** |
| | (0.157) | (0.143) |
| Evangelical Protestant | 1.013** | −0.126 |
| | (0.523) | (0.504) |
| Mormon | −0.008 | 0.321 |
| | (0.989) | (1.386) |
| White Catholic | 0.704 | 0.200 |
| | (0.620) | (0.548) |
| Mainline Protestant | 1.150** | 0.331 |
| | (0.600) | (0.540) |
| No religion | −0.559 | −0.731* |
| | (0.613) | (0.437) |
| Secular salience | −0.151 | 0.216** |
| | (0.174) | (0.135) |
| Religiosity | −0.211 | −0.724*** |
| | (0.241) | (0.219) |
| Age | 0.041*** | 0.034*** |
| | (0.010) | (0.009) |
| South | 0.298 | −0.192 |
| | (0.316) | (0.277) |
| Gender (Female) | −0.629** | 0.096 |
| | (0.314) | (0.264) |
| Income | 0.006 | 0.004 |
| | (0.005) | (0.005) |
| Black | −0.827 | 1.221** |
| | (1.052) | (0.483) |
| Hispanic | −0.220 | 0.325 |
| | (0.599) | (0.459) |
| Education | 0.571*** | 0.455*** |
| | (0.131) | (0.110) |
| Constant | −3.828*** | −1.466 |
| | (1.182) | (0.974) |
| Observations | 851 | |
| Pseudo R-squared | 0.57 | |

Standard errors in parentheses
*** $p < 0.01$, ** $p < 0.05$, * $p < 0.1$
Did not turn out to vote is the omitted category.
*Source:* Mormon Perceptions Study, 2012

# 10

# Seeking the Promised Land

Just as the 2012 presidential race was heating up, the Pew Mormons in America Survey[1] found that 68 percent of Mormons thought their fellow Americans did not consider Mormonism "mainstream." But a nearly identical number, 63 percent, also indicated that their fellow citizens were *becoming* more accepting of Mormons. And 56 percent of Mormons said Americans were ready to elect a Mormon president. Simultaneously believing that they are viewed with suspicion and that the suspicion is waning reflects the Mormon paradox of being a self-consciously peculiar people who are also quintessential Americans. The belief that full acceptance by society will come one day undoubtedly stems from the optimistic spirit of the proselytizing people Mormons are.

Mormons have long sought their own promised land, where they can be both clearly distinctive and fully at peace with their neighbors. Or, as Mormons themselves often put it, they want to be in the world, not of the world – yet also accepted by the world. They would like to be counted among the "mainstream" faiths, grouped in the public mind with Protestants, Catholics, and Jews rather than, say, Scientologists or Wiccans. Mormons have earned a measure of such acceptance in many other venues, including business, sports, entertainment, literature, and academia. But in a democratic society, a key measure of acceptance is politics – an area that has produced mixed results for the Latter-day Saints. Old secular and religious tensions persist, even with new allies, and a Mormon has yet to break the stained-glass ceiling to win the White House.

The Mormon experience thus reveals the continuing importance of ethno-religious groups in the United States. Many social scientists – including your authors – have written about the replacement of the old ethno-religious differences by a grand division between "orthodox" believers on the one hand and on the other, "progressive" believers and those who profess no belief at all (Wuthnow 1990). Latter-day Saints, however, are a notable exception to this

---

[1] See Data Appendix for details of the Pew Mormons in America survey.

trend. The tide of religious restructuring washed over the Mormons, leaving them standing outside of either coalition.

In this concluding chapter, we briefly summarize the arguments and evidence of the book thus far. We then consider the various ways that Mormons have attempted to address their paradox before glimpsing into the future.

## A BRIEF SUMMARY

In Part 1 (Chapters 1–3), we described how and why Mormons are distinctive. In Chapter 1 we met the Mormons, a proudly peculiar people. Mormons originated in America and undertook an epic journey in search of the promised land. This journey has left the legacy of a geographic concentration in the Mountain West and a distinctive religious worldview and lifestyle – wherever Mormons are found.

In Chapter 2, we argued that Mormons are a good example of an ethnoreligious group. More than just a denomination, Mormons are characterized by high internal solidarity, high external tensions, and a unique subculture. This subculture is defined by dual social boundaries, or what we have metaphorically called the "two-front war." One boundary is with secular society (the world), the second with other religions ("gentiles," although this term is not much used anymore). We identified this subculture as the "sacred tabernacle," drawing on the experience of the biblical Israelites – an apt metaphor since the children of Israel were also seeking a promised land. The Mormons' sacred tabernacle is both encompassing and portable.

Chapter 3 turned to the religious core of the sacred tabernacle. One way that the Latter-day Saints differentiate themselves from secular society is with a high level of religiosity – higher, in fact, than most other faiths in America. At the same time, Mormons differentiate themselves from the devout of other religions with an array of peculiar beliefs and behaviors. Within the sacred tabernacle, Mormons display a remarkable degree of unity on the essentials of their faith. But they are not completely homogeneous, showing internal variation on religious activity, Church authority, Mormon identity, and social insularity. Furthermore, because of its emphasis on continuing revelation, the sacred tabernacle has the capacity to adjust its boundaries over time.

Part 2 (Chapters 4–6) examined the political implications of the sacred tabernacle. Politically, Mormons' peculiarity has waxed and waned over time (Chapter 4). While during the early days of LDS Church history Mormons were actively courted by politicians from different parties, the second half of the nineteenth century was a period of Mormon exclusion from national politics – to the point that the peculiar people even had their own political party in Utah. A new century brought Mormons into a period of reinvolvement with national politics. Their participation was broad and bipartisan, as Latter-day Saints voted for both Democrats and Republicans. Among elected officials, Mormons could be found on both sides of the aisle. More recently, however, Mormons' political participation has narrowed, becoming more one-sidedly partisan. Over the last half century, Mormons have developed overwhelming support for the Republicans.

Yet in spite of their embrace of the GOP, Mormons are "peculiar partisans," as Chapter 5 showed. They tend to hold conservative views on many subjects, but do not always toe the line of conservative orthodoxy on issues like immigration, abortion, and even same-sex marriage. These deviations can be attributed to the sacred tabernacle. When asked to choose between their party and their Church, most Mormons go with the latter.

We presented further evidence of how Mormons "follow their leaders" on political issues in Chapter 6. The capacity of LDS leaders to change Church members' minds is an important precondition for political mobilization. Another is the social capital found in the sacred tabernacle. The same skills, networks, and organizations that foster religious voluntarism can be directed toward a political cause. Although such mobilization is infrequent – and perhaps because it is infrequent – when it does occur Mormons have responded in force, such as during the campaign for California's Proposition 8.

Part 3 (Chapters 7–9) turned to public reactions to Mormons' peculiarity. In Chapter 7, we showed that Americans have mixed views of Mormons, although the negatives outweigh the positives. Among the factors that ameliorate negative perceptions of Mormons are factual knowledge about the LDS faith and personal relationships with flesh-and-blood Latter-day Saints. Importantly, however, a little contact with Mormons elicits a more negative response than no contact at all – presumably because it brings exposure to Mormons' peculiarity without a counterbalancing knowledge of the people themselves.

Chapter 8 illustrated the political consequences of public attitudes toward Mormons. In reviewing seven campaigns of Mormon presidential candidates between 1967 and 2012, we found considerable variation in the linkage of generic public attitudes about Mormons to views of particular Mormon candidates. Such politicization was the product of particular campaigns as well as long-term political developments. These effects were largest in the 2008 and 2012 Republican nomination contests, but declined substantially during Mitt Romney's general election campaign against Barack Obama in 2012. Nevertheless, Romney failed to break the stained-glass ceiling in his quest for the White House.

Chapter 9 focused on public reaction to Mitt Romney's 2008 and 2012 presidential campaigns. Using a variety of data, we showed how voters reacted to information about Romney's Mormonism. While the reaction was strongly negative in 2008, by the 2012 general election the independent impact of such reactions had diminished, being largely subsumed under partisanship. However, while most attention has been paid to whether attitudes toward Mormons affected Mitt Romney, we also found that Mitt Romney's campaign affected public views of Mormons. Indeed, public attitudes toward Latter-day Saints were sharply polarized along partisan lines at the conclusion of the 2012 campaign, but only time will tell whether this effect endures or fades.

ADDRESSING THE MORMON PARADOX

Thus far, we have discussed the causes and consequences of the Mormon paradox – being simultaneously peculiar and as American as apple pie. However, these two sides of Mormonism are not constants, but variables. Since the founding of Mormonism, they have been balanced in different ways, at different times, with different results. By examining the strategies of the past, we can find clues as to what the future holds.

Mormons have employed a variety of strategies to address the paradox of peculiarity. They went from a strategy of separation to assimilation to engagement and, we suggest, might be moving to a new strategy of alignment. Each of these strategies has had its benefits and costs. These strategies are not unique to the Latter-day Saints, but they are easily illustrated in terms of Mormon history. Of course, any such account is an oversimplification. The LDS Church is a large, complex organization; Mormon culture is multifaceted. At any given point in time more than one of the following strategies was no doubt present, but typically one strategy has been favored over others, nudging Mormonism in a general direction.

The first strategy was *separation*. After the exodus to the Utah territory, Mormons consciously cut themselves off from American society and politics. Under Brigham Young, they avoided contact with "gentiles" and built a parallel society of their own. Most famously, polygamy meant a unique familial system, but Mormons' distinctive institutions also included their legal (Firmage 2001), economic (Arrington, Fox, and May 1992), and political systems (see Chapter 4). During these years of separation, the sacred tabernacle was nearly all-encompassing and hardly portable.[2] Mormonism pervaded every aspect of life and converts migrated to "Zion" rather than erect the sacred tabernacle where they lived.

Separation brought the benefit of high internal vitality for the faith. In this, Mormons are not alone as, historically, numerous American ethno-religious groups have employed a strategy of internal strength through separation from the outside world. Some still do, including Old Order Amish, ultraorthodox Jews, and, fittingly, fundamentalist polygamists. These groups are frequently seen as largely apolitical.[3]

For Mormons, the costs of separation were high, at least in terms of societal acceptance. They were reviled in the rest of the country; a federal military expedition was dispatched to keep them in check; Congress enacted laws to stamp out polygamy; and Utah's statehood was long delayed. Thus, in pursuing a strategy of separation, nineteenth-century Mormons tried to evade the Mormon paradox

---

[2] In keeping with Peter Berger's original terminology, Mormonism in this period could be described as a sacred canopy (1990).

[3] In terms of the Mormon presidential campaigns discussed in Chapter 8, there is no clear counterpart to separation. However, Morris Udall's "avoidance" approach is analogous – although Udall sought to avoid talking about his lack of religious activity rather than Mormon distinctiveness.

altogether, but instead ended up accentuating it.[4] Isolation ceased to be a viable option.

As the twentieth century began, Mormons then began to pursue a strategy of *assimilation*. The end of polygamy and statehood for Utah made Mormonism less distinctive in social and political terms. The faith was refocused on the story of its founder, Joseph Smith, a religious seeker whose restoration of New Testament Christianity was far less controversial than his revival of Old Testament-style polygamy (Flake 2004). As Mormonism was reintegrated into the cultural, economic, and political norms found within the rest of America, the sacred tabernacle become less encompassing but more portable, especially as Mormonism grew in areas outside of the Mountain West. In the early years of the twentieth century, LDS doctrine and practice adapted to the zeitgeist of the Progressive Era. Matthew Bowman describes how Mormonism even incorporated various ideas of the Progressive Era, as "[m]any Mormon leaders at the turn of the century found in Progressive ideas the way to harmonize their faith with their nation" (2012a, 154). According to Armand Mauss (1994), Mormonism's defining metaphor changed from the angel (a symbol of religious revelation) to the beehive (a symbol of industry and commerce with the world). The promised land was to be found through incorporation into American culture. Thus the paradox was less resolved than minimized.[5]

The benefit of assimilation was a reduction in both secular and religious tensions. Such a strategy is not unique to Mormons, either – indeed, some scholars have argued that assimilation is very nearly the norm among new (and newly arrived) religious groups in America (Finke and Stark 2005). The rabble-rousing, "shouting" Methodists evolved into conventional mainline Protestantism, while Jews went from being despised to admired. Perhaps the best case of assimilation is Catholics, who have gone from the margins to the mainstream partly by eliminating traditional boundaries between Catholicism and the dominant Protestant culture of the United States (Putnam and Campbell 2010). Finke and Stark argue that the end of mandatory meatless Fridays after the Second Vatican Council was especially significant:

[In] a pluralistic setting the observance had been a clear cultural marker and social boundary. When Catholic teenagers at drive-ins on Friday nights counted down to midnight before ordering their burgers, everyone present was reminded who was Catholic and who was not. To waive this very visible rule necessarily raised serious questions about the basis of religious truth and institutional credibility. (263–4)[6]

---

[4] Readers may note the similarity between the separation strategy and H. Richard Niebuhr's (2001 [1951]) category of "Christ against culture." As we have argued, Mormons do not just have tensions with American culture but also with other religions. In the nineteenth century, these tensions may well have overlapped to a high degree.

[5] Assimilation fits well with Niebuhr's (2001 [1951]) category "Christ of culture." One could imagine Mormons becoming just another denomination if enough assimilation occurred.

[6] Interestingly, these scholars go on to compare this change to a hypothetical decision by the Mormon Church to "authorize cola and coffee drinking" (264). In the years since these words were originally

Perhaps the most telling evidence of Catholic assimilation is in politics, including a Catholic president in 1960, a Catholic presidential nominee of the Democratic Party in 2004, and Catholic vice-presidential nominees in both parties in 2012.[7]

While the story of Catholics' assimilation is one of good feelings in a once hostile nation, their positive image has arguably come at a price. According to Finke and Stark, the loss of Catholic distinctiveness sapped the vitality of the Catholic faith writ large. Likewise, assimilation potentially threatened the vitality of the Mormon faith. To put it bluntly, if Mormons are fully in the world, then where exactly in the world are Mormons?

While Mormons may have started down the path of assimilation, they did not go very far before veering off into another direction. To return to Mauss's metaphors, Mormons swung back from the beehive to the angel, entering what he calls a period of "retrenchment." We prefer to describe it as *engagement* with secular society. Mormons would not retreat from or surrender to it, but instead choose their battles carefully. Mauss describes Mormons as reaching "ever more deeply into their bag of cultural peculiarities to find either symbolic or actual traits that will help them mark their subcultural boundaries and thus their very identity as a special people" (1994, 77).

In particular, Mormons maintained their traditionalist views on sex and gender roles even as the sexual revolution broke out all around them. Within the Church, there was renewed emphasis on the authority of Church leaders, more frequent participation in temple rites, increased proselytizing (that is, missionary work), the promotion of Church programs to strengthen the traditional family, and a reorientation of the Church's educational system toward promoting the faith rather than intellectual inquiry (Mauss 1994, 99). In many respects, Mormons continued the process of integration into American society – as evidenced by Latter-day Saints who have achieved worldly success. Mormons also became the most middle class of the middle class (see Chapter 1). But for all their integration, in important ways Mormons have also remained distinctive from much of secular society – in carefully selected ways. Examples of their distinctiveness include extraordinarily high levels of religious activity; no drinking, smoking, coffee or tea; and strict standards for sexual behavior, including a recent emphasis on modest (that is, nonrevealing) clothing. Politically, Mormons had considerable representation in both political parties.[8]

The period of engagement has also been marked by a movement within the Church known as "correlation," whereby the organizational structure, curriculum, and religious practices of the faith were consolidated and standardized to a greater extent than ever before. Mormonism's sharpened boundaries expanded

published in 1992 and revised in 2005, the LDS Church has quietly but officially noted that it does not prohibit cola consumption. Coffee, however, is still forbidden in policy and practice.

[7] In terms of the Mormon presidential campaigns discussed in Chapter 8, Jon Huntsman's "aloofness" approach fits well with assimilation.

[8] In terms of the Mormon presidential campaigns discussed in Chapter 8, George Romney's "affirmation" approach reflects the "engagement" strategy.

the reach of the sacred tabernacle; the correlation program ensured the tabernacle's uniformity, making it truly portable. The promised land was to be found in tight-knit communities distributed throughout society. Thus the paradox was not so much resolved as managed.[9]

Mormons are not alone in their strategy of engagement, as evangelical Protestants have done the same. Upon emerging from their self-imposed cultural isolation in the post-World War II era, evangelicals also opted for "integration with exceptions" (see Chapter 2). And like Mormons, evangelicals were "embattled and thriving" (Smith et al. 1998), but not concentrated in one political party. It is worth remembering that "born again" Jimmy Carter was a Democrat and that Jerry Falwell originally proposed a bipartisan Moral Majority.

As we described in Chapter 2, for Mormonism the benefit of engagement has been its religious energy. Clear boundaries foster a personal sense of meaning and strong communal bonds. However, there is no free lunch and engagement imposes costs as well. For one, the faith's leaders must constantly negotiate the precise points of distinction in the face of secular and religious changes. Finding the right dose of distinctiveness presents a challenge for a large, growing, diverse, and increasingly international Church. Too much distinctiveness and Mormons cease to be the biblical "salt of the earth," ending up cut off from their communities rather than full participants within them. Too little distinctiveness and they are no longer the "light of the world," exemplars of a distinctive gospel. No matter where the balance is struck, distinctiveness inevitably brings disapprobation from some quarters.

Engagement has also meant that the LDS Church has occasionally chosen to mobilize the Church's membership and/or resources on behalf of a political cause. In each case, the issue has reflected a point of Mormons' distinctiveness – alcohol, gambling, gender roles (the Equal Rights Amendment), and gay marriage.

While engagement has been the dominant LDS strategy of the last generation or two, in recent years there are signs that Mormons are adopting a new strategy of *alignment*, increasingly allying themselves with other religious and social conservatives. In a strategy of alignment, the promised land is to be found in a close alliance with the more traditional elements of American society. The Mormon paradox is thus partially resolved by identifying with a particular kind of American, but at the risk of diminishing the distinctiveness of the sacred tabernacle.[10]

We wish to be clear that the jury is still out on whether Mormons are shifting from engagement to alignment. What is the evidence? Certainly there has been a growing sociological and attitudinal affinity between Mormons with other demographic groups with conservative views (see Chapters 2 and 5). In an effort

---

[9] Engagement fits well with Niebuhr's (2001 [1951]) category "Christ and culture in paradox," although the Mormon paradox is complicated by the dual boundaries of the sacred tabernacle.

[10] Alignment resembles Niebuhr's (2001 [1951]) category "Christ above culture" in the sense that Mormons and their allies offer a common, moral alternative to the broader culture.

to ease tensions with other faiths – particularly evangelical Protestants – in recent years LDS leaders have stressed that Mormons are Christians (J. R. Holland 2012). Similarly, Mormon and evangelical Protestant intellectuals have engaged in inter-religious dialogue (Blomberg and Robinson 1997). However, the best case for the shift is found in electoral politics. As we discussed in Chapter 6, as an institution the LDS Church does not often enter into political combat, only doing so in initiative campaigns and not partisan elections. However, the issues on which the LDS Church has been most vocal, particularly opposition to same-sex marriage in California, nonetheless have a distinctly Republican cast. While the Church has supported some policies – specifically on immigration and Salt Lake City's antidiscrimination statute – that align better with the Democrats than Republicans, in the public eye Mormons are closely associated with the GOP. This public perception conforms to reality, as Mormon voters and officeholders are now overwhelmingly Republican (Harry Reid being a rare, albeit highly visible, exception). Furthermore, the Mormon-Republican connection was only strengthened by Mitt Romney's presidential candidacy.[11]

While it is too early to tell if alignment will supplant engagement as a strategy for addressing the Mormon paradox, we can nonetheless highlight its potential implications. The primary benefit of alignment over engagement is the defense of Mormons' interests in the public square, with the corollary benefit of potentially fostering better relations with their political allies such as conservative Catholics (successful) and evangelicals (less successful). Here, too, evangelical Protestants are a good example. Evangelicals were making very similar social and political choices at about the same time for many of the same reasons. They have defended their views on issues like abortion and homosexuality vociferously in the public square and, in so doing, made peace with Catholics, their previous theological nemeses.

As we have noted, Mormons have largely been excluded from this theological peace treaty. Accordingly, many evangelicals and Mormons found themselves at odds during Mitt Romney's campaigns for the Republican nomination. However, the times might be changing, as many evangelicals rallied behind Romney against a common opponent in the 2012 general election. At this point, we do not know if this coalition was a fleeting affair or will become a lasting relationship. Should it last, perhaps Mormons will be fully welcomed into the coalition of religious conservatives, much like the rapprochement between conservative Catholics and evangelical Protestants.

There are costs to an alignment strategy as well, both inside the sacred tabernacle and out. Within Mormonism, the close association between the LDS Church and the Republican Party could have a potentially detrimental impact on healthy civic dialogue. The fact that Mormons are heavily supportive of one party risks silencing the minority of Church members who support the other

---

[11]  In terms of the Mormon presidential campaigns discussed in Chapter 8, Mitt Romney's "alliance" approach fits well with the alignment strategy.

party. If Mormon Democrats feel uncomfortable expressing their political views to their fellow Church members, political discourse is impoverished. Both the Republican majority and Democratic minority miss out on the opportunity to exchange political views, and hear a different perspective on how Mormonism applies to politics.[12]

The political cohesiveness of Mormons could also hurt LDS interests outside the sacred tabernacle. Taking a partisan side links Mormons with the GOP and its interests, intensifying opposition from the other quarters, especially among the growing nonwhite and nonreligious populations. Consequently, LDS leaders would find it difficult to build coalitions with groups of a different partisan stripe on an issue like immigration.

Arguably, the greatest costs of all extend beyond politics to a higher realm. Evidence suggests that a rising share of Americans, especially those under thirty, have turned away from religion as a reaction to the mingling of faith and conservative politics (Hout and Fischer 2002; Putnam and Campbell 2010; Patrikios 2008). Likewise, the close connection between Mormons and Republicans could drive people of other political persuasions – or no persuasion at all – away from Mormonism, whether they are friends of the faith, potential converts, or even current members. The Church's perceived affinity for the Republican Party could also limit the effectiveness of LDS leaders' voices in the public square. Prophetic voices are most likely to be heard and heeded when they rise above the partisan fray (Campbell and Putnam 2012).

It is too soon to know whether we are correct to describe this as a new era of political alignment. At a minimum, it would require Mormons to maintain their support for the GOP and an enduring perception among the general public that Mormons are Republicans – both of which seem likely. However, to conclude that alignment has replaced engagement as a strategy for resolving the Mormon paradox would also require partisanship to seep into the religious aspects of Mormonism. While some observers might argue that this has already happened, the LDS Church remains officially nonpartisan and, as our data show, Mormons hear less politicking from the pulpit than any other religious group (see Chapter 4).

In fact, there have been signals from the LDS leadership suggesting that they would prefer to see more partisan balance among Church members. In 1998 Elder Marlin K. Jensen, one of the Church's general authorities, spoke at length in an interview with the *Salt Lake Tribune* about the need for greater partisan balance within the LDS rank and file. He noted that it is "not in our

---

[12] Mormon Republicans are indeed more likely to report talking about politics with other Mormons. Twenty-eight percent of Republicans say that they talk about politics with their fellow ward members (outside of church) several times a month, compared to 21 percent of Democrats. Likewise, there is a ten-point difference in having political conversations roughly once a month: 31 percent of Republicans, 21 percent of Democrats.

best interest to be known as a one-party church" (1998, 82). In response to the question of how Mormons might reconcile their religious views with some of the positions taken by the Democratic Party, he went on to say, "[W]e would probably hope that they wouldn't abandon a party necessarily because it has a philosophy or two that may not square with Mormonism. Because, as I say, they [i.e. parties] in their philosophies ebb and flow" (82). In responding to the specific claim that Mormonism and the Democratic Party are incompatible, he elaborated further.

> I think I could safely say that one of the things that prompted this discussion in the first place was the regret that's felt about the decline of the Democratic Party and the notion that may prevail in some areas that you can't be a good Mormon and a good Democrat at the same time. There have been some awfully good men and women who have, I think, been both and are today. (84)

This was one media interview given by a mid-level Church official, not an authoritative statement from the highest echelon of the LDS leadership, and so we would not have expected it to move the needle on Mormons' partisanship. And, judging from the trends in party affiliation among Latter-day Saints, it does not appear that his words have had much effect. In the years since Elder Jensen gave this unusually candid interview, Mormons have remained as Republican as ever. More recently, LDS leaders have used official channels to remind Church members in Utah that more than one party has principles compatible with Mormonism (see Chapter 5).

It is not hard to see why an alignment strategy alarms LDS Church leaders, as they look to the long-term mission of the Church as a whole. Here, too, the experience of evangelicals is worth noting. Many leaders within evangelical circles have soured on politics and their close identification with one party, worried that their religious message has been drowned out by their coreligionists' political activity (J. C. Hunter 2008; Thomas 2000).

If Mormons were to wholly adopt alignment as a strategy, it should be of concern to Mormons and non-Mormons alike. To have attitudes toward Mormons – or any religion – reinforce, and be reinforced by, the nation's ever-deepening political divisions risks hampering the spirit of religious tolerance within all of America. Indeed, if groups are too sharply aligned with and against one another, a potent source of inter-religious acceptance – personal contact among group members – may be severely limited. We can learn from the past, as ethno-religious politics has a history of prejudice and antagonism. We can also learn from the racial politics of the present; some scholars have argued that the close association of African Americans with the Democratic Party has exacerbated racial tensions in America (Tesler 2010).[13]

---

[13]  But see Goldman and Mutz (2014) for a contrary view.

## THE FUTURE

As Mormons have sought the promised land, they have had to balance their distinctiveness and their desire to be embraced as quintessential Americans. We would suggest, however, that the promised land *is* this balance. LDS Church spokesperson Michael Otterson writes that he does not see why Mormons should seek a spot in the mainstream, which "carries with it a sense of being part of the majority." Instead,

Mormons are deserving of acceptance and respect as part of the complex fabric of American society, not because they have passed some ill-defined test of orthodoxy, but because that is what America is at its core. Mormons want acceptance, but not assimilation. (2012)

The acceptance Mormons seek is in the face of – perhaps even in spite of – the very peculiarity that feeds their religious vitality that, in turn, fosters the quintessential American-ness of the Latter-day Saints.

What does the future hold for Mormonism in America? Given its past, we expect Mormonism to remain a dynamic faith, continuously negotiating the boundaries of the sacred tabernacle. In the course of this process, we would expect some aspects of the faith to be de-emphasized and perhaps even changed. As we have noted, attitudes toward gender roles are undergoing a subtle but profound shift within Mormonism (see Chapter 5). Similarly, the LDS Church has recently taken steps to soften its position on homosexuality. While homosexual sexual activity remains prohibited, Church members who identify as gays or lesbians but remain chaste can now be considered in good standing, able to hold callings and participate in temple worship – a new level of inclusion.

This is not to say that we expect Mormonism to revert to assimilation. To the contrary, many distinctive, and boundary-defining, features of the faith are nearly certain to continue. In particular, we suspect that the heavy time commitment that the LDS Church asks of its members will increasingly mark Mormons as distinctive, especially in an age of declining community engagement and rising secularism (Putnam 2001). There is no reason to think that the LDS Church will abandon its reliance on a lay clergy, which necessitates the high degree of Church-based voluntarism.

In fact, owing to a recent policy change, such voluntarism appears to be on the rise. The LDS Church has lowered the age at which its young members can serve as full-time missionaries. American men can now start their two years of missionary service at eighteen,[14] but even more significantly, the age for all women missionaries (American and otherwise) has been dropped from twenty-one to nineteen. This new policy has dramatically boosted the number of all missionaries, and female missionaries especially (Stack 2012e). If this trend persists, it

---

[14] In other nations, the age of eligibility for men (but not women) had already been lowered.

will expose more Mormon women to the intense socialization of missionary service, strengthening every dimension of their Mormon-ness, from religious activity to views of Church authority and Mormon identity, and even their degree of insularity – since the "refiner's fire" of the mission field leads to many deep friendships, not to mention marriages.


## LESSONS

In closing, we look beyond Mormonism, as the LDS experience can inform our understanding of other highly distinctive religious minorities that are also growing in size and salience. Mormons' peculiarity may be increasingly unusual among religions in America, but it is hardly unique. In this regard, the parallel between Mormons and Muslims is particularly illuminating. Like Muslims today, Mormons of yesteryear were often portrayed as disloyal Americans, prone to violence. Both groups even share a dark association with September 11. Not only is this the day in 2001 when Islamic terrorists committed the worst terrorist attack on U.S. soil, it was also on that date in 1857 that a band of Mormons committed the Mountain Meadows Massacre, killing 120 unarmed men, women, and children who were traveling in a wagon train through Southern Utah (Walker, Turley, and Leonard 2011). Still another parallel is how their public perception is colored by partisanship. The Republican Party of the 1850s explicitly sought to stamp out polygamy; today, Republicans are far more likely than Democrats to have negative views toward Islamic beliefs and practices (Dionne and Galston 2010). Perhaps most importantly, American Muslims share with Mormons the duality of balancing their internal distinctiveness with the desire for acceptance by their fellow Americans (Pew Forum on Religion & Public Life 2011; Abu Dhabi Gallup Center 2011).

Distinctive minority religions, such as Muslims and Mormons, resist the trend in America toward ever-more-permeable boundaries among religions, and thus put religious tolerance to the test. It is one thing for Americans to tolerate and accept religions that minimize their differences with the broader culture, and it is quite another to tolerate, accept, and even embrace starkly different faiths. The challenge for Mormons – and Muslims, and other distinctive faiths – is to affirm their peculiarity in a pluralistic nation; the challenge for America is to accept that a pluralistic nation is made up of peculiar peoples.

# Data Appendix

This book employed several special surveys conducted by the authors as well as secondary analysis of other data sets. The details are listed below. All links were live as of October 7, 2013.

SPECIAL SURVEYS CONDUCTED BY AUTHORS

**Peculiar People Survey 2012.** Self-identified Mormons; YouGov online panel; N = 500; http://csed.byu.edu/Research/PeculiarPeopleSurvey.aspx.

**Mormon Perceptions Study 2012.** General population, pre- and post-election interviews; YouGov online panel; N = 1,349; http://csed.byu.edu/Research/MormonPerceptionsSurvey.html.

**YouGov Daily Omnibus Survey 2014 (replication of feeling thermometer from Mormon Perceptions Survey).** General population; YouGov online panel; N = 1,000; http://csed.byu.edu/Research/MormonPerceptionsSurvey.aspx.

**Cooperative Congressional Election Study 2012.** Akron, BYU, and Notre Dame pre-election modules; YouGov online panel; N = 3,000; http://projects.iq.harvard.edu/cces/data.

**Cooperative Campaign Analysis Project 2008.** Akron, BYU, and Notre Dame January modules 2008; YouGov online panel; N = 3,000; http://ccap.yougov.com/.

*Methodological Note*: YouGov online panel surveys employ a matching procedure to representative samples; see Jackman and Vavreck (2010) for the details of matching process, and Vavreck and Rivers (2008) on the representativeness of the samples drawn using this method. Overall, the results of these surveys are consistent with findings from telephone surveys.

## SURVEYS USED FOR SECONDARY ANALYSIS

**Pew Mormons in America Survey 2012.** Self-identified Mormons; telephone; N = 1,000; http://www.pewforum.org/christian/mormon/mormons-in-america-executive-summary.aspx.

**Pew Political Survey 2012.** General population; telephone; N = 1,503; http://www.pewforum.org/Christian/Mormon/attitudes-toward-mormon-faith.aspx.

**Pew Religion and Politics Survey 2012.** General population; telephone; N = 2,973; http://www.pewforum.org/Politics-and-Elections/2012-romney-mor monism-obamas-religion.aspx.

**Pew Post-Election Survey 2012.** General population; telephone; N = 1,206; http://www.people-press.org/2012/11/15/low-marks-for-the-2012-election.

**Pew Religion and Politics Survey 2011.** General population; telephone; N = 2,001; http://www.pewforum.org/Politics-and-Elections/Romneys-Mormon-Faith-Likely-a-Factor-in-Primaries-Not-in-a-General-Election.aspx.

**Pew Political Typology Survey 2011.** General population; telephone; N = 1,504; http://www.people-press.org/2011/05/04/beyond-red-vs-blue-the-political-typology.

**Pew U.S. Religious Landscape Survey 2007.** General population; telephone; N = 35,556; http://religions.pewforum.org/.

**Pew Religion and Public Life Survey 2007.** General population; telephone; N = 3,002; http://www.people-press.org/2007/09/06/clinton-and-giuliani-seen-as-not-highly-religious-romneys-religion-raises-concerns/.

**Faith Matters Survey 2006–2011.** General population; telephone; N = 3,108; (Harvard University); http://www.thearda.com/Archive/Files/Descriptions/FTH MATT.asp.

**Gallup Presidential Election/Religion 2012.** (#2012–08) General population; telephone; N = 1,004; http://www.ropercenter.uconn.edu/.

**Gallup Immigration/Abortion 2011.** (#2011–11) General population; telephone; N = 1,020; http://www.ropercenter.uconn.edu/.

**Gallup Lifestyles – Economy/Religion 2007.** (#2007–40) General population; telephone; N = 1,027; http://www.ropercenter.uconn.edu/.

**Gallup Election/Social Security 2007.** (#2007–08) General population; telephone; N = 1,010; http://www.ropercenter.uconn.edu/.

**Gallup Presidential Election 2007.** (#2007–06) General population; telephone; N = 1,006; http://www.ropercenter.uconn.edu/.

**Gallup Kosova/Hillary Clinton 1999.** (#1999–02012) General population; telephone; N = 1,014; http://www.ropercenter.uconn.edu/.

**Gallup Presidential Election 1967.** (#1967–0744) General population; face-to-face; N = 3,519; http://www.ropercenter.uconn.edu/.

**Michigan Exit Poll 1976.** (USCBSNYT1976-STPRIM-MIDM). Democratic primary voters; face-to-face, N = 838; http://www.ropercenter.uconn.edu/.

**Wisconsin Exit Poll 1976.** (USCBSNYT1976-STPRIM-WI) Primary voters; face-to-face; N = 1,835; http://www.ropercenter.uconn.edu/.

**American National Elections Study (ANES).** 1948–2008 Cumulative File (University of Michigan); http://www.electionstudies.org/studypages/cdf/cdf.htm.

**General Social Survey (GSS).** Cumulative Data File 1972–2010 (University of Chicago) http://www.ropercenter.uconn.edu/data_access/data/datasets/general_social_survey.html.

**Utah Colleges Exit Polls.** 1982–2012 General election voters; face-to-face (Brigham Young University); http://exitpolldata.byu.edu.

**Utah Delegate Surveys 2012.** State convention delegates; Internet survey (Brigham Young University); http://csed.byu.edu/Research/2012UtahDelegateSurveys.html.

**Secularism Study 2012.** General population; GfK (formerly Knowledge Networks) online panel; N = 1,412; Data not yet released in the public domain.

# Bibliography

"A Man's Religion and American Politics: An Interview with Governor Romney." 1967. *Dialogue: A Journal of Mormon Thought* 3: 23–41.

ABC News. 2012. "Second Presidential Debate Full Transcript." http://www.abcnews.com.

Abu Dhabi Gallup Center. 2011. *Muslim Americans: Faith, Freedom, and the Future.* Abu Dhabi, United Arab Emirates: Abu Dhabi Gallup Center.

Alexander, Thomas G. 1996. *Mormonism in Transition: A History of the Latter-Day Saints, 1890–1930.* Urbana: University of Illinois Press.

Allot, Daniel. 2012. "Ted Kennedy's Anti-Mormon Moment." *American Spectator*, May 23.

Allport, Gordon W. 1979. *The Nature of Prejudice: 25th Anniversary Edition.* New York: Basic Books.

Arrington, Leonard J. 1986. *Brigham Young: American Moses.* Urbana: University of Illinois Press.

Arrington, Leonard J., and Davis Bitton. 1992. *The Mormon Experience: A History of the Latter-day Saints.* Urbana: University of Illinois Press.

Arrington, Leonard J., Feramorz Y. Fox, and Dean L. May. 1992. *Building the City of God: Community and Cooperation among the Mormons.* Urbana: University of Illinois Press.

Asay, Carlos E. 1997. "The Temple Garment: 'An Outward Expression of an Inward Commitment.'" *Ensign*, August. https://www.lds.org/ensign/1997/08/the-temple-gar ment-an-outward-expression-of-an-inward-commitment?lang=eng#footnote2-97908_ 000_008.

Associated Press. 1988. "Apostles Talk about Reasons for Lifting Ban." *Provo Daily Herald*, June 5.

2011. "Texas: Polygamist Leader Gets Life Sentence." *New York Times*, August 9. http://www.nytimes.com/2011/08/10/us/10brfs-POLYGAMISTLE_BRF.html.

Bacon, Jr., Perry. 2007. "Romney Reaches to the Christian Right." *Washington Post*, May 6. http://www.washingtonpost.com/wp-dyn/content/article/2007/05/05/ AR2007050501081.html.

Ball, Molly, and Jonathan Martin. 2011. "The Mormon Primary: Mitt Romney vs. Jon Huntsman." *Politico*, February 3. http://www.politico.com/news/stories/0211/48753. html.

Bardsley, J. Roy. 1980. "Voters Opposed to ERA, but Support Its Concept." *Salt Lake Tribune*, May 11.

Barrus, Roger M. 1992. "Political History." In *Encyclopedia of Mormonism*, edited by Daniel H. Ludlow. New York: Macmillan.

Bellah, Robert N. 1967. "Civil Religion in America." *Daedalus* 96 (1): 1–21.

Benson, Ezra Taft. 1980. "Fourteen Fundamentals in Following the Prophet." Brigham Young University in Provo, UT. February 28. Speech.

    1987. "The Constitution – A Glorious Standard." *LDS.org*. September. http://www.lds. org/ensign/1987/09/the-constitution-a-glorious-standard?lang=eng&query=united+ states+constitution.

Berger, Peter L. 1990. *The Sacred Canopy: Elements of a Sociological Theory of Religion*. New York: Anchor Books.

Bergera, Gary James. 2002. *Conflict in the Quorum: Orson Pratt, Brigham Young, Joseph Smith*. Salt Lake City, UT: Signature Books.

Bernick, Jr., Bob. 1999a. "Hatch Sees His Religion as Asset in Politics." *Deseret News*, June 25.

    1999b. "Straw Poll Is a Big Deal to Utah Senator – Will Iowa's LDS Church Members Surprise Nation?" *Deseret News*, July 28. http://www.deseretnews.com/article/ 709722/Straw-poll-is-a-big-deal-to-Utah-senator.html?pg=all.

Blomberg, Craig L. and Stephen E. Robinson. 1997. *How Wide the Divide? A Mormon & an Evangelical in Conversation*. Downers Grove, IL: InterVarsity Press.

Bloom, Harold. 1992. *The American Religion: The Emergence of the Post-Christian Nation*. New York: Simon & Schuster.

Blumell, Bruce D. 1980. "The LDS Response to the Teton Dam Disaster in Idaho." *Sunstone* 5 (March–April): 35–42.

Bowman, Matthew. 2012a. *The Mormon People: The Making of an American Faith*. New York: Random House.

    2012b. "Mormon Temple Garments – They're Not Magic." *Huffington Post*, July 14. http://www.huffingtonpost.com/matthew-bowman/mormon-temple-garments-_b_ 1673617.html.

    2012c. "Is This the Mormon Moment?" *Time.com*, September 27. http://ideas.time. com/2012/09/27/is-this-the-mormon-moment/.

Bringhurst, Newell G., and Craig L. Foster. 2011. *The Mormon Quest for the Presidency: From Joseph Smith to Mitt Romney and Jon Huntsman*. Independence, MO: John Whitmer Books.

Brooks, Joanna. 2012. *The Book of Mormon Girl: A Memoir of an American Faith*. New York: Free Press.

Brower, Brock. 1967. "Puzzling Front Runner." *LIFE*, May 5.

Burr, Thomas. 2008. "Romney's Big Investment in Iowa Turns Bitter." *Salt Lake Tribune*, January 3. http://www.sltrib.com/ci_7875772.

    2012a. "Marco Rubio's Book Explains Why He Left Mormonism." *Salt Lake Tribune*, June 20. http://www.sltrib.com/sltrib/news/54325018-78/rubio-church-family-faith. html.csp.

2012b. "Harry Reid: Mitt Romney Is Not the Face of Mormonism." *Salt Lake Tribune*, September 24. http://www.sltrib.com/sltrib/politics/54958981-90/rom ney-reid-mormonism-prince.html.csp.

Bush, Jr., Lester E. 1973. "Mormonism's Negro Doctrine: An Historical Overview." *Dialogue: A Journal of Mormon Thought* 8 (1): 11–68.

Bushman, Richard Lyman. 2005. *Joseph Smith: Rough Stone Rolling*. New York: Knopf Doubleday Publishing Group.

2008. *Mormonism: A Very Short Introduction*. New York: Oxford University Press.

California Fair Political Practices Commission. 2010. "In the Matter of The Church of Jesus Christ of Latter-day Saints; Late Contribution Violations, Stipulation, Decision, and Order; FPPC No. 2008–7035." June 10. www.fppc.ca.gov/agendas/06-10/Church.pdf.

Camia, Catalina. 2012. "Pastor Who Sparked Mormon Flap Backs Romney." *USA Today*, April 18. http://content.usatoday.com/communities/onpolitics/post/2012/04/robert-jeffress-mitt-romney-endorse-mormon-cult-/1#.USPfYYJVAig.

Campbell, David E. 2004. "Acts of Faith: Churches and Political Engagement." *Political Behavior* 26 (2): 155–180.

2006. *Why We Vote: How Schools and Communities Shape Our Civic Life*. Princeton, NJ: Princeton University Press.

Campbell, David E., John C. Green, and J. Quin Monson. 2012. "The Stained Glass Ceiling: Social Contact and Mitt Romney's 'Religion Problem'." *Political Behavior* 34 (2): 277–299.

Campbell, David E., Chris Karpowitz, and J. Quin Monson. Forthcoming. "A Politically Peculiar People: How Mormons Moved Into and Then Out Of the Political Mainstream." In *Mormonism and American Politics*, edited by Randall Balmer and Jana Riess. New York: Columbia University Press.

Campbell, David E., and J. Quin Monson. 2003. "Following the Leader? Mormon Voting on Ballot Propositions." *Journal for the Scientific Study of Religion* 42 (4): 605–619.

2007. "Dry Kindling: A Political Profile of American Mormons." In *From Pews to Polling Places: Faith and Politics in the American Religious Mosaic*, edited by J. Matthew Wilson, 105–129. Washington, DC: Georgetown University Press.

Campbell, David E., and Robert D. Putnam. 2012. "God and Caesar in America: Why Mixing Religion and Politics Is Bad for Both." *Foreign Affairs* 91 (2): 34–43.

Campbell, David E., and Steven J. Yonish. 2003. "Religion and Volunteering in America." In *Religion as Social Capital: Producing the Common Good*, edited by Corwin Smidt, 87–106. Waco, TX: Baylor University Press.

Canham, Matt. 2013. "Mormon Leader: Obama's Immigration Plan Matches LDS Values." *Salt Lake Tribune*, March 8. http://www.sltrib.com/sltrib/politics/55974230-90/church-faith-immigrants-immigration.html.csp?page=1.

Canham, Matt, Derek P. Jensen, and Rosemary Winters. 2009. "Salt Lake City Adopts Pro-Gay Statutes – with LDS Church Support." *Salt Lake Tribune*, November 10. http://archive.sltrib.com/article.php?id=13758070&itype=NGPSID.

Carmines, Edward G., and James A. Stimson. 1990. *Issue Evolution: Race and the Transformation of American Politics*. Princeton, NJ: Princeton University Press.

Carson, Donald W., and James W. Johnson. 2001. *Mo: The Life & Times of Morris K. Udall*. Tucson: University of Arizona Press.

Casey, Shaun. 2008. *The Making of a Catholic President: Kennedy vs. Nixon 1960*. New York: Oxford University Press.

Catanese, David. 2012. "Hatch: Obama Camp Will 'Throw Mormon Church' at Romney." *Politico.com*, April 4. http://www.politico.com/blogs/david-catanese/2012/04/hatch-obama-camp-will-throw-mormon-church-at-romney-119564.html.

Chafets, Zev. 2007. "The Huckabee Factor." *New York Times Magazine*, December 12. http://www.nytimes.com/2007/12/12/magazine/16huckabee.html.

Chandra, Kanchan. 2006. "What Is Ethnic Identity and What Does It Matter?" *Annual Review of Political Science* 9: 397–424.

Chong, Dennis, and James N. Druckman. 2007. "Framing Theory." *Annual Review of Political Science* 10: 103–126.

Christofferson, D. Todd. 2012. "The Doctrine of Christ." Talk delivered in the General Conference of the Church of Jesus Christ of Latter-day Saints. April. https://www.lds.org/general-conference/2012/04/the-doctrine-of-christ.

Church of Jesus Christ of Latter-day Saints. 1980a. "The Church and the Proposed Equal Rights Amendment: A Moral Issue." The Church of Jesus Christ of Latter-day Saints. http://www.lds.org/ensign/1980/03/the-church-and-the-proposed-equal-rights-amendment-a-moral-issue?lang=eng.

1980b. "Easter Message – A Plea for Peace." *LDS Church News*, April 18.

1980c. "Christmas Message from the First Presidency." *LDS Church News*, December 20.

1981. "First Presidency Statement on Basing of MX Missile." *Ensign*, June. http://www.lds.org/ensign/1981/06/news-of-the-church/first-presidency-statement-on-basing-of-mx-missile?lang=eng.

1995. "The Family: A Proclamation to the World." https://www.lds.org/topics/family-proclamation.

2008a. "First Presidency Letter, Preserving Traditional Marriage and Strengthening Families." *Newsroom: The Official Resource for News Media, Opinion Leaders, and the Public*, June 30. http://www.mormonnewsroom.org/ldsnewsroom/eng/commentary/california-and-same-sex-marriage.

2008b. "The Divine Institution of Marriage." *Newsroom: The Official Resource for News Media, Opinion Leaders, and the Public*, August 13. http://www.mormonnewsroom.org/article/the-divine-institution-of-marriage.

2009a. "Mormon Helping Hands Completes First Decade of Service." *Ensign*, January.

2009b. "Church Clarifies Proposition 8 Filing, Corrects Erroneous News Reports." *Newsroom: The Official Resource for News Media, Opinion Leaders, and the Public*, February 2. http://www.mormonnewsroom.org/article/church-clarifies-proposition-8-filing-corrects-erroneous-news-reports.

2010a. "Church Statement on 'White Horse Prophecy' and Political Neutrality." *Newsroom: The Official Resource for News Media, Opinion Leaders, and the Public*, January 6. http://www.mormonnewsroom.org/blog/church-statement-on-white-horse-prophecy-and-political-neutrality.

2010b. "Church Supports Principles of Utah Compact on Immigration." *Newsroom: The Official Resource for News Media, Opinion Leaders, and the Public*, November 11. http://www.mormonnewsroom.org/article/church-supports-principles-of-utah-compact-on-immigration.

2012a. "Mormons Continue Aid for Neighbors of Sandy Disaster into New Year." *Newsroom: The Official Resource for News Media, Opinion Leaders, and the*

*Public,* December 27. http://www.mormonnewsroom.org/article/mormons-con
tinue-aid-for-sandy-disaster-into-new-year.

2012b. "Mormonism in the News: Getting It Right | August 29." *Newsroom Blog,*
August 29. http://www.mormonnewsroom.org/article/mormonism-news-getting-it-
right-august-29.

2012c. "Handbook 2: Administering the Church." Intellectual Reserve, Inc. http://www.
lds.org/handbook/handbook-2-administering-the-church/introduction?lang=eng.

Clapp, Rodney. 1996. *A Peculiar People: The Church as Culture in a Post-Christian
Society.* Downers Grove, IL: InterVarsity Press.

Cnaan, Ram, Van Evans, and Daniel W. Curtis. 2012. *Called to Serve: The Prosocial
Behavior of Active Latter-day Saints.* University of Pennsylvania School of Social
Policy and Practice. www.sp2.upenn.edu/docs/people/faculty/cnaan_lds_giving.pdf.

Coit, Margaret L. 1968. "The Dream Nobody Wanted to Hear." *Saturday Review*
(April 6): 27–38.

Converse, Philip E. 1966. "Religion and Politics: The 1960 Election." In *Elections and the
Political Order,* edited by Philip E. Converse, Warren E. Miller, Donald E. Stokes,
and Angus Campbell, 96–124. New York: John Wiley and Sons.

Cook, Quentin L. 2011. "LDS Women Are Incredible!" Talk delivered in the General
Conference of the Church of Jesus Christ of Latter-day Saints. April. https://www.
lds.org/general-conference/2011/04/lds-women-are-incredible?lang=eng.

Coppins, McKay. 2012. "Exclusive: Marco Rubio's Mormon Roots." *Buzzfeed,* February
23. http://www.buzzfeed.com/mckaycoppins/exclusive-marco-rubios-mormon-roots.

Cornwall, Marie. 1989. "The Determinants of Religious Behavior: A Theoretical Model
and Empirical Test." *Social Forces* 68 (2): 572–592.

Cornwall, Marie, Stan L. Albrecht, Perry H. Cunningham, and Brian L. Pitcher. 1986.
"The Dimensions of Religiosity: A Conceptual Model with an Empirical Test."
*Review of Religious Research* 27 (3): 226–244.

Covey, Stephen R. 1970. *The Spiritual Roots of Human Relations.* Salt Lake City: Deseret
Book. Co.

1990. The Seven Habits of Highly Effective People: Restoring the Character Ethic. 1st
Fireside ed. New York: Fireside Books.

1997. *The Seven Habits of Highly Effective Families: Building a Beautiful Family
Culture in a Turbulent World.* New York: Golden Books.

Crapo, Richley H. 1987. "Grassroots Deviance from the Official Doctrine: A Study of
Latter-day Saint (Mormon) Folk-Beliefs." *Journal for the Scientific Study of Religion*
26 (December): 465–486.

Crawford, Alan Pell. 1980. *Thunder on the Right: The "New Right" and the Politics of
Resentment.* New York: Pantheon Books.

Cross, Whitney R. 1981. *The Burned-Over District: The Social and Intellectual History
of Enthusiastic Religion in Western New York, 1800–1850.* Ithaca, NY: Cornell
University Press.

D'Antonio, William V. 1994. "Autonomy and Democracy in an Autocratic Organization:
The Case of the Roman Catholic Church." *Sociology of Religion* 55 (4): 370-396.

2001. *American Catholics: Gender, Generation, and Commitment.* Walnut Creek, CA:
AltaMira Press.

D'Antonio, William V., Michele Dillon, and Mary L. Gautier. 2013. *American Catholics
in Transition: Persisting and Changing.* Lanham, MD: Rowman & Littlefield.

Davidson, Lee. 1999. "What Do You Call Hatch Donor List? Try Eclectic." *Deseret News*, October 20. http://www.deseretnews.com/article/723674/What-do-you-call-Hatch-donor-list-Try-eclectic.html?pg=all.

Daynes, Kathryn M. 2001. *More Wives Than One: Transformation of the Mormon Marriage System, 1840–1910*. Urbana: University of Illinois Press.

Delli Carpini, Michael X, and Scott Keeter. 1996. *What Americans Know about Politics and Why It Matters*. New Haven, CT: Yale University Press.

Deseret News. 1980. "Opposition throughout Utah Strong and Growing." *Deseret News*, April 21.

Dionne, E. J., and William A. Galston. 2010. *The Old and New Politics of Faith: Religion and the 2010 Election*. Washington, DC: Brookings Institution.

Djupe, Paul A, and Christopher P. Gilbert. 2009. *The Political Influence of Churches*. Cambridge; New York: Cambridge University Press.

Douthat, Ross. 2012. *Bad Religion: How We Became a Nation of Heretics*. New York: Free Press.

Druckman, James N. 2001. "The Implications of Framing Effects for Citizen Competence." *Political Behavior* 23 (3): 225–256.

"Equal Rights Amendment." 1975. *LDS Church News*, January 11.

Economist. 2012. "Stephen Covey, RIP." *Economist*, July 21, 58.

Ertl, Gretchen. 2012. "Mitt Romney's Years as a Mormon Church Leader." *Washington Post*, August 19. http://www.washingtonpost.com/politics/mitt-romneys-years-as-a-mormon-church-leader/2012/08/19/88360dda-ea40-11e1-9ddc-340d5efb1e9c_gallery.html#photo=3.

Evans, Steve. 2012. "Man on a Mission: Mitt Romney in France." *Washington Post*, May 13. http://articles.washingtonpost.com/2012-05-13/national/35456591_1_mormonism-mitt-romney-elder-romney.

Ewing, Katherine Pratt. 2008. *Being and Belonging: Muslims in the United States Since 9/11*. New York: Russell Sage Foundation.

"Faith in America: Interviews with President Barack Obama and Governor Mitt Romney." 2012. *Cathedral Age*. http://www.nationalcathedral.org/age/CAA-66319-MM000A.shtml -. UtrYcWQo4y4.

Finke, Roger, and Rodney Stark. 2005. *The Churching of America, 1776–2005: Winners and Losers in Our Religious Economy*. Revised and expanded ed. New Brunswick, NJ: Rutgers University Press.

Firmage, Edwin Brown. 1983. "Allegiance and Stewardship: Holy War, Just War, and the Mormon Tradition in the Nuclear Age." *Dialogue: A Journal of Mormon Thought* 16 (1): 47–61.

——— 2001. *Zion in the Courts: A Legal History of the Church of Jesus Christ of Latter-day Saints, 1830–1900*. 1st paperback ed. Urbana: University of Illinois Press.

Flake, Kathleen. 2004. *The Politics of American Religious Identity: The Seating of Senator Reed Smoot, Mormon Apostle*. Chapel Hill: University of North Carolina Press.

Flanders, Robert Bruce. 1975. *Nauvoo: Kingdom on the Mississippi*. Urbana: University of Illinois Press.

Fluhman, J. Spencer. 2012. *A Peculiar People: Anti-Mormonism and the Making of Religion in Nineteenth-Century America*. Chapel Hill: University of North Carolina Press.

Fox, Jeffrey Carl. 2006. *Latter-Day Political Views*. Lanham, MD: Lexington Books.

Garr, Arnold K. 2007. *Joseph Smith: Presidential Candidate*. Orem, UT: Millennial Press.

Gehrke, Steve. 2008. "Seven LDS Wardhouses Vandalized over Weekend." *Salt Lake Tribune*, November 11. http://archive.sltrib.com/article.php?id=10957167&itype=NGPSID.

Georgetown/On Faith. 2012. "Mitt Romney: I Believe in Heavenly Father, Jesus Christ, and the Holy Ghost." *Washington Post*. http://www.washingtonpost.com/blogs/under-god/post/mitt-romney-i-believe-in-heavenly-father-jesus-christ-and-the-holy-ghost/2012/06/01/gJQApeQD7U_blog.html.

Givens, Terryl L. 1997. *The Viper on the Hearth: Mormons, Myths, and the Construction of Heresy*. New York: Oxford University Press.

   2007. *People of Paradox: A History of Mormon Culture*. New York: Oxford University Press.

Givens, Terryl L., and Fiona Givens. 2012. *The God Who Weeps: How Mormonism Makes Sense of Life*. Salt Lake City, UT: Ensign Peak.

Gold, Matea. 2012. "Salt Lake Olympics Were Romney's Golden Moment." *Los Angeles Times*, July 27. http://articles.latimes.com/2012/jul/27/nation/la-na-romney-olympics-20120727-1.

Goldman, Seth, and Diana Mutz. 2014. *The Obama Effect: How the 2008 Campaign Changed White Racial Attitudes*. New York: Russell Sage Foundation.

Gordon, Elizabeth Ellen, and William L. Gillespie. 2012. "The Culture of Obedience and the Politics of Stealth: Mormon Mobilization against ERA and Same-Sex Marriage." *Politics and Religion* 5 (2): 343–366.

Gordon, Milton. 1966. *Assimilation in American Life: The Role of Race, Religion, and National Origins*. New York: Oxford University Press.

Gordon, Sarah Barringer. 2002. *The Mormon Question: Polygamy and Constitutional Conflict in Nineteenth-Century America*. Chapel Hill: University of North Carolina Press.

Grammich, Clifford. 2012. *2010 U.S. Religion Census: Religious Congregations & Membership*. Lenexa, KS: Association of Statisticians of American Religious Bodies.

Greeley, Andrew M. 1967. *The Catholic Experience: An Interpretation of the History of American Catholicism*. Garden City, NY: Doubleday.

   1976. *Ethnicity, Denomination, and Inequality*. Beverly Hills, CA: Sage Publications.

   1977. *The American Catholic: A Social Portrait*. New York: Basic Books.

Greeley, Andrew M., and Michael Hout. 2006. *The Truth about Conservative Christians: What They Think and What They Believe*. Chicago: University of Chicago Press.

Green, John C. 2007. *The Faith Factor: How Religion Influences American Elections*. Westport, CT: Greenwood Publishing Group.

Greene, Steven. 1999. "Understanding Party Identification: A Social Identity Approach." *Political Psychology* 20 (2): 393–403.

Gregory, Sean. 2011. "Brandon Davies: Is BYU's Premarital Controversy Good for College Sports?" *Time.com*, March 4. http://keepingscore.blogs.time.com/2011/03/04/brandon-davies-is-byus-premarital-sex-controversy-good-for-college-sports/#ixzz1G7F7zZ11.

Guth, James L. 2012. "The Religious Roots of Foreign Policy Exceptionalism." *Review of Faith and International Affairs* 10 (2): 77–85.

Haight, David B. 1984. "Personal Morality." *Ensign*, November.

Hamby, Peter. 2011. "Romney Jabs Controversial Speaker at Values Voter Summit." *CNN.com,* October 8. http://politicalticker.blogs.cnn.com/2011/10/08/romney-jabs-controversial-speaker-at-values-voter-summit/.

Harrie, Dan. 1992. "LDS Church Shows Its Hand, Speaks Against Gambling." *Salt Lake Tribune,* January 5.

Harrie, Dan, and Peggy Fletcher Stack. 1992. "LDS Church Turns up Heat on Horse-race Betting." *Salt Lake Tribune,* June 1.

Hart, John L. 2005. "Help: LDS Volunteers Get to Work." *Deseret News,* September 11.

Hartz, Louis. 1955. *The Liberal Tradition in America: An Interpretation of American Political Thought Since the Revolution.* New York: Harcourt, Brace.

Heaton, Tim B., and Cardell K. Jacobson. Forthcoming. "The Social Life of Mormons." In *Oxford Handbook of Mormonism,* edited by Terryl L. Givens and Philip Barlow. New York: Oxford University Press.

Heilprin, John. 1999. "Did Hatch Allude to LDS Prophecy?" *Salt Lake Tribune,* November 11.

Henneberger, Melinda. 2011. "Huntsman, the Cool Kid." *Time,* May 12.

Herberg, Will. 1960. *Protestant, Catholic, Jew: An Essay in American Religious Sociology.* Garden City, NY: Anchor Books.

Hewitt, Hugh. 2007. *A Mormon in the White House? 10 Things Every American Should Know About Mitt Romney.* Washington, DC: Regnery Publishing.

Hildreth, Steven A. 1984. "Mormon Concern over MX: Parochialism or Enduring Moral Theology?" *Journal of Church and State* 26 (Spring): 240–244.

Hill, Greg. 2005. "City of Prophecy: Charleston, S.C., Relates to Scripture as Well as Church Growth." *LDS Church News,* February 19. http://www.ldschurchnews.com/articles/46893/City-of-prophecy.html.

Hill, Norman C., and Richard M. Romney. 2007. "Storming Back." *Ensign,* March. https://www.lds.org/ensign/2007/03/storming-back.

Hinckley, Gordon B. 1996. "Women of the Church." Talk delivered in the General Conference of the Church of Jesus Christ of Latter-day Saints. October. https://www.lds.org/ensign/1996/11/women-of-the-church.

    1999. "Why We Do Some of the Things We Do." Talk delivered in the General Conference of the Church of Jesus Christ of Latter-day Saints. October. https://www.lds.org/general-conference/1999/10/why-we-do-some-of-the-things-we-do

    2005. "The Symbol of Our Faith." *Ensign.* April. https://www.lds.org/ensign/2005/04/the-symbol-of-our-faith?lang=eng.

Holland, Jeffrey R. 2012. "Standing Together for the Cause of Christ." *Ensign,* August. https://www.lds.org/ensign/2012/08/standing-together-for-the-cause-of-christ?lang=eng.

Holland, Steve. 2012. "In Testimonials, Romney's Mormon Faith Takes Spotlight." *Chicago Tribune,* August 30. http://articles.chicagotribune.com/2012-08-30/news/sns-rt-us-usa-campaign-romney-mormonsbre87u03f-20120830_1_romney-s-mormon-mormon-faith-mormon-church.

Holman, Marianne. 2010. "A New Mormon.org: Design Encourages Saints Worldwide to Create Profiles to Share the Gospel." *LDS Church News,* July 17. http://www.ldschurchnews.com/articles/59596/A-new-Mormonorg.html.

Horowitz, Donald. 1985. *Ethnic Groups in Conflict.* Berkeley: University of California Press.

Horowitz, Jason. 2012. "The Genesis of a Church's Stand on Race." *Washington Post*, February 28. http://www.washingtonpost.com/politics/the-genesis-of-a-churchs-stand-on-race/2012/02/22/gIQAQZXyfR_story.html.

Hout, Michael, and Claude S. Fischer. 2002. "Why More Americans Have No Religious Preference: Politics and Generations." *American Sociological Review* 67 (2) (April 1): 165–190.

Huefner, Dixie Snow. 1978. "Church and Politics at the Utah IWY Conference." *Dialogue: A Journal of Mormon Thought* 11 (1): 58–75.

Hunter, James Davison. 1983. *American Evangelicalism: Conservative Religion and the Quandary of Modernity*. New Brunswick, NJ: Rutgers University Press.

1991. *Culture Wars: The Struggle to Define America*. New York: Basic Books.

Hunter, Joel C. 2008. *A New Kind of Conservative*. Ventura, CA: Regal.

Huntington, Samuel P. 1981. *American Politics: The Promise of Disharmony*. Cambridge, MA: Belknap Press.

Iannaccone, Laurence R. 1994. "Why Strict Churches Are Strong." *American Journal of Sociology* 99: 1180–1211.

Iannaccone, Laurence R., and Carrie A. Miles. 1990. "Dealing with Social Change: The Mormon Church's Response to Changes in Women's Roles." *Social Forces* 68 (4): 1231–1250.

Issenberg, Sasha. 2012. "Anatomy of a Narrow Victory." *Slate*, January 4. http://www.slate.com/articles/news_and_politics/victory_lab/2012/01/romney_s_iowa_win_it_took_a_lot_more_than_money_.html.

Jackman, Simon, and Lynn Vavreck. 2010. "Primary Politics: Race, Gender, and Age in the 2008 Democratic Primary." *Journal of Elections, Public Opinion, and Policy* 20 (2): 153–186.

Jardin, Xeni. 2011. "The Book of Mormon, Matt Stone, and Trey Parker's Broadway Musical." *BoingBoing.net*. http://boingboing.net/2011/03/09/the-book-of-mormon-m.html.

Jensen, Marlin K. 1998. "To Have a Robust, Multiparty System: Transcript of Salt Lake Tribune Interview with Elder Marlin K. Jensen." *Sunstone*, August.

Jensen, Richard J. 1971. *The Winning of the Midwest: Social and Political Conflict, 1888–1896*. Chicago: University of Chicago Press.

Jesse, Dean C. 1979. "Joseph Smith's 19 July 1849 Discourse." *BYU Studies* 19 (3): 390–94.

Jones, Jeffrey M. 2007. "Some Americans Reluctant to Vote for Mormon, 72-Year-Old Presidential Candidates: Strong Support for Black, Women, Catholic Candidates." *Gallup News Service*. www.gallup.com/poll/26611/some-americans-reluctant-vote-mormon-72yearold-presidential-candidate.aspx.

Kane, Paula M. 1994. *Separatism and Subculture: Boston Catholicism, 1900–1920*. Chapel Hill: University of North Carolina Press.

Kantor, Jodi. 2012. "How the Mormon Church Shaped Mitt Romney." *NYTimes.com*, May 19. http://www.nytimes.com/2012/05/20/us/politics/how-the-mormon-church-shaped-mitt-romney.html?pagewanted=all.

Keith, Bruce E., David B. Magleby, Candice J. Nelson, Elizabeth Orr, and Mark C. Westlye. 1992. *The Myth of the Independent Voter*. Berkeley: University of California Press.

Kellstedt, Lyman A., John C. Green, James L. Guth, and Corwin E. Smidt. 1996. "Grasping the Essentials: The Social Embodiment of Religion and Political Behavior." In *Religion and the Culture Wars: Dispatches from the Front*, In *Religion and the Culture Wars:*

*Dispatches from the Front*, edited by John C. Green, James L. Guth, Corwin E. Smidt, and Lyman A. Kellstedt, 174–192. Lanham, MD: Rowman & Littlefield.

Kellstedt, Lyman, and Corwin Smidt. 1996. "Measuring Fundamentalism: An Analysis of Different Operational Strategies." In *Religion and the Culture Wars: Dispatches from the Front*, edited by John C. Green, James L. Guth, Corwin E. Smidt, and Lyman A. Kellstedt, 193–218. Lanham, MD: Rowman & Littlefield.

Kennedy, John F. 1960. "Speech to the Houston Ministerial Association." Houston, TX. September 12. Speech.

Kilpatrick, James J. 1967. "Romney: Salesman on the Move." *National Review*, December 12.

Kimball, Kara. 2014. "Hi, I'm Kara." *Mormon.org*. Accessed January 31. http://mormon.org/me/D71H/Kara.

King, Gary. 1997. *A Solution to the Ecological Inference Problem: Reconstructing Individual Behavior from Aggregate Data*. Princeton, NJ: Princeton University Press.

King, Robert R., and Kay Atkinson King. 2000. "Mormons in Congress, 1951–2000." *Journal of Mormon History* 26 (2): 1–50.

Kleppner, Paul. 1979. *The Third Electoral System, 1853–189: Parties, Voters, and Political Cultures*. Chapel Hill: University of North Carolina Press.

   1987. *Continuity and Change in Electoral Politics, 1893–1928*. New York: Greenwood Press.

Knight, Hal, and Dan Jones. 1974. "Most Favor Full Rights for Women." *Deseret News*, November 15.

Kotkin, Joel. 1993. *Tribes: How Race, Religion, and Identity Determine Success in the New Global Economy*. New York: Random House.

Kranish, Michael, and Scott Helman. 2012. *The Real Romney*. New York: HarperCollins.

Kuruvila, Matthai. 2008. "Mormons Face Flack for Backing Prop. 8." *San Francisco Chronicle*, October 27. http://www.sfgate.com/bayarea/article/Mormons-face-flak-for-backing-Prop-8-3264077.php.

Lassen, David. 2009. "You Raise Me Up: The Social Identity Underpinnings of Campaign Contributions." Presented at the annual meeting of the Pacific chapter of the American Association of Public Opinion Research, San Francisco. December 10–11.

Lawrence, Gary. 2008. "Update." *Yes on Prop 8*. http://yesonprop8.blogspot.com/2008/08/gary-lawrence-grass-roots-coordinator.html.

Layman, Geoffrey. 2001. *The Great Divide: Religious and Cultural Conflict in American Party Politics*. New York: Columbia University Press.

Layman, Geoffrey C., Thomas M. Carsey, John C. Green, Richard Herrera, and Rosalyn Cooperman. 2010. "Activists and Conflict Extension in American Party Politics." *American Political Science Review* 104 (2): 324–346.

Lee, Rex E. 1992. *What Do Mormons Believe?* Salt Lake City, UT: Deseret Book Co.

Leege, David C., Joel Lieske, and Kenneth D. Wald. 1991. "Toward Cultural Theories of American Political Behavior: Religion, Ethnicity, Race, and Class Outlook." In *Political Science: Looking toward the Future*, edited by William Crotty, 193–238. Evanston, IL: Northwestern University Press.

Leege, David C., Kenneth D. Wald, Brian S. Krueger, and Paul D. Mueller. 2002. *The Politics of Cultural Differences: Social Change and Voter Mobilization Strategies in the Post–New Deal Period*. Princeton, NJ: Princeton University Press.

Leege, David C., and Michael R. Welch. 1989. "The Religious Roots of Political Orientations: Variations among American Catholic Parishioners." *Journal of Politics* 51 (1): 137–162.

Levenson, Michael. 2007a. "Methodical Style Sets Romney Apart from GOP Rivals." *Boston Globe*, November 13. http://www.boston.com/news/nation/articles/2007/11/13/methodical_style_sets_romney_apart_from_gop_rivals/.

———. 2007b. "Pressed, Romney to Speak on His Mormonism." *Boston Globe*, December 3. http://www.boston.com/news/nation/articles/2007/12/03/pressed_romney_to_speak_on_his_mormonism/.

Linker, Damon. 2006. "The Big Test." *New Republic*, December 23.

Lyman, Edward Leo. 1986. *Political Deliverance: The Mormon Quest for Utah Statehood*. Urbana: University of Illinois Press.

Lythgoe, Dennis L. 1971. "The 1968 Presidential Decline of George Romney: Mormonism or Politics?" *BYU Studies* 11 (3): 219–240.

Mael, Fred A., and Lois E. Tetrick. 1992. "Identifying Organizational Identification." *Educational and Psychological Measurement* 52 (4): 813–824.

Mansbridge, Jane J. 1986. *Why We Lost the ERA*. Chicago: University of Chicago Press.

Martin, Clint, David Tedder, Loyd Ericson, Adam Fisher, Rebecca Ellsworth, Michelle Larson, Benson Dastrup, et al. 2008. "Reflections on Proposition 8." *Sunstone*, December.

Martin, Douglas. 2012. "Stephen R. Covey, Herald of Good Habits, Dies at 79." *New York Times*, July 16.

Marwell, Gerald. 1996. "We Still Don't Know If Strict Churches Are Strong, Much Less Why: Comment on Iannaccone." *American Journal of Sociology* 101 (4): 1097–1103.

Mason, Patrick Q. 2011. *The Mormon Menace: Violence and Anti-Mormonism in the Postbellum South*. New York: Oxford University Press.

Mauss, Armand L. 1994. *The Angel and the Beehive: The Mormon Struggle with Assimilation*. Urbana: University of Illinois Press.

———. 2003. *All Abraham's Children: Changing Mormon Conceptions of Race and Lineage*. Urbana: University of Illinois Press.

May, Dean L. 1980. "Mormons." In *Harvard Encyclopedia of American Ethnic Groups*, edited by Stephan Thernstrom, 720–731. Cambridge, MA: Belknap Press of Harvard University Press.

McCormick, Richard L. 1974. "Ethno-Cultural Interpretations of Nineteenth-Century American Voting Behavior." *Political Science Quarterly* 89 (2): 351–377.

McKinley, Jesse, and Kirk Johnson. 2008. "Mormons Tipped Scale in Ban on Gay Marriage." *New York Times*, November 14. http://www.nytimes.com/2008/11/15/us/politics/15marriage.html.

Memoli, Michael. 2012. "CPAC: Mitt Romney Tells Conservatives He's One of Them." *Los Angeles Times*, February 10. http://articles.latimes.com/2012/feb/10/news/la-pn-mitt-romney-cpac-20120210.

Millet, Robert L. 2007. *Grace Works*. Salt Lake City, UT: Deseret Book. Co.

Mollenhoff, Clark R. 1968. *George Romney, Mormon in Politics*. New York: Meredith Press.

Monson, J. Quin, Leah A. Murray, Kelly D. Patterson, and Sven E. Wilson. 2006. "Dominant Cue Givers and Voting on Ballot Propositions." Working Paper.

Monson, J. Quin, Brian Reed, and Zach Smith. 2013. "Religion and Secular Realignment: Explaining Why Mormons Are So Republican." Presented at the annual meeting of the American Political Science Association, Chicago. August 30.

Monson, J. Quin, and Jordan Stauss. 2011. "Did the Utah Compact Actually Change Attitudes about Immigration?" *Utahdatapoints.com*. http://utahdatapoints.com/2011/04/did-the-utah-compact-actually-change-attitudes-about-immigration/.

Montgomery, Lori, Jia Lynn Yang, and Philip Rucker. 2012. "Mitt Romney's Tax Returns Shed Some Light on His Investment Wealth." *Washington Post*, January 24. http://www.washingtonpost.com/politics/2012/01/23/gIQAj5bUMQ_story.html?wpisrc=al_comboNP.

Moore, Deborah Dash. 1981. "Defining American Jewish Ethnicity." *Prospects* 6: 387–409.

Moore, R. Laurence. 1986. *Religious Outsiders and the Making of Americans*. New York: Oxford University Press.

Moskin, Julia. 2012. "A New Generation Redefines Mormon Cuisine." *NYTimes.com*, January 24. http://www.nytimes.com/2012/01/25/dining/a-new-generation-redefines-mormon-cuisine.html?pagewanted=all.

Mutz, Diana C. 2006. *Hearing the Other Side: Deliberative Versus Participatory Democracy*. Cambridge; New York: Cambridge University Press.

    2011. *Population-Based Survey Experiments*. Princeton, NJ: Princeton University Press.

*New York Times*. 2012. "Romney's Speech from Mother Jones Video." *New York Times*, September 19. http://www.nytimes.com/2012/09/19/us/politics/mitt-romneys-speech-from-mother-jones-video.html.

Newport, Frank, and Igor Himelfarb. 2013. *In U.S., Strong Link between Church Attendance, Smoking: Mormons Least Likely to Smoke, Those with No Religious Identity Most Likely*. Gallup, Inc. http://www.gallup.com/poll/163856/strong-link-church-attendance-smoking.aspx.

Newsweek. 1967a. "Mormons and the Negro." *Newsweek*, March 6.

    1967b. "It's Official." *Newsweek*, November 27.

Niebuhr, H. Richard. 2001 [1951]. *Christ and Culture*. 1st ed. San Francisco: HarperSanFrancisco.

Noll, Mark A., and Luke E. Harlow, eds. 2007. *Religion and American Politics: From the Colonial Period to the Present*. 2nd ed. New York: Oxford University Press.

Norris, Pippa, and Ronald Inglehart. 2011. *Sacred and Secular: Religion and Politics Worldwide*. Cambridge; New York: Cambridge University Press.

O'Brien, David J. 1968. *American Catholics and Social Reform: The New Deal Years*. New York: Oxford University Press.

O'Dea, Thomas F. 1957. *The Mormons*. Chicago: University of Chicago Press.

Oaks, Dallin H. 2010. "The Only True and Living Church." *LDS.org*. https://www.lds.org/youth/article/only-true-living-church?lang=eng.

    1992. "The Divinely Inspired Constitution." *Ensign*, February. http://www.lds.org/ensign/1992/02/the-divinely-inspired-constitution?lang=eng.

Obama, Barack. 2004. *Dreams from My Father: A Story of Race and Inheritance*. 1st paperback ed. New York: Three Rivers Press.

Oppel, Richard A., and Erik Eckholm. 2011. "Prominent Pastor Calls Romney's Church a Cult." *New York Times*, October 7. http://www.nytimes.com/2011/10/08/us/politics/prominent-pastor-calls-romneys-church-a-cult.html?_r=0.

Otterson, Michael. 2012. "Mormons in the Mainstream." *On Faith: Washington Post.com*. http://archive.is/IpiMa.

Packer, Boyd K. 2012. "How to Survive in Enemy Territory." *New Era*, April. http://
www.lds.org/new-era/2012/04/how-to-survive-in-enemy-territory?lang=eng.

Passel, Jeffrey S., and D'Vera Cohn. 2011. *Unauthorized Immigrant Population: National
and State Trends, 2010*. Pew Research Hispanic Center. http://www.pewhispanic.org/
2011/02/01/unauthorized-immigrant-population-brnational-and-state-trends-2010/.

Patashnick, Josh. 2007. "Latter-Day Skeptics." *New Republic*, November 19. http://
www.newrepublic.com/article/latter-day-skeptics.

Patrikios, Stratos. 2008. "American Republican Religion?" *Political Behavior* 30 (3):
367–389.

Paulson, Michael. 2002. "Romney Win Seen Sign of Acceptance of Mormons." *Boston
Globe*, November 9. https://secure.pqarchiver.com/boston/access/234795231.html?
FMT=ABS&FMTS=ABS:FT&type=current&date=Nov+9%2C+2002&author=Mic
hael+Paulson%2C+Globe+Staff&pub=Boston+Globe&edition=&startpage=B.1&
desc=ROMNEY+WIN+SEEN+SIGN+OF+ACCEPTANCE+OF+MORMONS.

Perry, Luke, and Christopher Cronin. 2012. *Mormons in American Politics: From
Persecution to Power*. Santa Barbara, CA: Praeger.

Pettigrew, T. F., and L. R. Tropp. 2000. "Does Intergroup Contact Reduce Prejudice?"
In *Reducing Prejudice and Discrimination*, edited by Stuart Oskamp, 93–114.
Mahwah, NJ: Lawrence Erlbaum.

Pew Forum on Religion & Public Life. 2006. *Many Americans Uneasy with Mix of
Religion and Politics*. Washington, DC. http://www.pewforum.org/Politics-and-
Elections/Many-Americans-Uneasy-with-Mix-of-Religion-and-Politics.aspx.

——— 2007. *Public Expresses Mixed Views of Islam, Mormonism*. Washington, DC. http://
www.pewforum.org/Public-Expresses-Mixed-Views-of-Islam-Mormonism.aspx.

——— 2011. *Muslim Americans: No Signs of Growth in Alienation or Support for Extremism*.
Washington, DC. http://www.pewforum.org/Muslim/Muslim-Americans–No-Signs-
of-Growth-in-Alienation-or-Support-for-Extremism.aspx.

——— 2012a. *Mormons in America: Certain of Their Beliefs, Uncertain of Their Place in
Society*. Washington, DC. http://www.pewforum.org/mormons-in-america/.

——— 2012b. *Little Voter Discomfort with Romney's Mormon Religion*. Washington, DC.
http://www.pewforum.org/politics-and-elections/2012-romney-mormonism-obamas-
religion.aspx.

——— 2012c. *How the Faithful Voted: 2012 Preliminary Analysis*. Washington, DC. http://
www.pewforum.org/Politics-and-Elections/How-the-Faithful-Voted-2012-Preli
minary-Exit-Poll-Analysis.aspx.

——— 2012d. *Impact of the Romney Campaign: Americans Learned Little About the
Mormon Faith, but Some Attitudes Have Softened*. Washington, DC. http://www.
pewforum.org/files/2012/12/Knowledge-and-Attitudes-about-Mormons.pdfhttp://
www.pewforum.org/Christian/Mormon/attitudes-toward-mormon-faith.aspx.

Phillips, Rick, and Ryan T. Cragun. 2011. *Mormons in the United States 1990–2008:
Socio-Demographic Trends and Regional Differences*. Hartford, CT: Trinity
College.

Podhoretz, John. 2012. "Mitt Romney's Vast Charitable Giving." *New York Post*.
September 22. http://www.nypost.com/p/news/opinion/opedcolumnists/romney_the_
giver_7nLMOZGuIo2zq1LmrNInjN.

Poll, Richard Douglas. 2001. "What the Church Means to People Like Me." *Dialogue: A
Journal of Mormon Thought* 34 (1 and 2): 11–22.

Popkin, Samuel L. 1994. *The Reasoning Voter: Communication and Persuasion in Presidential Campaigns*. 2nd ed. Chicago: University of Chicago Press.

Prendergrast, William B. 1999. *The Catholic Voter in American Politics: The Passing of the Democratic Monolith*. Washington, DC: Georgetown University Press.

Prince, Gregory A., and William Robert Wright. 2005. *David O. McKay and the Rise of Modern Mormonism*. Salt Lake City, UT: University of Utah Press.

Prothero, Stephen. 2003. *American Jesus: How the Son of God Became a National Icon*. New York: Farrar, Straus and Giroux.

2007. *Religious Literacy: What Every American Needs to Know – And Doesn't*. San Francisco: HarperSanFrancisco.

Public Broadcasting Service (PBS). 2006. "The Mormons: Interview. Jeffrey Holland." March 4. http://www.pbs.org/mormons/interviews/holland.html.

Putnam, Robert D. 2001. *Bowling Alone: The Collapse and Revival of American Community*. New York: Simon & Schuster.

Putnam, Robert D., and David E. Campbell. 2010. *American Grace: How Religion Divides and Unites Us*. New York: Simon & Schuster.

Quinn, D. Michael. 2005. "Exporting Utah's Theocracy Since 1975: Mormon Organizational Behavior and America's Culture Wars." In *God and Country: Politics in Utah*, edited by Jeffrey E. Sells, 129–168. Salt Lake City, UT: Signature Books.

Reilly, Adam. 2006. "Take My Wives. . . Please!" *Slate*, April 26. http://www.slate.com/articles/news_and_politics/politics/2006/04/take_my_wives_please.html.

Riccardi, Nicholas. 2008. "Mormons Feel the Backlash over Their Support of Prop. 8." *Los Angeles Times*, November 17. http://articles.latimes.com/2008/nov/17/nation/na-mormons17.

Riess, Jana. 2011. "Normal Mormons." *Christian Century*, September 26.

Rimer, Sara. 1994. "The 1994 Campaign: Massachusetts; Religion Is Latest Volatile Issue to Ignite Kennedy Contest." *New York Times*, September 29. http://www.nytimes.com/1994/09/29/us/1994-campaign-massachusetts-religion-latest-volatile-issue-ignite-kennedy.html.

Robertson, Margaret. 2000. "The Campaign and the Kingdom: The Activities of the Electioneers in Joseph Smith's Presidential Campaign." *BYU Studies* 39 (3): 147-180.

Roderick, Lee. 2000. *Gentleman of the Senate: Orrin Hatch, a Portrait of Character*. Washington, DC: Probitas Press.

Romney, Mitt. 2007. "Faith in America." George Bush Presidential Library, College Station, TX. December 6. Speech.

Rosenstone, Steven J., John Mark Hansen. 2009. *Mobilization, Participation, and Democracy in America*. New York: Macmillan.

Rusli, Evelyn M. 2012. "Giving Some Muscle to a Growing Fitness Trend." *Dealbook: NYTimes.com*, March 8. http://dealbook.nytimes.com/2012/03/08/giving-some-muscle-to-a-growing-fitness-trend/.

Rutenberg, Jim. 2012. "Mormons' First Families Rally Behind Romney." *New York Times*, July 16. http://www.nytimes.com/2012/07/17/us/politics/support-for-romney-by-old-mormon-families.html?pagewanted=all&_r=0.

Samuel, Ebenezer. 2011. "Amar'e Stoudemire Takes BYU to Task via Twitter for Kicking Brandon Davies off Team over Honor Code." *New York Daily News*, March 4. http://www.nydailynews.com/sports/basketball/knicks/amar-stoudemire-takes-byu-task-twitter-kicking-brandon-davies-team-honor-code-article-1.116724.

Schoofs, Mark. 2008. "Mormons Boost Antigay Marriage Effort." *Wall Street Journal*, September 20. http://online.wsj.com/article/SB122186063716658279.html.

Schubert, Frank, and Jeff Flint. 2009a. "Case Studies: Passing Prop 8." *Campaigns & Elections*, February. http://www.campaignsandelections.com/case-studies/176127/passing-prop-8.thtml.

2009b. "Proposition 8: A Case Study." Presented at the 18th Annual Pollie Awards and Conference of the American Association of Political Consultants, Washington, DC. March 28. The presentation can be viewed online at http://www.youtube.com/watch?v=9suhzVjoS90.

Seidler, John. 1986. "Contested Accommodation: The Catholic Church as a Special Case of Social Change." *Social Forces* 64 (4): 847–874.

Shahid, Aliyah. 2011. "Presidential Contender Mitt Romney's New Ad Touts Family Life and Marriage." *New York Daily News*, December 8. http://www.nydailynews.com/news/politics/mitt-romney-new-ad-touts-family-life-marriage-slam-thrice-divorced-newt-gingrich-article-1.988549.

Shannon, William. 1967. "George Romney: Holy and Hopeful." *Harper's Monthly*, February.

Shepherd, Gordon, and Gary Shepherd. 1984. *A Kingdom Transformed: Themes in the Development of Mormonism*. Salt Lake City: University of Utah Press.

Shipps, Jan. 1985. *Mormonism: The Story of a New Religious Tradition*. Urbana: University of Illinois Press.

Sides, John, and Lynn Vavreck. 2013. *The Gamble: Choice and Chance in the 2012 Presidential Election*. Princeton, NJ: Princeton University Press.

Smith, Christian, Michael Emerson, Sally Gallagher, Paul Kennedy, and David Sikkink. 1998. *American Evangelicalism: Embattled and Thriving*. Chicago: University of Chicago Press.

Snell, Steven. 2013. Telephone interview by J. Quin Monson, February 13.

Sokhey, Anand, and Stephen Mockabee. 2012. "Reexamining Political Discussion and Disagreement in Church Networks: An Exit Poll Assessment." *Politics and Religion* 5 (2): 253–279.

Spangler, Jerry, and Bob Bernick Jr. 1999. "Religious Bigotry Plagues Hatch." *Deseret News*, August 13. http://www.deseretnews.com/article/712391/Religious-bigotry-plagues-Hatch.html?pg=all.

Spencer, Jason. 2007. "Critics Target Romney's Mormonism." *Spartanburg Herald-Journal*, May 11.

Squires, Dee Dee. 2012. "Hi, I'm Dee Dee Squires." *Mormon.org*. Accessed December 24. http://mormon.org/me/7C32/DeeDeeSquires.

Stack, Peggy Fletcher. 2009. "Mormons and the Cross." *Salt Lake Tribune*, May 1. http://www.sltrib.com/faith/ci_12256269.

2011. "LDS Church Takes Public Stance on Immigration Legislation." *Salt Lake Tribune*, March 17. http://www.sltrib.com/sltrib/home/51439173-76/bills-burton-church-immigration.html.csp.

2012a. "Mormons Warned Against Baptizing Holocaust Victims." *USA Today*, March 5. http://usatoday30.usatoday.com/news/religion/story/2012-03-05/mormons-proxy-baptism-holocaust-jews/53372816/1.

2012b. "Change Lowers Mormonism's Growth Rate." *Salt Lake Tribune*, May 18. http://www.sltrib.com/sltrib/news/54036926-78/church-lds-membership-growth.html.csp.

2012c. "Shake-Up Hits BYU's Mormon Studies Institute." *Salt Lake Tribune*, June 26. http://www.sltrib.com/sltrib/utes/54358137-78/mormon-institute-peterson-studies. html.csp.

2012d. "OK, Mormons, Drink up – Coke and Pepsi Are OK." *Salt Lake Tribune*, September 5. http://www.sltrib.com/sltrib/news/54797595-78/church-drinks-caf feine-lds.html.csp.

2012e. "Mormon Missionary Applications Explode 471%; Half Are Women." *Salt Lake Tribune*, October 22. http://www.sltrib.com/sltrib/news/55129357-78/mis sionaries-lds-missionary-mormon.html.csp.

2012f. "Sunstone: Designer Recalls History of LDS Church's 'Visual Identity.' Salt Lake Tribune, July 27, http://www.sltrib.com/sltrib/lifestyle/54575040-80/church-logo-lds-smith.html.csp.

Stack, Peggy Fletcher, and Jessica Ravitz. 2008. "Thousands in Salt Lake City Protest LDS Stance on Same-sex Marriage." *Salt Lake Tribune*, November 8. http://archive. sltrib.com/article.php?id=10929992&itype=NGPSID.

Stark, Rodney. 1984. "The Rise of a New World Faith." *Review of Religious Research* 26 (1): 18–27.

1996. "So Far, So Good: A Brief Assessment of Mormon Membership Projections." *Review of Religious Research* 38 (2): 175–178.

Steensland, Brian, Jerry Z. Park, Mark D. Regnerus, Lynn D. Robinson, W. Bradford Wilcox, and Robert D. Woodberry. 2000. "The Measure of American Religion: Toward Improving the State of the Art." *Social Forces* 79 (1): 291–318.

Steinfels, Margaret O'Brien. 2004a. *American Catholics and Civic Engagement: A Distinctive Voice*. American Catholics in the Public Square Series v. 1. Lanham, MD: Rowman & Littlefield.

2004b. *American Catholics, American Culture: Tradition and Resistance*. American Catholics in the Public Square Series v. 2. Lanham, MD: Rowman & Littlefield.

Steinfels, Peter. 2003. *A People Adrift: The Crisis of the Roman Catholic Church in America*. New York: Simon & Schuster.

Stephanopoulos, George. 2007. "Mitt Romney: The Complete Interview." http://abc news.go.com/ThisWeek/Politics/story?id=2885156&page=1.

Stuart, Elizabeth. 2011. "Mormon Ousts Mormon in Arizona Recall Race about Immigration." *Deseret News*, November 10. http://www.deseretnews.com/article/ 700196515/Mormon-ousts-Mormon-in-Arizona-recall-race-about-immigration.html? pg=all.

Swierenga, Robert P. 1971. "Ethnocultural Political Analysis: A New Approach to American Ethnic Studies." *Journal of American Studies* 5 (1): 59–79.

Terry, Thomas C. 2012. "An Acceptable Prejudice?" *Inside Higher Ed*, May 29. http:// www.insidehighered.com/views/2012/05/29/essay-about-prejudice-academe-against-mormons.

Tesler, Michael. 2010. *Obama's Race: The 2008 Election and the Dream of a Post-Racial America*. Chicago: University of Chicago Press.

Thomas, Cal. 2000. *Blinded by Might: Why the Religious Right Can't Save America*. Grand Rapids, MI: Zondervan.

Trapasso, Clare. 2012. "Mormon Helping Hands Mobilizes for Storm-Ravaged Rockaways Broad Channel." *New York Daily News*, November 14. http://www.nydailynews.com/ new-york/queens/mormon-helping-hands-queens-article-1.1201469.

Trepanier, Lee, and Lynita Newswander. 2012. *LDS in the USA: Mormonism and the Making of American Culture*. Waco, TX: Baylor University Press.

Turner, John G. 2012. *Brigham Young, Pioneer Prophet*. Cambridge, MA: Belknap Press of Harvard University Press.

Van Wagoner, Richard S. 1989. *Mormon Polygamy: A History*. Salt Lake City, UT: Signature Books.

Varshney, Ashutosh. 2007. "Ethnicity and Ethnic Conflict." In *Oxford Handbook of Comparative Politics*, edited by Carles Boix and Susan Stokes, 274–294. New York: Oxford University Press.

Vavreck, Lynn, and Douglas Rivers. 2008. "The 2006 Cooperative Congressional Election Study." *Journal of Elections, Public Opinion, and Parties* 18 (4): 355–366.

Verba, Sidney, Kay Lehman Schlozman, and Henry E. Brady. 1995. *Voice and Equality: Civic Voluntarism in American Politics*. Cambridge, MA: Harvard University Press.

Voas, David, Daniel V. Olson, and Alasdair Crockett. 2002. "Religious Pluralism and Participation: Why Previous Research Is Wrong." *American Sociological Review* 67 (2): 212–230.

Wade, Pam. 1981a. "Scales Tilt to Less MX Opposition." *Deseret News*, March 20.

1981b. "65 Pct. of Utahns Opposed to MX." *Deseret News*, September 14.

Walch, Tad. 2007. "Reid Gets Warm Reaction at BYU." *Deseret Morning News*, October 10.

Wald, Kenneth D., Adam Silverman, and Kevin Fridy. 2005. "Making Sense of Religion in Political Life." *Annual Review of Political Science* 8: 121–141.

Walker, Ronald W., Richard E. Turley, and Glen M. Leonard. 2011. *Massacre at Mountain Meadows*. New York: Oxford University Press.

Weaver, Warren. 1967. "Romney Sounds an Uncertain Trumpet." *New York Times Magazine*, November 19.

Weisberg, Jacob. 2006. "Romney's Religion: A Mormon President? No Way." *Slate*, December 20. http://www.slate.com/articles/news_and_politics/the_big_idea/2006/12/romneys_religion.html.

Welch, Michael R., and David C. Leege. 1991. "Dual Reference Groups and Political Orientations: An Examination of Evangelically Oriented Catholics." *American Journal of Political Science* 35 (1): 28–56.

Welch, Reed L., and Ric Jensen. 2007. "When Should a Political Candidate's Religion Become a Campaign Issue? How Mitt Romney's Mormonism Has Become a Factor in His Previous and Current Races." *American Communication Journal* 9 (3). http://ac-journal.org/journal/2007/Fall/4WhenShouldaPoliticalCandidatesReligionBec.pdf.

White, O. Kendall. 1989. "Mormonism and the Equal Rights Amendment." *Journal of Church and State* 31 (2): 249–267.

Wicks, Robert S., and Fred R. Foister. 2005. *Junius and Joseph: Presidential Politics and the Assassination of the First Mormon Prophet*. Logan: Utah State University Press.

Wilcox, Clyde, and Carin Robinson. 2010. *Onward Christian Soldiers?: The Religious Right in American Politics*. Boulder, CO: Westview Press.

Williams, Alex. 2011. "To Be Young, Hip, and Mormon." *NYTimes.com*. October 26. http://www.nytimes.com/2011/10/27/fashion/young-mormons-find-ways-to-be-hip.html?pagewanted=all&_r=1&.

Wilson, Matthew J. 2007. "The Changing Catholic Voter: Comparing Responses to John F. Kennedy in 1960 and John Kerry in 2004." In *A Matter of Faith: Religion in the*

*2004 Presidential Election,*, edited by David E. Campbell, 163–179. Washington, DC: Brookings Institution Press.

Witcover, Jules. 1977. *Marathon: The Pursuit of the Presidency, 1972–1976.* New York: Viking Press.

Wolbrecht, Christina. 2000. *The Politics of Women's Rights: Parties, Positions, and Change.* Princeton, NJ: Princeton University Press.

Wood, Michael, and Michael Hughes. 1984. "The Moral Basis of Moral Reform: Status Discontent vs. Culture and Socialization as Explanations of Anti-Pornography Social Movement Adherence." *American Sociological Review* 49 (1): 86–99.

Wuthnow, Robert. 1990. *The Restructuring of American Religion: Society and Faith Since World War II.* Princeton, NJ: Princeton University Press.

Wuthnow, Robert, and Virginia Ann Hodgkinson. 1990. *Faith and Philanthropy in America: Exploring the Role of Religion in America's Voluntary Sector.* San Francisco: Jossey-Bass.

Zaimov, Stoyan. 2012. "Evangelist Laments Billy Graham's Support of Romney, Says Mormon 'Lies' Spreading." *Christian Post*, October 23. http://global.christianpost. com/news/evangelist-laments-billy-grahams-support-of-romney-says-mormon-lies-spreading-83804/.

Zaller, John R. 1992. *The Nature and Origins of Mass Opinion.* Cambridge; New York: Cambridge University Press.

1994. "Elite Leadership of Mass Opinion: New Evidence from the Gulf War." In *Taken by Storm: The Media, Public Opinion, and U.S. Foreign Policy in the Gulf War,* edited by W. Lance Bennett and David L Paletz, 186–209. Chicago: University of Chicago Press.

Zoglin, Richard. 2011. "Book of Mormon: South Park Creators Hit Broadway." *Time. com*, March 22. http://www.time.com/time/magazine/article/0,9171,2059601,00. html.

# Index